E · H · GOMBRICH

ART AND ILLUSION

t'AMSTERDAM.
by FREDERICK DE WIT,
in de Kalverſtraet by den Dam in de Witte Paskaert.

1

ART AND ILLUSION

A STUDY IN THE PSYCHOLOGY OF
PICTORIAL REPRESENTATION

BY

E·H·GOMBRICH

WITH 320 ILLUSTRATIONS

PHAIDON PRESS·LONDON

FIRST PUBLISHED 1960
SECOND EDITION 1962
THIRD EDITION 1968

SBN 7148 1329 X

PUBLISHED BY PHAIDON PRESS LTD · 5 CROMWELL PLACE · LONDON SW7
MADE IN GREAT BRITAIN
PRINTED BY LONSDALE & BARTHOLOMEW (LEICESTER) LTD · LEICESTER

CONTENTS

To the Memory of my Teachers

EMANUEL LOEWY
1857 – 1938

JULIUS VON SCHLOSSER
1866 – 1938

ERNST KRIS
1900 – 1957

PREFACE

WHEN I was honoured by an invitation to deliver the A. W. Mellon Lectures in the Fine Arts, at the National Gallery in Washington, I proposed as my subject the psychology of representation. I was very grateful to the Trustees for agreeing to a field of inquiry that extends beyond the frontiers of art to the study of perception and optical illusion. For the mysterious way in which shapes and marks can be made to signify and suggest other things beyond themselves had intrigued me since my student days. In my book *The Story of Art*, I had sketched the development of representation from the conceptual methods of the primitives and the Egyptians, who relied on 'what they knew', to the achievements of the impressionists, who succeeded in recording 'what they saw'. While thus making use of the traditional distinction between 'knowing' and 'seeing', I ventured to suggest in my last chapter that the self-contradictory nature of the impressionist programme contributed to the collapse of representation in twentieth-century art. My assertions to the effect that no artist can 'paint what he sees' and discard all conventions were of necessity somewhat aphoristic and dogmatic. To clarify and substantiate them I had to re-examine the very theory of perception I had found so serviceable. This book is a record of this re-examination. It does not aim at upsetting the previous interpretation but at justifying and refining it in the light of contemporary work in psychology. The earlier book, in short, applied a traditional hypothesis about the nature of vision to the history of representational styles; this book has the more ambitious aim of using the history of art, in its turn, to probe and test the hypothetical framework itself. Thus I had to assume that the reader would know the main phases of representational styles which are described in the earlier book. No more specialized knowledge than that is required. Even less do I assume a knowledge of psychology, for in this field I am myself a layman and a learner. In stressing this fact, however, I do not want to sound unduly apologetic. As I see it, the great purpose for which the A. W. Mellon Lectures were founded was to keep the discussion of art in flux and to advance the subject. I believe we can do so only if we learn from the artists to shun the ready-made and to take intellectual risks. All I promised my understanding audience in Washington was not to play safe.

The seven lectures I gave in the spring of 1956 were entitled 'The Visible World and the Language of Art'. All of them are incorporated in this book, the majority with only slight changes (Chapters I, III, X, XI). Of the remaining three, one survives in a considerably extended form as Chapter IX; the other two have expanded into several chapters and constitute sections of Chapters II and V, VII and VIII respectively. A good deal of supplementary matter also came from lectures on this general topic which I gave at various times during my tenure of the Slade

Professorship at Oxford, at various institutions of the University of London to which I belong, during a visit to Harvard University, and at the annual congress of the British Psychological Society in Durham in 1955, where I outlined my programme of research.

Such a process of expansion was probably inevitable as soon as the material here presented was released from the tyranny of the clock. Indeed, my main difficulty was to make the underlying argument sufficiently explicit without allowing every chapter to swell into a volume. Despite much recasting and rewriting, therefore, I decided to take advantage of the lecture form, which enjoys the privilege of leaving stones unturned and avenues unexplored. It also encourages the optimistic assumption that the reader will settle down in a chair, as the listener has to, and will follow the arguments and the illustrations in the sequence in which they are presented. For it should be clear by now that this is not a picture book with explanatory letterpress. It is reading matter with explanatory pictures. The publishers have spared no effort to keep the illustrations close to the passage which they support. The arrangement of the notes serves a similar purpose. We don't interrupt our lectures, as a rule, to bombard the audience with bibliographical data. I have kept the references out of the reader's sight and assembled all the notes at the end, referring back to the pagination of the text and to the topic there discussed. Any reader looking for chapter and verse and seeking a way to further literature should find it easy to spot the relevant information. The full titles of books sometimes cited in a shortened form are listed on page 334.

It was no lack of gratitude towards the authors I have used which made me thus remove the titles of their works from immediate view. On the contrary, I should like at this point to acknowledge my profound indebtedness to the self-denying work of those experts, who must have sacrificed years of their lives and much rewarding research to make their knowledge available to nonspecialists. The fact, for instance, that the notes contain some of the quoted passages in the original language and that I have sometimes used my own translations should not obscure my indebtedness to the editors and translators of the Loeb Classical Library. Nor should an occasional reference to individual papers in psychological periodicals hide my dependence on the books which stood on my shelf throughout the time of writing: I have in mind such indispensable surveys as C. E. Osgood, *Method and Theory in Experimental Psychology* (1953), R. S. Woodworth and Harold Schlosberg, *Experimental Psychology* (1954), and also the compact, small volume by O. L. Zangwill, *An Introduction to Modern Psychology* (1950). Among specialized studies of vision, M. D. Vernon, *A Further Study of Visual Perception* (1952), presents an admirable conspectus, while Wolfgang Metzger, *Gesetze des Sehens* (2nd edn., 1953), surveys the whole field from the point of view of the Gestalt school. I also owe much to Ralph M. Evans, *An Introduction to Color* (1948), but most of all to J. J. Gibson,

The Perception of the Visual World (1950), which, I hope, prevented me from underrating what the author calls 'the awe-inspiring intricacy of vision'.

Even closer to the fringe of my intellectual horizon I hope to have profited from D. O. Hebb, *The Organization of Behavior* (1949), Viktor von Weizsäcker, *Der Gestaltkreis* (1950), F. H. Allport, *Theories of Perception and the Concept of Structure* (1955), and most of all, perhaps, F. A. Hayek, *The Sensory Order* (1952).

The enumeration of books representing different schools of psychology will arouse, in the mind of the specialist, the suspicion that my approach must be fundamentally eclectic. Up to a point this suspicion would be justified, but my selection was not without a bias of its own. If any student of the subject should wish to know at this stage what direction this bias took, I would refer him to the famous joint paper by E. C. Tolman and E. Brunswik, 'The Organism and the Causal Texture of Environment', *Psychological Review*, 1935, which stresses the hypothetical character of all perceptual processes.

It so happens that I saw this paper only after having completed my book. I do not mention this fact in order to claim originality; I rather want to emphasize the part played by living traditions in the shaping of our selective interests. The paper was written in Vienna in 1934, at a time when I had some fleeting contact with Egon Brunswik, who kindly served as a subject in a series of experiments on the reading of facial expressions in art which I helped to organize under the direction of my late friend Ernst Kris. Above all it was Ernst Kris, the art historian turned psycho-analyst, who, during a friendship lasting more than twenty years, taught me the fruitfulness of a psychological approach. Our joint research into the problem of caricature first brought me up against the question of what is involved in accepting an image as a likeness. The basic results of our research are embodied in an essay in his book *Psychoanalytic Explorations in Art* (1952), on which I have drawn in these chapters. What the printed word can hardly convey was the passion and versatility of his ever-inquiring mind, to which I owe the conviction that the history of art will become sterile unless it is constantly enriched by a close contact with the study of man.

It was in the same years, before Hitler's occupation of Vienna, that I was fortunate enough to meet Karl R. Popper, who had just published his book *The Logic of Scientific Discovery* (Eng. tr., 1959), in which he established the priority of the scientific hypothesis over the recording of sense data. Any acquaintance I may have with problems of scientific method and philosophy I owe to his constant friendship. I should be proud if Professor Popper's influence were to be felt everywhere in this book, though naturally he is not responsible for its many shortcomings.

It was from Dr. Gottfried Spiegler, a medical physicist, that I learned to see the interpretation of all images as a philosophical problem. Professor Wolfgang Köhler generously gave me of his time in Princeton and reassured me that the complex questions encountered in the practice of art are still of potential interest to psychological research. Professor Richard Held, of Brandeis University, elucidated several points and introduced me to the department of psychology at Princeton University, where I saw the Ames Demonstrations. Oskar Kokoschka, who invited me to speak at the 'School of Seeing' at the Salzburg Summer Academy, convinced me that the mysteries of perception can still fascinate a great artist of our time. Conversations with Professor Roman Jakobson, of Harvard University, and with Professor Colin Cherry, of the Imperial College of Science in London, have given me tantalizing glimpses into the exciting fields of linguistic theory and information theory.

Naturally I cannot enumerate all my immediate colleagues at the Warburg Institute and the Slade School of Art of the University of London to whom I owe stimulation and encouragement. But I should at least like to mention those who kindly read the manuscript of this book at various stages and offered suggestions for its improvement: they are Professor Ian Bialostocki, Professor Gertrud Bing, Professor Harry Bober, Mr. B. A. R. Carter (who also contributed diagrams), Professor Philipp Fehl, Mrs. Ellen Kann, Mr. H. Lester Cooke, Miss Jennifer Montagu, Mr. Michael Podro, and Mrs. Ruth Rubinstein. Mr. William McGuire at the publishing end and my wife and my son Richard on this side helped nursing the book and its author.

For permission to quote in the text I acknowledge gratefully as follows: to Random House for a passage from a poem by W. H. Auden; to Dent and Sons Ltd. for a passage from the Ellis translation of *The Romance of the Rose;* to George Allen and Unwin Ltd. for extracts from *The Works of John Ruskin;* and to Phaidon Press Ltd. for extracts from the Mayne edition of Leslie's *Memoirs of the Life of John Constable* as well as extracts from my book *The Story of Art.*

E. H. G.

January 1959

PREFACE TO THE SECOND EDITION

CHANGES in the body of the book are restricted to a few corrections of fact or of wording. Any major alterations would have thrown the careful layout which so successfully dovetails text and illustrations fatally out of gear. But I gladly accepted my publisher's invitation to write a Preface to this second edition.

My first duty is surely to thank all those whose interest and understanding have made this reprinting necessary after less than a year. My second duty would be to take account of all criticisms and to remove all sources of misunderstanding that these may have revealed. I cannot do this in a preface, but I can at least draw attention to a few of them. One such stumbling block is still the rash assumption that a book on the rise of illusionist art must want to set up fidelity to nature as the standard of artistic perfection. If my disclaimers on pages 6 and 7 did not suffice, my discussion of caricature and other nonillusionist aspects of representation should have saved me from this misinterpretation. It is an interesting and un-contested fact that many great artists of the past were fascinated by problems of visual truth, but none of them can ever have thought that visual truth alone will make a picture into a work of art.

Another group of readers have sought support from this book for the opposite view, according to which the demand for fidelity to nature must always be meaning-less since everybody sees nature differently. Actually I have tried to show (e.g., on pages 233f. and 252) that the undeniable subjectivity of vision does not preclude objective standards of representational accuracy. A wax dummy can be in-distinguishable from its prototype, and a view through a peephole at a picture may look the same as the view at a solid object quite regardless of who does the viewing or whether he admires or despises the trick.

What may have caused this misunderstanding (apart from overstatements on pages 33 and 41, which I have now rectified) is my repeated assertion that no artist can copy what he sees. There is no contradiction here, for the successful *trompe l'œil* no less than the striking caricature are not only the result of careful looking but also the fruit of experimentation with pictorial effects. The invention of these effects, as I have tried to show, was stimulated by the dissatisfaction which certain periods of Western civilization felt with images that failed to look convincing. It is the gradual modification of the traditional schematic conventions of image making under the pressure of novel demands that forms one of my main themes.

Here I should perhaps point to a less obvious difficulty, which should, however, not be too hard for the reader to overcome. As an historian of art I took the existence and frequency of such schematic vocabularies as my starting point with-out demonstrating their character in detail. It lies in the nature of this problem that it would need a disproportionate number of illustrations merely to show vast numbers of Egyptian servant figures, Chinese bamboo paintings, Byzantine madonnas, Gothic angels, or Baroque putti in order to prove what an attentive look at museums and art books will confirm—how narrow is the range and how subtle are the variations within which the craftsmen and artists of the past created their masterpieces. For the real purpose of this book is not to describe but to explain the reasons for the unexpected difficulty which artists encountered who clearly wanted to make their images look like nature.

I admit that this intention is not always easy to prove, and I am grateful to one of my painter friends, who helped me to formulate my problem afresh by asking me to tell quite simply what would be the opposite of the view I hold. It would be a state of affairs in which every person wielding a brush could always achieve fidelity to nature. The mere desire to preserve the likeness of a beloved person or of a beautiful view would then suffice for the artist to 'copy what he sees'. Those would be right who regard all deviations from nature in non-naturalistic styles as intentional. This view looks plausible in our own world because most city dwellers have absorbed a great deal of knowledge of pictorial effects from posters and picture postcards. We have no right whatever to assume a similar freedom of choice for those who cannot pick up the trick at second hand. I recently came across an episode in the memoirs of a painter that illustrates this point. Brought up among orthodox Jews in Poland who did not admit pictorial representations, Jehudo Epstein tells in *Mein Weg von Ost nach West* (Stuttgart, 1929) how pathetically he failed when he tried for the first time to sketch a castle on a hill in his home town and what a revelation it was to him when somebody then lent him a textbook on perspective.

To explain this need of the painter to profit from the experiences of preceding generations I had to investigate in my turn the working of pictorial effects and to ask how they relate to the way we normally process the information that reaches us from the visible world in which we live and move. In my treatment of this question, some philosophical critics from the neopositivist camp have objected to my equation of seeing and interpreting. They fear, I suspect, that this approach might undermine the faith in the reliability of sense observations and thus give aid and comfort to their enemies. I do not share their apprehensions, but I am not wedded to any form of words. I would be ready to substitute another for the offensive term 'interpretation', provided it described the same process of trial and error by which alone we weed out illusions and test and revise our beliefs about the world, in perception no less than in science. Perhaps I should have been a little more explicit in the presentation of this hypothesis, since no critic has, to my knowledge, taken up the central arguments on pages 231 and 278.

None of these discussions about perception will ever solve the mystery of art. I do not believe that any book that claimed to do so could be worth reading. The disappointment which a few critics seem to have felt when they discovered the limited nature of my problem reflects, I fear, the immaturity of the study of art as compared with the study of nature. Those who have made a little progress in the understanding of the metabolism of the heart are rarely reproached nowadays for having failed to solve the mystery of life. Whether or not this book represents such progress in the understanding of pictorial representation and its history depends on the validity of its arguments. And so I return to the great debt of gratitude I owe the many readers whose willingness to enter into these arguments and to join in their examination surpassed my boldest dreams.

E. H. G.

London, January 1961

PREFACE TO THE THIRD EDITION

I T would be a task beyond my powers to bring this book 'up to date' by taking account of all publications in psychology, philosophy and in the history of art which may have a bearing on its argument. But the reader may like to know that the conclusion of my central chapter on *The Analysis of Vision in Art* for which I quoted an 'aside' by Professor J. J. Gibson (p. 277) can now rest on the solid support of a closely reasoned book by that great student of perception, *The Senses Considered as Perceptual Systems* (Boston, 1966). I should also like to draw attention to an important article I overlooked and to which I should have referred in my attack on the idea of the 'innocent eye'; R. Blanché, 'La Vision du Peintre et la Psychologie de la Perception', *Journal de Psychologie Normale et Pathologique*, April-June, 1946 (pp. 153–80). As for myself, I have reviewed some of the problems of this book from a slightly different vantage point in a lecture on 'Visual Discovery through Art' at Austin, Texas, published in the *Arts Magazine*, November 1965.

Not that there are no contradictions between these various approaches to the same problems. On the contrary, many of the most basic questions raised by this book still remain open. My colleagues know that I am still apt to pounce on them in a College Common Room or Refectory and make them look with me at some indifferent portrait of an academic worthy, not for the sake of its artistic merit, but to help sorting out what is going on when we look at such a painting. They may have to walk with me from one corner of the room to the other in order to watch the apparent shift in the sitter's orientation, they may have to try to screen off the frame with their hands and report on the degree to which they 'lose the surface' of the painting, they may be cross-examined about their capacity to remain aware of the picture plane while scrutinizing the make of the sitter's gown or the expression on his face. Strangely enough there is no agreement about the way these experiences should be described, though I have not been convinced that my account is much in need of revision. I believe, moreover, that some of these questions could be amenable to experimental investigation. Should I hear of any conclusive results I venture to hope that I may be able, one day, to refer to them in yet another Preface.

E. H. G.

London, November 1967

ART AND ILLUSION

*A Study in the Psychology
of Pictorial Representation*

1. Drawing by ALAIN   © 1955 *The New Yorker Magazine, Inc.*

INTRODUCTION

Psychology and the Riddle of Style

Art being a thing of the mind, it follows that any scientific study of art will be psychology. It may be other things as well, but psychology it will always be.

MAX J. FRIEDLÄNDER, *Von Kunst und Kennerschaft*

I

THE ILLUSTRATION in front of the reader should explain much more quickly than I could in words what is here meant by the 'riddle of style'. Alain's cartoon neatly sums up a problem which has haunted the minds of art historians for many generations. Why is it that different ages and different nations have represented the visible world in such different ways? Will the paintings we accept as true to life look as unconvincing to future generations as Egyptian paintings look to us? Is everything concerned with art entirely subjective, or are there objective standards in such matters? If there are, if the methods taught in the life class today result in more faithful imitations of nature than the conventions adopted by the Egyptians, why did the Egyptians fail to adopt them? Is it possible, as our cartoonist hints, that they perceived nature in a different way? Would not such a variability of artistic vision also help us to explain the bewildering images created by contemporary artists?

These are questions which concern the history of art. But their answers cannot be found by historical methods alone. The art historian has done his work when he has described the changes that have taken place. He is concerned with the differences in style between one school of art and another, and he has refined his methods of description in order to group, organize, and identify the works of art which have survived from the past. Glancing through the variety of illustrations we find in this book, we all react, to a major or minor extent, as he does in his studies: we take in the subject of a picture together with its style; we see a Chinese landscape here and a Dutch landscape there, a Greek head and a seventeenth-century portrait. We have come to take such classifications so much for granted that we have almost stopped asking why it is so easy to tell whether a tree was painted by a Chinese or by a Dutch master. If art were only, or mainly, an expression of personal vision, there could be no history of art. We could have no reason to assume, as we do, that there must be a family likeness between pictures of trees

3

produced in proximity. We could not count on the fact that the boys in Alain's life class would produce a typical Egyptian figure. Even less could we hope to detect whether an Egyptian figure was indeed made three thousand years ago or forged yesterday. The art historian's trade rests on the conviction once formulated by Wölfflin, that 'not everything is possible in every period'. To explain this curious fact is not the art historian's duty, but whose business is it?

II

THERE WAS a time when the methods of representation were the proper concern of the art critic. Accustomed as he was to judging contemporary works first of all by standards of representational accuracy, he had no doubt that this skill had progressed from rude beginnings to the perfection of illusion. Egyptian art adopted childish methods because Egyptian artists knew no better. Their conventions could perhaps be excused, but they could not be condoned. It is one of the permanent gains we owe to the great artistic revolution which has swept across Europe in the first half of the twentieth century that we are rid of this type of aesthetics. The first prejudice teachers of art appreciation usually try to combat is the belief that artistic excellence is identical with photographic accuracy. The picture post card or pin-up girl has become the conventional foil against which the student learns to see the creative achievement of the great masters. Aesthetics, in other words, has surrendered its claim to be concerned with the problem of convincing representation, the problem of illusion in art. In certain respects this is indeed a liberation and nobody would wish to revert to the old confusion. But since neither the art historian nor the critic still wishes to occupy himself with this perennial problem, it has become orphaned and neglected. The impression has grown up that illusion, being artistically irrelevant, must also be psychologically very simple.

We do not have to turn to art to show that this view is erroneous. Any psychology textbook will provide us with baffling examples that show the complexity of the issues involved. Take the simple trick drawing which has reached the philosophical seminar from the pages of the humorous weekly *Die Fliegenden Blätter* [2]. We can see the picture as either a rabbit or a duck. It is easy to discover both readings. It is less easy to describe what happens when we switch from one interpretation to the other. Clearly we do not have the illusion that we are confronted with a 'real' duck or rabbit. The shape on the paper resembles neither

2. Rabbit or duck?

animal very closely. And yet there is no doubt that the shape transforms itself in some subtle way when the duck's beak becomes the rabbit's ears and brings an otherwise neglected spot into prominence as the rabbit's mouth. I say 'neglected', but does it enter our experience at all when we switch back to reading 'duck'? To answer this question, we are compelled to look for what is 'really there', to see the shape apart from its interpretation, and this, we soon discover, is not really possible. True, we can switch from one reading to another with increasing rapidity; we will also 'remember' the rabbit while we see the duck, but the more closely we watch ourselves, the more certainly will we discover that we cannot experience alternative readings at the same time. Illusion, we will find, is hard to describe or analyse, for though we may be intellectually aware of the fact that any given experience *must* be an illusion, we cannot, strictly speaking, watch ourselves having an illusion.

If the reader finds this assertion a little puzzling, there is always an instrument of illusion close at hand to verify it: the bathroom mirror. I specify the bathroom because the experiment I urge the reader to make succeeds best if the mirror is a little clouded by steam. It is a fascinating exercise in illusionist representation to trace one's own head on the surface of the mirror and to clear the area enclosed by the outline. For only when we have actually done this do we realize how small the image is which gives us the illusion of seeing ourselves 'face to face'. To be exact, it must be precisely half the size of our head. I do not want to trouble the reader with geometrical proof of this fact, though basically it is simple: since the mirror will always appear to be halfway between me and my reflection, the size on its surface will be one half of the apparent size. But however cogently this fact can be demonstrated with the help of similar triangles, the assertion is usually met with frank incredulity. And despite all geometry, I, too, would stubbornly contend that I really see my head (natural size) when I shave and that the size on the mirror surface is the phantom. I cannot have my cake and eat it. I cannot make use of an illusion and watch it.

Works of art are not mirrors, but they share with mirrors that elusive magic of transformation which is so hard to put into words. A master of introspection, Kenneth Clark, has recently described to us most vividly how even he was defeated when he attempted to 'stalk' an illusion. Looking at a great Velázquez, he wanted to observe what went on when the brush strokes and dabs of pigment on the canvas transformed themselves into a vision of transfigured reality as he stepped back. But try as he might, stepping backward and forward, he could never hold both visions at the same time, and therefore the answer to his problem of how it was done always seemed to elude him. In Kenneth Clark's example, the issues of aesthetics and of psychology are subtly intertwined; in the examples of the psychology textbooks, they are obviously not. In this book I have often found it convenient to isolate the discussion of visual effects from the discussion of works of art. I realize this may sometimes lead to an impression of irreverence; I hope the opposite is the truth.

Representation need not be art, but it is none the less mysterious for that. I well remember that the power and magic of image making was first revealed to me, not by Velázquez, but by a simple drawing game I found in my primer. A little rhyme explained how you could first draw a circle to represent a loaf of bread (for loaves were round in my native Vienna); a curve added on top would turn the loaf into a shopping bag, two little squiggles on its handle would make it shrink into a purse; and now by adding a tail, here was a cat [3]. What intrigued me, as I

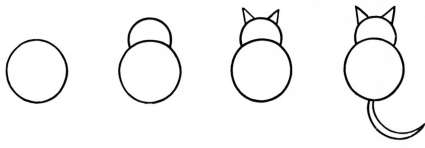

3. How to draw a cat

learned the trick, was the power of metamorphosis: the tail destroyed the purse and created the cat; you cannot see the one without obliterating the other. Far as we are from completely understanding this process, how can we hope to approach Velázquez?

I had hardly anticipated, when I embarked on my explorations, into what distant fields the subject of illusion would take me. I can only appeal to the reader who wishes to join in this Hunting of the Snark to train himself a little in the game of self-observation, not so much in museums as in his daily commerce with pictures and images of all kinds—while sitting on the bus or standing in the waiting room. What he will see there will obviously not count as art. It will be less pretentious but also less embarrassing than poor works of art that ape the tricks of Velázquez.

When we deal with masters of the past who were both great artists and great 'illusionists', the study of art and the study of illusion cannot always be kept apart. I am all the more anxious to emphasize as explicitly as I possibly can that this book is not intended as a plea, disguised or otherwise, for the exercise of illusionist tricks in painting today. I should like to prevent this particular breakdown of communication between myself and my readers and critics because I am, in fact, rather critical of certain theories of nonfigurative art and have alluded to some of these issues where they seemed relevant. But to chase this hare would be to miss the point of the book. That the discoveries and effects of representation which were the pride of earlier artists have become trivial today I would not deny for a moment. Yet I believe that we are in real danger of losing contact with the great masters of the past if we accept the fashionable doctrine that such matters never had anything to do with art. The very reason why the representation of nature can now be looked upon as something commonplace should be of the greatest interest to the historian. Never before has there been an age like ours when the visual image was so cheap in every sense of the word. We are surrounded and assailed by posters and advertisements, by comics and magazine illustrations. We see aspects of reality represented on the television screen and in the cinema, on postage stamps and on food packages. Painting is taught at school and practised at home as therapy and as a pastime, and many a modest amateur has mastered tricks that would have looked like sheer magic to Giotto. Perhaps even the crude coloured renderings we find on a box of breakfast cereal would have made Giotto's contemporaries gasp. I do not know if there are people who conclude from this that the box is superior to a Giotto. I am not one of them. But I think that the victory and vulgarization of representational skills create a problem for both the historian and the critic.

The Greeks said that to marvel is the beginning of knowledge and where we cease to marvel we may be in danger of ceasing to know. The main aim I have set myself in these chapters is to restore our sense of wonder at man's capacity to conjure up by forms, lines, shades, or colours those mysterious phantoms of visual reality we call 'pictures'. 'Should we not say', said Plato in the *Sophist*, 'that we make a house by the art of building, and by the art of painting we make another house, a sort of man-made dream produced for those who are awake?' I know of no better description to teach us the art of wonder again—and it detracts nothing from Plato's definition that many of these man-made dreams, produced for those who are awake, are banished by us from the realm of art, perhaps rightly, because they are almost too effective as dream substitutes, whether we call them pin-ups or comics. Even pin-ups and comics, rightly viewed, may provide food for thought. Just as the study of poetry remains incomplete without an awareness of the language of prose, so, I believe, the study of art will be increasingly supplemented by inquiry into the linguistics of the visual image. Already we see the outlines of iconology, which investigates the function of images in allegory and symbolism and their reference to what might be called the 'invisible world of ideas'. The way the language of art refers to the visible world is both so obvious and so mysterious that it is still largely unknown except to the artists themselves who can use it as we use all languages—without needing to know its grammar and semantics.

A great deal of practical knowledge is stored in the many books written by artists and art teachers for the use of students and amateurs. Not being an artist myself, I have refrained from enlarging on such technical matters beyond the needs of my argument. But I should be happy if each chapter of this book could be seen as a provisional pier for the much-needed bridge between the field of art history and the domain of the practising artist. We want to meet in Alain's life class and discuss the problems of the boys in a language that makes sense to both of us and, if luck will have it, even to the scientific student of perception.

III

THE READER who likes to be plunged *in medias res* is advised to turn from here to the first chapter. There is a good old tradition, however (as good and as old, in fact, as Plato and Aristotle), which demands that those who tackle a philosophical problem and propose a new solution should first give a critical account of its history. In the next three sections of this Introduction, therefore, I shall briefly survey the growth of our ideas about style and explain how the history of representation in art became increasingly mixed up with the psychology of perception. The final section will be devoted to the present situation and to the programme of this book.

The word 'style', of course, is derived from '*stilus*', the writing instrument of the Romans, who would speak of an 'accomplished style' much as later generations spoke of a 'fluent pen'. Classical education was centred on the student's power of expression and persuasion, and thus a great deal of thought was given by the ancient teachers of rhetoric to all aspects of style in speech and writing. Their discussions provided a storehouse of ideas on art and expression that had a lasting influence on criticism. Most of these efforts were concerned with analysing the psychological effects of various stylistic devices and traditions and the development of a rich terminology to describe the 'categories of expression', the ornate and the humble, the sublime and the bombastic. But characters of this kind are notoriously hard to describe, except in metaphors: we speak of a 'scintillating' or a 'woolly' style. Without this need, the terminology of style might never have spread to the visual arts. Casting around for vivid methods of characterization, the ancient writers on rhetoric liked to bring in comparisons with painting and sculpture. Quintilian, in particular, inserts a brief history of art from the 'hard' manner of archaic sculpture to the 'softness' and 'sweetness' of fourth-century masters to illustrate the rise of Latin oratory and its change in character from rough vigour to smooth polish. Fascinating as these discussions are, they frequently suffer from a confusion which we have inherited. The problems of expressive modes are rarely disentangled from that of varying skills. Thus what looks like progress from the point of view of the mastery of a medium can also be viewed as decline into empty virtuosity. Polemics between the various schools of rhetoric make ample use of such moral arguments. Asiatic bombast is decried as a sign of moral decay, and the return to a pure Attic vocabulary is hailed as a moral victory. There exists an essay by Seneca in which the corruption of style at the hands of Maecenas is mercilessly analysed as a manifestation of a corrupt society in which affectation and obscurity count for more than straightforward lucidity. But arguments of this kind did not remain unanswered. Tacitus, in his dialogue on oratory, presents a case against the Jeremiahs of his time who decried contemporary styles. Times have changed and so have our ears. We demand a different style of oratory. This reference to the conditions of the time and the diversity of 'ears' is perhaps the first fleeting contact between the psychology of style and that of perception. I know of no such explicit reference in ancient writings on art. Not that the bearing of the painter's skill on the psychology of perception was lost on antiquity. In one of Cicero's philosophical dialogues, the *Academica*, the argument turns on the status of sense perceptions as a source of knowledge. The skeptic who denies the possibility of any knowledge is reminded of the acuteness and perfectibility of our eyes: 'How much painters see in shade and protrusions that we do not see!' exclaims the speaker, only to be reminded later that this argument merely proves how feeble the vision of an ordinary Roman must be, for how many painters are Romans?

There is no evidence, however, that classical antiquity fully realized the implications of this observation. Strictly speaking, it poses a question which is still unsolved. Are painters successful in the imitation of reality because they 'see more', or do they see more because they have acquired the skill of imitation? Both views are somehow supported by commonsense experience. Artists know that they learn by looking intensely at nature, but obviously looking alone has never sufficed to teach an artist his trade. In antiquity the conquest of illusion by art was such a recent achievement that the discussion of painting and sculpture inevitably centred on imitation, *mimesis*. Indeed it may be said that the progress of art toward that goal was to the ancient world what the progress of technics is to the modern: the model of progress as such. Thus Pliny told the history of sculpture and painting as the history of inventions, assigning definite achievements in the rendering of nature to individual artists: the painter Polygnotus was the first to represent people with open mouths and with teeth, the sculptor Pythagoras was the first to render nerves and veins, the painter Nicias was concerned with light and shade. In the Renaissance it was Vasari who applied this technique to the history of the arts of Italy from the thirteenth to the sixteenth century. Vasari never fails to pay tribute to those artists of the past who made a distinct contribution, as he saw it, to the mastery of representation. 'Art rose from humble beginnings to the summit of perfection' because such natural geniuses as Giotto blazed the trail and others were thus enabled to build on their achievements. Thus we read of the mysterious Stefano: 'Although the foreshortenings which he made are faulty in manner . . . owing to the difficulty of execution, yet, as the first investigator of these difficulties, he deserves much greater fame than do those who follow after him with a more orderly and regulated style.' Vasari, in other words, saw the invention of the means of representation as a great collective enterprise of such difficulty that a certain division of labour was inevitable. Thus he says of Taddeo Gaddi: 'Taddeo always adopted Giotto's manner but did not greatly improve it except in the colouring, which he made fresher and more vivid. Giotto had paid so much attention to the improvement of other aspects and difficulties of this art that although he was adequate in colouring, he was not more than that. Hence Taddeo, who had seen and learned what Giotto had made easy, had time to add something of his own by improving colouring.'

I hope to show in the course of this book that this view is by no means as naïve as it is sometimes made out to be. It appears naïve only because Vasari, too, could not disentangle the idea of invention from that of the imitation of nature. This contradiction nearly comes to the surface in Vasari's treatment of Masaccio, whom he credits with the discovery that 'painting is nothing more than the simple portrayal of all things alive in nature by means of design and colour as nature herself produces them.' Masaccio, for instance, 'loved to paint drapery with few folds and an easy fall just as they are in natural life, and this has been of great use to artists, so that he deserves to be commended as if he had invented it.'

It is at such moments the reader will ask himself what difficulty there could have been in this simple portrayal which prevented artists before Masaccio from looking at the fall of drapery for themselves. It took some time for this question to emerge in an articulate form, but its formulation and the first attempts to answer it are still bound up with the academic tradition of art teaching.

The question of what is involved in 'looking at nature'—what we today call the psychology of perception—first entered into the discussion of style as a practical problem in art teaching. The academic teacher bent on accuracy of representation found, as he still will find, that his pupils' difficulties were due not only to an inability to copy nature but also to an inability to see it. Discussing this observation, Jonathan Richardson remarked, early in the eighteenth century: 'For it is a certain maxim, no man sees what things are, that knows not what they ought to be. That this maxim is true, will appear by an academy figure drawn by one ignorant in the structure, and knitting of the bones, and anatomy, compared with another who understands these thoroughly . . . both see the same life, but with different eyes.'

It was but a step from such observations to the idea that the changes in style such as Vasari had described were not only based on an improvement of skill but were the result of different modes of seeing the world. This step had already been taken in the eighteenth century and, appropriately, by an academic teacher, James Barry, in one of the lectures delivered at the Royal Academy. Barry was puzzled by Vasari's story that Cimabue's Madonna Rucellai [4] (now generally attributed to Duccio) was acclaimed as a masterpiece in the thirteenth century. 'The very great deficiencies of this work of Cimabue,' Barry said, 'might, perhaps, induce

4. *The Madonna Rucellai.* About 1285

some to think that he could not possibly have availed himself of the inspection of nature when he painted it. But the imitations of early art are exactly like those of children; nothing is seen even in the spectacle before us, until it be in some measure otherwise previously known and sought for, and numberless observable differences between the ages of ignorance and those of knowledge show how much the contraction or extension of our sphere of vision depends upon other considerations than the simple return of our mere natural optics. The people, then, of those ages only saw so much, and admired it, because they knew no more.'

Stimulated by the rise of science and the new interest in factual observation, these questions of vision were much debated by artists at the start of the nineteenth century. 'The art of seeing nature,' said Constable in his pungent way, 'is a thing almost as much to be acquired as the art of reading the Egyptian hieroglyphs.' There is a new edge to this utterance, for this time it is addressed to the public rather than to artists. The public has no right to judge the veracity of a painting, Constable implies, because its vision is clouded by ignorance and prejudice. It was this same conviction that led Ruskin, in 1843, to publish his *Modern Painters* in defence of Turner. This vast treatise is perhaps the last and most persuasive book in the tradition that starts with Pliny and Vasari in which the history of art is interpreted as progress toward visual truth. Turner is better than Claude or Canaletto, Ruskin argues, because he knows demonstrably more about natural effects than his predecessors. But this 'truth of nature is not to be discerned by the uneducated senses'. Let the doubting critic analyse the structure of waves and clouds, of rocks and vegetation, and he will have to admit that Turner is correct every time. The progress of art here becomes a triumph over the prejudices of tradition. It is slow because it is so hard for us all to disentangle what we really see from what we merely know and thus to recover the innocent eye, a term to which Ruskin gave currency.

Without being aware of the fact, Ruskin had thus laid the explosive charge which was to blow the academic edifice sky-high. For Barry 'the simple return of our natural optics' had appeared insufficient to produce anything better than the Madonna Rucellai. For Ruskin and those who followed him, the painter's aim was to be to return to the unadulterated truth of natural optics. The discoveries of the impressionists and the heated debates which they aroused increased the interest of artists and critics in these mysteries of perception. Had the impressionists really the right to claim that they saw the world as they painted it, that they reproduced 'the image on the retina'? Was that the goal toward which the whole history of art had been moving? Would the psychology of perception finally solve the artist's problems?

IV

THIS DEBATE revealed what it was bound to reveal: science is neutral, and the artist will appeal to its findings at his peril. The distinction between what we really see and what we infer through the intellect is as old as human thought on perception. Pliny had succinctly summed up the position in classical antiquity when he wrote that 'the mind is the real instrument of sight and observation, the eyes act as a sort of vessel receiving and transmitting the visible portion of the consciousness'. Ptolemy devotes much thought in his *Optics* (*c.* A.D. 150) to the role of judgment in the process of vision. The greatest Arab student of the subject, Alhazen (d. A.D. 1038), taught the medieval West the distinction between sense, knowledge, and inference, all of which come into play in perception. 'Nothing visible is understood by the sense of sight alone', he says, 'save light and colours.' The problem raised by this tradition acquired fresh urgency when John Locke came to deny all innate ideas and insisted that all knowledge comes to us through the senses. For if the eye reacts only to light and colour, where does our knowledge of the third dimension come from? It was Berkeley who, in his *New Theory of Vision* (1709), explored the ground afresh and reached the conclusion that all our knowledge of space and solidity must be acquired through the sense of touch and movement. This analysis into 'sense data', begun by the British empiricists, continued to dominate psychological research in the nineteenth century when intellectual giants such as Helmholtz developed the science of physiological optics. But neither Berkeley nor Helmholtz made the mistake of confusing 'seeing' with the visual sensation. On the contrary, the distinction between what came to be known as 'sensation'—the mere registering of 'stimuli'—and the mental act of perception based, as Helmholtz put it, on 'unconscious inference' was a commonplace of nineteenth-century psychology.

It was thus not difficult to counter the psychological arguments of the impressionists that their paintings showed the world 'as we really see it' with equally valid psychological arguments for the reliance of traditional art on intellectual knowledge. In the course of this debate, which began toward the end of the nineteenth century, the whole comfortable idea of the imitation of nature disintegrated, leaving artists and critics perplexed.

Two German thinkers are prominent in this story. One is the critic Konrad Fiedler, who insisted, in opposition to the impressionists, that 'even the simplest sense impression that looks like merely the raw material for the operations of the mind is already a mental fact, and what we call the external world is really the result of a complex psychological process'.

But it was Fiedler's friend, the neoclassical sculptor Adolf von Hildebrand who set out to analyse this process in a little book called *The Problem of Form in the Figurative Arts*, which came out in 1893 and gained the ear of a whole generation. Hildebrand, too, challenged the ideals of scientific naturalism by an appeal to the psychology of perception: if we attempt to analyse our mental images to discover their primary constituents, we will find them composed of sense data derived from vision and from memories of touch and movement. A sphere, for instance, appears to the eye as a flat disc; it is touch which informs us of the properties of space and form. Any attempt on the part of the artist to eliminate this knowledge is futile, for without it he would not perceive the world at all. His task is, on the contrary, to compensate for the absence of movement in his work by clarifying his image and thus conveying not only visual sensations but also those memories of touch which enable us to reconstitute the three-dimensional form in our minds.

It is hardly an accident that the period when these ideas were so eagerly debated was also the period when the history of art emancipated itself from antiquarianism, biography, and aesthetics. Issues which had been taken for granted so long suddenly looked problematic and required reassessment. When Bernard Berenson wrote his brilliant essay on the Florentine painters, which came out in 1896, he formulated his aesthetic creed in terms of Hildebrand's analysis. With his gift for the pregnant phrase, he summed up almost the whole of the sculptor's somewhat turgid book in the sentence 'The painter can accomplish his task only by giving tactile values to retinal impressions'. For Berenson, Giotto's or Pollaiuolo's claim on our attention is that they had done precisely this. Like Hildebrand, he was concerned with aesthetics rather than with history.

Three years later, in 1899, Heinrich Wölfflin paid tribute to Hildebrand in the preface to his classic book on *Classic Art*. The ideal of clarity and spatial order presented by Wölfflin in his descriptions of Raphael's masterpieces shows the marks of Hildebrand's influence no less vividly than does Berenson's image of Giotto. But Wölfflin saw that Hildebrand's categories were suitable not only as an aid to appreciation but also as a tool for the analysis of various modes of representation. The final 'polarities' he was to evolve in his *Principles of Art History*, the distinction between the solid clarity of Renaissance modes and the 'painterly' complexities of the Baroque, still owe much to Hildebrand's approach. It was Wölfflin who gave currency to the catchword of the 'history of seeing' in art history, but it was also he who warned against taking this metaphor too seriously. Wölfflin, in fact, never mistook description for explanation. Few historians were more acutely aware than he of the problem posed by the very existence of representational styles, but with that restraint which he had inherited from his great predecessor Jakob Burckhardt, he never entered into speculations about the ultimate causes of historical change.

It was thus left to the third of the founding fathers of stylistic history, Alois Riegl, to marry Hildebrand's ideas to the study of artistic evolution. Riegl's ambition was to make the history of art scientifically respectable by eliminating all subjective ideals of value. He was favoured in this approach by his work in a museum of arts and crafts. Studying the history of decorative art, of pattern and ornament, he had become convinced of the inadequacy of those assumptions which had dominated the scene—the 'materialist' assumption that pattern depended on such techniques as weaving and basketry and the technological assumption that what counts in art is skill of hand. After all, the decorative patterns of many so-called 'primitive tribes' testify to an amazing manual dexterity. If styles have differed it must be because intentions have changed. In his first book, the *Stilfragen* of 1893, Riegl showed that questions of this kind could and should be discussed in a purely 'objective' manner without introducing subjective ideas of progress and decline. He sought to demonstrate that plant ornament evolves and changes in one continuous tradition, from the Egyptian lotus to the arabesque, and that these changes, far from being fortuitous, express a general reorientation of artistic intentions, of the 'will-to-form' which manifests itself in the smallest palmette no less than in the most monumental building. To this approach, the notion of a 'decline' was meaningless. The historian's task is not to judge but to explain.

It so happens that another art historian in Vienna, the great Franz Wickhoff, was also bent, at the same time, on clearing a period of the stigma of decline. In 1895 he was publishing the *Vienna Genesis*, a precious manuscript of late antiquity, and he wanted to demonstrate that what had been considered the debased and slovenly style of Roman imperial art deserved such an accusation as little as did the modern impressionists, whose much-maligned paintings Wickhoff had learned to love. The art of the Romans, Wickhoff concluded, was as progressive in the direction of visual subjectivity as the art of his own time.

Riegl seized on this interpretation as the basis for an even bolder generalization. In 1901 he defined his position toward Hildebrand's much-discussed theories: The historian could accept Hildebrand's psychological analysis; he could not share his artistic bias. Reliance on touch was neither better nor worse than reliance on vision; each was justified in its own right and in its own period. Having been commissioned to publish archaeological finds from the period of declining antiquity, Riegl wrote his famous book *Spätrömische Kunstindustrie* ('Late Roman Arts and Crafts'), which represents the most ambitious attempt ever made to interpret the whole course of art history in terms of changing modes of perception.

The book is hard to read and even harder to summarize, but Riegl's main argument is that ancient art was always concerned with the rendering of individual objects rather than with the infinite world as such. Egyptian art shows this attitude in its extreme form, for here vision is only allowed a very subsidiary part; things are rendered as they appear to the sense of touch, the more 'objective' sense which reports on the permanent shape of things irrespective of the shifting viewpoint. Here, too, is the reason why Egyptians shunned the rendering of the third dimension, because recession and foreshortening would have introduced a subjective element. An advance toward the third dimension, which grants the eye its share in the perception of modelling, was made in Greece. It needed, however, the third and last phase of ancient art—late antiquity—to develop a purely visual mode of rendering objects as they appear from a distance. But paradoxically this advance strikes the modern observer as a regression because it makes bodies look flat and shapeless, and since only individual things are rendered, irrespective of their surroundings, these lumpy figures look doubly harsh as they stand out against an indefinite foil of shadowy depth or golden ground. Within the context of world history, however, late antique art was not a decline but a necessary phase of transition. The intervention of Germanic tribes, whom Riegl considered more inclined to subjectivity, enabled art to continue its transformations on a higher plane, from a tactile conception of three-dimensional space as conceived in the Renaissance to a further increase in visual subjectivity in the Baroque and so to the triumph of pure optical sensations in impressionism: 'Every style aims at a faithful rendering of nature and nothing else, but each has its own conception of Nature. . . .'

There is a touch of genius in the single-mindedness with which Riegl tries by one unitary principle to account for all stylistic changes in architecture, sculpture, painting, and patternmaking. But this single-mindedness, which he took to be the hallmark of a scientific approach, made him a prey to those prescientific habits of mind by which unitary principles proliferate, the habits of the mythmakers. The 'will-to-form', the *Kunstwollen*, becomes a ghost in the machine, driving the wheels of artistic developments according to 'inexorable laws'. In fact, as Meyer Schapiro has pointed out, Riegl's 'motivation of the process and his explanation of its shifts in time and space are vague and often fantastic. Each great phase corresponds to a racial disposition. . . . Each race plays a prescribed role and retires when its part is done. . . .'

It is not difficult to see in this picture of world history a revival of those romantic mythologies which found their climax in Hegel's philosophy of history. To classical antiquity and to the Renaissance, the history of art had reflected the increase in technical skill. In this context the arts themselves were sometimes spoken of as having a childhood, maturity, and decline. But the romantics saw the whole of history as the great drama of mankind's evolution from childhood to maturity. Art became the 'expression of the age' and a symptom of the phase which the World Spirit had reached at any given point. In the context of such speculations, the German romantic physician Carl Gustav Carus had actually anticipated Riegl in his interpretation of the history of art as a movement from touch to vision. Wanting to plead for the recognition of landscape painting as the great art of the future, he based his advocacy on the laws of historical inevitability: 'The development of the senses in any organism begins with feeling, with touch. The more subtle senses of hearing and seeing emerge only when the organism perfects itself. In almost the same manner, mankind began with sculpture. What man formed had to be massive, solid, tangible. This is the reason why painting . . . always belongs to a later phase. . . . Landscape art . . . pre-supposes a higher degree of development.'

I have discussed elsewhere why this reliance of art history on mythological explanations seems so dangerous to me. By inculcating the habit of talking in terms of collectives, of 'mankind', 'races', or 'ages', it weakens resistance to totalitarian habits of mind. I do not make these accusations lightly. Indeed I can quote chapter and verse by enumerating the lessons which Hans Sedlmayr wanted the reader to draw from reading Riegl's collected essays, the introduction to which he wrote in 1927.

Having presented what he considered the 'quintessence' of Riegl's doctrine, Sedlmayr proceeded to enumerate the false intellectual positions which those who embrace Riegl's views of history must give up as untenable. Among the convictions we are asked to surrender is the idea that 'only individual human beings are real, while groups and spiritual collectives are mere names'. It follows for Sedlmayr that we must also 'reject the belief in the unity and immutability of human nature and human reason' no less than the idea that 'nature remains the same and is only "represented" in different modes'. Finally, we must renounce the causal analysis of history 'which conceives of historical change merely as a resultant of blind and isolated chains of causation'. There is such a thing as the 'meaningful self-movement of the Spirit which results in genuine historical totalities of events'.

I happen to be a passionate believer in all those outmoded ideas which Sedlmayr in 1927 asked a gullible public to discard in favour of a Spenglerian historicism. Like K. R. Popper, on whose words in *The Poverty of Historicism* I cannot improve, 'I have not the slightest sympathy with these "spirits"; neither with their idealistic prototype nor with their dialectical and materialistic incarnations, and I am in full sympathy with those who treat them with contempt. And yet I feel that they indicate, at least, the existence of a vacuum, of a place which it is the task of sociology to fill with something more sensible, such as an analysis of problems arising within a tradition.' Styles, I believe, are instances of such traditions. As long as we have no better hypothesis to offer, the existence of uniform modes of representing the world must invite the facile explanation that such a unity must be due to some supraindividual spirit, the 'spirit of the age' or the 'spirit of the race'.

Not that I deny that historians, like other students of groups, often find attitudes, beliefs, or tastes that are shared by many and might well be described as the mentality or outlook dominant in a class, generation, or nation. Nor do I doubt that changes in the intellectual climate and changes in fashion or taste are often symptomatic of social change, or that an investigation of these connections can be worth while. Both in the writings of Riegl himself and in those of his followers and interpreters, such as Worringer, Dvořák, and Sedlmayr, there is a wealth of challenging historical problems and suggestions, but I would assert that what is their greatest pride is in fact their fatal flaw: by throwing out the idea of skill they have not only surrendered vital evidence, they have made it impossible to realize their ambition, a valid psychology of stylistic change.

The history of taste and fashion is the history of preferences, of various acts of choice between given alternatives. The rejection by the Pre-Raphaelites of the academic conventions of their day is an example, and so is the Japonism of *art nouveau*. Such changes in style and in the prestige of styles might be described (though hardly exhaustively) in terms of a 'will-to-form'; no one doubts they were symptomatic of a whole cluster of attitudes. But what matters here from the point of view of method is that an act of choice is only of symptomatic significance, is expressive of something only if we can reconstruct the choice situation. The captain on the bridge who could have left the sinking ship but stayed must have been a hero; the man who was trapped in his sleep and drowned may also have been heroic, but we shall never know. If we really want to treat styles as symptomatic of something else (which may, on occasion, be very interesting), we cannot do without some theory of alternatives. If every change is inevitable and total, there is nothing left to compare, no situation to reconstruct, no symptom or expression to be investigated. Change becomes the symptom of change as such, and to hide this tautology, some grandiose scheme of evolution has to be called in, as happened not only to Riegl but to many of his successors. There are few historians today, and even fewer anthropologists, who believe that mankind has undergone any marked biological change within historical periods. But even those who might admit the possibility of some slight oscillation in the genetic make-up of mankind would never accept the idea that man has changed as much within the last three thousand years, a mere hundred generations, as have his art and his style.

V

EVOLUTIONISM is dead, but the facts which gave rise to its myth are still stubbornly there to be accounted for. One of these facts is a certain kinship between child art and primitive art that had suggested to the unwary the false alternatives that either these primitives could not do better because they were as unskilled as children or that they did not want to do anything else because they still had the mentality of children. Both these conclusions are obviously false. They are due to the tacit assumption that what is easy for us must always have been easy. It seems to me one of the permanent gains of the first contacts between art history and the psychology of perception that we need no longer believe this. Indeed, though I regret the misuse of this psychology in its historicist form, I admit to a certain nostalgia for the speculative boldness of those nineteenth-century optimists. Perhaps this is due to the fact that I still had the privilege of being taught by such bold minds who, at the turn of this century, tried to tackle the problem of why art has a history. One of them was Emanuel Loewy, whose famous study *The Rendering of Nature in Early Greek Art* came out in 1900. That book, it seems to me, contains most of what is worth preserving in evolutionism.

Loewy, too, was influenced by Hildebrand and by the outlook of sense-data psychology. Like other critics of his period, Hildebrand had attributed the peculiarities of child art to a reliance on vague memory images. These images were conceived of as the residue of many sense impressions that had been deposited in the memory and there coalesced into typical shapes, much in the way typical images can be created by the superimposition of many photographs. In this process, Loewy thought, the memory sifted out the characteristic features of objects, those aspects which show them in their most distinctive form. The primitive artist, like the child, takes these memory images as his starting point. He will tend to represent the human body frontally, horses in profile, and lizards from above. Loewy's analysis of these 'archaic' modes is still basically accepted, though his explanation is really circular: since the primitive artist obviously does not copy the outside world, he is believed to copy some invisible inside world of mental images. For these mental images, in their turn, however, the typical pictures of primitives are the only evidence. None of us, I believe, carries in his head such schematic pictures of bodies, horses, or lizards as Loewy's theory postulates. What these words conjure up will be different for all of us, but it will always be an elusive welter of fleeting events which can never be communicated in full. But this criticism cannot detract from the value of Loewy's analysis of those features which the works of children, untutored adults, and primitives have in common. By taking as his subject not the evolution of mankind but the first occasion in history when these features were slowly and methodically eliminated in early Greek art, Loewy taught us to appreciate the forces which have to be overcome by an art aiming at the illusion of reality. Each of these steps appears as a conquest of hitherto unknown territory that had to be secured and fortified in a new tradition of image making. Thus arises the tenacity of the newly invented types that no theory of art in terms of 'sense impressions' was able to account for.

It so happens that my teacher in the history of art, Julius von Schlosser, was also particularly interested in the role of the type and even of the stereotype in tradition. His starting point had been in numismatics, and he soon found his way to the study of medieval art, where the sway of the formula is so marked. The problem of the use of 'precedents' or 'similes' in medieval art never ceased to fascinate Schlosser despite the fact that the influence of Croce made him increasingly suspicious of psychological explanations. Those who know his meditations on these problems will recognize some of their recurrent themes in this book.

What Schlosser did for the Middle Ages, his contemporary Aby Warburg did for the Italian Renaissance. In pursuing the problem that governed his life, the problem of what exactly it was that the Renaissance sought in classical antiquity,

Warburg was led to investigate the rise of Renaissance styles in terms of the adoption of a new visual language. He saw that the borrowings of Renaissance artists from classical sculpture were not haphazard. They occurred whenever a painter felt in need of a particularly expressive image of movement or gesture, of what Warburg came to call *Pathosformel*. His insistence that *quattrocento* artists, who had previously been regarded as the champions of pure observation, so frequently took recourse to a borrowed formula made a great impression. Aided by interest in iconographic types, his followers found increasingly that dependence on tradition is the rule even with works of art of the Renaissance and the Baroque that had hitherto been regarded as naturalistic. Investigations of these continuities have now largely replaced the older preoccupation with style.

It was André Malraux who seized upon the significance of these findings in his captivating volumes on *The Psychology of Art*. There is much of Hegel and Spengler in Malraux's rhapsodic hymns to myth and to change, but he has at last disposed of the misunderstanding which comes in for its share of ridicule in Alain's cartoon, the idea that the styles of the past literally reflect the way these artists 'saw' the world. Malraux knows that art is born of art, not of nature. Yet, for all its fascination and its brilliant psychological asides, Malraux's book fails to give us what its title promises, a psychology of art. We still have no satisfactory explanation for the puzzle of Alain's cartoon. But we may be better prepared than Riegl was to attempt such an explanation. We have learned a good deal about the grip of conventions and the power of traditions in more fields than one. Historians have investigated the hold which the formula has over the chronicler who means to record recent events; students of literature, such as Ernst Robert Curtius, have demonstrated the role of the 'topos', the traditional commonplace, in the warp and woof of poetry. The time seems ripe to approach the problem of style once more, fortified by this knowledge of the force of traditions.

I realize that this insistence on the tenacity of conventions, on the role of types and stereotypes in art, will be met with scepticism by those who have not worked in this field. It has almost become the stock accusation against art history that it concentrates on a search for influences and thereby misses the mystery of creativity. But this is not necessarily the case. The more we become aware of the enormous pull in man to repeat what he has learned, the greater will be our admiration for those exceptional beings who could break this spell and make a significant advance on which others could build.

Even so, I have sometimes asked myself whether my assumptions are really borne out by the facts of art history, whether the need for a formula is as universal as I postulated it to be. I remembered a beautiful passage from Quintilian where he speaks of the creativity of the human mind and uses the artist as an illustration:

'Not everything that art can achieve can be passed on. What painter ever learned to represent everything that exists in nature ? But once he has grasped the principles of imitation, he will portray whatever presents itself. Which craftsman has not made a vessel of a shape he has never seen ?'

It is an important reminder, but it does not account for the fact that even the shape of the new vessel will somehow belong to the same family of forms as those the craftsman has seen, that his representation of 'everything that exists in nature' will still be linked with those representations that were handed on to him by his teachers. It is once more the stubborn fact of Alain's Egyptian boys that has to be accounted for, and no historian of art will be inclined to underrate the sway of style, least of all the historian who maps the long road to illusion.

VI

TO TACKLE these central problems of our discipline, I believe, it cannot be sufficient to repeat the old opposition between 'seeing' and 'knowing', or to insist in a general way that all representation is based on conventions. We have to get down to analysing afresh, in psychological terms, what is actually involved in the process of image making and image reading. But here a formidable obstacle arises. The simple type of psychology on which Barry and Ruskin, Riegl and Loewy relied with such confidence no longer exists to guide us. Psychology has become alive to the immense complexity of the processes of perception, and no one claims to understand them completely.

Bernard Berenson could introduce his excursion into these fields with the words 'psychology has ascertained. . . .' Those who consult more recent books will not find the same tone of assured authority. J. J. Gibson, for instance, writes in his exciting study *The Perception of the Visual World*, 'Learning to attend to novel features of the world, to explore it, is something which psychologists do not understand at present'—and down go the hopes of the historian. D. O. Hebb in his well-known book *The Organization of Behavior* even tells us that 'the perception of size, brightness and pitch should be written down for the present as not yet accounted for by any theory'. Nor is this perplexity confined to basic questions. Discussing the so-called 'spreading effect', the unexpected way superimposed colours may affect each other, which is so important for the painter, Ralph M. Evans in his basic *Introduction to Color* says: 'The writer feels that until this effect can be explained without elaborate assumptions we cannot say that we understand the way in which the visual process operates.'

In these circumstances it may seem foolhardy to invoke the results of one field of uncertain study for the explanation of our own uncertainties. Yet, encouragement for this kind of venture comes precisely from one of the greatest pioneers in the field of perceptual psychology, Wolfgang Köhler. In his lectures on *Dynamics in Psychology* (1940), Köhler extols the virtues of 'trespassing as a scientific technique':

'The most fortunate moments in the history of knowledge occur when facts which have been as yet no more than special data are suddenly referred to other apparently distant facts, and thus appear in a new light. For this to happen in psychology we should keep ourselves informed about more than our subject-matter in the narrowest sense.' And Köhler asks: 'If the present situation of psychology offers us an excellent reason—or should I say a marvellous pretext—for extending our curiosity beyond our limited field, should we not rather be impatient to seize this opportunity at once?'

At least one of Köhler's followers has seized the opportunity and has ventured from psychology into the field of art. Rudolf Arnheim's book *Art and Visual* *Perception* deals with the visual image from the point of view of Gestalt psychology. I have read it with much profit. His chapter on growth, which deals with child art, seems to me so instructive that I was relieved to be able to exclude this much-discussed example from the field of my inquiry. For the historian and his problems of style, on the other hand, the book yields less. Perhaps its author is too eager to follow Riegl in his 'objectivity', too eager also to vindicate the experiments of twentieth-century art to see the problem of illusion as anything but a Philistine prejudice. The fact that different periods are known to have had different standards of 'lifelikeness' makes him hope that a 'further shift of the artistic reality level' will make works of Picasso, Braque, or Klee 'look exactly like the things they represent'. If he is right, the Sears Roebuck catalogue of the year 2000 will represent the mandolins, jugs, or twittering machines for sale on this new reality level.

The book by W. M. Ivins, Jr., *Prints and Visual Communication*, is an astringent antidote to these intellectual fashions. For Ivins has shown that the history of representation can indeed be treated in the context of the history of science without reference to aesthetic issues.

It is in this context that I should also like to mention Anton Ehrenzweig's book *The Psychoanalysis of Artistic Vision and Hearing*. The speculative boldness with which the author tries to fit the findings of Gestalt psychology into a system of Freudian ideas deserves attention and respect. Ehrenzweig certainly does not make the mistake of underrating those forces that have to be overcome by scientific naturalism in art. He gives us challenging descriptions of the visual chaos that art seeks to dominate, but he, too, I believe, mars his analysis by a refusal to discuss objective reality tests and by a flight into evolutionist speculations.

The three books I have mentioned prove what we all know, that certain problems are 'in the air' and clamour for solutions. Being already at work when the books came out, I cannot claim that my judgment about them is unbiased. But to me they seemed to demonstrate most forcefully the necessity for the historian of style to stage a counterraid across the psychologist's frontier. It is more than a few isolated results of psychological experiments that I hope to bring back from this foraging expedition. It is the news of a radical reorientation of all traditional ideas about the human mind, which cannot leave the historian of art unaffected. This reorientation is implicit in Arnheim's treatment of child art and in Ehrenzweig's ideas of unconscious perception, but their insistence on the ideas and terminology of one particular school of psychological theory has perhaps somewhat obscured its general nature and importance. The basic terms which critics, artists, and historians have hitherto used with confidence have lost much of their validity in this assessment. The whole idea of the 'imitation of nature', of 'idealization', or of 'abstraction' rests on the assumption that what comes first are 'sense impressions' that are subsequently elaborated, distorted, or generalized.

K. R. Popper has dubbed these assumptions the 'bucket theory of the mind', the picture, that is, of a mind in which 'sense data' are deposited and processed. He has shown the unreality of this basic assumption in the field of scientific method and the theory of knowledge, where he insists on what he calls the 'searchlight theory', emphasizing the activity of the living organism that never ceases probing and testing its environment. The fruitfulness of this approach is increasingly felt in many fields of psychology. However much theories may differ, their emphasis shifts steadily from the stimulus to the organism's response. This response, it is becoming clear, will be vague and general at first and gradually will become more articulate and differentiated.

'The progress of learning is from indefinite to definite, not from sensation to perception. We do not learn to have percepts but to differentiate them', writes J. J. Gibson, discussing vision.

'Modern research makes it probable that at first there are yet unorganized and amorphous wholes which progressively differentiate', writes L. von Bertalanffy on his problems of theoretical biology.

It would be easy to parallel these quotations in the writings of Jean Piaget on the intellectual growth of children or in those on children's emotional development by Freud and his disciples. Even recent studies of the way machines can be said to 'learn' stress this same direction—from the general to the particular. In the course of this book I have sometimes referred to such parallels. I have done so with diffidence, for in these fields I am not even a trespasser. Moreover, I am aware of the dangers of amateurishness and the drift of fashion in such matters. In the end there can be only one justification for the approach I advocate in this book, if it proves useful in the day-to-day work of the historian. But in a study of illusion I could not very well do without a theory of perception. It was here that I found it most useful to think along the lines I have indicated, in terms of sorting and categorizing rather than in terms of associations. The theoretical model for this approach, which ultimately goes back to Kant, is worked out most consistently in F. A. Hayek's book *The Sensory Order*. But I have profited most of all from Popper's insistence on the role of anticipation and tests. In psychology this approach is adopted in the theories of Bruner and Postman that 'all cognitive processes, whether they take the form of perceiving, thinking, or recalling, represent "hypotheses" which the organism sets up. . . . They require "answers" in the form of some *further* experience, answers that will either confirm or disprove them.'

It is in the logic of this situation, as Popper has shown, that confirmations of these 'hypotheses' can never be more than provisional while their refutation will be final. There is no rigid distinction, therefore, between perception and illusion. Perception employs all its resources to weed out harmful illusions, but it may sometimes fail to 'disprove' a false hypothesis—for instance, when it has to deal with illusionist works of art.

I firmly believe that some such theory of perceptual trial and error will prove fruitful in other fields than mine, but I have endeavoured to keep it in the background. My main concern was with the analysis of image making—the way, that is, in which artists discovered some of these secrets of vision by 'making and matching'. What Alain's Egyptian boys had to learn before they could create an illusion of reality was not to 'copy what they saw' but to manipulate those ambiguous cues on which we have to rely in stationary vision till their image was indistinguishable from reality. In other words, instead of playing 'rabbit or duck' they had to invent the game of 'canvas or nature', played with a configuration of coloured earth which—at a distance at least—might result in illusion. Artistic or not, this is a game which could emerge only as a result of countless trials and errors. As a secular experiment in the theory of perception, illusionist art perhaps deserves attention even in a period which has discarded it for other modes of expression.

At the risk of giving away my plot, I will confess to the hurried reader or critic that these conclusions, here anticipated, will only be presented in full in the ninth chapter of this book, where some of the problems discussed in this introduction will be taken up again. I cannot now prevent him from going to those pages at once, but I should like to plead that a book that centres on an argument must be built like an arch. The coping stone will look as if it is hanging in the air unless it is seen to be supported by the neighbouring stones. Each chapter of this book somehow tends inwards toward the centre of the problem, but the results of each should receive support from the whole structure. The limits of likeness imposed by the medium and the schema, the links in image making between form and function, most of all, the analysis of the beholder's share in the resolution of ambiguities will alone make plausible the bald statement that art has a history because the illusions of art are not only the fruit but the indispensable tools for the artist's analysis of appearances. I hope the reader will not stop at this point but will test this idea with me in its application to physiognomic expression and beyond that to the borders of aesthetics, that promised land which he will only glimpse from afar.

I am well aware that this lengthy approach through the quicksands of perceptual theory puts a considerable strain on the reader who is in a hurry to get to the emotional core of art. But I feel that these vital matters can be discussed with greater chance of success once the ground has been cleared a little. I am confirmed in this conviction by a passage in *Psychoanalytic Explorations in Art* by my late friend and mentor Ernst Kris, with whom I so often discussed these matters and who did not live to read this final version of the book:

'We have long come to realize that art is not produced in an empty space, that no artist is independent of predecessors and models, that he no less than the scientist and the philosopher is part of a specific tradition and works in a structured area of problems. The degree of mastery within this framework and, at least in certain periods, the freedom to modify these stringencies are presumably part of the complex scale by which achievement is being measured. However, there is little which psychoanalysis has as yet contributed to an understanding of the meaning of this framework itself; the psychology of artistic style is unwritten.'

The reader must not expect the subsequent chapters to fill the gap which Kris has shown. The psychology of representation alone cannot solve the riddle of style. There are the unexplored pressures of fashions and the mysteries of taste. But if we ever want to understand the impact of these social forces on our attitude toward representation in art—the changing prestige of mastery or the sudden disgust with triviality, the lure of the primitive and the hectic search for alternatives that may determine the fluctuations of style—we must first try to answer the simpler questions posed by Alain's cartoon.

Part One

THE LIMITS OF LIKENESS

---

5. CONSTABLE: *Wivenhoe Park, Essex.* 1816

I

From Light into Paint

Painting is the most astounding sorceress. She can persuade us through the most evident falsehoods that she is pure Truth.

JEAN ETIENNE LIOTARD, *Traité des principes et des règles de la peinture*

I

AMONG the treasures of the National Gallery of Art in Washington hangs a painting of Wivenhoe Park in Essex by John Constable [5]. No historical knowledge is needed to see its beauty. Anyone can enjoy the rural charm of the scene, the artist's skill and sensitivity in rendering the play of sunlight on the green pastures, the gentle ripples on the lake with its swans, and the beautiful cloudscape that encloses it all. The picture looks so effortless and natural that we accept it as an unquestioning and unproblematic response to the beauty of the English countryside.

But for the historian there is an added attraction in this painting. He knows that this freshness of vision was won in a hard struggle. The year 1816, in which Constable painted this countryseat of one of his first patrons, marks a turning point in his artistic career. He was moving toward that conception of painting which he was later to sum up in his lectures at Hampstead. 'Painting is a science,' Constable said, 'and should be pursued as an inquiry into the laws of nature. Why, then, may not landscape painting be considered as a branch of natural philosophy, of which pictures are but the experiments?'

What Constable called 'natural philosophy' we today call 'physics'; the assertion that the quiet and unassuming painting of Wivenhoe Park should be classed with the abstruse experiments of physicists in their laboratories must sound puzzling at first. Yet it is my conviction that Constable's statement should not be confused with those wild utterances with which artists sometimes like to startle and shake their complacent contemporaries. He knew what he was talking about. In the Western tradition, painting has indeed been pursued as a science. All the works of this tradition that we see displayed in our great collections apply discoveries that are the result of ceaseless experimentation.

If this sounds a little paradoxical, it is only because much of the knowledge gained by these experiments in the past has become common property today. It can be taught and applied with the same ease with which we use the laws of the

29

pendulum in a grandfather clock, though it needed a Galileo to discover and a Huygens to apply them. Indeed, there are artists who think the field to which Constable devoted his scientific endeavours has been fully investigated by now and that they must turn to different areas for experiment. Instead of exploring the visible world, they probe the mysteries of the unconscious mind or test our response to abstract shapes. Compared with these hectic activities, Constable's painting of Wivenhoe Park looks so natural and obvious that we are inclined to overlook its daring and its success. We accept it as simply a faithful record of what the artist saw in front of him—'a mere transcript of nature', as paintings of this kind are sometimes described, an approximation at least to that photographic accuracy against which modern artists have rebelled. Let us admit there is something in this description. Constable's painting is surely much more like a photograph than the works of either a Cubist or a medieval artist. But what do we mean when we say that a photograph, in its turn, is like the landscape it represents? This is not a problem which is very easily discussed with the aid of illustrations alone because illustrations will inevitably beg the question. But it should not be too hard to demonstrate at least one of the points where the painter's experiments adjoin those of the physicists. The two photographs here reproduced [6, 7] were taken on the spot where Constable must have stood when he painted Wivenhoe Park. For the park still exists, though the house was much altered and the view of the lake is now obscured by rhododendrons. What is it these pictures 'transcribe'? Surely there is not one square inch in the photograph which would be identical with, say, a mirror image, such as one might have produced on the spot. The reason is obvious. The black-and-white photograph only reproduces gradations of tone between a very narrow range of greys. Not one of these tones, of course, corresponds to what we call 'reality'. Indeed, the scale depends largely on the photographer's choice in the darkroom and is partly a matter of processing. It so happens that the two photographs illustrated here were printed from one and the same negative. The one printed within a narrow scale of greys produces the effect of misty light; the other, where stronger contrasts were used, gives a different effect. The print, therefore, is not even a 'mere' transcript of the negative. The photographer who wanted to get the most out of this snapshot taken on a rainy day would himself have to turn experimenter with different exposures and different papers. If this is true of his humble activity, how much more will it apply to the artist's.

For the artist, too, cannot transcribe what he sees; he can only translate it into the terms of his medium. He, too, is strictly tied to the range of tones which his medium will yield. Where the artist works in black and white this transposition is easily seen. We happen to have two drawings made by Constable on almost the same spot. In one [8] he seems to have used a rather hard-pointed pencil. He had therefore to adjust all his gradations to what is objectively a very narrow range of

6. *Wivenhoe Park, Essex.* Pale print

7. *Wivenhoe Park, Essex.* Contrast print

8. CONSTABLE: *Dedham Vale*. About 1811, pencil

tones, from the black horse in the foreground to the distant trees through which the light of the sky appears to shine, as represented by the greyish paper. In a later drawing [9] he used a darker and cruder medium which allowed more forceful contrast. But what we call 'contrast' here is actually a very small step in the intensity of the light reflected from different areas of the drawing. He also represented the identical view in an oil sketch [10] now in Oxford, where the tonal gradations

9. CONSTABLE: *Dedham from Langham*. 1813, pencil

10. CONSTABLE: *Dedham Vale*. 1812 (oil sketch)

are translated into coloured areas. Does it therefore reproduce what the artist had in front of his eyes?

It is tempting to think so. Why should not the painter be able to imitate the colours of any object if the maker of wax images manages this trick so remarkably well? He certainly can, if he is willing to sacrifice that aspect of the visible world that is likely to interest him most, the aspect of light. When we say that an image looks exactly like its prototype we usually mean that the two would be indistinguishable when seen side by side in the same light. Place them in different lights and the similarity will disappear. If the difference is small we can still restore the match by brightening the colours of the object in the dimmer light, but not if the one is in the shade and the other in sunlight. It was not for nothing that painters were advised since ancient times to have their studios facing north. For if the painter of a portrait or a still life hopes to copy the colour of his motif area by area, he must not allow a ray of sunlight to play havoc with his procedure. Imagine him matching a white tablecloth with his whitest white—how could his palette then still yield the extra brightness of a sunlit patch or the brilliance of a sparkling reflection? The landscape painter has even less use for literal imitation. Remember once more the photographer's troubles. If he wants us to admire the wonderful autumn tints he photographed on his latest trip he will lure us into a darkened room where he displays his transparencies on a silver screen. Only the borrowed light of the projector lamp, aided by the adaptability of our eyes, will allow him to match the range of light intensities he had enjoyed in nature.

It so happens that Constable himself had occasion to comment on a similar expedient. He describes in a letter the new invention called the 'diorama', which was on view in the 1820's. 'It is in part a transparency; the spectator is in a dark chamber, and it is very pleasing, and has great illusion. It is without [i.e., outside] the pale of the art, because its object is deception. The art pleases by *reminding*, not by *deceiving*.'

Had Constable written today he would probably have used the word 'suggesting'. The artist cannot copy a sunlit lawn, but he can suggest it. Exactly how he does it in any particular instance is his secret, but the word of power which makes this magic possible is known to all artists—it is 'relationships'.

No professional critic saw the nature of this problem more clearly than a famous amateur artist who had taken up painting as a pastime. But then this was no ordinary amateur but Sir Winston Churchill:

'It would be interesting if some real authority investigated carefully the part which memory plays in painting. We look at the object with an intent regard, then at the palette, and thirdly at the canvas. The canvas receives a message dispatched usually a few seconds before from the natural object. But it has come through a post office *en route*. It has been transmitted in code. It has been turned from light into paint. It reaches the canvas a cryptogram. Not until it has been placed in its correct relation to everything else that is on the canvas can it be deciphered, is its meaning apparent, is it translated once again from mere pigment into light. And the light this time is not of Nature but of Art.'

I am not that 'real authority' on memory to whom Sir Winston appealed for an explanation of this mystery, but it seems to me that we will be able to tackle this aspect only after we have learned more about that 'transmission in code' which he discusses.

II

I AM NOT sure we are ever quite sufficiently surprised at our capacity to read images, that is, to decipher the cryptograms of art. To Sir Winston, the 'post office' and its code were no more than a brilliant metaphor, but we might do worse than take it literally. After all, post offices (in England, at least) do transmit such visual information as weather charts and photographs by means of telegraph and radio, and to do so they must in fact 'code' them into simple signalling systems. The technicalities of this process need not concern us, suffice it to show that a simple but serviceable image can be translated into equal units which are either filled or empty. Any large street sign composed of electric bulbs will demonstrate this principle—a notation of which are to be 'off' or 'on' will create the required configuration of light. The telegraphed picture and indeed the television screen,

11. *Pattern for drawn work.* Venice, 1568

produced as they are by the varying intensities of one beam scanning the field, illustrate the principle involved. But before I get out of my depth I prefer to withdraw to the safer example of art forms in which this creation of cryptograms can be studied with greater ease. There are many media of art in which such an 'on' or 'off' principle is applied—let us think of certain types of drawn work or lace in which the netting is filled in or left empty of pattern but still gives perfect images of men and beasts [11]. It does not matter in such a medium whether the filled-in squares represent 'figure' or 'ground'. All that counts is the relationship between the two signals.

Maybe it was some textile technique in which reversal of relationships was frequent and automatic that first brought home to craftsmen the fact that the negative image is as easy to decode as the positive. It is well known that the Greek vase painters made use of this principle of reversal when they switched over from the earlier black-figured technique [12] to the red-figured style in which the tone of burnt clay is reserved for the figure [13]. They knew that what is needed to set off the intended shape against the nonintended ground is the relationship of contrast, of 'yes' or 'no', regardless of the direction of the change.

The Greeks went on from there and developed the cryptograms for the rounded form as distinct from the flat silhouette, that is, the three-tone code for 'modelling' in light and shade which remained basic to all later developments of Western art. Its system is well exemplified on a South Italian vase, where the shape of the head

12, 13. *Andokides Amphora. Herakles and the Cretan Bull.* About 520 B.C.
Black-figured side/Red-figured side

is 'heightened' with whitish paint on one side of the vase to suggest light [14] and 'shaded' with a darker tone on the other side [15]. Instead of having a mere 'yes' indicate the intended form, we have the neutral tone and its two modifications toward light and darkness.

14, 15. *South Italian vase*. Third century B.C. Details, opposite sides

No medium illustrates the code character of this gradation more clearly than that of the mosaic. Four graded tones of tesserae will suffice for the mosaicists of classical antiquity to suggest the basic relationships of form in space. I confess to being naïve enough to admire these simple tricks of the craftsmen who laid down the floor mosaics for villas and baths throughout the Roman Empire [16]. They exemplify the relational cryptograms which remained in use throughout Western art, the contrast of figure and ground on the one hand and, within the figure, the modifications of the 'local colour' through the simple 'more' or 'less' of light.

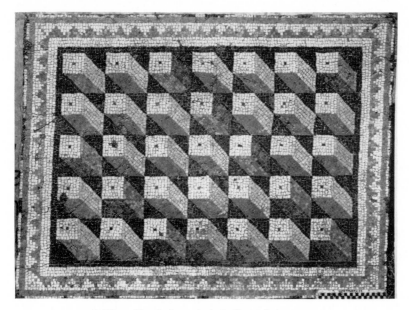

16. *Floor Mosaic from Antioch*. Second century A.D.

17. BALDUNG GRIEN: *The Fall of Man.*
1511. Woodcut

18. BALDUNG GRIEN: *The Fall of Man.*
1511. Chiaroscuro woodcut

As a matter of fact, we have become so obedient to the artist's suggestions that we respond with perfect ease to the notation in which black lines indicate both the distinction between ground and figure and the gradations of shading that have become traditional in all graphic techniques. Baldung Grien's woodcut of the Fall

19. Detail of 18

[17] looks perfectly complete and legible to us in its notation of black and white. It is all the more interesting to study the additional effect of the second plate [18]—one of the earliest examples of the chiaroscuro woodcut technique. By lowering the tone of the ground the artist can now use the white of the paper to indicate light. The gain from this modest extension of range is dramatic, for these indications of light not only increase the sense of modelling but also convey to us what we call 'texture'—the way, that is, in which light behaves when it strikes a particular surface. It is only in the chiaroscuro version of the woodcut, therefore, that we get the 'feel' of the scaly body of the serpent [19].

20. URS GRAF: *Standard Bearer*. 1514. Pen and white ink on tinted paper

The three-step relationship has certainly proved an ideal instrument for Western art in exploring our response to light. But we are also capable of reading a two-step system in reverse, as it were. Such artists as Urs Graf successfully experimented with a technique that cuts out any indication of shading and renders only the incidence of light [20] against a dark background. Our response to relationships suffices to make this curious notation look perfectly 'natural'.

The fact that all graphic techniques operate with conventional notation is, of course, familiar ground, but when it comes to painting, there is still a certain amount of confusion in the minds of the public and of the critics as to what we mean by 'true to nature'. The task of the painter with his many colours seems so much simpler than that of the graphic artist with his limited cryptograms. It is in fact more complex. His aim of 'imitation' may cut across the need for that basic information about relationships which we need for our decoding. I must plead guilty to sharing this confusion in my *Story of Art* when I quoted a well-known anecdote about Constable and his patron, Sir George Beaumont: 'The story goes that a friend remonstrated with him for not giving his foreground the requisite mellow brown of an old violin, and that Constable thereupon took a violin and put it before him on the grass to show the friend the difference between the fresh green as we see it and the warm tones demanded by convention.'

It was an amusing gesture, but obviously we must not infer that Sir George had never noticed that grass was green and violins brown, or that Constable made that momentous discovery. Both of them knew, of course, that such matching will never do. The point at issue was a much more subtle one—how to reconcile what we call 'local colour' with the range of tonal gradations which the landscape painter needs to suggest depth.

We find an echo of these discussions in an observation by Benjamin West recorded in *The Farington Diary*: 'He thinks Claude [23] began his pictures by laying in simple gradations of flat colours from the Horizon to the top of the sky,—and from the Horizon to the foreground, witht. putting clouds into the sky or specific forms into the landscape till He had fully settled those gradations.—When He had satisfied himself in this respect, He painted in his forms, by that means securing a due gradation,—from the Horizontal line to the top of his sky,—and from the Horizontal line to the foreground.—Smirke remarked how entirely all *positive* colour was avoided, even to the draperies of the figures.—Turner said He was both pleased and unhappy while He viewed it,—it seemed to be beyond the power of imitation'.

These experiments with gradations from a pale blue to a mellow brown by seventeenth- and eighteenth-century artists taught Sir George Beaumont how to suggest light and distance in a landscape. The eighteenth century had even invented a mechanical device to aid the painter in this transposition of local colour into a narrower range of tones. It consisted of a curved mirror with a toned surface that was appropriately often called the 'Claude glass' and was supposed to do what the black-and-white photograph does for us, to reduce the variety of the visible world to tonal gradations. That this method had its merits we need not doubt. Eighteenth-century masters achieved most pleasing effects with foregrounds of warm brown and fading distances of cool, silvery blues.

Looking at Reynolds' *Lady Elizabeth Delmé and Her Children* in the National Gallery in Washington [29] or, for that matter, at Gainsborough's *Landscape with a Bridge* [21, page 49], we realize the value of an even gradation based on the brown of the foreground. Indeed, a glance at Constable's *View of Salisbury Cathedral* [24] convinces us that he, too, achieved the impression of light and depth by modulating tone. The difference is one of degree. Constable questioned the need to remain within the compass of one scale. He wanted to try out the effect of respecting the local colour of grass somewhat more—and, indeed, in his *Wivenhoe Park* he is seen pushing the range more in the direction of bright greens. Only in the direction of—for, needless to say, if we would match fresh green grass against the canvas it would still be nearer to the Cremona fiddle. It is a transposition, not a copy.

Once we realize this basic fact, the master's contention that all paintings should be viewed as experiments in natural science loses much of its puzzling character. He is trying to produce what he called the 'evanescent effects of nature's chiaroscuro' on canvas, within a medium which excludes matching. Indeed his experiments resulted in discoveries. For instance, there was a resistance at first against so much green, which was thought to upset the needed tonal gradation. There is a pathetic story about Constable's sitting on the jury of the Royal Academy, of which he was a member, when by mistake one of his own paintings was put on the easel for judgment, and one of his colleagues said rashly, 'Take that nasty green thing away'. But we also know that when his *Hay Wain* was shown in Paris, French artists were stimulated to repeat his experiments and lightened their palettes. We need only walk through any major gallery to see that in the end Constable's method found acceptance. Green is no longer considered 'nasty'. We can read much brighter pictures, such as the landscapes by Corot [22] and, what is more, enjoy the suggestion of light without missing the tonal contrasts which were thought indispensable. We have learned a new notation and expanded the range of our awareness.

This is the main lesson the historian should learn from the measurements of the physicists. The truth of a landscape painting is relative and the more so the more the artist dares to accept the challenge of light. Great scientists, such as Brücke in the nineteenth century, even drew the conclusion from this fact that painters should not attempt sunlit scenes. 'A little more poetry and a little less midday sun would do our modern landscape painters a lot of good', he wrote in 1877. We now know that he was wrong, but then it is easy for us to know it. The experiments of the impressionist painters have convinced us that these limitations of the medium can be overcome: a painter like Monet [25] can suggest the effect of the midday sun by exploiting the dazzle that results from its glare, and such pictures will even gain in poetry from the artist's determination to achieve the

21. GAINSBOROUGH: *Landscape with a Bridge*. About 1780–1788

22. COROT: *View near Epernon*. About 1850–1860

23. CLAUDE LORRAIN: *The Herdsman*. About 1655/1660

24. CONSTABLE: *A View of Salisbury Cathedral*. About 1825

25. MONET: *Rouen Cathedral, West Façade, Sunlight.* 1894

impossible. To predict this success, Brücke would have had to be a creative artist himself. For a scientist his objections were perfectly rational. Too often the conflict between the artist and the public, between tradition and innovation, is told without regard for that simple fact. On the one side we are shown the purblind public, bred on falsehoods; on the other the artist, who sees the truth. History based on this fallacy can never be good history. And nothing may help us to overcome these limitations better than Constable's description of landscape painting as an inquiry into the laws of nature.

It is only in one respect that we should perhaps amend his formulation. What a painter inquires into is not the nature of the physical world but the nature of our reactions to it. He is not concerned with causes but with the mechanisms of certain effects. His is a psychological problem—that of conjuring up a convincing image despite the fact that not one individual shade corresponds to what we call 'reality'. In order to understand this puzzle—as far as we can claim to understand it as yet—science had to explore the capacity of our minds to register relationships rather than individual elements.

III

WE WERE not endowed with this capacity by nature in order to produce art: it appears that we could never find our way about in this world if we were not thus attuned to relationships. Just as a tune remains the same whatever the key it is played in, so we respond to light intervals, to what have been called 'gradients', rather than to the measurable quantity of light reflected from any given object. And when I say 'we', I include newly hatched chickens and other fellow-creatures who so obligingly answer the questions psychologists put to them. According to a classic experiment by Wolfgang Köhler, you can take two grey pieces of paper— one dark, one bright—and teach the chickens to expect food on the brighter of the two. If you then remove the darker piece and replace it by one brighter than the other one, the deluded creatures will look for their dinner, not on the identical grey paper where they have always found it, but on the paper where they would expect it in terms of relationships—that is, on the brighter of the two. Their little brains are attuned to gradients rather than to individual stimuli. Things could not go well with them if nature had willed it otherwise. For would a memory of the exact stimulus have helped them to recognize the identical paper? Hardly ever! A cloud passing over the sun would change its brightness, and so might even a tilt of the head, or an approach from a different angle. If what we call 'identity' were not anchored in a constant relationship with environment, it would be lost in the chaos of swirling impressions that never repeat themselves.

What we get on the retina, whether we are chickens or human beings, is a welter of dancing light points stimulating the sensitive rods and cones that fire their messages into the brain. What we see is a stable world. It takes an effort of the imagination and a fairly complex apparatus to realize the tremendous gulf that exists between the two. Consider any object, such as a book or a piece of paper.

When we scan it with our eyes it projects upon our two retinas a restless, flitting pattern of light of various wave lengths and intensities. This pattern will hardly ever repeat itself exactly—the angle at which we look, the light, the size of our pupils, all these will have changed. The white light a piece of paper reflects when turned toward the window is a multiple of what it reflects when turned away. It is not that we do not notice some change; indeed, we must if we want to form an estimate of the illumination. But we are never conscious of the objective degree of all these changes unless we use what psychologists call a 'reduction screen', in essence a peephole that makes us see a speck of colour but masks off its relationships. Those who have used this magic instrument report the most striking discoveries. A white handkerchief in the shade may be objectively darker than a lump of coal in the sunshine. We rarely confuse the one with the other because the coal will on the whole be the blackest patch in our field of vision, the handkerchief the whitest, and it is relative brightness that matters and that we are aware of. The coding process of which Sir Winston Churchill speaks begins while en route between the retina and our conscious mind. The term which psychology has coined for our relative imperviousness to the dizzy variations that go on in the world around us is 'constancy'. The colour, shape, and brightness of things remain to us relatively constant, even though we may notice some variation with the change of distance, illumination, angle of vision, and so on. Our room remains the same room from dawn through midday to dusk, and the objects in it retain their shape and colour. Only when we are faced with special tasks involving attention to these matters do we become aware of uncertainties. We would not judge the colour of an unfamiliar fabric in artificial light, and we step into the middle of the room if we are asked whether a picture hangs straight on the wall. Otherwise our capacity to make allowances, to infer from relationships alone, is astounding. We all know the experience at the moving pictures when we are ushered to a seat very far off-centre. At first the screen and what is on it look so distorted and unreal we feel like leaving. But in a few minutes we have learned to take our position into account, and the proportions right themselves. And as with shapes, so with colours. A faint light is disturbing at first, but with the aid of the physiological adaptation of the eye we soon get the feel of relationships, and the world assumes its familiar face.

Without this faculty of man and beast alike to recognize identities across the variations of difference, to make allowance for changed conditions, and to preserve the frame work of a stable world, art could not exist. When we open our eyes under water we recognize objects, shapes, and colours although through an unfamiliar medium. When we first see pictures we see them in an unfamiliar medium. This is more than a mere pun. The two capacities are interrelated. Every time we meet with an unfamiliar type of transposition, there is a brief moment of shock and a period of adjustment—but it is an adjustment for which the mechanism exists in us.

IV

I SUSPECT that somewhere here lies the preliminary answer to the question of how far we must learn to read such images as line drawings or black-and-white photographs and of how far this capacity is inborn. As far as I can make out, primitive tribes that have never seen such images are not necessarily able to read them. But it would be wrong to conclude from this fact that the symbolism of photography is merely conventional. It appears to be learned with surprising speed once the nature of the required adjustment is understood.

26. FANTIN-LATOUR: *Portrait of Sonia.*   27. MANET: *Madame Michel-Lévy.* 1882.
1890   Pastel and oil

I believe that something similar accounts for both the initial difficulty and the subsequent ease in adjusting ourselves to new types of notations in painting. To eyes used to the style of Fantin-Latour's *Portrait of Sonia* [26], Manet's *Madame Michel-Lévy* [27] must at first have looked as harsh and glaring as sunlight looks to the deep-sea diver.

It is once more in Constable's correspondence that we find rich documentation of this difficulty which besets the path of the artist-innovator. Hearing of that rare bird, a prospective buyer for one of his landscapes, the embittered painter writes: 'Had I not better grime it down with slime and soot, as he is a connoisseur, and perhaps prefers filth and dirt to freshness and beauty?' 'Rubbed out and dirty canvases,' he writes elsewhere, 'take the place of God's own works.' Intent as he was on the rendering of light, he could not but deplore and despise the visual habits of the public that had adjusted its eyes to the gloom of old varnish. His point of view, as we know, has prevailed. The yellow varnish that was spread over paintings in the nineteenth century to give them what was called a 'gallery tone' has disappeared with the Claude glass. We have been taught to look into light without putting on black spectacles.

But it would be a little rash to assume that this revolution has at last given us the truth and that we now know what pictures should look like. Constable rightly deplored the visual habits of those who were used to looking at dirty canvases, and he went so far as to deplore the founding of the National Gallery in London, which would mean 'the end of art in poor old England'. But today the position may be reversed. The brighter palette, the strong and even loud colours to which first impressionism and then twentieth-century paintings (not to mention posters and neon lights) have inured us may have made it difficult for us to accept the quiet tonal gradations of earlier styles. The National Gallery in London has now become the focus of discussion about the degree of adjustment we should be prepared to make when we look at old paintings.

I venture to think this issue is too frequently described as a conflict between the objective methods of science and the subjective impressions of artists and critics. The objective validity of the methods used in the laboratories of our great galleries is as little in doubt as the good faith of those who apply them. But it may well be argued that restorers, in their difficult and responsible work, should take account not only of the chemistry of pigments, but also of the psychology of per-ception—ours and that of the chicken. What we want of them is not to restore individual pigments to their pristine colour, but something infinitely more tricky and delicate—to preserve rela-tionships. It is particularly the impres-sion of light, as we know, that rests exclusively on gradients and not, as one might expect, on the objective bright-ness of the colours. Wherever we observe a sudden steep rise in the brightness of a tone we accept it as a token of light. A typical tonal picture such as Daumier's *Advice to a Young Artist* [28] reminds us of this basic fact. The abrupt change of tone brings the sunlight into the gloomy nineteenth-century interior. Study the clever effect

28. DAUMIER: *Advice to a Young Artist.*
After 1860

29. REYNOLDS: *Lady Elizabeth Delmé and Her Children.* 1777–1789

30. PANNINI: *The Interior of the Pantheon.*   31. JOSEPH BIEDER: *Poster.* 1953
About 1740

of the daylight streaming through the eye of the Pantheon in Pannini's attractive picture [30]. Once more it is the sharp edge of the patch of light that creates the illusion. Mask it off and the impression of light will largely disappear. I am told that this fact presents a problem of which the restorer must learn to be aware. Whenever he starts the process of cleaning, he will produce a similar difference in brightness, an unexpected gradient which will look as if light were streaming into the picture. It is a psychological effect cleverly exploited by an amusing poster of the National Clean-up Paint-up Fix-up Bureau [31]. But I would not send my pictures to that admirable institution for treatment. This seductive impression of daylight dispelling the gloom is created within the picture; the gradient which causes it will disappear when the cleaning is finished. As soon as we are then attuned to the new key of brightness, the constancies come into their own and the mind returns to its proper business of assessing gradients and relationships. We adapt ourselves to different varnishes as we adapt ourselves to different conditions of light in the gallery, provided, of course, that visibility is not completely obscured. The added brilliance, I feel, often sinks back as soon as the shock wears off. It is an effect which resembles, to me at any rate, that of turning the knob of the radio from bass to treble. At first the music seems to acquire a new, sharp edge, but here, too, I adjust my expectations and return to the constancies with the added worry whether all gradients have been respected and preserved by those invisible ghosts, the tone engineers.

I fear it is in the nature of things that the historian will always be distrustful of the man of action in these difficult and delicate matters. We are as appalled as any to see our documents fading and our pictures dirty, but we also know how little we know about the past. About one thing we are quite certain: our reactions and our taste must of necessity differ from that of past generations. If it is true that the Victorians erred so frequently, it is all the more likely that we, too, will often be mistaken despite the improvement in our techniques. We know, moreover, that there were other periods besides the nineteenth century that looked upon brilliance of colour as a disturbing element. To Cicero, for instance, it seemed obvious that a cultivated taste grew tired of such brilliance no less than of a surfeit of sweetness. 'How strongly,' he writes, 'do new paintings usually appeal to us at first for the beauty and variety of their colours, and yet it is the old and rough picture that will hold our attention.' Even more telling is a passage in Pliny where we read of Apelles' inimitable way of toning down his pigments with a dark glazing 'so that the brightness of colours should not hurt the eyes'. We do not know what degree of brightness offended the sensitive taste of a fourth-century Greek or a first-century Roman. But is it conceivable that such famous testimonies would never have induced a master of the sixteenth or seventeenth century to emulate Apelles and apply a darkening varnish to achieve a more subtle tonal unity? I do not think it is even claimed that our 'safe' cleaning methods could detect such a varnish, let alone that they could preserve it. Admittedly, the man of action confronted with a deteriorating canvas may have to take the risk—but need he deny its existence?

32. REMBRANDT: *The Young Haaring*. 1655. Etching

The question of what paintings looked like when they were made is more easily asked than answered. Luckily we have additional evidence in images that neither fade nor change—I mean particularly the works of graphic art. Some of Rembrandt's prints [32], I believe, provide an astounding object lesson in reliance on dark tones and subdued contrasts. Is it an accident that there are fewer print lovers now than there ever were? Those who got used to the sound of the concert grand find it difficult to adjust their ears to the harpsichord.

We do well to remember that relationships matter in art not only within any given painting but also between paintings as they are hung or as they are seen. If

33. HOBBEMA: *Village with Watermill among Trees.* About 1670

34. CONSTABLE: *The White Horse.* 1819

we look, in the Frick Collection, from Hobbema's *Village with Watermill among Trees* [33] to Constable's *White Horse* [34], the latter painting will look as full of light and atmosphere as Constable meant us to see it. Should we choose another route in the gallery and come to it with our eye adjusted to the palette of the school of Barbizon, of Corot [cf. 22], for instance, Constable's painting will seem to be eclipsed. It recedes behind the ridge which separates, for us, the contemporary vision from that of the past.

The reason, I believe, lies precisely in the role which our own expectations play in the deciphering of the artists' cryptograms. We come to their works with our receivers already attuned. We expect to be presented with a certain notation, a certain sign situation, and make ready to cope with it. Here sculpture is an even better example than painting. When we step in front of a bust we understand what we are expected to look for. We do not, as a rule, take it to be a representation of a cut-off head; we take in the situation and know that this belongs to the institution or convention called 'busts' with which we have been familiar even before we grew up. For the same reason, perhaps, we do not miss the absence of colour in the marble any more than we miss its absence in black-and-white photographs. On the contrary. Some who are so attuned will register a shock, not necessarily of pleasure, when they discover that a bust has been slightly tinted. Such a bust may even look to them unpleasantly lifelike, transcending, as it were, the symbolic sphere in which it was expected to dwell, although objectively it may still be very remote indeed from the proverbial wax image which often causes us uneasiness because it oversteps the boundary of symbolism.

Psychologists call such levels of expectation 'mental set', and this concept will still engage our attention in future chapters. All culture and all communication depend on the interplay between expectation and observation, the waves of fulfillment, disappointment, right guesses, and wrong moves that make up our daily life. If somebody arrives at the office we may be set to hear him say 'good morning', and the fulfillment of our expectation is hardly registered. If he fails to say 'good morning' we may, on occasion, adjust our mental set and watch out for other symptoms of rudeness or hostility. It is one of the problems of the foreigner in a strange country that he lacks a frame of reference that allows him to take the mental temperature around him with assurance. A German will expect a handshake where an Englishman will scarcely nod his head. An Italian peasant may be scandalized by a tourist's dress which may seem to us a model of propriety. The point to remember is that here, as elsewhere, it is the 'more' or 'less' that counts, the relationship between the expected and the experienced.

The experience of art is not exempt from this general rule. A style, like a culture or climate of opinion, sets up a horizon of expectation, a mental set, which registers deviations and modifications with exaggerated sensitivity. In noticing relationships the mind registers tendencies. The history of art is full of reactions that can only be understood in this way. To those used to the style we call 'Cimabue' [35] and expecting to be presented with a similar notation, the paintings of Giotto [36] came with a shock of incredible lifelikeness. 'There is nothing,' writes Boccaccio, 'which Giotto could not have portrayed in such a manner as to deceive the sense of sight.' It may seem strange to us, but have we not experienced a similar shock, if on a very much lower level? When the cinema introduced '3-D', the distance between

35. CIMABUE: *Madonna and Child Enthroned with Angels and Prophets*. About 1275–1280

36. GIOTTO: *Madonna and Child Enthroned with Saints and Angels*. About 1310

expectation and experience was such that many enjoyed the thrill of a perfect illusion. But the illusion wears off once the expectation is stepped up; we take it for granted and want more.

To us historians these simple psychological facts present some difficulties when we discuss the relation between art and what we call reality. We cannot but look at the art of the past through the wrong end of the telescope. We come to Giotto on the long road which leads from the impressionists backward via Michelangelo and Masaccio, and what we see first in him is therefore not lifelikeness but rigid restraint and majestic aloofness. Some critics, notably André Malraux, have concluded from this that the art of the past is closed to us altogether, that it survives only as what he calls 'myth', transformed and transfigured as it is seen in the ever-changing contexts of the historical kaleidoscope. I am a little less pessimistic. I believe the historical imagination can overstep these barriers, that we can attune ourselves to different styles no less than we can adjust our mental set to different media and different notations. Of course some effort is needed. But this effort seems to me eminently worth while—which is one of the reasons why I have selected the problem of representation as the topic of these lectures.

II

Truth and the Stereotype

> The schematism by which our understanding deals with the phenomenal world . . . is a skill so deeply hidden in the human soul that we shall hardly guess the secret trick that Nature here employs.
>
> IMMANUEL KANT, *Kritik der reinen Vernunft*

I

IN HIS charming autobiography, the German illustrator Ludwig Richter relates how he and his friends, all young art students in Rome in the 1820's, visited the famous beauty spot of Tivoli and sat down to draw. They looked with surprise, but hardly with approval, at a group of French artists who approached the place with enormous baggage, carrying large quantities of paint which they applied to the canvas with big, coarse brushes. The Germans, perhaps roused by this self-confident artiness, were determined on the opposite approach. They selected the hardest, best-pointed pencils, which could render the motif firmly and minutely to its finest detail, and each bent down over his small piece of paper, trying to transcribe what he saw with the utmost fidelity. 'We fell in love with every blade of grass, every tiny twig, and refused to let anything escape us. Every one tried to render the motif as objectively as possible.'

Nevertheless, when they then compared the fruits of their efforts in the evening, their transcripts differed to a surprising extent. The mood, the colour, even the outline of the motif had undergone a subtle transformation in each of them. Richter goes on to describe how these different versions reflected the different dispositions of the four friends, for instance, how the melancholy painter had straightened the exuberant contours and emphasized the blue tinges. We might say he gives an illustration of the famous definition by Emile Zola, who called a work of art 'a corner of nature seen through a temperament'.

It is precisely because we are interested in this definition that we must probe it a little further. The 'temperament' or 'personality' of the artist, his selective preferences, may be one of the reasons for the transformation which the motif undergoes under the artist's hands, but there must be others—everything, in fact, which we bundle together into the word 'style', the style of the period and the style of the artist. When this transformation is very noticeable we say the motif has been greatly 'stylized', and the corollary to this observation is that those who happen to be interested in the motif, for one reason or another, must learn to discount the style. This is part of that natural adjustment, the change in what I called 'mental

37. *Hastings.* From the Bayeux Tapestry. About 1080

set', which we all perform quite automatically when looking at old illustrations. We can 'read' the Bayeux tapestry [37] without reflecting on its countless 'deviations from reality'. We are not tempted for a moment to think the trees at Hastings looked like palmettes and the ground at that time consisted of scrolls. It is an extreme example, but it brings out the all-important fact that the word 'stylized' somehow tends to beg the question. It implies there was a special activity by which the artist transformed the trees, much as the Victorian designer was taught to study the forms of flowers before he turned them into patterns. It was a practice which chimed in well with ideas of Victorian architecture, when railways and factories were built first and then adorned with the marks of a style. It was not the practice of earlier times.

The very point of Richter's story, after all, is that style rules even where the artist wishes to reproduce nature faithfully, and trying to analyse these limits to objectivity may help us get nearer to the riddle of style. One of these limits we know from the last chapter; it is indicated in Richter's story by the contrast between coarse brush and fine pencil. The artist, clearly, can render only what his tool and his medium are capable of rendering. His technique restricts his freedom of choice. The features and relationships the pencil picks out will differ from those the brush can indicate. Sitting in front of his motif, pencil in hand, the artist will, therefore, look out for those aspects which can be rendered in lines—as we say in a pardonable abbreviation, he will tend to see his motif in terms of lines, while, brush in hand, he sees it in terms of masses.

The question of why style should impose similar limitations is less easily answered, least of all when we do not know whether the artist's intentions were the same as those of Richter and his friends.

Historians of art have explored the regions where Cézanne and van Gogh set up their easels and have photographed their motifs [38, 39]. Such comparisons will always retain their fascination since they almost allow us to look over the

38. CÉZANNE: *Mont Sainte-Victoire*. About 1905

artist's shoulder—and who does not wish he had this privilege? But however instructive such confrontations may be when handled with care, we must clearly beware of the fallacy of 'stylization'. Should we believe the photograph represents the 'objective truth' while the painting records the artist's subjective vision—the way he transformed 'what he saw'? Can we here compare 'the image on the retina' with the 'image in the mind'? Such speculations easily lead into a morass of un-provables. Take the image on the artist's retina. It sounds scientific enough, but actually there never was *one* such image which we could single out for comparison with either photograph or painting. What there was was an endless succession of innumerable images as the painter scanned the landscape in front of him, and these images sent a complex pattern of impulses through the optic nerves to

39. *Mont Sainte-Victoire seen from Les Lauves*. Photograph by John Rewald

his brain. Even the artist knew nothing of these events, and we know even less. How far the picture that formed in his mind corresponded to or deviated from the photograph it is even less profitable to ask. What we do know is that these artists went out into nature to look for material for a picture and their artistic wisdom led them to organize the elements of the landscape into works of art of marvellous complexity that bear as much relationship to a surveyor's record as a poem bears to a police report.

Does this mean, then, that we are altogether on a useless quest? That artistic truth differs so much from prosaic truth that the question of objectivity must never be asked? I do not think so. We must only be a little more circumspect in our formulation of the question.

II

THE NATIONAL GALLERY in Washington possesses a landscape painting by a nineteenth-century artist which almost seems made to clarify this issue.

40. INNESS: *The Lackawanna Valley*. 1855

It is an attractive picture by George Inness of *The Lackawanna Valley* [40], which we know from the master's son was commissioned in 1855 as an advertisement for a railroad. At the time there was only one track running into the roundhouse, 'but the president insisted on having four or five painted in, easing his conscience by explaining that the road would eventually have them'. Inness protested, and we can see that when he finally gave in for the sake of his family, he shamefacedly hid the patch with the nonexistent tracks behind puffs of smoke. To him this patch was a lie, and no aesthetic explanation about mental images or higher truth could have disputed this away.

But, strictly speaking, the lie was not in the painting. It was in the advertisement, if it claimed by caption or implication that the painting gave accurate information about the facilities of the railway's roundhouses. In a different context the same picture might have illustrated a true statement—for instance, if the president had taken it to a shareholders' meeting to demonstrate improvements he was anxious to make. Indeed in that case, Inness' rendering of the nonexistent tracks might conceivably have given the engineer some hints about where to lay them. It would have served as a sketch or blueprint.

Logicians tell us—and they are not people to be easily gainsaid—that the terms 'true' and 'false' can only be applied to statements, propositions. And whatever may be the usage of critical parlance, a picture is never a statement in that sense of the term. It can no more be true or false than a statement can be blue or green. Much confusion has been caused in aesthetics by disregarding this simple fact. It is an understandable confusion because in our culture pictures are usually labelled, and labels, or captions, can be understood as abbreviated statements. When it is said 'the camera cannot lie', this confusion is apparent. Propaganda in wartime often made use of photographs falsely labelled to accuse or exculpate one of the warring parties. Even in scientific illustrations it is the caption which determines the truth of the picture. In a *cause célèbre* of the last century, the embryo of a pig, labelled as a human embryo to prove a theory of evolution, brought about the downfall of a great reputation. Without much reflection, we can all expand into statements the laconic captions we find in museums and books. When we read the name 'Ludwig Richter' under a landscape painting, we know we are thus informed that he painted it and can begin arguing whether this information is true or false. When we read 'Tivoli', we infer the picture is to be taken as a view of that spot, and we can again agree or disagree with the label. How and when we agree, in such a case, will largely depend on what we want to know about the object represented. The Bayeux tapestry, for instance, tells us there was a battle at Hastings. It does not tell us what Hastings 'looked like'.

Now the historian knows that the information pictures were expected to provide differed widely in different periods. Not only were images scarce in the past, but so were the public's opportunities to check their captions. How many people ever saw their ruler in the flesh at sufficiently close quarters to recognize his likeness? How many travelled widely enough to tell one city from another? It is hardly surprising, therefore, that pictures of people and places changed their captions with sovereign disregard for truth. The print sold on the market as a portrait of a king would be altered to represent his successor or enemy.

There is a famous example of this indifference to truthful captions in one of the most ambitious publishing projects of the early printing press, Hartmann Schedel's so-called 'Nuremberg Chronicle' with woodcuts by Dürer's teacher Wolgemut. What an opportunity such a volume should give the historian to see what the world was like at the time of Columbus! But as we turn the pages of this big folio, we find the same woodcut of a medieval city recurring with different

41, 42. WOLGEMUT: *Woodcuts from the 'Nuremberg Chronicle'*. 1493

captions as Damascus, Ferrara, Milan, and Mantua [41, 42]. Unless we are prepared to believe these cities were as indistinguishable from one another as their suburbs may be today, we must conclude that neither the publisher nor the public minded whether the captions told the truth. All they were expected to do was to bring home to the reader that these names stood for cities.

These varying standards of illustration and documentation are of interest to the historian of representation precisely because he can soberly test the information supplied by picture and caption without becoming entangled too soon in problems of aesthetics. Where it is a question of information imparted by the image, the comparison with the correctly labelled photograph should be of obvious value. Three topographical prints representing various approaches to the perfect picture postcard should suffice to exemplify the results of such an analysis.

The first [43] shows a view of Rome from a German sixteenth-century news-sheet reporting a catastrophic flood when the Tiber burst its banks. Where in Rome could the artist have seen such a timber structure, a castle with black-and-white walls, and a steep roof such as might be found in Nuremberg? Is this also a view of a German town with a misleading caption? Strangely enough, it is not. The artist, whoever he was, must have made some effort to portray the scene, for this curious building turns out to be the Castel Sant' Angelo in Rome, which guards the bridge across the Tiber. A comparison with a photograph [45] shows that it does embody quite a number of features which belong or belonged to the castle: the angel on the roof that gives it its name, the main round bulk, founded on Hadrian's mausoleum, and the outworks with the bastions that we know were there [44].

I am fond of this coarse woodcut because its very crudeness allows us to study the mechanism of portrayal as in a slow-motion picture. There is no question here of the artist's having deviated from the motif in order to express his mood or his aesthetic preferences. It is doubtful, in fact, whether the designer of the woodcut ever saw Rome. He probably adapted a view of the city in order to illustrate the sensational news. He knew the Castel Sant' Angelo to be a castle, and so he selected from the drawer of his mental stereotypes the appropriate cliché for a castle—a German *Burg* with its timber structure and high-pitched roof. But he did not simply repeat his stereotype —he adapted it to its particular function by embodying certain distinctive features which he knew belonged to that particular building in Rome. He supplies some information over and above the fact that there is a castle by a bridge.

Once we pay attention to this principle of the adapted stereotype, we also find it where we would be less likely to expect it: that is, within the idiom of illustrations, which look much more flexible and therefore plausible.

The example from the seventeenth century, from the views of Paris by that well-known and skilful topographical artist Matthäus Merian, represents Notre Dame and gives, at first, quite a convincing rendering of that

43. ANONYMOUS: *Castel Sant' Angelo, Rome.* 1557. Woodcut

44. ANONYMOUS: *Castel Sant' Angelo, Rome.* About 1540. Pen and ink

45. *Castel Sant' Angelo, Rome.* Modern photograph

famous church [46]. Comparison with the real building [47], however, demonstrates that Merian has proceeded in exactly the same way as the anonymous German woodcutter. As a child of the seventeenth century, his notion of a

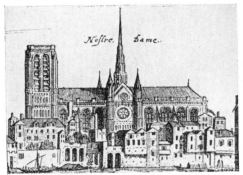

46. MERIAN: *Cathedral of Notre Dame, Paris.*
Detail. About 1635. Engraving

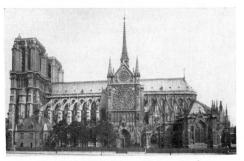

47. *Cathedral of Notre Dame, Paris.*
Modern photograph

church is that of a lofty symmetrical building with large, rounded windows, and that is how he designs Notre Dame. He places the transept in the centre with four large, rounded windows on either side, while the actual view shows seven narrow, pointed Gothic windows to the west and six in the choir. Once more portrayal means for Merian the adaptation or adjustment of his formula or scheme for churches to a particular building through the addition of a number of distinctive features—enough to make it recognizable and even acceptable to those who are not in search of architectural information. If this happened to be the only document extant to tell us about the Cathedral of Paris, we would be very much misled.

One last example in this series: a nineteenth-century lithograph [48] of Chartres Cathedral, done in the heyday of English topographical art. Here, surely, we might expect a faithful visual record. By comparison with the previous instances, the artist really gives a good deal of accurate information about that famous building. But he, too, it turns out, cannot escape the limitations which his time and interests impose on him. He is a romantic to whom the French cathedrals are the greatest flowers of the Gothic centuries, the true age of faith. And so he conceives of Chartres as a Gothic structure with pointed arches and fails to record the Romanesque rounded windows of the west façade, which have no place in his universe of form [49].

I do not want to be misunderstood here. I do not want to prove by these examples that all representation must be inaccurate or that all visual documents before the advent of photography must be misleading. Clearly, if we had pointed out to the artist his mistake, he could have further modified his scheme and rounded the windows. My point is rather that such matching will always be a step-by-step process—how long it takes and how hard it is will depend on the choice of the initial schema to be adapted to the task of serving as a portrait. I believe that in this respect these humble documents do indeed tell us a lot about the procedure of any artist who wants to make a truthful record of an individual form. He begins not with his visual impression but with his idea or concept: the

48. GARLAND: *Cathedral of Notre Dame, Chartres.* 1836. Engraving after lithograph

49. *Cathedral of Notre Dame, Chartres.* Modern photograph

German artist with his concept of a castle that he applies as well as he can to that individual castle, Merian with his idea of a church, and the lithographer with his stereotype of a cathedral. The individual visual information, those distinctive features I have mentioned, are entered, as it were, upon a pre-existing blank or formulary. And, as often happens with blanks, if they have no provisions for certain kinds of information we consider essential, it is just too bad for the information.

The comparison, by the way, between the formularies of administration and the artist's stereotypes is not my invention. In medieval parlance there was one word for both, a *simile*, or pattern, that is applied to individual incidents in law no less than in pictorial art.

And just as the lawyer or the statistician could plead that he could never get hold of the individual case without some sort of framework provided by his forms or blanks, so the artist could argue that it makes no sense to look at a motif unless one has learned how to classify and catch it within the network of a schematic form. This, at least, is the conclusion to which psychologists have come who knew nothing of our historical series but who set out to investigate the procedure anyone adopts when copying what is called a 'nonsense figure', an inkblot, let us say, or an irregular patch. By and large, it appears, the procedure is always the same. The draughtsman tries first to classify the blot and fit it into some sort of familiar schema—he will say, for instance, that it is triangular or that it looks like a fish. Having selected such a schema to fit the form approximately, he will proceed to adjust it, noticing for instance that the triangle is rounded at the top, or that the fish ends in a pigtail. Copying, we learn from these experiments, proceeds through the rhythms of schema and correction. The schema is not the product of a process of 'abstraction', of a tendency to 'simplify'; it represents the first approximate, loose category which is gradually tightened to fit the form it is to reproduce.

III

ONE MORE important point emerges from these psychological discussions of copying: it is dangerous to confuse the way a figure is drawn with the way it is seen. 'Reproducing the simplest figures,' writes Professor Zangwill, 'constitutes a process itself by no means psychologically simple. This process typically displays an essentially constructive or reconstructive character, and with the subjects employed, reproduction was mediated pre-eminently through the agency of verbal and geometrical formulae. . . .'

If a figure is flashed on a screen for a short moment, we cannot retain it without some appropriate classification. The label given it will influence the choice of a

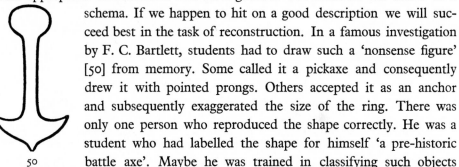

schema. If we happen to hit on a good description we will succeed best in the task of reconstruction. In a famous investigation by F. C. Bartlett, students had to draw such a 'nonsense figure' [50] from memory. Some called it a pickaxe and consequently drew it with pointed prongs. Others accepted it as an anchor and subsequently exaggerated the size of the ring. There was only one person who reproduced the shape correctly. He was a student who had labelled the shape for himself 'a pre-historic

50   battle axe'. Maybe he was trained in classifying such objects and was therefore able to portray the figure that happened to correspond to a schema with which he was familiar.

Where such a pre-existing category is lacking, distortion sets in. Its effects become particularly amusing when the psychologist imitates the parlour game of 'drawing consequences'. Thus F. C. Bartlett had an Egyptian hieroglyph copied and recopied till it gradually assumed the familiar shape and formula of a pussycat [51].

To the art historian these experiments are of interest because they help to clarify certain fundamentals. The student of medieval art, for instance, is constantly brought up against the problem of tradition through copy. Thus the copies of classical coins by Celtic and Teutonic tribes have become fashionable of late as

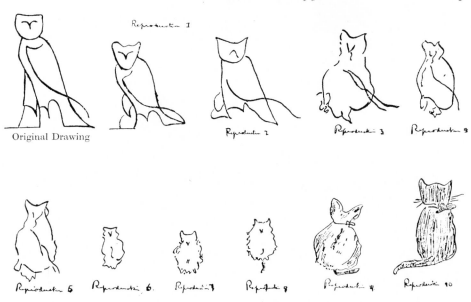

Original Drawing

51. Bartlett's transformations of a hieroglyph

witnesses to the barbaric 'will-to-form' [52]. These tribes, it is implied, rejected classical beauty in favour of the abstract ornament. Maybe they really disapproved of naturalistic shapes, but if they did we would need other evidence. The fact that in being copied and recopied the image became assimilated into the schemata of their own craftsmen demonstrates the same tendency which made the German woodcut transform the Castel Sant' Angelo into a timbered *Burg*. The 'will-to-form' is rather a 'will-to-make-conform', the assimilation of any new shape to the schemata and patterns an artist has learned to handle.

52. Ancient British coins and (*left*) the Greek models

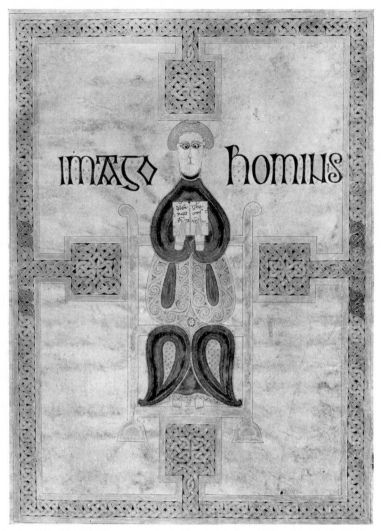

53. *The Symbol of St. Matthew.* About 690. Illuminated page from the Echternach Gospels

The Northumbrian scribes were marvellously skilled in the weaving of patterns and the shaping of letters. Confronted with the task of copying the image of a man, the symbol of St. Matthew, from a very different tradition, they were quite satisfied to build it up from those units they could handle so well. The solution in the famous Echternach Gospels [53] is so ingenious as to arouse our admiration. It is creative, not because it differs from the presumed prototype—Bartlett's pussycat also differs from the owl—but because it copes with the challenge of the unfamiliar in a surprising and successful way. The artist handles the letter forms as he handles his medium, with complete assurance in creating from it the symbolic image of a man.

But did the designer of the Bayeux tapestry [37] act very differently? He was obviously trained in the intricate interlace work of eleventh-century ornament and adjusted these forms as far as he thought necessary to signify trees. Within his universe of form this procedure was both ingenious and consistent.

Could he have done otherwise? Could he have inserted naturalistic renderings of beeches or firs if only he had wanted to? The student of art is generally discouraged from asking this question. He is supposed to look for explanations of style in the artist's will rather than in his skill. Moreover, the historian has little use for questions of might-have-been. But is not this reluctance to ask about the degree of freedom that exists for artists to change and modify their idiom one of the reasons why we have made so little progress in the explanation of style?

In the study of art no less than in the study of man, the mysteries of success are frequently best revealed through an investigation of failures. Only a pathology of representation will give us some insight into the mechanisms which enabled the masters to handle this instrument with such assurance.

Not only must we surprise the artist when he is confronted with an unfamiliar task that he cannot easily adjust to his means; we must also know that his aim was in fact portrayal. Given these conditions, we may do without the actual comparison between photograph and representation that was our starting point. For, after all, nature is sufficiently uniform to allow us to judge the information value of a picture even when we have never seen the specimen portrayed. The beginnings of illustrated reportage, therefore, provide another test case where we need have no doubt about the will and can, consequently, concentrate on the skill.

IV

PERHAPS the earliest instance of this kind dates back more than three thousand years, to the beginnings of the New Kingdom in Egypt, when the Pharaoh Thutmose included in his picture chronicle of the Syrian campaign a record of plants he had brought back to Egypt [54]. The inscription, though somewhat mutilated, tells us that Pharaoh pronounces these pictures to be 'the truth'. Yet botanists have found it hard to agree on what plants may have been meant by these renderings. The schematic shapes are not sufficiently differentiated to allow secure identification.

An even more famous example comes from the period when medieval art was at its height, from the volume of plans and drawings by the Gothic masterbuilder, Villard de Honnecourt, which tells us so much about the practice and outlook of the men who created the French cathedrals. Among the many architectural, religious, and symbolic drawings of striking skill and beauty to be found in this

54. *Plants brought by Thutmose III from Syria*. About 1450 B.C. Limestone relief

55. VILLARD DE HONNECOURT: *Lion and Porcupine*. About 1235. Pen and ink

volume, there is a curiously stiff picture of a lion, seen *en face* [55]. To us, it looks like an ornamental or heraldic image, but Villard's caption tells us that he regarded it in a different light: '*Et saves bien,*' he says, '*qu'il fu contrefais al vif.*' 'Know well that it is drawn from life.' These words obviously had a very different meaning for Villard than they have for us. He can have meant only that he had drawn his schema in the presence of a real lion. How much of his visual observation he allowed to enter into the formula is a different matter.

Once more the broadsheets of popular art show us to what extent this attitude survived the Renaissance. The letterpress of a German woodcut from the sixteenth century informs us that we here see 'the exact counterfeit' of a kind of locust that invaded Europe in

Natürliche Contrasepbung des gewaltigen flugs der Hew=
schrecken/welcher gefangen worden ist der gröffest/zu Mayland am andern
tag des Hewmonats im 1556. Jars.

56. ANONYMOUS: *Locust*. 1556. Woodcut

menacing swarms [56]. But the zoologist would be rash to infer from this inscription that there existed an entirely different species of creatures that has never been recorded since. The artist had again used a familiar schema, compounded of animals he had learned to portray, and the traditional formula for locusts that he knew from an Apocalypse where the locust plague was illustrated. Perhaps the fact that the German word for a locust is *Heupferd* (hay horse) tempted him to adopt a schema of a horse for the rendering of the insect's prance.

The creation of such a name and the creation of the image have, in fact, much in common. Both proceed by classifying the unfamiliar with the familiar, or more exactly, to remain in the zoological sphere, by creating a subspecies. Since the locust is a kind of horse it must therefore share some of its distinctive features.

The caption of a Roman print of 1601 [57] is as explicit as that of the German woodcut. It claims the engraving represents a giant whale that has been washed ashore near Ancona the same year and 'was drawn accurately from nature' ('*Ritratto qui dal naturale appunto*'). The claim would be more trustworthy if there did not exist an earlier print recording a similar 'scoop' from the Dutch coast in 1598 [58]. But surely the Dutch artists of the late sixteenth century, those masters of realism, would be able to portray a whale? Not quite, it seems, for the creature looks suspiciously as if it had ears, and whales with ears, I am assured on higher authority, do not exist. The draughtsman probably mistook one of the whale's flippers for an ear and therefore placed it far too close to the eye. He, too, was misled by a familiar schema, the schema of the typical head. To draw an

57. ANONYMOUS ITALIAN: *Whale Washed Ashore at Ancona.* 1601. Engraving

58. AFTER GOLTZIUS: *Whale Washed Ashore in Holland.* 1598. Engraving

unfamiliar sight presents greater difficulties than is usually realized. And this, I suppose, was also the reason why the Italian preferred to copy the whale from another print. We need not doubt the part of the caption that tells the news from Ancona, but to portray it again 'from the life' was not worth the trouble.

In this respect, the fate of exotic creatures in the illustrated books of the last few centuries before the advent of photography is as instructive as it is amusing. When Dürer published his famous woodcut of a rhinoceros [59], he had to rely on secondhand evidence which he filled in from his own imagination, coloured, no doubt, by what he had learned of the most famous of exotic beasts, the dragon with its armoured body. Yet it has been shown that this half-invented creature served as a model for all renderings of the rhinoceros, even in natural-history books, up to the eighteenth century. When, in 1790, James Bruce published a drawing of the beast [60] in his *Travels to Discover the Source of the Nile*, he proudly showed that he was aware of this fact:

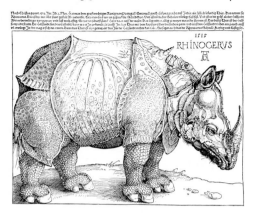

59. DÜRER: *Rhinoceros.* 1515. Woodcut

'The animal represented in this drawing is a native of Tcherkin, near Ras el Feel . . . and this is the first drawing of the rhinoceros with a double horn that has ever yet been presented to the public. The first figure of the Asiatic rhinoceros, the species having but one horn, was painted by Albert Durer, from the life. . . . It was wonderfully ill-executed in all its parts, and was the origin of all the monstrous forms under which that animal has been painted, ever since. . . . Several modern philosophers have made amends for this in our days; Mr. Parsons, Mr. Edwards, and the Count de Buffon, have given good figures of it from life; they have indeed some faults, owing chiefly to preconceived prejudices and inattention. . . . This . . . is the first that has been published with two horns, it is designed from the life, and is an African'.

60. HEATH: *Rhinoceros of Africa.* 1789. Engraving

61. *African rhinoceros*

If proof were needed that the difference between the medieval draughtsman and his eighteenth-century descendant is only one of degree, it could be found here. For the illustration, presented with such flourishes of trumpets, is surely not free from 'preconceived prejudices' and the all-pervading memory of Dürer's woodcut. We do not know exactly what species of rhinoceros the artist saw at Ras el Feel, and the comparison of his picture with a photograph taken in Africa [61] may not, therefore, be quite fair. But I am told that none of the species known to zoologists corresponds to the engraving claimed to be drawn *al vif!*

The story repeats itself whenever a rare specimen is introduced into Europe. Even the elephants that populate the paintings of the sixteenth and seventeenth centuries have been shown to stem from a very few archetypes and to embody all their curious features, despite the fact that information about elephants was not particularly hard to come by.

These examples demonstrate, in somewhat grotesque magnification, a tendency which the student of art has learned to reckon with. The familiar will always remain the likely starting point for the rendering of the unfamiliar; an existing representation will always exert its spell over the artist even while he strives to record the truth. Thus it was remarked by ancient critics that several famous artists of antiquity had made a strange mistake in the portrayal of horses: they had represented them with eyelashes on the lower lid, a feature which belongs to the human eye but not to that of the horse. A German ophthalmologist who studied the eyes of Dürer's portraits, which to the layman appear to be such triumphs of painstaking accuracy, reports somewhat similar mistakes. Apparently not even Dürer knew what eyes 'really look like'.

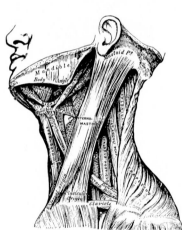

This should not give us cause for surprise, for the greatest of all the visual explorers, Leonardo himself, has been shown to have made mistakes in his anatomical drawings. Apparently he drew features of the human heart which Galen made him expect but which he cannot have seen.

The study of pathology is meant to increase our understanding of health: the sway of schemata did not prevent the emergence of an art of scientific illustration that sometimes succeeds in packing more correct visual information into the image than even a photograph contains. But the diagrammatic maps of mucles in our illustrated anatomies

62. *Muscles of the neck.* From Gray's 'Anatomy'

[62] are not 'transcripts' of things seen but the work of trained observers who build up the picture of a specimen that has been revealed to them in years of patient study.

Now in this sphere of scientific illustration it obviously makes sense to say that Thutmose's artists or Villard himself could not have done what the modern illustrator can do. They lacked the relevant schemata, their starting point was too far removed from their motif, and their style was too rigid to allow a sufficiently supple adjustment. For so much certainly emerges from a study of portrayal in art: you cannot create a faithful image out of nothing. You must have learned the trick if only from other pictures you have seen.

V

IN OUR CULTURE, where pictures exist in such profusion, it is difficult to demonstrate this basic fact. There are freshmen in art schools who have facility in the objective rendering of motifs that would appear to belie this assumption. But those who have given art classes in other cultural settings tell a different story. James Cheng, who taught painting to a group of Chinese trained in different conventions, once told me of a sketching expedition he made with his students to a famous beauty spot, one of Peking's old city gates. The task baffled them. In the end, one of the students asked to be given at least a picture post card of the building so that they would have something to copy. It is stories such as these, stories of breakdowns, that explain why art has a history and artists need a style adapted to a task.

I cannot illustrate this revealing incident. But luck allows us to study the next stage, as it were—the adjustment of the traditional vocabulary of Chinese art to the unfamiliar task of topographical portrayal in the Western sense. For some decades Chiang Yee, a Chinese writer and painter of great gifts and charm, has delighted us with contemplative records of the Silent Traveller, books in which he tells of his encounters with scenes and people of the English and Irish countryside and elsewhere. I take an illustration [63] from the volume on the English Lakeland.

It is a view of Derwentwater. Here we have crossed the line that separates documentation from art. Mr. Chiang Yee certainly enjoys the adaptation of the Chinese idiom to a new purpose; he wants us to see the English scenery for once 'through Chinese eyes'. But it is precisely for this reason that it is so instructive to compare his view with a typical 'picturesque' rendering from the Romantic period [64]. We see how the relatively rigid vocabulary of the Chinese tradition acts as a selective screen which admits only the features for which schemata exist. The artist will be attracted by motifs which can be rendered in his idiom. As he scans the landscape, the sights which can be matched successfully with the schemata he has learned to handle will leap forward as centres of attention. The style, like the medium, creates a mental set which makes the artist look for certain aspects in the scene around him that he can render. Painting is an activity, and the artist will therefore tend to see what he paints rather than to paint what he sees.

63. CHIANG YEE: *Cows in Derwentwater*. 1936. Brush and ink

64. ANONYMOUS: *Derwentwater, looking toward Borrowdale*. 1826. Lithograph

It is this interaction between style and preference which Nietzsche summed up in his mordant comment on the claims of realism:

> *'All Nature faithfully'—But by what feint*
> *Can Nature be subdued to art's constraint?*
> *Her smallest fragment is still infinite!*
> *And so he paints but what he likes in it.*
> *What does he like? He likes, what he can paint!*

There is more in this observation than just a cool reminder of the limitations of artistic means. We catch a glimpse of the reasons why these limitations will never obtrude themselves within the domain of art itself. Art presupposes mastery, and the greater the artist the more surely will he instinctively avoid a task where his mastery would fail to serve him. The layman may wonder whether Giotto could have painted a view of Fiesole in sunshine, but the historian will suspect that, lacking the means, he would not have wanted to, or rather that he could not have wanted to. We like to assume, somehow, that where there is a will there is also a way, but in matters of art the maxim should read that only where there is a way is there also a will. The individual can enrich the ways and means that his culture offers him; he can hardly wish for something that he has never known is possible.

The fact that artists tend to look for motifs for which their style and training equip them explains why the problem of representational skill looks different to the historian of art and to the historian of visual information. The one is concerned with success, the other must also observe the failures. But these failures suggest that we sometimes assume a little rashly that the ability of art to portray the visible world developed, as it were, along a uniform front. We know of specialists in art— of Claude Lorrain, the master of landscape whose figure paintings were poor, of Frans Hals who concentrated almost exclusively on portraits. May not skill as much as will have dictated this type of preference? Is not all naturalism in the art of the past selective?

A somewhat Philistine experiment would suggest that it is. Take the next magazine containing snapshots of crowds and street scenes and walk with it through any art gallery to see how many gestures and types that occur in life can be matched from old paintings. Even Dutch genre paintings that appear to mirror life in all its bustle and variety will turn out to be created from a limited number of types and gestures, much as the apparent realism of the picaresque novel or of Restoration comedy still applies and modifies stock figures which can be traced back for centuries. There is no neutral naturalism. The artist, no less than the writer, needs a vocabulary before he can embark on a 'copy' of reality.

VI

EVERYTHING POINTS to the conclusion that the phrase 'the language of art' is more than a loose metaphor, that even to describe the visible world in images we need a developed system of schemata. This conclusion rather clashes with the traditional distinction, often discussed in the eighteenth century, between spoken words which are conventional signs and painting which uses 'natural' signs to 'imitate' reality. It is a plausible distinction, but it has led to certain difficulties. If we assume, with this tradition, that natural signs can simply be copied from nature, the history of art represents a complete puzzle. It has become increasingly clear since the late nineteenth century that primitive art and child art use a language of symbols rather than 'natural signs'. To account for this fact it was postulated that there must be a special kind of art grounded not on seeing but rather on knowledge, an art which operates with 'conceptual images'. The child—it is argued—does not look at trees; he is satisfied with the 'conceptual' schema of a tree that fails to correspond to any reality since it does not embody the characteristics of, say, birch or beech, let alone those of individual trees. This reliance on construction rather than on imitation was attributed to the peculiar mentality of children and primitives who live in a world of their own.

But we have come to realize that this distinction is unreal. Gustaf Britsch and Rudolf Arnheim have stressed that there is no opposition between the crude map of the world made by a child and the richer map presented in naturalistic images. All art originates in the human mind, in our reactions to the world rather than in the visible world itself, and it is precisely because all art is 'conceptual' that all representations are recognizable by their style.

Without some starting point, some initial schema, we could never get hold of the flux of experience. Without categories, we could not sort our impressions. Paradoxically, it has turned out that it matters relatively little what these first categories are. We can always adjust them according to need. Indeed, if the schema remains loose and flexible, such initial vagueness may prove not a hindrance but a help. An entirely fluid system would no longer serve its purpose; it could not register facts because it would lack pigeonholes. But how we arrange the first filing system is not very relevant.

The progress of learning, of adjustment through trial and error, can be compared to the game of 'Twenty Questions', where we identify an object through inclusion or exclusion along any network of classes. The traditional initial schema of 'animal, vegetable, or mineral' is certainly neither scientific nor very suitable, but it usually serves us well enough to narrow down our concepts by submitting them to the corrective test of 'yes' or 'no'. The example of this parlour game has become popular of late as an illustration of that process of articulation through which we learn to adjust ourselves to the infinite complexity of this world. It indicates, however crudely, the way in which not only organisms, but even machines may be said to 'learn' by trial and error. Engineers at their thrilling work on what they call 'servo mechanisms', that is, self-adjusting machines, have recognized the importance of some kind of 'initiative' on the part of the machine. The first move such a machine may make will be, and indeed must be, a random movement, a shot in the dark. Provided a report of success or failure, hit or miss, can be fed back into the machine, it will increasingly avoid the wrong moves and repeat the correct ones. One of the pioneers in this field has recently described this machine rhythm of schema and correction in a striking verbal formula: he calls all learning 'an arboriform stratification of guesses about the world'. Arboriform, we may take it, here describes the progressive creation of classes and subclasses such as might be described in a diagrammatic account of 'Twenty Questions'.

We seem to have drifted far from the discussion of portrayal. But it is certainly possible to look at a portrait as a schema of a head modified by the distinctive features about which we wish to convey information. The American police some-times employ draughtsmen to aid witnesses in the identification of criminals. They may draw any vague face, a random schema, and let witnesses guide their modifica-tions of selected features simply by saying 'yes' or 'no' to various suggested standard alterations until the face is sufficiently individualized for a search in the files to be profitable. This account of portrait drawing by remote control may well be over-tidy, but as a parable it may serve its purpose. It reminds us that the starting point of a visual record is not knowledge but a guess conditioned by habit and tradition.

Need we infer from this fact that there is no such thing as an objective likeness? That it makes no sense to ask, for instance, whether Chiang Yee's view of Derwent-water is more or less correct than the nineteenth-century lithograph in which the formulas of classical landscapes were applied to the same task? It is a tempting conclusion and one which recommends itself to the teacher of art appreciation because it brings home to the layman how much of what we call 'seeing' is condi-tioned by habits and expectations. It is all the more important to clarify how far this relativism will take us. I believe it rests on the confusion between pictures, words, and statements which we saw arising the moment truth was ascribed to paintings rather than to captions.

If all art is conceptual, the issue is rather simple. For concepts, like pictures, cannot be true or false. They can only be more or less useful for the formation of descriptions. The words of a language, like pictorial formulas, pick out from the flux of events a few signposts which allow us to give direction to our fellow-speakers in that game of 'Twenty Questions' in which we are engaged. Where the needs of users are similar, the signposts will tend to correspond. We can mostly find equivalent terms in English, French, German, and Latin, and hence the idea has taken root that concepts exist independently of language as the constituents of 'reality'. But the English language erects a signpost on the roadfork between 'clock' and 'watch' where the German has only '*Uhr*'. The sentence from the German primer, '*Meine Tante hat eine Uhr*', leaves us in doubt whether the aunt has a clock or a watch. Either of the two translations may be wrong as a description of a fact. In Swedish, by the way, there is an additional roadfork to distinguish between aunts who are 'father's sisters', and those who are 'mother's sisters', and those who are just ordinary aunts. If we were to play our game in Swedish we would need additional questions to get at the truth about the timepiece.

This simple example brings out the fact, recently emphasized by Benjamin Lee Whorf, that language does not give names to pre-existing things or concepts so much as it articulates the world of our experience. The images of art, we suspect, do the same. But this difference in styles or languages need not stand in the way of correct answers and descriptions. The world may be approached from a different angle and the information given may yet be the same.

From the point of view of information there is surely no difficulty in discussing portrayal. To say of a drawing that it is a correct view of Tivoli does not mean, of course, that Tivoli is bounded by wiry lines. It means that those who understand the notation will derive *no false information* from the drawing—whether it gives the contour in a few lines or picks out 'every blade of grass' as Richter's friends wanted to do. The complete portrayal might be the one which gives as much correct information about the spot as we would obtain if we looked at it from the very spot where the artist stood.

Styles, like languages, differ in the sequence of articulation and in the number of questions they allow the artist to ask; and so complex is the information that reaches us from the visible world that no picture will ever embody it all. That is not due to the subjectivity of vision but to its richness. Where the artist has to copy a human product he can, of course, produce a facsimile which is indistinguishable from the original. The forger of banknotes succeeds only too well in effacing his personality and the limitations of a period style.

But what matters to us is that the correct portrait, like the useful map, is an end product on a long road through schema and correction. It is not a faithful record of a visual experience but the faithful construction of a relational model.

Neither the subjectivity of vision nor the sway of conventions need lead us to deny that such a model can be constructed to any required degree of accuracy. What is decisive here is clearly the word 'required'. The form of a representation cannot be divorced from its purpose and the requirements of the society in which the given visual language gains currency.

Part Two

_____

FUNCTION AND FORM

_____

III

Pygmalion's Power

Once there was an old man whose name was Nahokoboni. He was troubled in his mind because he had no daughter, and who could look after him if he had no son-in-law? Being a witch doctor, he therefore carved himself a daughter out of a plum tree. . . .

A fairy tale of the Guiana Indians

I

EVER SINCE the Greek philosophers called art an 'imitation of nature' their successors have been busy affirming, denying, or qualifying this definition. The first two chapters of this book have the same purpose. They try to show some of the limits of this aim toward a perfect 'imitation' set by the nature of the medium on the one hand and by the psychology of artistic procedure on the other. Everybody knows that this imitation has ceased to be the concern of artists today. But is this a new departure? Were the Greeks right even in their description of the aims of the artists in the past?

Their own mythology would have told them a different story. For it tells of an earlier and more awe-inspiring function of art when the artist did not aim at making a 'likeness' but at rivalling creation itself. The most famous of these myths that crystallize belief in the power of art to create rather than to portray is the story of Pygmalion. Ovid turned it into an erotic novelette, but even in his perfumed version we can feel something of the thrill which the artist's mysterious powers once gave to man.

In Ovid, Pygmalion is a sculptor who wants to fashion a woman after his own heart and falls in love with the statue he makes. He prays to Venus for a bride modelled after that image, and the goddess turns the cold ivory into a living body. It is a myth that has naturally captivated the imagination of artists, the solemn and somewhat maudlin dreams of Burne-Jones [65] no less than the irreverent mockery of Daumier [66]. Without the underlying promise of this myth, the secret hopes and fears that accompany the act of creation, there might be no art as we know it. One of the most original young painters of England, Lucien Freud, wrote very recently: 'A moment of complete happiness never occurs in the creation of a work of art. The promise of it is felt in the act of creation, but disappears towards the completion of the work. For it is then that the painter realises that it is only a picture he is painting. Until then he had almost dared to hope that the picture might spring to life.'

65. BURNE-JONES: *Pygmalion.* 1878   66. DAUMIER: *Pygmalion.* 1842. Lithograph

'Only a picture', says Lucien Freud. It is a motif we find in the whole history of Western art; Vasari tells of Donatello at work on his *Zuccone* [69] looking at it suddenly and threatening the stone with a dreadful curse, 'Speak, speak—*favella, favella, che ti venga il cacasangue!*' And the greatest wizard of them all, Leonardo da Vinci, extolled the power of the artist to create. In that hymn of praise to painting, the 'Paragone', he calls the painter 'the Lord of all manner of people and of all things'. 'If the painter wishes to see beauties to fall in love with, it is in his power to bring them forth, and if he wants to see monstrous things that frighten or are foolish or laughable or indeed to be pitied, he is their Lord and God.' [67, 68].

67, 68. LEONARDO DA VINCI: *Grotesque heads.* About 1495. *Leda.* About 1509. Pen and ink

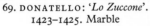

69. DONATELLO: '*Lo Zuccone*'.   70. (*Attributed to*) LEONARDO DA VINCI: *Bacchus*.
1423–1425. Marble   About 1508–1513

Indeed, the power of art to rouse the passions is to him a token of its magic. Unlike the poet, he writes, the painter can so subdue the minds of men that they will fall in love with a painting that does not represent a real woman. 'It happened to me,' he continues, 'that I made a religious painting which was bought by one who so loved it that he wanted to remove the sacred representation so as to be able to kiss it without suspicion. Finally his conscience prevailed over his sighs and lust, but he had to remove the picture from his house.' If we think of a work like the *St. John* and its transformation into a *Bacchus* [70], we may accept the plausibility of Leonardo's account.

And yet Leonardo, if anyone, knew that the artist's desire to create, to bring forth a second reality, finds its inexorable limits in the restrictions of his medium. I feel we catch an echo of the disillusionment with having created only a picture that we found in Lucien Freud when we read in Leonardo's notes: 'Painters often fall into despair . . . when they see that their paintings lack the roundness and the liveliness which we find in objects seen in the mirror . . . but it is impossible for a painting to look as rounded as a mirror image . . . except if you look at both with one eye only.'

Perhaps the passage betrays the ultimate reason for Leonardo's deep dissatisfaction with his art, his reluctance to reach the fatal moment of completion: all the artist's knowledge and imagination are of no avail, it is only a picture that he has been painting, and it will look flat. Small wonder that contemporaries describe him in his later years as most impatient of the brush and engrossed in mathematics. Mathematics was to help him to be the true maker. Today we read of Leonardo's project to build a 'flying machine', but if we look into Leonardo's notes we will not find such an expression. What he wants to make is a bird that will fly, and once more there is an exultant tone in the master's famous prophecy that the bird *would* fly. It did not. And shortly afterward we find Leonardo lodging in the Vatican— at the time when Michelangelo and Raphael were there creating their most renowned works—quarrelling with a German mirror-maker and fixing wings and a beard to a tame lizard in order to frighten his visitors. He made a dragon, but it was only a whimsical footnote to a Promethean life. The claim to be a creator, a maker of things, passed from the painter to the engineer—leaving to the artist only the small consolation of being a maker of dreams.

II

THIS FATEFUL DISTINCTION goes back to the very period when the 'imitation of nature' was first discovered and defined by the Greeks of the fourth century. There are few more influential discussions on the philosophy of representation than the momentous passage in the *Republic* where Plato introduces the comparison between a painting and a mirror image. It has haunted the philosophy of art ever since. To re-examine his theory of ideas, Plato contrasts the painter with the carpenter. The carpenter who makes the couch translates the idea, or concept, of the couch into matter. The painter who represents the carpenter's couch in one of his paintings only copies the appearance of one particular couch. He is thus twice removed from the idea. The metaphysical implications of Plato's condemnation of art need not concern us. It is possible to translate his statement into terminology which does not operate with Platonic ideas. If you telephone a carpenter to order a couch, he must know what the word means, or, to put it somewhat pedantically, what pieces of furniture are subsumed under the concept 'couch'. A painter who draws the interior of a room need not trouble his head about the names given in the furniture trade to the objects in front of him. He is not concerned with concepts or classes but with particular things.

But it is just because this analysis looks so plausible that we must probe it carefully. Is there really this difference between the carpenter who makes the couch and the painter who imitates it? Surely the difference cannot lie in the medium. Many a couch is designed first and worked out in a blueprint before it is made. In this case, Plato would have to admit the designer into his Ideal State because he, too, imitated the idea of the couch rather than any deceptive reality. But the example of Inness' painting of the roundhouse in the previous chapter has shown that we cannot tell in any particular case whether the design is to serve as an instruction or as an imitation. A series of pictures of couches in a sales catalogue may be a promise that such pieces of furniture will be made to order, or that they have already been made; in an illustrated dictionary of English words they may be an 'iconic sign', a device to impart information about the meaning of the term.

The more we think about Plato's famous distinction between making and imitating, the more these border lines become blurred. Plato speaks of the painter who 'paints both reins and bit'. Unlike the horseman and the harness-maker, Plato thought, the painter need have no knowledge of these things. It is a doubtful assertion even in the case of painters. But what about the sculptor who fits a real metal bit to his marble horse, as many a sculptor has done? Or what, for that matter, of a sculptor who represents a figure lying on a couch? Is he not also a maker?

Must it always be true that the sculptor's couch is a representation? If we mean by this term that it must refer to something else, that it is a sign, then this will surely depend on the context. Put a real couch into a shop window and you thereby turn it into a sign. It is true that once this is its only function, you may choose a couch which is not good for anything else. You may also make a cardboard dummy. In other words, there is a smooth and even transition, dependent on function, between what Plato called 'reality' and what he called 'appearance'. On the stage no less than in the shop window, we can find the real couch side by side with flimsy imitations or furniture painted on a backdrop. Any one of these may become a sign to us if we question it for information about the type of object it stands for. To one person, let us say, the model airplane may be interesting for its reference; to the child, it will be just a toy that really works.

In the world of the child there is no clear distinction between reality and appearance. He can use the most unlikely tools for the most unlikely purposes—a table upside down for a spaceship, a basin for a crash helmet. For the context of the game it will serve its purpose rather well. The basin does not 'represent' a crash helmet, it *is* a kind of improvised helmet, and it might even prove useful. There is no rigid division between the phantom and reality, truth and falsehood, at least not where human purpose and human action come into their own. What we call 'culture' or 'civilization' is based on man's capacity to be a maker, to invent unexpected uses, and to create artificial substitutes.

To us the word 'artificial' seems immensely far removed from art. But this was not always so. The works of cunning craftsmen in myth and story include precious toys and intriguing machines, artificial singing birds, and angels blowing real trumpets. And when men turned from the admiration of artifice to the worship of nature, the landscape gardener was called in to make artificial lakes, artificial waterfalls, and even artificial mountains. For the world of man is not only a world of things; it is a world of symbols where the distinction between reality and make-believe is itself unreal. The dignitary who lays the foundation stone will give it three taps with a silver hammer. The hammer is real, but is the blow? In this twilight region of the symbolic, no such questions are asked, and therefore no answers need be given.

When we make a snowman we do not feel, I submit, that we are constructing a phantom of a man. We are simply making a man of snow. We do not say, 'Shall we represent a man who is smoking?' but 'Shall we give him a pipe?' For the success of the operation, a real pipe may be just as good or better than a symbolic one made of a twig. It is only afterward that we may introduce the idea of reference, of the snowman's representing somebody. We can make him a portrait or a carica-ture, or we can discover a likeness to someone and elaborate it. But always, I contend, making will come before matching, creation before reference. As likely as not, we will give our snowman a proper name, call him 'Jimmie' or 'Jeeves', and will be sorry for him when he starts to slump and melt away.

But are we not still matching something when we make the snowman? Are we not at least modelling our creation after the idea of a man, like Plato's craftsman who copied the idea of the couch? Or, if we reject this metaphysical interpretation, are we not imitating the image of a man we have in our mind? This is the traditional answer, but we have seen in the last chapter that it will not quite do. First of all, it makes the created image into a replica of something nobody has ever seen, the snowman we allegedly carry in our heads before we body it forth. Moreover there was no such pre-existent snowman. What happens is rather that we feel tempted to work the snow and balance the shapes till we recognize a man. The pile of snow provides us with the first schema, which we correct until it satisfies our minimum definition. A symbolic man, to be sure, but still a member of the species man, subspecies snowman. What we learn from the study of symbolism, I contend, is precisely that to our minds the limits of these definitions are elastic.

This, once more, is the real issue. For Plato and those who followed him, definitions were something made in heaven. The idea of man, couch, or basin was something fixed eternally with rigid outlines and immutable laws. Most of the tangles into which the philosophy of art and the philosophy of symbolism got themselves can be traced back to this awe-inspiring starting point. For once you accept the argument that there are rigid classes of things, you must also describe their image as a phantom. But a phantom of what? What is the artist's task when he represents a mountain—does he copy a particular mountain, an individual member of the class, as the topographic painter does, or does he, more loftily, copy the universal pattern, the idea of a mountain?

We know this to be an unreal dilemma. It is up to us how we define a mountain. We can make a mountain out of a molehill, or ask our landscape gardener to make one. We can accept the one or the other according to our wish or whim. There is a fallacy in the idea that reality contains such features as mountains and that, looking at one mountain after another, we slowly learn to generalize and to form the abstract idea of mountaineity. We have seen that both philosophy and psychology have revolted against this time-honoured view. Neither in thought nor in perception do we learn to generalize. We learn to particularize, to articulate, to make distinctions where before there was only an undifferentiated mass.

III

NOWHERE, I believe, has more spectacular progress been made in the last few decades than in the investigation of the filing systems of the mind. Psychoanalysis has shown us one aspect of those reasons of which reason knows nothing, the study of animal behaviour another.

In a previous chapter I called in aid those newly hatched chickens who categorize the shades of their dinner plates, not according to colour, but according to brightness relationships. Their mother, the hen, will sit on a marble egg in the Pygmalion hope, we must assume, that it will come to life. This type of behaviour has been investigated in sea gulls. If you remove an egg from the gull's nest and put it nearby it will retrieve it. It will also retrieve other round objects—pebbles or potatoes, if they are sufficiently close in shape and touch to the egg—but it will leave angular and soft shapes untouched. For the gull, the class of egglike things is larger than our class of eggs. Its filing system is a little too wide, which makes errors possible, but not likely, in its wild state. It is on this range of classification that the scientist plays when he wants to deceive the gull. He cannot make eggs which would answer his own definition, to be sure, but he can make eggs which answer the gull's definition and study the bird's reactions to the image or counterfeit.

In recent years this making of dummies and images has become one of the most rewarding tools of the student of animal behaviour. Following the thrilling discoveries of Konrad Lorenz about the way animals react to certain inborn cues, the scientist's laboratory has turned into an artist's workshop. In a famous series of experiments, N. Tinbergen made dummies of sticklebacks to probe the reactions of the male fish [71]. The naturalistic dummy does not impress it much, unless it is red below, but the caricature with plenty of red arouses violent reaction. Indeed, there are cases when dummies arouse more reaction than the real thing—they exhibit what are called the 'releasers' in a purer, more recognizable form than life situations ever provide. But sometimes life also plays its tricks, particularly on animals in captivity. Tinbergen's sticklebacks always postured in their aquarium when red mail trucks passed the window at some distance, for to their brains red stands for danger and rivalry.

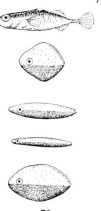

71

On the theory of abstraction you would be forced to say the gull knew what potatoes had in common with eggs, or the stickleback generalized to such an extent from the fact that red sticklebacks are dangerous that he concluded the same must be true of red trucks. Not that anybody ever held this view, but it must be made explicit if we are to combat the idea that the creation of a symbol, or image, constitutes a particular feat of abstraction. On the contrary. It could not happen if we, too, were not prone to extend the classes of things beyond their rational groups—if we, too, did not react to minimum images.

Now, I do not believe that the mystery of Raphael will one day be solved through the study of gulls. My sympathies are all with those who warn us against rash speculations about inborn reactions in man—whether they come from the racialist camp or that of Jung. The dignity of man, as Pico della Mirandola felt, lies precisely in his Protean capacity for change. We are not simple slot machines which begin to tick when coins are dropped into us, for, unlike the stickleback, we have what psychoanalysts call an 'ego' which tests reality and shapes the impulses from the id. And so we can remain in control while we half-surrender to counterfeit coins, to symbols and substitutes. Our twin nature, poised between animality and rationality, finds expression in that twin world of symbolism with its willing suspension of disbelief.

One example must suffice. It can be argued, and has been argued, that we respond with particular readiness to certain configurations of biological significance for our survival. The recognition of the human face, on this argument, is not wholly learned. It is based on some kind of inborn disposition.

Whenever anything remotely facelike enters our field of vision, we are alerted and respond. We all know the feeling when fever or fatigue has loosened the triggers of our reactions and a pattern on the wallpaper suddenly appears to look or leer at us with a threatening grin. The English humorist Fougasse has made clever use of this propensity of ours to see faces, in his plea for more functional

72. FOUGASSE: *Illustration*　　　　　73. PICASSO: *Baboon and Young.*
          for a leaflet　　　　　　　　　　　　1951. Bronze

furniture [72]. Objectively, this chair is not very much like any known physiognomy, but given this disposition of ours to meet the design halfway, the artist
may find he has accidentally made a face. A daring exploitation of our disposition
to read faces into things is in Brueghel's *Dulle Griet* [74]. Here the building on

74. BRUEGHEL: *Dulle Griet (Mad Meg).* 1562

the right with its one window becomes a devouring face, aided by the juxtaposition with a more realistic image of the mouth of hell. And do not language and metaphor testify that the class of things which subjectively cluster round the ideas of eye, mouth, or face is much wider than the anatomist's concept? To our emotion, a window can be an eye and a jug can have a mouth; it is reason which insists on the difference between the narrower class of the real and the wider class of the metaphorical, the barrier between image and reality.

The headlights of a car may look to us like a pair of glowing eyes, and we may even call them so. The artist may use this similarity to work his magic of transformation. Picasso did precisely that when he created his wonderful bronze baboon with its young [73]. He took a toy car, perhaps from the nursery of his children, and turned it into a baboon's face. He could see the hood and windshield of the car as a face, and this fresh act of classification inspired him to put his find to the test. Here, as so often, the artist's discovery of an unexpected use for the car has a twofold effect on us. We follow him not only in seeing a particular car as a baboon's head but learn in the process a new way of articulating the world, a new metaphor, and when we are in the mood we may suddenly find the cars that block our way looking at us with that apish grin that is due to Picasso's classification.

IV

I HAVE SPOKEN of classification, but in psychology this process is more frequently labelled 'projection'. We say we 'project' the familiar form of a face into the configuration of a car just as we project familiar images into vaguely similar shapes of clouds. It is well known that this propensity of our minds is used in modern psychiatry as a diagnostic tool. In the so-called 'Rorschach test', standard inkblots are offered to the subject for interpretation [75]. The same blot will be interpreted as a bat or as a butterfly, not to speak of the countless other possibilities we find listed in the vast literature accumulated on this method of testing. Rorschach himself stressed that there is only a difference of degree between ordinary perception, the filing of impressions in our mind, and the interpretations due to 'pro-

75. *Rorschach inkblot*

jection'. When we are aware of the process of filing we say we 'interpret', where we are not we say 'we see'. From this point of view, there is also a difference of degree rather than of kind between what we call a 'representation' and what we call an 'object of nature'. To the primitive, the tree trunk or rock which looks like an animal may become a kind of animal.

The idea that we may find the roots of art in this mechanism of projection, in the filing systems of our mind, is not of recent origin. It was first expressed more than five hundred years ago in the writings of Leon Battista Alberti. The passage is little known because it occurs, not in Alberti's famous book on painting, but in his little treatise on sculpture, *De Statua*:

'I believe that the arts which aim at imitating the creations of nature originated in the following way: in a tree trunk, a lump of earth, or in some other thing were accidentally discovered one day certain contours that needed only a very slight change to look strikingly like some natural object. Noticing this, people tried to see if it were not possible by addition or subtraction to complete what still was lacking for a perfect likeness. Thus by adjusting and removing outlines and planes in the way demanded by the object itself, men achieved what they wanted, and not without pleasure. From that day, man's capacity to create images grew apace until he was able to create any likeness, even when there was no vague outline in the material to aid him.'

Today we lack Alberti's boldness in speculating about origins. Nobody was present when 'the first image was made'. And yet I think Alberti's theory about the role of projection in the origins of art deserves to be taken seriously. There is one area at least where we can check and confirm the importance which the discovery of accidental similarity has for the mind of primitive man: the images which all peoples project onto the night sky. I need hardly enlarge on the spell these discoveries cast over the mind of man. To find the image of an animal in the scattered pattern of luminous points in heaven was to imagine it ruling over that part of the sky and over all creatures which came under its influence. We know that the slightest resemblance sufficed to suggest such identification. The constellations have changed since the time when the names of the zodiac were first given them several thousand years ago. But at no time can it have been easy to find the ram or the scorpion, the lion or the bull. We know in fact that different tribes projected different images into this first Rorschach test. And nothing is more instructive than to compare the different interpretations given to the same group of stars.

The constellation of the zodiac which the ancients called the Lion provides a good example: if you approach it with the appropriate mental set you can read a lion, or at least a quadruped, into that group by drawing lines between the main stars [76]. Indians of South America react differently. They do not see a lion shown sideways because they disregard what we would call the animal's tail and hind legs and make of the rest a lobster seen from above. The ethnologist Koch-Grünberg some fifty years ago was inspired to let experienced Indian hunters draw the night sky for him. One of them produced a version enumerating the principal constellations in schematic form, and his lobster is easily recognized [77]. An Indian from a different tribe showed more imagination and less regard for the

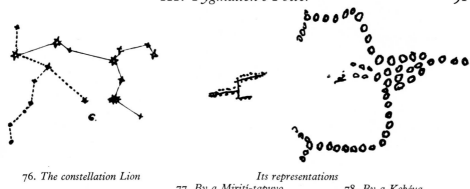

76. *The constellation Lion*

Its representations

77. *By a Miriti-tapuyo*   78. *By a Kobéua*

real position of the stars [78]; his lobster is an even more convincing creature, which shows how actively he projected the image of the animal he knew onto the constellation.

If we meditate on the hold which these images in the sky still have on the imagination of Western man, we will perhaps be less reluctant to consider Alberti's suggestion that projection was one of the roots of art. For in a state of tension primitive man must have been as prone as we are to project his fears and his hopes into any shape which remotely permitted such identification. Not only the night sky but anything that could not be classified otherwise may have offered such shapes. At least I can see no reason why we should not extend our Just So Story to include strange rock formations and cracks and veins in the walls of caves. Could it not be that bulls and horses were first 'discovered' by man in these mysterious haunts before they were fixed and made visible to others by means of coloured earth ?

It is true that the Abbé Breuil's famous water-colour copies, which are frequently used as illustrations, make such an explanation look implausible. But then their whole purpose was to sort out the painted silhouette from the surface of the stone. What this surface was like in the ice age, how much it may have been covered by moss or stained by water, we will never know. Perhaps a photograph of the sculptured horse from Cap Blanc [79] gives a better idea of the way these man-made shapes rose from the irregular rock. Admittedly there are prehistoric paintings, notably the famous masterpieces of Lascaux, that look far too controlled and deliberate to be the result of accident and projection. But these certainly do not stand at the beginning of cave art. Thousands of years of image-making must have preceded them. It is important to keep this possibility in mind because the naturalistic art of the caves is often used as an argument against the view that the imitation of appearances is a complex and late achievement, the result of tradition and learning. Thus cave art and its relation, the art of the Bushmen, have given rise to far-reaching speculations concerning the psychological make-up of these

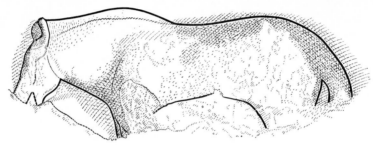

79. *Horse*. Prehistoric, from Cap Blanc near Les Eyzies (Dordogne)

primitive hunters and their uncanny powers of visualization, their alleged grasp of the visible world unspoiled by the intervention of logic and the ravages of analytical reasoning. But these evolutionist ideas that looked so plausible to the nineteenth century are everywhere in retreat. The best working hypothesis in such matters is the assumption that there was not much biological and psychological difference between our cave men ancestors and ourselves. I see no reason, therefore, to believe that these early artists were exempt from the rhythm of schema and correction. Once the animal shape had been discovered somewhere in a rock, as the lobster was discovered in the stars by the Indian, it should have proved easier to transfer and adjust it till the tribe or the caste of medicine men engaged in some magic ritual acquired a specialized skill in the making of such images. In this respect, the cave art we know may be anything but primitive. It may be a very developed style. And yet the priority of projection may still determine the character of the style. We have frequently seen to what an extent the artist's starting point will determine the final product. The schema on which a representation is based will continue to show through the ultimate elaboration. It would be tempting to assume that the most striking feature of cave art, its lack of geometrical rigidity, may be thus connected with its distant roots in indeterminate forms discovered and elaborated by subsequent generations.

Perhaps the conditions of their lives encouraged the early hunters to look for animal shapes in sacred caves rather than to make animals, to scan the vague forms of patches and shadows for the revelation of a bison, much as the hunter must scan the dusky plains for the outline of the hoped-for prey. He was better trained in finding than in making. The construction of tool-like minimum images may have lain largely outside the experience of these earliest artists. The geometric schema requires something of the constructor's engineering skill, and this skill and habit may have developed with the needs of settled communities. These speculations would, at any rate, fit in with the general assumption that the rigid style of neolithic art coincided with the development of agriculture and its technology. There were some advantages in the construction of basic images which may have recommended the new methods to these cultures. Only the construction of the basic forms offers the possibility of strict control, the safety of the repeatable, which cave art may never have completely attained.

V

WHAT WE KNOW of the beginnings of image-making confirms the continuous link between finding and making. Recent excavations in Jericho have brought to light a series of images some seven thousand years old that must be the earliest portraits known [80]. They exemplify the Pygmalion story in reverse. In the latter,

a statue came to life, while in these early practices the living man becomes an image after his death. The skull was used as the armature for the modelling. Onto this skull the craftsman spread earth to represent the flesh which had decayed. The head has suffered a sea change into something rich and strange, but it is still the head of the dead. Since eyes, too, decay, the artist had to give the skull artificial eyes, and he found them in the shape of cowrie shells. We know that these shells are used in other contexts as sexual symbols betokening fertility. The difference between symbolization and representation is one of use, of context, of metaphor. In

80. *Modelled skull from Jericho.*
About 6000 B.C.

both cases, similarities present a starting point for what I have described somewhat pedantically as the 'extension of a class'. Here the class of eyelike objects can take the place of eyes because when they are put in position the skull will suddenly 'look' at us.

The representation, then, is not a replica. It need not be like the motif. The craftsman of Jericho did not think eyes indistinguishable from cowrie shells any more than Picasso thinks baboons indistinguishable from motorcars, but in certain contexts the one can represent the other. They belong to the same class because they release a similar response.

The farther back we go in history, the more important this principle appears to be. The test of the image is not its lifelikeness but its efficacy within a context of action. It may be lifelike if that is thought to contribute to its potency, but in other contexts the merest schema will suffice, provided it retains the efficacious nature of the prototype. It must work as well or better than the real thing.

There is a gruesome but characteristic story told by the Alaskan Eskimos of Nunivak which illustrates this point.

'Once there was a man whose grandmother was a powerful magician. The man often had trouble with his kayak, which kept capsizing, and so when his grand-mother died, he had the idea of using the powers that were in her to stabilize his kayak. He flayed her corpse and fixed the skin with outspread arms and legs under the boat—and lo, it never capsized again. Unfortunately, however, the skin decayed and wore off, and so the pious grandson replaced it by an image that turned out to have the same effect. And to this very day, kayaks in these regions are adorned with schematic images that keep them in balance.'

Once more, as in the case of the Jericho heads, we have that uncanny transition from life to image or substitute. What matters in the image is that it should preserve and repeat those features of the witch that worked the magic.

The substitute may well be a magic rune rather than a naturalistic image. A pair of schematic eyes may serve to deter evil spirits, an indication of claws may protect the bedstead or chair. Indeed, the tool-like precision of 'primitive art' often goes hand in hand with a reduction of the image to its bare essentials. It is tempting to regard this tendency to abbreviation as a consequence of the belief in 'Pygmalion's power'. For if to represent is to create, there must indeed be safe-guards against this power which might easily get out of control. There is a fascinat-ing book by Ernst Kris and Otto Kurz on the legends connected with art and artists that suggests such fears may indeed become very real. There are stories all over the world of images that had to be chained to prevent their moving of their own accord and of artists who had to refrain from putting the finishing touch to their paintings to prevent the images from coming to life.

We know of similar tensions caused by belief in the potency of symbols in the

81. *Prisoners of Seti I.* About 1300 B.C. Relief

realms of language and writing. Certain words must not be uttered because they would cast a spell, and holy names must not be spelled out in written texts because they are too sacred and potent to be entrusted to paper. There is at least one parallel to this practice which reaches back to the dawn of civilization. In the hieroglyphic inscriptions on the pyramids, all signs which are formed by the images of noxious animals are either avoided or 'abbreviated'—the scorpion is left without its dangerous tail, the lion cut in two. In this context there is no doubt the image was seen as more than a sign; do not put scorpions in graves lest they harm the dead.

When we speak of 'stylized' images we should always keep in mind the possibility that the belief in making engendered the opposite pull of fears and precautions, limiting the artist's freedom. Egyptian art again provides the most famous but also the most difficult example; its rules of schematic rendering, the familiar profile figure, cannot be explained through the sway of the stereotype alone. Foreign prisoners, dead enemies on the battlefield, and slave girls were sometimes rendered *en face* [81], as if certain taboos did not apply to such low creatures.

In this case we have to rely on speculation, but there is one tradition where the selective restraints of religious prohibitions are very well documented: in the tradition of Judaism. It has been argued that the Old Testament ban on 'graven images' is connected not only with a fear of idolatry but with the more universal fear of encroaching on the creator's prerogatives. Rabbinical commentaries permit sealing rings in the form of intaglios because the negative shape is not an image in the forbidden sense, and Jewish households are said to exist in Poland that even admit statuettes, provided they are not quite complete—if, for instance, a finger is missing. Certain Jewish manuscripts from the Middle Ages show figures without faces, and it has been suggested that the first artist at work in the Synagogue of

82. *The Sacrifice of Isaac.*
Wall painting, Dura-Europos
synagogue, third century A.D.

Dura-Europos of the third century also obeyed similar scruples in his rendering of the sacrifice of Isaac [82]. There is a good deal of evidence of similar fears in related traditions. The Eastern Church, which came to admit sacred images, made a distinction between sculpture in the round, which was too real for admission, and painted icons. The test was whether you could take the image by the nose. But even the painted image is restricted in scope. In Byzantium and Ethiopia, evil figures such as Judas are never shown looking out of the picture for fear their evil eye may harm the onlooker.

But do we not all feel that certain portraits look at us? We are familiar with the guide in a castle or country house who shows the awe-struck visitors that one of the pictures on the wall will follow them with its eyes. Whether they want to or not, they endow it with a life of its own. Propagandists and advertisers have exploited this reaction to reinforce our natural tendency to endow an image with a 'presence'; Alfred Leete's famous recruiting poster of 1914 gave every passerby the feeling of being addressed by Lord Kitchener in person [83].

Are these magic beliefs? Do we really think the image on the wall comes to life? The question may allow no more of a clear-cut answer than does any such question connected with symbolism. 'We realize more to-day than was realized before,' said Edwyn Bevan in his book *Holy Images*, 'how the mind of man is on various levels, and how, beneath an articulate intellectual theory, a belief inconsistent with that theory, closely connected with unavowed feelings and desires, may still subsist.'

No lesson of psychology is perhaps more important for the historian to absorb than this multiplicity of layers, the peaceful coexistence in man of incompatible attitudes. There never was a primitive stage of man when all was magic; there never happened an evolution which wiped out the earlier phase. What happens is rather that different institutions and different situations favour and bring out a different approach to which both the artist and his public learn to respond. But beneath these new attitudes, or mental sets, the old ones survive and come to the surface in play or earnest.

I remember a visit I made to one of Queen Victoria's residences, Osborne on the Isle of Wight, which is still the principal monument to that incredible taste

83. ALFRED LEETE: *Recruiting poster.* 1914

which seems more remote to us, and inexplicable to my generation, than the taste of primitive cultures. Prominent among the works displayed there was a life-size marble sculpture of a large furry dog, a portrait of the Queen's beloved pet 'Noble'. The portrait must have been as faithful as the dog undoubtedly was—but for the lack of colour it might have been stuffed. I do not know what impelled me to ask our guide, 'May I stroke him?' She answered, 'Funny you want to do that; all the visitors who pass stroke him—we have to wash him every week.' Now, I do not think the visitors to Osborne, myself included, are particularly prone to magic beliefs. We did not think the image was real. But if we had not thought it somewhere we would not have reacted as we did—that stroking gesture may well have been compounded of irony, playfulness, and a secret wish to reassure ourselves that after all the dog was only of marble.

When we write in our museums, 'Visitors are forbidden to touch the exhibits'— remembering Noble—we are not only using a very necessary precaution for the preservation of works of art: we might argue with André Malraux that the museum turns images into art by establishing that new category, a new principle of classification that creates a different mental set. Take any object from a museum, say

Riccio's *Box in the Shape of a Crab* from the Kress Collection [84]. If I had it in my hand or, better still, on my desk, I might well be tempted to play with it, to poke it with my pen, or to warn a child, most unpsychologically, not to touch any paper on my desk or the crab would bite it. Indeed, who knows whether its spiky legs and claws were not made both to conceal and to protect the contents of the box from prying fingers? On the desk, in short, this object would belong to the species crab, subspecies bronze crab. As I contemplate it in its glass case, my reaction is different. I think of certain trends in Renaissance realism which lead to Palissy and his *style rustique*. The object belongs to the species Renaissance bronzes, subspecies bronzes representing crabs. Small wonder that our artists are in revolt against this devitalizing of the image and yearn all the more desperately for the lost secret of Pygmalion's power. And yet we may have made quite a good bargain when we exchanged the archaic magic of image-making for the more subtle magic we call 'art'. For without this new category of 'pictures', image-making would still be hedged in by taboos. Only in the realm of dreams has the artist found full freedom to create. I think the difference is well summed up in the anecdote about Matisse. When a lady visiting his studio said, 'But surely, the arm of this woman is much too long,' the artist replied politely, 'Madame, you are mistaken. This is not a woman, this is a picture.'

84. RICCIO: *Box in the shape of a crab*. Early sixteenth century. Bronze

IV

Reflections on the Greek Revolution

> Our sculptors say that if Daidalos were born today and
> created such works as those that made him famous, he
> would be laughed at.
>
> PLATO, *The Greater Hippias*

I

IF I HAD to reduce the last chapter to a brief formula it would be 'making comes before matching'. Before the artist ever wanted to match the sights of the visible world he wanted to create things in their own right. Nor is this true only of some mythical past. For in a way our formula dovetails with the findings of the preceding chapter, that the matching process itself proceeds through the stages of 'schema and correction'. Every artist has to know and construct a schema before he can adjust it to the needs of portrayal.

We have seen that Plato objected to this change. What the artist can match, he reminded his contemporaries, is only 'appearances'; his is the world of illusion, the world of mirrors that deceive the eye. Were he a maker, like the carpenter, the lover of truth could put up with him. But as an imitator of this shifting world of the senses he leads us away from truth and must be banished from the state.

The very violence with which Plato denounces this trickery reminds us of the momentous fact that at the time he wrote, mimesis was a recent invention. There are many critics now who share his distaste, for one reason or another, but even they would admit there are few more exciting spectacles in the whole history of art than the great awakening of Greek sculpture and painting between the sixth century and the time of Plato's youth toward the end of the fifth century B.C. Its dramatic phases have often been told in terms of the episode from 'The Sleeping Princess' when the kiss of the prince breaks the thousand-year-old spell and the whole court begins to stir from the rigours of unnatural sleep. We are shown how the stiff and frozen figures we call Apollines, or *kouroi* [85], first move one foot forward, then bend their arms [86], how their masklike smile softens, and how, at the time of the Persian wars, the symmetry of their tense posture is finally broken when their bodies receive a slight twist, so that life seems to enter the marble [87]. There are the refined figures of maidens, the *korai*, to confirm this picture. There is finally the history of Greek painting, as we can follow it in painted pottery, which tells of the discovery of foreshortening and the conquest of space

99

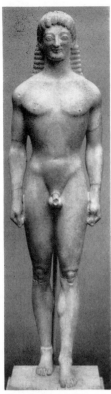  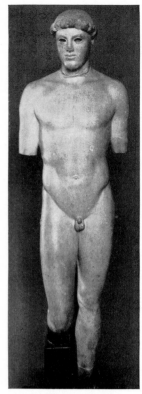

85. *Apollo of Tenea.*
Sixth century B.C.
Parian marble

86. *Apollo of Piombino.*
About 500 B.C. Bronze

87. *The Kritian Boy.*
About 480 B.C.
Parian marble

in the fifth century and of light in the fourth. The whole process looks so logical and
inevitable that it appears easy to arrange the various types of figures so as to show
their gradual approximation to life. It is true that in creating these sequences
classical archaeologists may not always have escaped the danger of a circular
argument. What is more rigid is called 'early', and what looks 'lifelike' is dated
later. There are not many monuments from this crucial period that can be dated
on independent evidence. But even though our reading of the history of Greek art
may have made it look a little too tidy, the essential lines of this astounding development have been established beyond any doubt.

It is a development which neatly illustrates our formulas of schema and correction, of making before matching. Indeed, it was in this area that Emanuel Loewy
at the turn of the century first developed his theories about the rendering of nature
in Greek art that stressed the priority of conceptual modes and their gradual adjustment to natural appearances. Archaic art starts from the schema, the symmetrical
frontal figure conceived for one aspect only, and the conquest of naturalism may be
described as the gradual accumulation of corrections due to the observation of reality.

As a description of what happened, Loewy's account still seems to me unsurpassed. But in itself it explains little. For why was it that this process started comparatively so late in the history of mankind? In this respect our perspective has very much changed. To the Greeks the archaic period represented the dawn of history, and classical scholarship has not always quite shaken off this inheritance. From this point of view it appeared quite natural that the awakening of art from primitive modes should have coincided with the rise of all those other activities that, for the humanist, belong to civilization: the development of philosophy, of science, and of dramatic poetry.

It needed the extension of our historical horizon and our increased awareness of the art of other civilizations to bring home to us what has rightly been called the 'Greek miracle', the uniqueness of Greek art. Indeed it was an Egyptologist, Heinrich Schäfer, who extended Loewy's findings and brought out the Greek achievement through his analysis of the Egyptian ways of rendering the visible world. Schäfer stressed that the 'corrections' introduced by the Greek artist in order to 'match' appearances are quite unique in the history of art. Far from being a natural procedure, they are the great exception. What is normal to man and child all over the globe is the reliance on schemata, on what is called 'conceptual art'. What needs explanation is the sudden departure from this habit that spread from Greece to other parts of the world.

II

AS HISTORIANS we have learned to use the word 'explanation' with caution. The scientist can test his explanations by a systematic variation of conditions in experiment, the historian obviously cannot. But this need not prevent him from rejecting spurious explanations, such as 'the evolution of mankind' or 'the spirit of the Greeks', and searching instead for conditions that would make the adoption of one or the other way of rendering nature intelligible. It is precisely because mankind can hardly have changed in the period which separates us from the archaic Greeks that we are entitled to expect these conditions still to be intelligible if we ask the simple question of how the function of an image will influence its form.

As soon as we approach pre-Greek art from this angle, the familiar comparison between the conceptual modes of child art and that of the ancient Orient lets us down. From the point of view of function, the child art of our age is a most impure example. The motives and purpose for which children draw are very mixed. They grow up in our world where the image has already assumed its manifold functions: to portray, to illustrate, to decorate, to entice or to express emotion. Our children know picture books and magazines, the cinema and the television screen, and the pictures they make reflect this experience in more ways than the child psychologist realizes. In a 'mosaic test' a high score was given to a child who used its geometric shapes to represent a fox, seen from behind, in the act of watching something in front of him. No doubt the solution was ingenious and the high score well deserved, but it is most unlikely that this child ever saw a fox in that attitude. It must have seen picture books, and one of them may have offered a convenient schema ready-made for adaptation to the medium of mosaic. Children make such pictures to amuse themselves, to show off, or because their mothers want to keep them quiet. All the time they are absorbing and adapting the standards and schemata of the grown-up world, even though they may not all be as sophisticated as the four-year-old son of a German philosopher who was questioned about his drawings: 'What is this?'—'A steamboat.' 'And that scribble over there?'—'That is art.' The approval which such 'creative activity' earns from the adults must soon reassure the child that it is safer to be naughty on paper than in real life. But the very idea of this licence presupposes the belief that art is a kind of fool's paradise, a realm of phantoms where we develop our dreams, the belief, that is, that aroused the protest of Plato.

Those who want to study the relation between form and function in a contemporary setting may do better to turn from child art to the rigid context of games. For here the purpose of the image or symbol imposes strict limits on the fancy of the designer. This purpose demands one thing above all: clear distinctions. It does not matter whether the fields of the checkerboard are white and black or red and green so long as they remain distinct. And so with the colours of the opponent's pieces. How far the pieces themselves will be articulated by distinctive features will depend on the rules of the game. In checkers, where each player needs only two categories of pieces, we make our own queens simply by putting one checker on top of the other. In chess we must distinguish more categories; no designer of chessmen, however, will be concerned with the real appearance of castles or bishops, knights or kings, but only with the creation of clear, distinctive features which set off one piece from the other. Provided these distinctions are respected, he is free to indulge his fancy in any way he likes. I have chosen this rather far-fetched example of games because it allows us to study articulation, the creation of distinctions without the intrusion of the problem of likeness or representation. But we also know of contexts in our culture where some degree of 'representation' is admitted into symbolism without being allowed to blur the conceptual clarity demanded by its function. Maps are an example. The map-maker will generally represent water by blue and vegetation by green. Where the purpose of the map demands a distinction between fields and forests, he will introduce a further articulation of his greens and select the darker shade for the woods. But beyond the indication of this difference, the 'real' tones of the particular scenery will obviously not concern him.

III

IF ONE READS Schäfer's analysis of Egyptian conventions, one is more often reminded of such conventionalized representations than one is of child art. The Egyptian painter distinguished, for instance, between a dark brown for men and a pale yellow for women's bodies. The real flesh tone of the person portrayed obviously mattered as little in this context as the real colour of a river matters to the cartographer.

It is for this very reason that the analysis of such a style in terms of 'knowing' and 'seeing', or of 'tactile' versus 'optic', does not appear to take us very far. Would the Egyptian embalmer have known less about the human body than the Greek sculptor? May not the conceptual, diagrammatic character of Egyptian images which has so often been described have as much to do with the function of these images as with the hypothetical 'mentality' of the Egyptian? It would be tempting to equate this function with the idea of 'making' which was the concern of the last chapter. But we may do well to remember that this ideal can never survive on the surface, as it were, without being modified by the harsh realities of frustrated dreams. No belief in magic ever extinguished the sanity of man; and the Egyptian artist surely knew that in this world he is not a maker. That this aspiration lay closer to the surface than it does in other cultures we need not doubt. Has it not been suggested that the Great Sphinx was not conceived as the representation of a divinity but rather as a watchful guardian in her own right? There is no doubt, however, that Egyptian art had long been adapted to the function of portrayal, of presenting visual information and memories of campaigns and ceremonies. The records of an expedition to the land of Punt and of plants brought back from Syria by Thutmose III [54] would suffice to remind us of this possibility. But what these records confirm is the interest of Egyptian artists in distinctive features. It is sometimes thought paradoxical that the Egyptian artists showed themselves such keen observers of animals and foreign races [81] while they were satisfied with the conventional stereotypes of the ordinary human figure. But from the point of view of a diagrammatic art, this habit looks less puzzling. Whenever the difference between species matters, the schema is modified to admit the distinction. What may confuse the issue in these discussions is only the word 'observation'. There must have been keen observers among the Egyptians, but observation is always for a purpose. The Egyptian had sharpened his eyes to the different profiles of Nubians and Hittites, he knew how to characterize fish and flowers, but he had no reason to observe what he was not asked to convey. Perhaps only Ikhnaton demanded that his personal, distinctive features should be entered on the map of history, but even these became a stereotype that was applied to the whole royal family. Admittedly

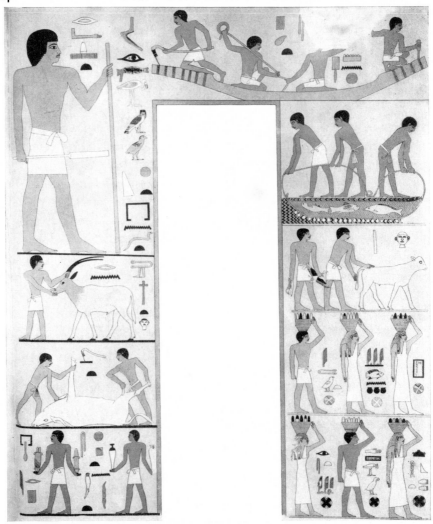

88. *Wall painting from the Tomb of Ra-hotep.* About 2600 B.C.

the art of Tell el 'Amarna is altogether richer in schemata and also more flexible, but these diagrammatic refinements, however striking they may be, should not mislead the historian into speaking of a naturalistic revolution. To do so is to obscure the cataclysmic effect of the 'Greek miracle'.

We must never forget that we look at Egyptian art with the mental set we have all derived from the Greeks. So long as we assume that images in Egypt mean much the same as they do in the post-Greek world, we are bound to see them as rather childlike and naïve. Nineteenth-century observers frequently made this mistake. They described the reliefs and paintings in Egyptian tombs as 'scenes from the daily life' of the Egyptians. But recently it has been pointed out by Mrs. Frankfort-

To Keats, addressing the images of the Grecian urn, there was a sweet melancholy in the contrast between the changeless realm of art and the irretrievable evanescence of human life. For the Egyptian, the newly discovered eternity of art may well have held out a promise that its power to arrest and to preserve in lucid images might be used to conquer this evanescence. Perhaps it was not only as the maker of 'substitute heads' and other dwellings for the 'ka' that the Egyptian sculptor could lay claim to the famous appellation of 'one who keeps alive'. His images weave a spell to enforce eternity. Not our idea of eternity, to be sure, which stretches backward and forward in an infinite extension, but rather the ancient conception of recurrent time that a later tradition embodied in the famous 'hieroglyph' of the serpent biting its own tail. Clearly an 'impressionist' art could never have served this outlook. Only the complete embodiment of the typical in its most lasting and changeless form could assure the magic validity of these pictographs for the 'watcher' who could here see both his past and his eternal future removed from the flux of time.

IV

THERE COULD BE no more poignant contrast to this confidence in the spells of art than a passage from Plato's older contemporary Euripides that also deals with a tomb sculpture. When Alcestis is going to die, her grieving husband Admetus speaks of the work he will commission for his solace:

> *And represented by the skillful hands*
> *Of craftsmen, on the bed the body shall*
> *Be laid; whereon I shall fall in embrace*
> *And clasp my hands around it, call thy name,*
> *And fancy in my arms my darling wife*
> *To hold, holding her not; perhaps, I grant,*
> *Illusory delight, yet my soul's burden*
> *Thus should I lighten. . . .*

What Admetus seeks is not a spell, not even assurance, only a dream for those who are awake; in other words, precisely that state of mind to which Plato, the stern seeker after truth, objected.

Plato, we know, looked back with nostalgia at the immobile schemata of Egyptian art. In the work of his old age, the *Laws*, he speaks with disapproval of the licence the Greeks allow their musicians 'to teach whatever rhythm or tune', and he commends the Egyptians, who long ago 'determined on the rule . . . that the youth of a State should practise in their rehearsals only postures and tunes that are good: these they prescribed in detail and posted up in the temples, and outside this official list it was and still is forbidden to painters and all other producers of postures and representations to introduce any innovation or invention, whether in such productions or in any other branch of music over and above the traditional forms. And if you look there, you will find the things depicted or graven there 10,000 years ago (I mean what I say, not loosely but literally 10,000) and no whit better or worse than the productions of today, but wrought with the same art. . . .'

Is it too much to infer Plato saw in the conceptual style of Egypt a nearer approach to the art of the couch-maker, who imitates changeless ideas rather than fleeting appearances? For this is precisely what the famous passage in the *Republic* suggests. 'Does a couch differ from itself according to how you view it from the side or the front or in any other way? Or does it differ not at all in fact though it appears different . . . ?' It is first of all for this reason—for his failure to represent the couch as it is by itself and for including only one aspect of it in his picture—that the artist is condemned as a maker of phantoms. But that is not all. 'The same magnitude, I presume, viewed from near or far does not appear equal.— Why, no.—And the same things appear bent and straight to those who view them in water and out, or concave and convex, owing to similar errors of vision about colours and there is obviously every confusion of this sort in our souls. And so scene-painting in its exploitation of this weakness of our nature falls nothing short of witchcraft, and so do jugglery and many other such contrivances.'

The picture conjured up by art is unreliable and incomplete, it appeals to the lower part of the soul, to our imagination rather than to our reason, and must therefore be banished as a corrupting influence.

For us, who have lived with the heritage of Greek and post-Greek art throughout our lives, it may need a good deal of historical imagination to recapture the thrill and the shock which the first illusionist images must have caused when shown on the stage or on the walls of Greek houses. There is reason to believe that this did not happen before Plato's lifetime and that his outburst against the trickeries of painting was an outburst against 'modern art'. For it was only in Plato's period, toward the middle of the fourth century, that the Greek revolution was moving toward its climax, only then that the tricks of foreshortening were joined by those of modelling in light and shade to produce the possibility of a real *trompe l'œil*. If we place the beginning of the revolution somewhere in the middle of the sixth century, when archaic art begins to stir to life, it took the Greeks some two hundred years, scarcely more than six generations, to arrive at that point. How did they achieve, in this brief moment of time, what had been denied the Egyptians, the Mesopotamians, and even the Minoans? Surely only a change in the whole function of art can explain such a revolution. It is well to remember here that Plato's attack is not directed against the visual arts only. As a matter of fact the painter's tricks are used by him only as an illustration of a more decisive issue: the banishment of Homer from the ideal Republic. The arts must go, we learn, because they blur the only distinction which mattered to Plato, that between truth and falsehood. Not that Plato failed to enjoy them—there is no evidence of that. But it is hard enough, he would have pleaded, to sort out scientific knowledge from myth, reality from mere appearance, without interposing a twilight realm which is neither the one nor the other.

Now it is precisely the acknowledgment of such a twilight realm, of 'dreams for those who are awake', which may constitute the decisive discovery of the Greek mind. To the unsophisticated mind—which may well be a mind as yet uninfluenced by the ideas of the Sophists—a story is either true or false. The recitals of mythical events and the chronicles of battles are received as accounts of actual happenings. Even today the idea of 'fiction' is not immediately accessible to everyone. John Forsdyke has shown how reluctantly the Greeks admitted this newcomer into their midst, how even they feared the loss of face that goes with being duped by a liar. The story of the gradual emancipation of conscious fiction from myth and moral parable has not yet been told. Obviously it could not be treated in isolation from the rise of critical reason in Greek culture. But here I am concerned with its bearing on the history of art. For it is tempting to think it was the impact of this idea that led to the emancipation of the visual image from the near-Pygmalion phase of 'making'. This impact would first make itself felt where the realm of poetry meets that of art, in the sphere of illustration.

I know of a small girl who became worried and pensive when many Christmas cards began to arrive in her home. How could one tell which was the 'correct' rendering of Holy Night? It is a natural question and one which even engaged the mind of Christian theologians in the East and the West. But where it is asked in all seriousness, illustration in our sense of the term cannot exist. It demands the freedom of the artist to picture to himself what it may have been like when the heavenly child lay in the manger and the shepherds came to adore it.

Now this very freedom does not appear to have existed in the ancient Orient. I am glad in this context to be able to refer to the results of a symposium on narration in ancient art recently held in Chicago by leading experts in various fields. Egyptian art scarcely knows narrative illustration in our sense. There are no mythological cycles telling of the exploits of gods and heroes. There are only some standardized pictographs which were surely thought to symbolize the truth. Nor can the attitude of Mesopotamian cultures have differed greatly. It is hard for us to interpret the scenes on cylinder seals and similar monuments, but none of them looks like a free evocation of mythological events such as we know them from the arts of Greece and its successors.

It has been suggested that this limitation is due to a limitation of means that prevented pre-Greek art from conjuring up a lifelike scene. Their stereotypes of gestures and grouping, their inability to represent a spatial setting, prevented an art of mythological narrative. This, in fact, is the hypothesis implied by the specialist on Greek art in the Chicago symposium, Professor Hanfmann, who succinctly sums up the prevailing view: 'When classical sculptors and painters discovered a convincing method of representing the human body, they set up a chain reaction which transformed the character of Greek narration.'

As the reader may have guessed, I feel prompted to put forward the opposite hypothesis: when classical sculptors and painters discovered the character of Greek narration, they set up a chain reaction which transformed the methods of representing the human body—and indeed more than that.

For what is the character of Greek narration as we know it from Homer? Briefly, it is concerned not only with the 'what' but also with the 'how' of mythical events. Obviously this is not a very strict distinction. There can be no recital of events that does not include description of one kind or another, and nobody would claim that the Gilgamesh Epic or the Old Testament is devoid of vivid accounts. But maybe there is still a difference in the way Homer presents the incidents in front of Troy, the very thoughts of the heroes, or the reaction of Hector's small son, who takes fright from the plumes of his father's helmet. The poet is here an eye-witness. If he were asked how he could know so exactly how it actually happened, he would still invoke the authority of the Muse who told him all and enabled his inner eye to see across the chasm of time. We do not know whether painters and sculptors invoked a similar sanction when they first ventured into the realm of genuine mythological narrative. But one thing was bound to follow: in a narrative illustration, any distinction between the 'what' and the 'how' is impossible to maintain. The painting of the creation will not tell you, like the Holy Writ, only that 'in the beginning God created the heaven and the earth'. Whether he wants to or not, the pictorial artist has to include unintended information about the way God proceeded and, indeed, what God and the world 'looked like' on the day of creation. The Christian Church has had to battle with this unwelcome concomitant of illustration since the very beginnings of Biblical cycles. It may well have been the same difficulty that restrained earlier cultures from embarking on pictorial narrative of sacred themes. But where the poet was given the licence to vary and embroider the myth and to dwell on the 'how' in the recital of epic events, the way was open for the visual artist to do likewise.

It was only this freedom that would enable an artist to tackle a subject such as the judgment of Paris, for how could he render it without adding to the bare story? Not that he would have invented deliberately. On the contrary. Originally he probably did what we have known artists to do in such circumstances: he cast around for an existing schema that would lend itself to adaptation. It has been

90. *The Judgment of Paris*. 'Pontic' vase, sixth century B.C.

conjectured that the first illustrations of this story are adaptations of a traditional cult image showing Hermes leading the three Graces. In the famous 'Pontic' vase of the sixth century [90], this hieratic formula is still noticeable, but the artist clearly amused himself in trying to picture the curious tale of the three irate goddesses being led toward the great beauty contest by Hermes and a bearded old man. We do not know whether his public found his version very convincing, but if it did not there was now every incentive to try again, to amend the formula, and to bring it closer to a plausible narrative. The cup in Berlin from the fifth-century workshop of Hieron and Makron [91] may stand for the success that would have attended such successive efforts. Now we can see much better how it was when the god hailed the princely shepherd, how Athene beckoned, how Hera maintained a dignified reserve becoming to her character, and how Aphrodite, surrounded and adorned by winged cupids, had her victory assured. But even this narrative is still

91. *The Judgment of Paris*. From a cup by Hieron and Makron. About 480 B.C.

92. *Paris on Mount Ida.*
Pompeian wall painting, first century A.D.

'conceptual', intent on that almost pictographic clarity of form that Greek art inherited from Egypt where it served such a different purpose. The shepherd with his goats is a fine pictogram rather than a visual evocation of Mount Ida at that fateful hour, and so there would be every incentive for artists to explore the possibility of a convincing stage on which to place the hero in convincing light and space. It is surely no accident that the tricks of illusionist art, perspective and modelling in light and shade, were connected in classical antiquity with the design of theatrical scenery. It is here, in the context of plays based on the ancient mythical tales, that the re-enactment of events according to the poet's vision and insight comes to its climax and is increasingly assisted by the illusions of art. The records of this development are irretrievably lost, but a Pompeian wall painting of Paris on Mount Ida [92] may illustrate its direction. Here the artist invites us to picture the shepherd dreaming idly by the rural shrine before the quarrel of the goddesses shattered the peace of the scene for ever.

In the whole history of Western art we have this constant interaction between narrative intent and pictorial realism. To ask which came first, the idea of evocation or the means of representation, may therefore seem a rather idle exercise. But where we are confronted with the origins of this entire tradition, the problem of the cause of the Greek revolution, these speculations may at least help to formulate the whole question afresh. What one would like to know is whether the idea of a convincing rather than an effective or lucid image existed in the pre-Greek Orient. Is there any passage in a pre-Homeric text which compares with the description in the *Odyssey* of a gold brooch?

'There was a device on the face of it: a hound holding down a dappled fawn in his forepaws and ripping it as it struggled. Everyone admired the workmanship, the hound ripping and throttling the fawn, the fawn lashing out with its feet in his efforts to escape—and the whole thing done in gold.'

We cannot tell what the brooch which Homer's listeners imagined from this description may have looked like. Possibly it would appear less lifelike to us. But in our context it matters more how it was seen: the attitude, or mental set, which enters into the evocation of the scene at the hunt and tries to imagine with the artist how the hound went in for the kill and how the victim struggled. Would not such an attitude inevitably set up that 'chain reaction' of which Professor Hanfmann speaks?

I do not want to claim that the existence of Homeric poetry alone can suffice to explain the rise of Greek art. In ancient India, for instance, the development of the epic and drama did not lead to the same consequence, but then India lacked the Egyptian heritage of image-making. If one may here apply the scholastic distinction between necessary and sufficient conditions, my hypothesis would be merely that the Homeric freedom of narration was as necessary as was the acquired skill of craftsmanship to open the way for the Greek revolution.

V

IF I AM RIGHT, the traditional picture of the awakening of Greek art which I presented at the beginning of this chapter may give a slightly misleading idea of the sequence of events. By taking this history of the freestanding figure more or less in isolation we arouse the impression of the Sleeping Beauty, but we miss the life-giving kiss. Is it not much more likely that the discoveries which infused life into the freestanding single statue were first made in narrative contexts that demanded a convincing re-creation of a situation—for instance, in the narrative groups of pediments with their dramatic evocation of mythical episodes?

This need not mean that the Greek revolution was more sudden than we thought

93. *The priest Kuy-Em-Snewy.*
About 2400 B.C. Wood

or that we must discard the tidy sequences of *kouroi*. No revolution in art can ever be quite abrupt without sinking into chaos, for we have seen that no attempt to create an image is exempt from the rhythm of schema and correction. To create that realm of mimesis to which Plato objected, the Greek artist, like any artist, needed a vocabulary which could only be articulated in a gradual learning process. No one doubts archaeologists are right if they see the starting point of this vocabulary in the art of the ancient Orient; but may the Greek artists not have modified and adapted it precisely because they made it serve a different purpose? In other words, they approached it with a different mental set and therefore saw it with different eyes.

For as soon as the Greeks looked at the Egyptian figure type from the aspect of an art which wants to 'convince', it undoubtedly raised the question why it looks unconvincing. It is the reaction we express when we speak of its 'rigid posture'. It might be argued that this reaction itself is due to our Greek education; it was the Greeks who taught us to ask '*How* does he stand?' or even 'Why does he stand like that?' Applied to a pre-Greek work of art, it may be senseless to ask this question. The Egyptian statue does not represent a man standing rigidly or a man standing at ease [93]—it is concerned with the what, not the how. To ask for more might have struck an Egyptian artist as it would strike us if someone inquired the age or mood of the king on the chessboard.

We have no early documents to prove that the Greeks did begin to ask such 'inappropriate' questions, but later texts illustrate the fact that from a new point of view, Egyptian art provoked such misunderstanding. We have seen, after all, that Plato considered that Egyptian reliefs represented certain sanctified *postures*. We also know that Heliodorus puzzled his mind over why the Egyptians rendered their gods with closed feet and that he suggested this was intended to symbolize their swiftness. But the most telling document of this change of attitude toward the symbolic image concerns not an Egyptian but an archaic Greek work and the way it was reinterpreted in a narrative context in a later period. We know from Philostratus' life of Apollonius that there was an archaic statue of one Milo in Olympia, standing on a disc with his two feet close together; in his left hand he grasped a pomegranate; the fingers of his right hand were extended and held tightly together. 'The people of Olympia thought that these features showed Milo to have been so inflexible and firm that he could never be induced to budge from the spot where he stood; and this is the meaning of the clinched fingers . . . and why they look as if they could not be separated . . . however much you struggled. . . .' Apollonius knew better. He told his guides that these puzzling traits were due to the archaic style of sculpture.

I do not want to adduce this document of the third century A.D. as decisive evidence for attitudes which I surmise existed some one thousand years earlier. But there are indications in works of art to confirm that the Greeks of the archaic period were in fact inclined to read the pictograms of Egypt as if they were representations of an imagined reality. The most striking and most amusing example is the so-called Busiris vase in Vienna, of the sixth century B.C. [94]. There is little doubt that this humorous account of Herakles' exploits among the Egyptians was inspired by Egyptian renderings of some victorious campaign. We are familiar with the type of pictorial chronicle that shows the gigantic figure of Pharaoh confronting an enemy stronghold with its diminutive defenders begging for mercy [95]. Within the conventions of Egyptian art the difference in scale marks the difference in importance. To the Greek who looked at pictures as evocations of a possible event, the type must have suggested the story of a giant among pygmies. And so he turns the Pharaoh into Herakles wreaking havoc among the puny Egyptians. The pictograph for a whole city becomes a real altar onto which two of the victims have climbed, and climbed in vain, stretching out their hands in comic despair. Many of the gestures of this vase could be matched in Egyptian reliefs, and yet their meaning is transformed: these men are no longer the anonymous tokens for a defeated tribe, they are individual people—laughable, to be sure, in their helpless confusion, but our very laughter presupposes an imaginative effort to see the scene enacted in front of us, to think not only of the 'what' but also of the 'how'.

Once this effort of imaginative sympathy becomes self-understood, the course of art is set for new continents of human experience. When a Greek artist who stood at the end of this tradition was given the task of glorifying a historic victory, he created not a juxtaposition of pictographs but that great history picture, the Battle of Alexander and Darius, of which the Pompeian mosaic copy [97] gives us at least an idea. We need not doubt that the artist and his patron intended to celebrate Alexander's triumph. But it is not only the triumph of victory we are made to share but also the tragedy of defeat. The despairing gesture of the defeated King [96] may ultimately derive from those tokens of helpless surrender we know from the chronicles of the ancient East—but in the context of the eyewitness account it gains a new meaning; it compels us to look at the scene of slaughter not only through the eyes of the victors but also through those of the man in flight. We

94. *Herakles slaying Busiris and his followers.* From a Greek vase, sixth century B.C.

feel how he looks back in agony at the young Alexander, who has just run his lance through a Persian noble; panic has seized the Persian army, the warriors have fallen, the horses shy. The bold foreshortening of the foreground figures, the fallen Persian whose face is reflected in his shield, all draw us into the scene. We are forced to sort out the puzzling shapes to build up the image of events in our mind, and in thus lingering on the situation we come to share the experience of those involved. I believe that the one response cannot be separated from the other. Once we are 'set' for this kind of appeal to our imagination, we will try to look through the picture into the imagined space and the imagined minds behind its surface.

95. *Seti I attacks a town of Canaan.* About 1300 B.C. Relief

Autobiography of Ludwig Richter.

P 56 "Style rules even where the artist
wishes to reproduce nature faithfully"

P 65 "The 'will-to-form' is rather a 'will-to-
make-conform', the assimilation of any
new shape to the schemata and patterns
an artist has learned to handle"

a process by which an image can
be incorporated into the artist's own
pictorial language.

P 78 "The correct portrait, too like the
useful map, is an end product
on a long road through schema
and correction. It is not a
faithful record of a visual
experience but the faithful
construction of a relational model"

P94   Book by Ernst Kris + Otto kurz
         Legends in Art

P116.   by engaging with a work of art
         and its subject the viewer comes
         to share the experience of those
         involved. (subject + Artist)
                         the concept of
         the creation of fiction arrives with
         the need to illustrate an event.
         detail must be added to develop a
         more complete scene and that is
         generated by the artist and is the
         beginning of fictional space.
         the detail draws the viewer in.

         the interpretation of images, itroduces
         variation that originate with the artist
         subconcious decision of colour + line.

         "Scheme and correction" for the expression
         of your own personality/Identity
         the dipping ← becomes the "schema" which is
         "corrected" to better express the personality
                                of the artist.

96. *Darius in defeat* (detail of 97)

97. *Alexander's victory over Darius*. Pompeian mosaic. About 100 B.C.

98. *Maiden gathering flowers.* Wall painting from Stabiae,
first century A.D.

Here, then, is another link in that 'chain reaction' of which Professor Hanfmann speaks. Narrative art is bound to lead to space and the exploration of visual effects, and the reading of these effects in their turn demands a different kind of 'mental set' from the magic rune with its enduring potency. But Plato was right when he felt that something had been sacrificed to this change: the timeless function of the potent image, the Pharaoh forever dominating his foes, had to be discarded in favour of an imaginary fleeting moment of time that might easily tempt an artist into triviality.

To us, this element of sacrifice that is involved in all naturalistic art has become somewhat obscured by the accident that the word 'Greek art' conjures up for most of us a picture of sculpture rather than painting. Yet it is in painting that the reduction to one moment of time and one angle of view will involve the more obvious loss. We remember that this was one of the shortcomings that Plato held against the painter, who could not represent the couch as it is but only as it appears

from one side. If the painting is to make us into specta-
tors of an imaginary scene, it has to sacrifice that diagrammatic completeness that was demanded by the
earlier functions of art. Pliny has preserved for us the
remark of a Hellenistic critic who praised the skill of
the famous painter Parrhasios in creating the illusion
of roundness by the outlines of his figures. This, we
read, is the most subtle part of painting, 'for the outline must go round and so end, that it promises something else to lie behind and thereby shows even what it
obscures'. It is a passage which has aroused much

99

puzzled comment. But I believe that when we compare any conceptual figure of pre-
Greek or early Greek art with the miracles of freely moving figures as we know them
from classical wall paintings [98], we may gather wherein the triumph of Parrhasios
lay. His figures suggest what they can no longer show. We feel the presence even of
the features we do not see, and so he can show us a dancing maiden turning into
the picture, an image that would have appeared senseless to any pre-Greek artist.
Imagine Pygmalion creating a figure with only one arm, or a head without eyes.
The figure in space can be conceived only when we have learned to see it as a sign
referring to an outer, imagined reality. We are expected to know that the arm must
be there but that the artist could not see it from where he stood, and neither
can we.

This understanding may not be very difficult to acquire, but it does demand an
adjustment of mental set. Psychologists who wanted to test the taste of Australian
aborigines and showed them pictures of birds [99] found it a disturbing element
that the natives 'disliked the absence of full representation, as when the foot of a
bird was missing in an attempt to convey perspective'. In other words, they share
Plato's objection to the sacrifices of illusionism.

We remember that this issue of the incomplete image also plays its part in the
context of Egyptian art—the mutilation of hieroglyphic signs that are to be prevented from harming the dead. There is perhaps no stronger confirmation of the
need for completeness in the potent image than this effect of a taboo. It throws an
unexpected light on the achievement of Greek art in breaking this spell for the
sake of illusion. Taken all in all it is not too fanciful, therefore, to compare the
Greek 'conquest of space' with the invention of flying. The pull of gravitation that
the Greek inventors had to overcome was the psychological pull toward the
distinctive 'conceptual' image that had dominated representation heretofore and
that we all have to counteract when we learn the skills of mimesis. Without these
systematic efforts art could never have soared on the wings of illusion into the
weightless zone of dreams.

VI

SURELY it is artificial in such a development to separate what we call 'form' from what we call 'content'. For that imaginative reconstruction which the new type of art demands from the beholder encompasses both. There is another famous passage in the writings of Pliny that also concerns an incomplete figure, but this time the appeal to the imagination is even greater: we hear that Timanthes painted the sacrifice of Iphigenia and expressed the grief of those around her in such a masterly way that when he came to represent her father Agamemnon, he had to suggest the climax of sorrow by representing him with his cloak drawn over his face, an enclosed world within the picture's world, which excited the admiration of the classical orators.

There is a painting on one of the walls of a Pompeian house that reflects this motif [100]. It is not a great work of art, and the same criticism applies to many other copies of Greek works found in Italy and elsewhere. But such criticism has tended to obscure the most astounding consequence of the Greek miracle: the fact that copies were ever made at all to be displayed in the houses and gardens of the educated. For this industry of making reproductions for sale implies a function of the image of which the pre-Greek world knew nothing. The image has been prised loose from the practical context for which it was conceived and is admired and enjoyed for its beauty and fame, that is, quite simply within the context of art. For this is the final consequence of that great 'chain reaction'. The creation of an imaginative realm led to an acknowledgment of what we call 'art' and to the celebration of those rare spirits who could explore and extend that realm.

It may sound paradoxical to say that the Greeks invented art, but from this point of view, it is a mere sober statement of fact. We rarely realize how much this concept owes to the heroic spirit of those discoverers who were active between 550 and 350 B.C. For the history of these years as it is reflected in Pliny or Quintilian was handed down like an epic of conquest, a story of inventions. When Quintilian called the contorted attitude of Myron's *Discobolos* 'particularly praiseworthy for its novelty and difficulty', he codified a standard of criticism that linked art with the solution of problems. The names of the artists who discovered new effects to increase illusion and lifelikeness, the names of Myron and Phidias, Zeuxis and Apelles, lived on in history and have retained their magic despite the fact we do not know one work from their hands. The legend of their triumphs remained as potent in the history of Western art as did the actual works that were recovered from the soil. The writers of the Renaissance echoed the anecdotes that extolled the powers of painting to deceive the eye—the very character which made Plato disapprove of art and prefer the immutable laws of the Egyptian canon.

100. *The Sacrifice of Iphigenia.* Pompeian wall painting, first century A.D.

The Greek revolution deserves its fame. It is unique in the annals of mankind. This should be acknowledged even by those who side with Plato in their taste for the archaic and ritualistic. What makes it unique is precisely the directed efforts, the continued and systematic modifications of the schemata of conceptual art, till making was replaced by the matching of reality through the new skill of mimesis. We mistake the character of this skill if we speak of the imitation of nature. Nature cannot be imitated or 'transcribed' without first being taken apart and put together again. This is not the work of observation alone but rather of ceaseless experimentation. For here, too, the term 'observation' has tended to mislead rather than enlighten.

There is no reason to think Greek artists offered a more complete or more accurate visual inventory of the world than did the art of Egypt, Mesopotamia, or

101. *Lioness under a palm tree.* From the palace of Assur-bani-pal. About 650 B.C.

Crete. On the contrary, in these early cultures the schemata of animals and plants were often refined to an astounding degree. One may well ask whether Greek art produced anything to surpass in this respect the *Lioness under a Palm Tree* from the palace of Assur-bani-pal [101]. After all, Greek art of the classical period concentrated on the image of man almost to the exclusion of other motifs, and even in the portrayal of man it remained wedded to types. This does not apply only to the idealized type of physique which we all associate with Greek art. Even in the rendering of movement and drapery the repertoire of Greek sculpture and painting has turned out to be strangely limited. There are a restricted number of formulas for the rendering of figures standing, running, fighting, or falling, which Greek artists repeated with relatively slight variations over a long period of time. Perhaps if a census of such motifs were taken, the Greek vocabulary would be found to be not much larger than the Egyptian.

It is not even necessarily true that individual observations, such as the existence of shadows or of foreshortening, were never made by pre-Greek artists. There are certain striking examples of such observations in Mexican art that would refute Schäfer's contention that all such departures from conceptual modes are directly dependent on the Greek revolution. But it was Schäfer himself who rightly pointed out that what is interesting in the isolated instances of such deviations, which can

102. *Men pulling a rope.* Relief from the mastaba of Ti, Sakkara. About 2400 B.C.

even be found in Egypt, is that they remained without consequence. They do not become part of the tradition to be improved and extended, as they do in Greece. On the contrary, one has the impression that they are accidents, random mutations which are weeded out by a process of natural selection. A careful scrutiny of Old Kingdom art in Egypt reveals figures as lifelike and unconventional as the one of the man pulling a rope, from the mastaba of Ti [102], which would look daring even in a Greek archaic relief. But from the point of view of function, the figure was perhaps considered a misfit, and the more Egyptian art develops, the less frequent are such variants. Maybe taboos played their part in this sorting-out process. But most of all, we may assume, tradition itself had this effect. Nothing succeeds like success, and nothing survives like survival. The very fact that certain images had survived for immeasurable periods must have appeared as a token of their magic potency.

It is well known that in spite of these powers of inertia the arts of the ancient Orient were not as static as Plato imagined. But this gradual adjustment and even the dramatic shocks of the Amarna period should not be equated in any way with the revolution we have described. The difference between a change in function and a change in formal treatment should not be blurred in the history of art.

Classical art also underwent an evolution, a sorting-out process after its heroic period. But it is no accident that Pliny and Quintilian stopped their story with Lysippus, who said of himself that earlier artists had represented people as they are, he represented them as they appeared to be. The conquest of appearances, sufficiently convincing to allow the imaginative reconstruction of mythological or historical events, was the end of classical art in more than one meaning of the word. The rise of the new religions from the East challenged this function. Perhaps that inevitable trivialization of the image which was the consequence of spreading

103. *The Emperor Justinian and his retinue*. Mosaic. San Vitale, Ravenna. About 550

skill and of joy in jugglery had made the art of mimesis vulnerable. In the time of Augustus there are already signs of a reversal of taste toward earlier modes of art and an admiration of the mysterious shapes of the Egyptian tradition. Quintilian tells us of connoisseurs who preferred the austere art of the 'primitive' Greeks to the more nearly perfect masterpieces of later times. The breakdown of classical standards was thus perhaps prepared by a lack of conviction. And yet I do not think this breakdown should be interpreted as a fresh revolution in favour of new ideals. What happened here looks much more like another process of natural selection, not a directed effort by a band of pioneers, but the survival of the fittest; in other words, the adaptation of the formulas to the new demands of imperial ceremony and divine revelation. In the course of this adaptation, the achievements of Greek illusionism were gradually discarded. The image was no longer asked questions of how and when: it was reduced to the what of impersonal recital. And with the beholder's questioning of the image, the artist's questioning of nature stopped. The schema was not criticized and corrected, and so it followed the natural pull toward the minimum stereotype, the 'gingerbread figure' of peasant art. The sacrifice of Iphigenia is followed by the sacrifice of Isaac as it appears on the walls of the synagogue of Dura-Europos [82].

It has become unfashionable to call this reorientation a 'decline' and, indeed, it is hard to use such a word when one stands in San Vitale in Ravenna [103]. The gleam of the mosaics, the intense gaze of the worshipping Emperor, the ceremonial dignity of the scene show the image has recovered something of the potency which it once had. But it owes its very strength to this direct contact with the beholder. It no longer waits to be wooed and interpreted but seeks to awe him into submission. Art has again become an instrument, and a change of function results in a change of form. The Byzantine icon is not conceived as free 'fiction'; it somehow partakes of the nature of a Platonic truth. Even the narrative cycles of the Byzantine Church, as Otto Demus has shown, are no longer to be understood as an imaginative account of a past event. They mark the annual cycle of feasts and the timeless re-enactment of the life of Christ in the liturgy of the Church. This is the closest approach to pre-Greek conceptions to which art could attain after the Greek revolution. Small wonder that it led to a concentration on distinctive features and came to restrict the free play of the imagination in artist and beholder alike. But in neither the East nor the West did medieval art ever eliminate the discoveries of Greek art, the modifications of the schema through foreshortening and modelling in light and shade. For the classical heritage of narrative was implicit in the illustration of the gospel story which challenged the imagination of poets and artists till the means of increasing the lifelikeness of re-presentations again became the object of systematic search.

V

Formula and Experience

Though their particulars are those
That each particular artist knows,
Unique events that once took place
Within a unique time and space,
In the new field they occupy
The unique serves to typify,
Becomes, though still particular,
An algebraic formula,
An abstract model of events
Derived from dead experiments,
And each life must itself decide
To what and how it be applied.

W. H. AUDEN, "The New Year Letter, 1940"

I

THE GREEK revolution may have changed the function and forms of art. It could not change the logic of image making, the simple fact that without a medium and without a schema which can be moulded and modified, no artist could imitate reality. We know what the ancients called their schemata; they referred to them as the canon, the basic geometric relationships which the artist must know for the construction of a plausible figure. But the problem of the canon has become overlaid in Greek art by the search for beauty and proportion, and so we may better select a starting point outside the realm of great art to continue our probing of mimesis. We may find such a starting point in a doctoral thesis on the psychology of drawing in which the author, F. C. Ayer, summarizes his conclusions as follows: 'The trained drawer acquires a mass of schemata by which he can produce a schema of an animal, a flower or a house quickly upon paper. This serves as a support for the representation of his memory images and he gradually modifies the schema until it corresponds with that which he would express. Many drawers who are deficient in schemata and can draw well from another drawing cannot draw from the object.'

We have seen in the second chapter that there is certainly some truth in Mr. Ayer's observations. Indeed, what I called the 'pathology of portrayal', the curious mistakes made by copyists and topographic artists, often turned out to be due to the lack of a schema. And yet I doubt whether many an artist today would like to see himself classified with those 'trained drawers' whom the psychologist observed and described. His account is rather reminiscent of those primers for amateurs which

126

104   105

promise to teach us 'how to draw trees', 'how to draw birds', sailingboats, aeroplanes, or horses. Where there is smoke there is fire. The mass of these books which pour from the printing presses year in year out must be as significant as the professional artist's horror of these 'tricks'. There are books for the studious on how to draw hands, feet, eyes, as well as comprehensive encyclopaedias teaching all this and more in a few lessons. Now, all these books work on the principle we would expect from the formula 'schema and correction'. They teach a simple canon and show how to construct the required vocabulary out of basic geometric forms, easy to remember and easy to draw, like the cat I learned to draw as a child [2]. At their simplest we find these tricks illustrated in such primers as Allen's *Graphic Art in Easy Stages* [104], but the principle is the same in more serious books, such as R. Sheppard's *How to Draw Birds* [105].

These lessons for the budding artist may be compared with certain methods of building images we observed in primitive art. Early civilizations learned how to represent eyes by classifying them with cowrie shells. The amateur now is taught to classify and sort out the basic shapes of things in terms of a few geometric distinctions. Only after he has learned to construct the image of a bird should he go out and look at birds he wishes to portray, and only at the end should he record such distinctive features as characterize first the species and then the individual bird.

Now the whole temper of art in our time revolts against such procedures. Have we not just struggled free of the dreary and melancholy methods by which Victorian boys were taught to draw the schema of a leaf they could hardly have seen from a

106. *A Victorian drawing class*

distance and which certainly looked quite different [106] ? Can anything be more deadening to spontaneity and imagination than the learning by rote recommended by these methods ?

II

THE HISTORIAN KNOWS that such revulsion from the formula is a comparatively recent development. Many earlier civilizations would scarcely have understood the contrast between convention and inspiration that plays such a part in our critical literature. No artistic tradition insists with greater force on the need for inspired spontaneity than that of ancient China, but it is precisely there we find a complete reliance on acquired vocabularies. The recent publication and translation of a Chinese standard textbook on painting from the seventeenth century [107] has made it easier for the Westerner to study this combination of traditionalism and respect for the uniqueness of every performance. 'In learning to write,' this work tells us, 'one begins with simple characters made up of a few strokes and proceeds to complicated characters with several strokes. In the same way, in learning to paint flowers, one begins with those with few petals and proceeds to those with many petals, from small leaves to large, and from single stems to bunches. . . . When the beginner has learned the basic steps, he will have started on the way to acquiring experience and skill.'

Some of these rules were summed up
in traditional four-word phrases which the
disciple could learn to memorize by chant-
ing, as in these hints for painting orchids:

'First draw four leaves. They should
vary in length. A fifth leaf crosses them.
In this there is grace and beauty. . . . Ink
tones should be varied. Old and young
leaves should mingle. Petals should be
light, stamens and calyx dark. The hand
should move like lightning; it should never
be slow or hesitant.'

107. *From the 'Mustard Seed Garden Manual
of Painting'. 1679–1701*

And so the minute rules of how to
create a convincing image of an orchid
would naturally include a quotation about
the mood which gives the best inspiration.
Chüeh Yin, Buddhist monk of the Yüan
period, said: 'When the emotions are strong
and one feels pent up, one should paint
bamboo; in a light mood one should paint
the orchid, for the leaves of the orchid
grow as though they were flying or fluttering, the buds open joyfully, and the
mood is indeed a happy one.'

It is clear even to the nonspecialist that the Chinese method must have been as
admirably adapted to the function of art in this beautifully consistent culture as
the formulas evolved by Egyptian art were adapted to their purpose. Its primary
concern was neither the perpetuation of images nor the plausible narrative but
something which is perhaps least inaccurately described as 'poetic evocation'. The
Chinese artist appears still as a 'maker' of mountains, trees, or flowers. He can
conjure them up because he has learned the secret of their being, but he does so to
record and evoke a mood which is deeply rooted in Chinese ideas about the nature
of the universe.

There is nothing in Western art which compares with this conception of painting; indeed, the language in which we discuss pictures differs so radically from the
critical terminology of the Far East that all attempts to translate from one into the
other are frustrated by this basic difference of categories. But it is all the more
interesting to continue the search for those common human traits which survive
any change of aesthetics and shift in purpose: the need for acquired formulas.

That this need is paramount in medieval art is universally recognized. For
almost a thousand years, between the third and the thirteenth centuries A.D., the

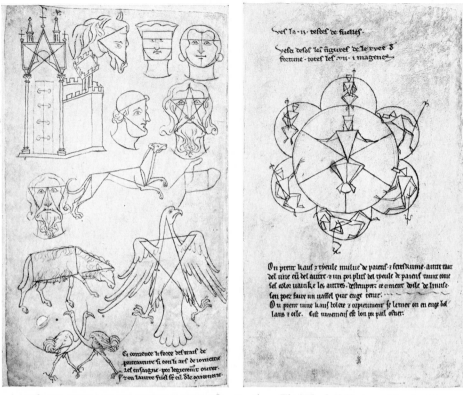

108–109. VILLARD DE HONNECOURT: *Constructions. The Wheel of Fortune.* About 1235.
Pen on vellum

contact of art with the visible world had been extremely tenuous. For the purpose
of narrative and of teaching the doctrine, the artist relied on the formulas evolved
by classical art, suitably adapted and transformed to fit the new contexts. Early
medieval art, as we know, is an art of copyists, of the transcription of traditional
picture cycles into a more or less individual idiom. We have seen the strange
results that ensued even in the thirteenth century when a skilled master like Villard
de Honnecourt wanted to use his art to record an individual and unique experience,
his encounter with a lion [55].

The character of this portrait contrasts significantly with the familiarity of the
trick figures which Villard included in his album of patterns [108]. One could find
a parallel for each of these diagrams in modern drawing books. Villard and his
workmates must have experienced the same difficulties and needed the same
psychological aids in learning to draw as we do. It is quite possible that he, too,
thought less of trained painters than of architects who should master the rudiments
of representation without needing refined skill. But most of all his pages indicate a
certain freedom of invention which leads away from reliance on individual narrative
cycles and dares to compose afresh.

The best way, perhaps, to clarify the basic difference between the function of art in medieval contexts and in later times is to make use of a terminology with which Villard would have been quite conversant: the philosophic distinction between 'universals' and 'particulars'. We have already encountered this main theme of Western philosophy in our discussions of Plato's couch. Ordinary nouns, such as 'man', 'sheep', 'hound', or 'lion', denote concepts, 'universals'. They refer to classes of things of which individuals are merely instances. A battle raged in the medieval schools whether these universals should be called more or less 'real' than such particular things as the man Villard, the dog Noble, or the lion Rex. In this terminology, what I have called the 'schema' refers to universals. Villard, no less than the Chinese or modern drawing books, teaches how to draw 'a man', or 'a dog', whenever the context demands it. In the contexts normal to medieval art, the schema could function like a hieroglyph or pictograph. It comes into its own in Villard's album where he shows how to draw the wheel of fortune [109], that tremendous image of the instability of the human lot that the Middle Ages had taken over from Boethius' vision in his adversity. These figures, rising and falling, are not particular men but are like the hero of the morality play 'Everyman', and it is for us to apply the concept to ourselves. With Villard's lion, of course, it is different. And yet in claiming he had drawn it '*al vif*', he probably wanted to say no more than we say when we use a 'universal' to tell that we have seen 'a lion'.

III

THE RETURN to the classical ideal of the 'convincing' image in the Renaissance did not necessarily change the nature of the problem, it only created more exacting standards for the rendering of universals, be they lions or men. But in one respect the importance of these fresh standards can hardly be overrated. As in classical times, the narrative was again to be presented to the beholder as if he were an eyewitness to imaginary events. Alberti drew the final conclusion from this reviving demand when he described the frame as a window through which the beholder looks into the world of the picture. To satisfy this demand you had to know the modifications of the schema caused by the angle of vision, or, in other words, you had to understand that branch of projective geometry known as 'perspective'. It was not enough to have a patternbook with graceful pictures of running hounds. You had to visualize the three-dimensional pattern of the hound if you wanted it to look convincing in many orientations, as it does in Uccello's *Hunt* [110].

With Uccello we still feel the schema very strongly. He may well have constructed first a wooden model and worked out the foreshortenings geometrically. But the Renaissance artist who wanted to people his stage freely with all manner and

110. UCCELLO: *The Hunt*. Detail. About 1460

classes of living things could not rely on such roundabout methods. He had to strive for a greater knowledge of universals and master the structure of things so thoroughly that he could visualize them in any spatial context.

The most illustrious instance of this natural union between knowledge and art is of course Leonardo da Vinci. It seems a far cry from Villard's geometric tricks and his heraldic lion to Leonardo's incessant search for the secret of organic form, and yet they belong together, for both are directed towards the 'universal'. One example must suffice. Leonardo was obviously dissatisfied with the current method of drawing trees. He knew a better way. 'Remember,' he taught, 'that wherever a branch divides, the stem grows correspondingly thinner, so that, if you draw a circle round the crown of the tree, the sections of every twig must add up to the thickness of the trunk' [111]. I do not know if this law holds. I do not think it quite does. But as a hint on 'how to draw trees', Leonardo's observation is invaluable. By teaching the assumed laws of growth he has given the artist a formula for construct-ing a tree—and so he can still feel like the creator, 'Lord and Master of all things', who knows the secrets of nature and can 'make' trees as he hoped to 'make' a bird that would fly.

I believe what we call the Renaissance artists' preoccupation with structure has a very practical basis in their needs to know the schema of things. For in a way our very concept of 'structure', the idea of some basic scaffolding or armature that determines the 'essence' of things, reflects our need for a schema with which to grasp the infinite variety of this world of change. No wonder these issues have become somewhat clouded by a metaphysical fog which settled over the discussions of art in the sixteenth and seventeenth centuries.

IV

THE MEDIEVAL DISTINCTION between universals and particulars was mainly a matter of logic. In these terms, Leonardo had discovered a law about the biological class called 'trees' to which every individual tree belonged. Those who wanted to portray a tree in their garden had first to know about the structure and proportion of trees. But thanks in part to the influence of Platonism, the whole distinction could be given a different twist. For Plato, the universal is the idea, the perfect pattern of the tree exists somewhere in a place beyond the heavens, or, to use the technical term, in the intelligible world. Individual trees or horses or men, such as the painter may encounter in real life, are only imperfect copies of these eternal patterns, imperfect because base matter will always resist the flawless seal and prevent the idea from realizing itself. It was on these grounds that Plato himself denied art its validity, for what value can there be in copying an imperfect copy of the idea? But on the same grounds, Neoplatonism tried to assign to art a new place that was eagerly seized upon by the emerging academies. It is just the point, they argued, that the painter, unlike ordinary mortals, is a person endowed with the divine gift of perceiving, not the imperfect and shifting world of individuals, but the eternal patterns themselves. He must purify the world of matter, erase its flaws, and approximate it to the idea. He is aided in this by the knowledge of the laws of beauty, which are those of harmonious, simple geometrical relationships, and by the study of those antiques that already represent reality 'idealized', i.e., approximated to the Platonic idea.

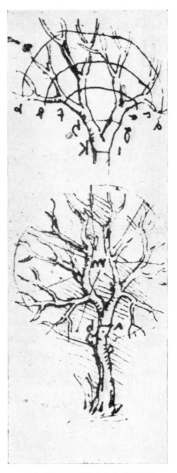

111. LEONARDO DA VINCI:
Diagram of the growth of trees

I believe this doctrine, which held sway in the academies for at least three hundred years, from 1550 to 1850, rests on self-deception. It endows the art of drawing, not a particular tree, but a tree, not a particular man, but a man—that is to say, a continuation of Villard's conceptual art—with a slightly specious philosophical halo. Mere portrayal is menial and low. You must recreate nature. If the tree or the man in front of you does not conform to that geometrical scaffolding now presented as the perfect canon, so much the worse for the tree or the man. The perfect painter is endowed with the gift of seeing the universal in the particular, of looking across the dross of matter at the 'essential form' which—in Aristotelian rather than in Platonic terms—shaped the resisting clay from within.

We need not doubt that painters experienced this very thrill. And yet one suspects that the pattern they found behind the visible world was not the one laid up in heaven but the remembered shapes they had learned in their youth. Would not a Chinese call that orchid 'perfect' which corresponds most closely to the rules he had absorbed? Do we not tend to judge human bodies by their resemblance to those Greek statues that have become traditionally identified with the canon of beauty?

V

I DO NOT CLAIM that this answer contains the whole truth about the changing ideals of natural beauty. But I do think the study of the metaphysics of art should always be supplemented by an analysis of its practice, notably the practice of teaching.

There are few aspects of the past that are more difficult for us to grasp and recapture than the old experience of schooling. The harshness and even cruelty of the demands it made on the young apprentice would certainly revolt us. Just as the young singer lived in the house of his master and learned and practised scales for many years under his constant supervision, so the painter's apprentice was delivered into the power of his taskmaster, who saw to it that he spent hours in the exercise of copying the works of the great. 'Draw, Antonio, draw, Antonio, draw and do not waste time', wrote the aged Michelangelo on a sheet of paper to urge a flagging apprentice on, and these words must have been echoed in workshops all over Europe. The aim of these exercises was clearly formulated in a seventeenth-century treatise by the German painter Joachim von Sandrart: 'When our Understanding issues its well-conceived concepts, and the hand, practised by many years of industrious drawing, puts them to paper according to reason, the perfect excellence of both the master and his art becomes manifest.'

No one doubted in those days that all art was 'conceptual' in the sense that you had first to learn and practise how to draw 'a man' before you were even allowed to try your hand in the life class. In the academies there was a carefully graded course from the copying of prints to the drawing after the antique that took years before the artist was permitted to wrestle with a real motif. It is this insistence on the mastery of tradition that secured the continuity of art between the Middle Ages and the eighteenth century, for all the time the sway of the pattern was unchallenged. Of course the material for copying had immeasurably increased with the coming of prints and the distribution of plaster casts. Moreover, it was supplemented by anatomy books and books on proportion, not to speak of the study of the nude in which the artist put his acquired knowledge to the test. But from no other source can we study the training of the artist's hand and eye as conveniently as in the drawing books. Within the context of this chapter I can only call attention to the unsuspected richness of this material. The *Catalogue of Books and Pamphlets in the National Art Library at South Kensington*, which came out in 1888, lists over five hundred titles of books that fall within this category, and yet this list is incomplete. It is no mere paradox to say that the scarcity of these books in our libraries is symptomatic of their past importance. They were simply used up, handled and torn in the workshops and studios, and even the existing ones are often misbound and incomplete.

The earliest printed patternbook came out in 1538 in Strasbourg. Its author, Heinrich Vogtherr, explicitly claims on the title page that his book is a novelty. In the introduction Vogtherr bewails the fate of art and artists in German lands because of the Reformation. He wants to prevent the arts from dying out lest Christendom decline into barbarism. Especially he thinks of those fellow-artists who are burdened with wives and children, or who cannot travel, and it is for their benefit he has compiled what he calls a *summa* of all the strange and most difficult pieces that usually demand much imagination and meditation, to save the weaker brethren trouble and to enable the subtle minds to rise still higher in order that the arts may rise again and Germany may return to her leading place among nations.

The means by which these great aims are to be achieved are the traditional patterns as we know them from late medieval workshop practices. There are pages with fantastic heads and headgear and others with hands in various attitudes, feet, and ornaments [112, 113].

Compared with Vogtherr's unassuming little book, Erhard Schön's *Underweisung der Proporzion* of 1538 is a sophisticated affair. Here we find a basic schema for the human head seen from all sides and a method of imagining the human body as composed of simple forms [115, 116], neither of which has lost anything in popularity. Schön owed his inspiration to Dürer's famous *Dresden Sketchbook* [114, 117] and its experiments with the geometrical and stereometrical structure of the human body, which have been compared with cubist methods. I do not think this comparison is illuminating. The cubist, as I hope to show in a future chapter,

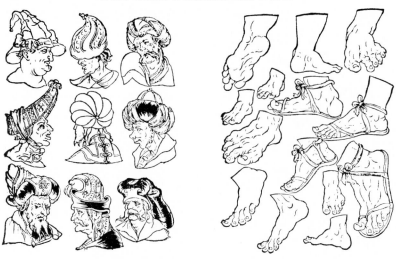

112, 113. VOGTHERR: *Heads and feet.* 1538

is not out to clarify a schema but to baffle our perception. Dürer's researches are linked with his quest for the secret of beauty but also with his practical aims as an educator. One can see he is interested in the construction of a suitable lay figure which might serve as a handy schema to future generations. One more German book from this tradition will suffice: Heinrich Lautensack's *Des Circkels unnd Richtscheyts . . . Underweisung*, which came out in Frankfurt in 1564. In its pages all the modern devices are exemplified: for instance, the hint of imagining the schema of the skeleton as a wire construction with dots for the joints [118].

On the whole, however, the sixteenth-century drawing books with their emphasis on projective geometry seem to have lacked the simplicity that was felt to be needed for the instruction of beginners. This, at least, is what we read in Carel van

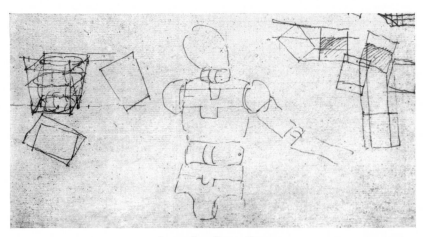

114. DÜRER: *Lay figure.* About 1513

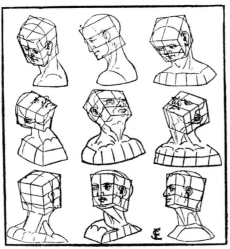

115, 116. SCHÖN: *Schematic heads and bodies.* 1538

Mander's poem on the art of painting which was written shortly before 1600. 'If only a great master,' he writes, 'would publish in print, for the use of youngsters, an A B C book on the first elements of our art. I am too clumsy to do it, and those who could, won't.'

But as so often happens, the demand elicited a supply. In 1608 there appeared in Venice what seems to be the first book of a new type, Odoardo Fialetti's 'The

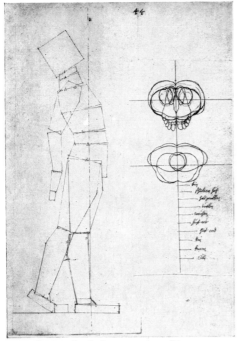

117. DÜRER: *Study in proportions.* About 1513   118. LAUTENSACK: *Schematic drawing.* 1564

119. FIALETTI: *Eyes.* 1608   120. AGOSTINO CARRACCI: *Features*

true method and order to draw all parts and limbs of the human body'. Some of
the pages are very much in the Vogtherr tradition, but Fialetti goes into much more
detail in his analysis of the various parts of the human body. He starts off with a
page on eyes [119] which combines the principle of 'graphic art in easy stages' with
a variety of examples. It seems this kind of detailed study was derived by Fialetti
from the workshop of a much greater artist, Agostino Carracci. Many of that
master's drawings have this analytic character, which confirms his reputation as

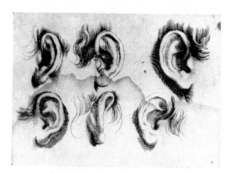

121. GUERCINO: *Ears.* 1619

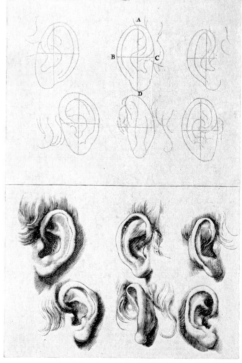

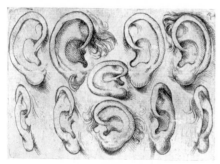

122. FIALETTI: *Ears.* 1608   123. VAN DE PASSE: *Ears, drawn after Guercino,
and diagrams.* 1643

one of the founders of the academic tradition [120]. Seventeenth-century sources mention that Agostino considered the ear the hardest of all features to draw and that he constructed a large plaster-cast model for the training of his students. There were in circulation in the seventeenth and eighteenth centuries a number of didactic prints attributed to Annibale Carracci, though their exact authorship is uncertain. The impact of the Carracci on drawing books can be studied in the work of two other members of the Bolognese school, Guercino and Guido Reni. Guercino's series was published in 1619. His dependence on Fialetti, or perhaps on a model provided in the Carracci workshop, becomes clear if we compare their pages of ears [121, 122]. This type of dependence is precisely what we would expect: it is easier to learn the drawing of ears from existing books than from nature. And so we cannot be surprised that Guercino in turn was asked to lend his ears to a northern patternbook, the large encyclopaedia of images by Crispyn van de Passe called *The Light of Painting and Drawing*, the first edition of which came out in Amsterdam in 1643. To meet the demand voiced by his compatriot van Mander for an ABC book, van de Passe copied Guercino [123] but also retranslated his patterns into simple diagrams that recall the modern drawing book. Into more than two hundred pages van de Passe also incorporates a visual inventory of the animal world that includes such delightful simplifications as the stag seen from behind [124] and the bird

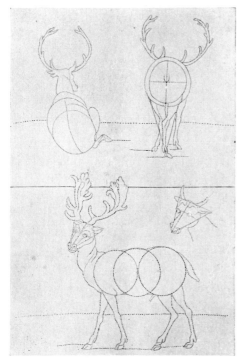

124. VAN DE PASSE: *Schematic stag.* 1643   125. VAN DE PASSE: *Birds and schema.* 1643

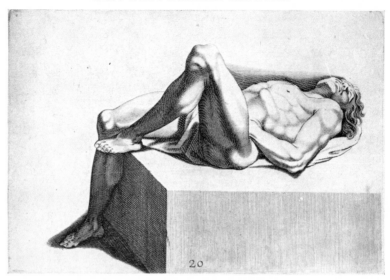

126. DE JODE: *Academy figure.* 1629

which anticipates the twentieth-century example [125]. But as so often in history, the similarity can help us to define the difference of attitude behind these almost

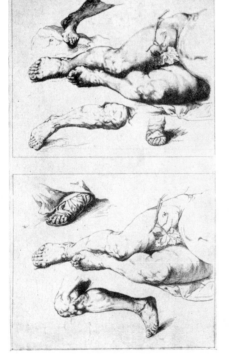

127. AFTER RIBERA:
Bacchic figure and outline. 1650

identical diagrams. What for us is only a shortcut method, a trick for the tyro, reveals to the seventeenth-century artist something also of the structure of the world. We read in the letterpress of the book that it is providential that birds, like all creatures, are composed of simple Euclidian forms. One might see in this confidence an echo of Plato's *Timaeus*, the idea that regular bodies are the ultimate constituents of the world. The regular schema which we call an abstraction was therefore 'found' by the artist in nature. It belongs to the laws of its being.

As luck will have it, the same century produced a parallel in the Far East. In the Chinese patternbook to which I referred before, we may read this: 'One should know well the whole form of the bird. Birds are born from eggs. And their forms resemble eggs, with head, tail, wings, and feet added.' In 'developing' the bird from

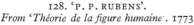

128. 'P. P. RUBENS'.
From 'Théorie de la figure humaine'. 1773

129. LAUTENSACK:
Schema of a running man. 1564

the egg form the artist followed the way of nature. But the book refrains from illustrating the diagrammatic tricks. As far as I know these only appear in the Far East in the eighteenth century. Hokusai made use of them. It would be interesting to know whether Western drawing books were responsible for this innovation. One tradition, of course, is peculiar to the West: the academy figure. This also formed part of the Carracci tradition, but the North contributed its share with a book by Pieter de Jode which came out in Antwerp in 1629 and bears the characteristic title *Various Academy Figures Newly Compiled from Life with Enormous Labour and at Great Cost, Most Convenient for Young People Who Enjoy the Art of Drawing* [126]. Here the tradition of Rubens merges with that of Italy.

It is never easy to decide what is original in this type of publication. De Jode and van de Passe, including his title, were taken over by Frederik de Wit, who prefaced his *Lumen picturae* with a striking variation on Ribera's etching *The Poet* [*frontisp*.]. By the time the book was out, a series of didactic prints after Ribera had been published in France by Poilly, with the device of showing each detail in contour for easy copying and with shading. This, too, is embodied in de Wit's volume [127]. These are just a few instances to demonstrate that such books really form a reservoir of formulas or schemata which spread through Europe. In 1773 there appeared a curious book of plates purporting to reproduce a treatise by Rubens, which contains, among other things, illustrations from Leonardo's

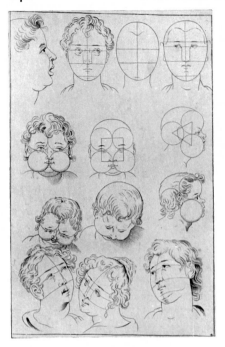

130. DE WIT: *Putti.* About 1660

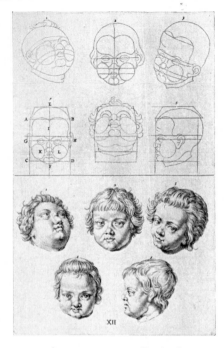

131. VAN DE PASSE: *Putti.* 1643

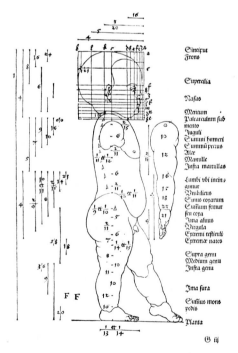

132. DÜRER: *Proportions of a child.* 1532

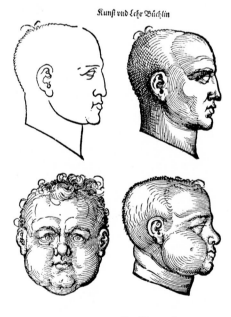

133. BEHAM: *Profiles.* 1565

134. RUBENS: *Portrait of his son*. Detail. About 1620

Trattato—but on one of its pages [128] we find the pose of Michelangelo's *David* together with the schema of a running man which turns out to be a copy from Lautensack [129].

In a way, then, these books can really be compared with vocabularies. After all, dictionaries, too, have grown through the ages by absorbing the wisdom and the errors of older dictionaries. One last example may illustrate the role of this visual vocabulary. Among de Wit's [130] formulas is a schema of how to draw children's heads which is traceable to van de Passe. The heads based on these curious constructions look rather like Rubens' *putti*. But if we look a little more closely we find that they, in turn, are only adaptations and modifications of a formula evolved by Dürer [132]. It was not directly from Dürer that they derived. Van de Passe [131] also embodied in his visual dictionary copies from a booklet by Sebald Beham [133], and I suspect that it was Beham who infected Rubens' *putti* with mumps. Now as long as these things remain on the level of patternbooks, they may be amusing but they cannot be very important. They become more exciting if one begins to ask oneself if it is possible that even a master such as Rubens might have been influenced in his portrayal of children, even in his portraits of his own boys [134], by the schema of proportion he had acquired in his youth.

For here we suddenly come up against the real problem of these teaching methods: the relation between the universal and the particular. It is the problem of portrayal which we looked at from another angle in the second chapter. What I called the 'pathology of portrayal' can only be studied from examples where we can still compare the 'accuracy' of the draughtsman's record. We shall never know what Rubens' children 'really looked like', but this need not mean we are forever barred from examining the influence which acquired patterns or schemata have on the organization of our perception. It would be interesting to examine this question in an experimental setting. But every student of art who has intensely occupied himself with a family of forms has experienced examples of such influence. In fact I vividly remember the shock I had while I was studying these formulas for chubby children: I never thought they could exist, but all of a sudden I saw such children everywhere.

This tendency of our minds to classify and register our experience in terms of the known must present a real problem to the artist in his encounter with the particular. Indeed, it may well be this difficulty which brought about the downfall of the formula in art.

VI

I SHOULD LIKE to illustrate this ambivalence through the most widespread and familiar of all the diagrammatic formulas taught in the Western tradition—the divided oval or egg shape that does duty for the head. Van Mander urges the apprentice diligently to practise the egg shape with the cross in it, without which no head can succeed, and so it quite appropriately is shown on a chapter heading of a popular drawing book of the time [135]. How should we describe the value of such a studio device? Maybe the egg shape is so useful because it acts as an effective corrective to one of the most frequent mistakes untrained persons make when they draw a head: the mistake of identifying what interests us, that is, the face, with the whole head. In the scrawl of a child the features which make up a face—the dots for the eyes, the strokes for the nose and for the mouth—are just surrounded any-how by a line which is used to support the ears or, if need be, a hat [136]. This crude conceptual schema is usually a flat disc. By asking the beginner to select another starting point, one which forces him to think of the head first and of the face as subordinated to its three-dimensional structure, the teacher will certainly induce progress.

Artists great and small have used this method of indicating a head. Indeed, the popularity of this formula with painters as different as Leonardo and Fra Barto-lommeo, Paolo Veronese and Rembrandt [137–40], testifies to that unity of language in representation which I am trying to emphasize in these chapters. In their drawings, the schema assumes the form of shorthand notations which the artist will expand and fill in when the time comes. And yet, I think, when we call such formulas

135. VAN DE PASSE: *From chapter title of a drawing book.* 1643

'abbreviations' or 'simplifications' we are not quite doing justice to their psychological status. The artist need not think first of a real head which he then reduces to the abstract oval—even for him the oval, the schema, is the starting point which he will then clothe with flesh and blood if the occasion requires.

But obviously such a reliance on the schema can block the path to effective portrayal unless it is accompanied by a constant willingness to correct and revise. We have a precious testimony to the existence of this danger even in the well-trained painters of the eighteenth century. The great eighteenth-century anatomist Pieter Camper tells us that 'the portrait painters of the present day generally describe an oval upon their panel before the person to be painted sits to be drawn, make a cross in the oval, which they divide into the length of four noses and the breadth of five eyes; and they paint the face according to these divisions to which it must be accommodated, let the proportions themselves be ever so much at variance.' Camper even goes further. He subjects the schema from a drawing book by Preissler [141] to a careful scrutiny and explains that in half profile the recipe goes wrong altogether because the mouth comes too close to the ear [142]. Yet he tells us that in contrast to van Dyck and the Italians, Northern painters usually make this mistake.

136. *Snowball fight*. Child's drawing

137. LEONARDO DA VINCI: *Schematic head*   138. FRA BARTOLOMMEO: *Drawings*

139. VERONESE: *Study for the 'Marriage at Cana'*. Detail   140. REMBRANDT: *Calvary*. Detail

It appears once more that the difference between Villard, who drew his schematic lion and
called it a portrait from life, and the eighteenth-
century painter criticized by Camper is only
one of degree. Both apply a universal stereotype to a member of a class, the Lion Rex or
Lord X Y Z. Now it may be true that once a
hack has learned how to make the image of a
tolerably convincing head, he may be tempted
to use this standard formula for the rest of his
days, merely adding just such distinguishing
features as will mark the admiral or the court
beauty. But obviously once he is in possession
of a standard head, he can also use it as a starting point for corrections, to measure all individual deviations against it. He may first draw it
on his canvas or in his mind, not in order to
complete it, but to match it against the sitter's
head and enter the differences onto his schema.

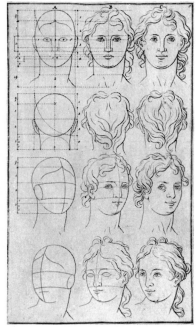

141. PREISSLER: *Schematic heads.* 1734

From what we have seen of the need for schemata, we need no longer be surprised
that even a wrong schema is a useful tool. Our perceptive apparatus is so built that
it only jumps into action when prodded in some such way. We hear a lot about
training the eye or learning to see, but this phraseology can be misleading if it hides
the fact that what we can learn is not to see but to discriminate. If seeing were a
passive process, a registration of sense data by the retina as a photographic plate,
it would indeed be absurd for us to need a wrong schema to arrive at a correct

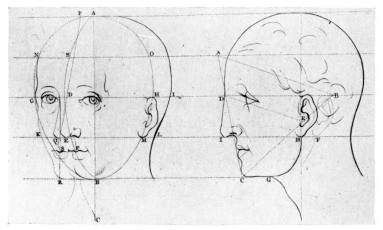

142. CAMPER: *The proportions of the head.* 1794

portrait. But every day brings new and startling confirmation from the psychology laboratories that this idea, or ideal, of passivity is quite unreal. 'Perception,' it has been recently said, 'may be regarded as primarily the modification of an anticipation.' It is always an active process, conditioned by our expectations and adapted to situations. Instead of talking of seeing and knowing, we might do a little better to talk of seeing and noticing. We notice only when we look *for* something, and we look when our attention is aroused by some disequilibrium, a difference between our expectation and the incoming message. We cannot take in all we see in a room, but we notice if something is changed. We cannot register all the features of a head, and as long as they conform to our expectations they fall silently into the slot of our perceptive apparatus. Similarly we have come to accept certain forms in pictures as representing heads, and we are not troubled before our attention is roused— though if somebody entered our room with an egg-shaped head, or even with a mouth misplaced like Preissler's, we would be sure to notice something wrong.

VII

SEEN IN THIS LIGHT, that dry psychological formula of schema and correction can tell us a good deal, not only about the essential unit between medieval and post-medieval art, but also of their vital difference. To the Middle Ages, the schema is the image; to the postmedieval artist, it is the starting point for corrections, adjustments, adaptations, the means to probe reality and to wrestle with the particular. The hallmark of the medieval artist is the firm line that testifies to the mastery of his craft [143]. That of the postmedieval artist is not facility, which he avoids, but constant alertness. Its symptom is the sketch [144], or rather the many sketches which precede the finished work and, for all the skill of hand and eye that marks the master, a constant readiness to learn, to make and match and remake till the portrayal ceases to be a secondhand formula and reflects the unique and unrepeatable experience the artist wishes to seize and hold.

It is this constant search, this sacred discontent, which constitutes the leaven of the Western mind since the Renaissance and pervades our art no less than our science. For it is not only the scientist of the stamp of Camper who can examine the schema and test its validity. Since the time of Leonardo, at least, every great artist has done the same, consciously or unconsciously.

Up to the nineteenth century, however, the patterns handed down by tradition derived some authority from those metaphysical views I have mentioned, the conviction that the artist snould represent the universal rather than the particular, that he should never slavishly copy the accidents of nature but keep his eye firmly on the ideal.

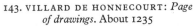

143. VILLARD DE HONNECOURT: *Page of drawings*. About 1235

144. LEONARDO DA VINCI: *Rearing horse*. About 1505

It was only when this metaphysical conviction faded that the real conflict started. Artists turned against the academies and the traditional methods of teaching because they felt it was the artist's task to wrestle with the unique visual experience which can never have been prefigured and can never recur. The history of late eighteenth- and nineteenth-century art thus became, in a way, the history of the struggle against the schema. Not entirely though. Some artists always kept their heads. Degas, for instance, dismissed the excited talk of his impressionist friends with the remark that painting was a conventional art and they would better occupy their time by copying drawings by Holbein. According to Meder, it was Rousseau who first held forth in *Emile* in 1763 against the traditional way of teaching the elements of drawing. Emile should never be taught to copy other men's work, he should copy only nature. This is one of those programmes which may be said to be charged with explosive ignorance. True, similar things had been said before ot or by Lysippus and Caravaggio, but in the eighteenth century the demand had a new ring. It is the time of 'original genius' and of nature worship. And so the break in tradition is heralded, which foreshadows the modern dilemma.

No artist embodies this dilemma more clearly than John Constable, with whose work I began these chapters. Nearly all his utterances betray this ambivalence toward tradition. 'I remember to have heard him say,' Leslie writes, 'when I sit down to make a sketch from nature the first thing I try to do is to forget that I have ever seen a picture.' The psychologist who hears of someone's 'trying to forget' will prick up his ears. In fact there is a strange irony in this manifesto of unconditional originality, for in itself it is not original. Cochin records a similar saying by Chardin and this, in its turn, may merely represent a variation on a theme intoned by the great traditionalist Poussin. Not that we need doubt that all these artists really strove to forget the formula. But the sober observer will realize there is all the difference in the world between trying to forget something and never having known it. The cynic may even be reminded of the sad story of the confidence man who promised his dupe a wonderful treasure-trove at a certain spot at midsummer midnight. There is only one condition attached to it—on no account must he think of a white crocodile while digging, or the treasure will vanish. The way to visual treasure-trove cannot lie that way. Nobody knew this better than Constable himself, who said that an artist who is self-taught is taught by a very ignorant person indeed. But the worship of tradition which he found prevalent among the public sometimes led him to talk as if the artist could ever do without it: 'In Art as in Literature, there are two modes by which men aim at distinction; in the one the Artist by careful application to what others have accomplished, imitates their works, or selects and combines their various beauties; in the other he seeks excellence at its primitive source NATURE. The one forms a style upon the study of pictures, and produces either imitative or eclectic art, as it has been termed; the other by a close observation of nature discovers qualities existing in her, which have never been portrayed before, and thus forms a style which is original.'

And yet in the very passage with which I began this series of lectures and to which I shall still revert, he makes this confession: 'I have endeavoured to draw a line between genuine art and mannerism, but even the greatest painters have never been wholly untainted by manner. Painting is a science and should be pursued as an inquiry into the laws of nature. Why, then, may not landscape painting be considered a branch of natural philosophy, of which pictures are but experiments?'

How did Constable come to link his admission that there is no art without 'mannerism' (we would say without traditional schemata) with his plea for experimentation? I think he felt that the history of science presented a story of continuous advance in which the achievements of one observer were used and extended by the next. No scientist would refuse to use the books of his predecessors for fear of becoming a slave to tradition. It so happens we can document the same attitude for Constable. The Courtauld Institute of Art in London possesses a moving testimony which has never been published before because its artistic value is as slight as its psychological significance seems to me great. It is a series of copies by Constable from a drawing book by Alexander Cozens, the eighteenth-century landscape painter who published for the use of his pupils a series of schemata for clouds [145].

Constable, the bold critic of tradition, sat down and carefully copied these plates, which teach the student a variety of typical skies: 'Streaky clouds at the top

145. COZENS: *Pattern of sky*. 1785

147. CONSTABLE: *Drawing after Cozens*

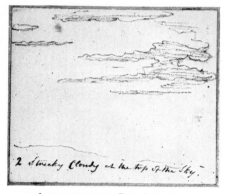

146. CONSTABLE: *Drawing after 145*

148. CONSTABLE: *Drawing after Cozens*

of the sky' [146]; 'Streaky clouds at the bottom of the sky' [147]; 'Half cloud, half plain, the clouds darker than the plain or blew part, and darker at the top than the bottom' [148]—and so forth through all manner of combinations and permutations.

We know by now what Cozens teaches Constable. Not, indeed, what clouds look like, but a series of possibilities, of schemata, which should increase his awareness through visual classification. It has recently been pointed out how close Constable's interest in the most elusive phenomena of the visible world comes to that of his countryman and contemporary Luke Howard, to whom we owe the classification of cloud forms into cumulus, cirrus, and stratus. Goethe, the great morphologist, hailed Howard's effort as a further conquest of the mind 'giving form to the indeterminate'. Cozens' schemata do the same for the artist who does not merely apply them in his searching study of phenomena but articulates and revises them beyond recognition. There are no more truthful images of clouds than those painted by Constable [149].

It matters little what filing system we adopt. But without some standards of comparison we cannot grasp reality. Having looked at Constable's creations we

149. CONSTABLE: *Cloud study*. Sept. 5, 1822

may also see clouds in a fresh way. If so, we will owe this heightened awareness to the memory of the images created by art. May it not be argued that when the grand classical manner of narrative painting died a natural death in the eighteenth century, it was this new function of art which brought landscape painting to the fore and compelled the artist to intensify the search for particular truths?

Part Three

_____

THE BEHOLDER'S SHARE

_____

VI

The Image in the Clouds

Sometimes we see a cloud that's dragonish;
A vapour sometime like a bear or lion,
A tower'd citadel, a pendent rock,
A forked mountain, or blue promontory
With trees upon't, that nod unto the world,
And mock our eyes with air. . . .

SHAKESPEARE, *Antony and Cleopatra*

I

THE MESSAGE from the visible world must be coded by the artist. We have seen how this code was adapted to the kind of signals that art was expected to transmit. It is time to return to the decoding end, the way we learn to read what Sir Winston Churchill called the 'cryptogram' on the canvas.

The most searching discussion of this aspect occurs in the work of an ancient writer who probed much more deeply into the nature of mimesis than Plato or Aristotle. It comes from that curious and moving document of declining paganism, the life of Apollonius of Tyana by Philostratus. Apollonius was a Pythagorean sage who lived at the time of Christ and travelled through the world preaching wisdom and working miracles. His biographer tells how on these travels he reached India, where he and his faithful disciple admired some metal reliefs in the Greek style which had been made at the time of Alexander the Great. As they were waiting to be called to the King, the philosopher cross-examined his companion Damis in the best Socratic manner: 'Tell me, Damis, is there such a thing as painting?' 'Of course,' says Damis. 'And what does this art consist of?' 'Well,' says Damis, 'in the mixing of colours.' 'And why do they do that?' 'For the sake of imitation, to get a likeness of a dog or a horse or a man, a ship, or anything else under the sun.' 'Then,' Apollonius asks again, 'painting is imitation, mimesis?' 'Well, what else?' answers the stooge. 'If it did not do that it would just be a ridiculous playing about with colours.' 'Yes,' says his mentor, 'but what about the things we see in the sky when the clouds are drifting, the centaurs and stag antelopes and wolves and horses? Are they also works of imitation? Is God a painter who uses his leisure hours to amuse himself in that way?' No, the two agree, these cloud shapes have no meaning in themselves, they arise by pure chance; it is we who by nature are prone to imitation and articulate these clouds. 'But does this not mean,' probes

154

Apollonius, 'that the art of imitation is twofold? One aspect of it is the use of hands and mind in producing imitations, another aspect the producing of likenesses with the mind alone?' The mind of the beholder also has its share in the imitation. Even a picture in monochrome, or a bronze relief, strikes us as a resemblance—we see it as form and expression. 'Even if we drew one of these Indians with white chalk,' Apollonius concludes, 'he would seem black, for there would be his flat nose and stiff curly locks and prominent jaw . . . to make the picture black for all who can use their eyes. And for this reason I should say that those who look at works of painting and drawing must have the imitative faculty and that no one could understand the painted horse or bull unless he knew what such creatures are like.'

I have quoted this long extract because it sums up the problem to which we now turn—our, the beholder's, share in the reading of the artist's image. In one respect we know a good deal more about what Apollonius calls our 'imitative faculty' than the sage can have thought possible. For we have seen that under the name of 'projection' this faculty has become the focus of interest for a whole branch of psychology. The description of the images we read into clouds reminds us of the psychological tests where symmetrical inkblots are used to diagnose a person's response. These inkblots, employed in the 'Rorschach test', have the advantage over clouds that we can repeat them and compare the interpretations offered by different subjects [75]. But what is important to us in looking at these instruments of psychiatry is that they confirm the intuition of the ancient philosopher. What we read into these accidental shapes depends on our capacity to recognize in them things or images we find stored in our minds. To interpret such a blot as, say, a bat or a butterfly means some act of perceptual classification—in the filing system of my mind I pigeonhole it with butterflies I have seen or dreamed of.

II

THIS FACULTY of projection has aroused the interest and curiosity of artists in many contexts. The most interesting for us is the attempt to use accidental forms for what we call 'schemata', the starting points of the artist's vocabulary. The inkblot becomes the rival of the patternbook. It so happens that the very patternbook discussed at the close of the last chapter, the models for skies and clouds which we saw Constable copy, demonstrates this dual possibility. For these permutations of possible types of sky formed part of Alexander Cozens' strange book called *A New Method of Assisting the Invention in Drawing Original Compositions of Landscape*. Cozens here advocates a method which he called 'blotting'—the use of accidental inkblots for the suggestion of landscape motif to the aspiring amateur [150–52,

153. CLAUDE LORRAIN: *Landscape drawing*

154. COZENS: *From 'A New Method'*

150–152. COZENS: *From 'A New Method'.*
1785

155. CLAUDE LORRAIN: *The Tiber above Rome.*
Brush in bister

154]. This method occasioned a good deal of ridicule at the time; Paul Oppé in his recent standard biography of the artist even felt compelled to defend the artist against the charge that he relied on mere accident. Cozens' preface shows more psychological understanding of what is involved in the invention of forms. His method is presented as a deliberate challenge to the traditional ways of teaching art.

'It cannot be doubted, that too much time is spent in copying the work of others, which tends to weaken the powers of invention; I scruple not to affirm that too much

time may be employed in copying the landscapes of nature herself.

'I lamented the want of a mechanical
method sufficiently expeditious . . . to draw
forth ideas of an ingenious mind disposed to
the art of designing.

'To sketch . . . is to transfer ideas from
the mind to the paper . . . to blot is to make
varied spots . . . producing accidental forms
. . . from which ideas are presented to the
mind . . . To sketch is to delineate ideas;
blotting suggests them.'

There may be a historical link between
the fashion started by Cozens and the diagnostic tool developed by Rorschach some
150 years later. The missing link may be
provided by the German romantic poet

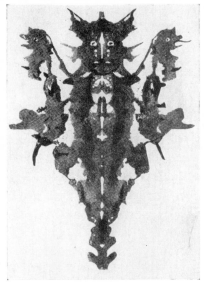

156. JUSTINUS KERNER:
From 'Kleksographien'. 1857

Justinus Kerner [156]. who used ink-blots on folded paper to stir his own imagination and that of his friends and wrote a number of poems on the weird apparitions
which these products suggested to him. Kerner was a spiritualist and saw mainly
ghosts in his symmetrical inkblots. To Cozens blotting was a method for suggesting
landscape motifs. The contrast points to the principle of selection which was at
work and which is described as mental set. We have met with this notion before.
It comprises the attitudes and expectations which will influence our perceptions
and make us ready to see, or hear, one thing rather than another. The psychiatrist
who uses the Rorschach test will avoid influencing the mental set of his patient—
though it has been doubted whether this is ever completely possible. Cozens, in
contrast, appeals to minds already attuned. His pupils should use the blots for
getting ideas for landscape painting, and so it is landscape motifs they will find
in them. If someone were shown a plate such as fig. 150 as representing a specimen
of anthracite, he would not necessarily find anything amiss.

But perhaps we still oversimplify if we say that Cozens' pupils were trained to see
landscapes in his blots. What they saw, and wanted to see, were landscape *paintings*.
They were men and women of the eighteenth century who had been brought up
in the admiration of Claude's sketches [153, 155]. It was these sketches that set the
standard of picturesque ideals, and it was these they wanted to emulate. A language of
forms was ready to be projected into the inkblots, and it was new combinations and
variations of these ideas which they desired rather than an entirely fresh vocabulary.

There are few examples, therefore, which show the complex process of interaction between making and matching, suggestion and projection, more clearly

than these demonstrations of Cozens' 'new method'. Without a knowledge of Claude's idiom, the English amateur would never have thought of discovering what he called 'picturesque motifs' in his native scenery. But this habit, and the pictures it produced in its turn, reinforced that readiness to see these cherished forms in everything that looked faintly like a landscape sketch, even if it was a blot made with Chinese ink on a piece of paper. A few adjustments would suffice to make it into a legible landscape picture that echoed the motifs of Claude [154].

This may be an extreme example of the predominance of making over matching. But the principle of which it makes use plays its part to a greater or smaller extent in all art. Perhaps the nearest approach to Cozens' method can be found in an anecdote told by the Dutch seventeenth-century author Hoogstraeten. There we read of three Dutch landscape painters wagering who among them could complete a landscape painting in the shortest time. One of them, Knipbergen, wrote his motif down 'like a ready scribe'—we may take it that he had learned the lessons we discussed in the last chapter. Jan van Goyen, however, proceeded in a very different way. He spread his paint on the canvas—here light, there dark—till it looked like a streaked agate stone, and then 'with little trouble', he made a finished painting emerge surprisingly out of the chaos of mixed paint. Van Goyen has used his preparation and priming of the canvas like an inkblot into which he projected his own favourite motifs. A glance at one of the artist's paintings [157] suggests a foundation for this anecdote. According to the Dutch author, neither of the two artists won. The palm was given to Perselles, who let hours pass without putting brush to canvas. He finished his picture in his mind and then completed it in no time.

Whatever the merits of this last procedure of rational planning may be, there is evidence that the value of projection was discovered independently by landscape painters in different parts of the globe. The most interesting parallel comes from China. The eleventh-century artist Sung Ti is reported to have criticized the landscape paintings of Ch'ên Yung-chih in the following way:

'The technique in this is very good but there is a want of natural effect. You should choose an old tumbledown wall and throw over it a piece of white silk. Then, morning and evening you should gaze at it until, at length, you can see the ruins through the silk, its prominences, its levels, its zig-zags, and its cleavages, storing them up in your mind and fixing them in your eyes. Make the prominences your mountains, the lower part your water, the hollows your ravines, the cracks your streams, the lighter parts your nearest points, the darker parts your more distant points. Get all these thoroughly into you, and soon you will see men, birds, plants, and trees, flying and moving among them. You may then ply your brush according to your fancy, and the result will be of heaven, not men. Ch'ên's eyes were opened and from that time his style improved.'

157. VAN GOYEN: *Landscape*. About 1635

It has often been remarked how strikingly close this advice of the Chinese artist comes to various passages in Leonardo da Vinci's *Treatise on Painting*. It was Leonardo, in fact, whose writings suggested the new method to Cozens, and it was on his authority Cozens relied. In the best-known of these passages Leonardo speaks of his method of 'quickening the spirit of invention'.

'You should look at certain walls stained with damp, or at stones of uneven colour. If you have to invent some backgrounds you will be able to see in these the likeness of divine landscapes, adorned with mountains, ruins, rocks, woods, great plains, hills and valleys in great variety; and then again you will see there battles and strange figures in violent action, expressions of faces and clothes and an infinity of things which you will be able to reduce to their complete and proper forms. In such walls the same thing happens as in the sound of bells, in whose stroke you may find every named word which you can imagine.'

There are other passages, even more interesting, in which Leonardo discusses the power of 'confused shapes', such as clouds or muddy water, to rouse the mind to new inventions. He goes so far as to advise the artist to avoid the traditional method of meticulous drawing because a rapid and untidy sketch may in its turn suggest new possibilities to the artist. Like van Goyen in the anecdote, he uses his own unfinished work as a screen onto which he projects his ideas.

Perhaps we may now be better equipped to reconsider the description of the 'trained drawer's' procedure given by the psychologist F. C. Ayer quoted in the preceding chapter. 'The trained drawer acquires a mass of schemata by which he can produce a schema of an animal, a flower, or a house quickly upon paper. This serves as a support for the representation of his memory images and he gradually modifies the schema until it corresponds to that which he would express.'

What the psychologist describes as the creation of a support for the artist's memory images is precisely the method of projection. It is another phase in the process of interaction between making and matching; the artist makes a configuration on paper which will suggest an image to him. But he will be well advised to keep his image flexible so that any difficulty he may experience in the process of projection can be adjusted and rectified.

Seen from this point of view, it really matters less whether the initial form into which the artist projects the image is man-made or found. What matters is rather what he can make of it.

Leonardo never omitted to drive home this lesson. In his treatise there is a fascinating echo of a conversation he must have had with Botticelli on the need of the artist to be universal and to know the structure of all the things he may have to include in a painting. 'Our Botticelli' had maintained that such study was unnecessary 'because by merely throwing a sponge full of paint at the wall it leaves a blot where one sees a fine landscape'. It is true, says Leonardo, that in such a blot you may see 'whatever you desire to seek in it'. But though they give you inventions, they do not teach you to finish any detail. 'And that painter,' Leonardo concludes, 'made the most wretched landscapes.' There are various memories in this studio talk of the Renaissance that may be worth pursuing. The story of throwing a sponge full of paint comes from Pliny, who extols the role of chance in the inventions of art; a painter who laboured at representing the foam at the mouth of a dog laboured in vain until, in despair, he threw a sponge at the panel and, lo! achieved the desired effect. But the real source of the new interest in accidental shapes and in the projection of images into them must be Alberti. I have had occasion in a previous chapter to quote his theory about the origins of art in accidental shapes and to speculate on the justification of his theory. In most cultures, of course, the finding of images in accidental shapes remains little more than a curiosity on the fringe of art. Fortunetellers may continue to read significant shapes into birthmarks or tea leaves, or study the forms of lead cast in play or in earnest on New Year's Eve. Travellers will see stones in animal shapes, and legends will always be woven round rocks in human form. At all times natural objects with a striking resemblance to familiar things have been collected as *lusus naturae* and regarded with awe. But unless a craftsman has put such a stone or pearl into its appropriate setting to complete the image, few artists take cognizance of these accidents. One of the early exceptions was Mantegna, who shows his interest in the workings of the imagination by making us see human faces in his clouds [158]. Only in recent

158. MANTEGNA: *Virtue Chasing Vice*. Detail. About 1490

years have some artists paid renewed attention to the *objet trouvé*, the pebble or piece of driftwood that suggests a weird presence. But it is neither in these oddities nor, indeed, in the methods of Leonardo and Cozens to stimulate the creative imagination by projection that we can gain a true idea of the importance of that force in the give and take of art. Its significance reveals itself only if we take account of the mind of the beholder.

III

AN AWARENESS of its role can be found, I believe, only where art becomes emancipated from its ritualistic context and appeals deliberately to man's imagination. We have seen the consequences of this momentous change in the writings of Leonardo, who equates the artist's work with the poet's dream. We find similar repercussions of this emancipation from rigid contexts in classical antiquity. At first they take the form of a protest. Plato, it will be remembered, objected to the art of his time because the artist did not create the thing itself but only a counterfeit, a mere dream or illusion. He was like the sophist who conjured up an impression in other people's minds which did not correspond to reality. The likeness which art creates exists in our imagination only. Plato especially denounced the practice of sculptors who stretched the proportion of figures destined for high buildings, thus making allowance for the spectator's viewpoint. 'If a person could get a correct view they would not even appear to be like to that to which they profess to be like.' There is an anecdote preserved by the Byzantine writer Tzetzes which illustrates this change of emphasis during the Great Revolution from the image itself to the impression it creates in the beholder's mind. It is quoted by the seventeenth-century writer Franciscus Junius in *The Painting of the Ancients*:

'The Athenians intending to consecrate an excellent image of Minerva upon a high pillar, set Phidias and Alcamenes to work, meaning to chuse the better of the two. Alcamenes being nothing at all skilled in Geometry and in the Optickes made the goddesse wonderfull faire to the eye of them that saw her hard by. Phidias on the contrary . . . did consider that the whole shape of his image should change according to the height of the appointed place, and therefore made her lips wide open, her nose somewhat out of order, and all the rest accordingly . . . when these two images were afterwards brought to light and compared, Phidias was in great danger to have been stoned by the whole multitude, untill the statues were at length set on high. For Alcamenes his sweet and diligent strokes beeing drowned, and Phidias his disfigured and distorted hardnesse being vanished by the height of the place, made Alcamenes to be laughed at, and Phidias to bee much more esteemed.'

By Horace's time the existence of paintings which should be seen at a distance had become a commonplace. 'Poetry is like painting,' he writes, 'there is a kind which appeals to you more when you stand near and others when you step back farther.' It is an experience which the classical writer handed on to the Middle Ages. In that curious encyclopaedia of all possible knowledge, the second part of the *Roman de la Rose*, we read these words:

> *We find that kings and pictures look*
> *Alike, for Ptolemy made note*
> *Of this when Almagest he wrote*
> *Saying: who would a picture see*
> *Right well, should at some distance be*
> *For all the faults we see anear*
> *Will at a distance disappear*
> *And things, which from afar we deem*
> *Most fair but rudely handled seem*
> *When closely viewed. . . .*

The *locus classicus* for this observation in the Italian Renaissance is to be found in Vasari's life of Luca della Robbia. Vasari there contrasts the two Singing Galleries for the Florentine cathedral, done respectively by Luca [159] and by Donatello [160]. His account comes so close to the anecdote told by the Byzantine writer about Phidias and Alcamenes that one wonders if Vasari knew it. Luca's work, we hear, was very neatly finished, but Donatello had proceeded with more judgment.

'He left it rough and unfinished,' wrote Vasari, 'so that from a distance it looked much better than Luca's; though Luca's is made with good design and diligence, its polish and refinement cause the eye from a distance to lose it and not

159. LUCA DELLA ROBBIA: *Singing Gallery.*
Florence, 1431–1438

160. DONATELLO: *Singing Gallery.*
Florence, 1433–1440

to make it out as well as that by Donatello, which is hardly more than roughed out.

'Artists should pay much attention to this, for experience shows that all things which are far removed, be they paintings, sculptures, or whatever, have more beauty and greater force when they are a beautiful sketch [*una bella bozza*] than when they are finished.

'And quite apart from the distance which has this effect, it also frequently appears in sketches which arise all of a sudden in the frenzy of art that expresses the idea in a few strokes, while a laboured effect and too much industry sometimes deprive of force and skill those who cannot ever leave their hand from the work they are doing.'

Vasari's account is so interesting because it shows his awareness of the link between the imagination of the artist and that of his public. Only works that are created in a state of heightened imagination, he said in effect, will appeal to the imagination. In the context of Renaissance theories and prejudices, insistence on inspiration and imagination goes hand in hand with emphasis on art as the high intellectual activity and the rejection of mere menial skill. Careful finish betrays the artisan who has to observe the standards of the guild. The true artist, like the true gentleman, will work with ease. This is Castiglione's famous doctrine of *sprezzatura*, the nonchalance which marks the perfect courtier and the perfect artist. 'One single unlaboured line, a single brushstroke, drawn with ease so that it seems that the hand moved without any effort or skill and reached its end all by itself, just as the painter intended it, reveals the excellence of the artist.'

161. TITIAN: *The Three Ages of Man.* Detail. About 1510

162. TITIAN: *Shepherd and Nymph.* About 1570

It is clear that an entirely new idea of art is taking shape here. It is an art in which the painter's skill in suggesting must be matched by the public's skill in taking hints. The literal-minded Philistine is excluded from this closed circle. He does not understand the magic of *sprezzatura* because he has not learned to use his own imagination to project. He lacks the appropriate mental set to recognize in the loose brushstrokes of a 'careless work' the images intended by the artist; least of all is he able to appreciate the secret skill and cunning which hide behind this lack of finish.

Vasari returns to this problem in his discussion of Titian's late manner. 'Certainly his way of procedure in these last works differs greatly from that of his youth, for the early works are executed with a certain refinement and an incredible industry so that they can be seen at close quarters and from afar [161], while his last ones are executed with crudely daubed strokes and blobs in such a way that one sees nothing at close quarters, though they look perfect from a distance [162]. That was the reason why many who wanted to imitate him in this to show themselves practised masters have made crude paintings, for though it may seem that such paintings are done without effort, this is not true at all.'

Titian's late manner became proverbial in the theory of art because of this magic of transformation. Lomazzo tells of a visit by Aurelio Luini to the workshop of the aged master: 'There he saw a miraculous landscape painting which at first glance appeared to Aurelio a mere daub, but when he stepped far back it looked to him as if the sun shone inside and made the roads recede here and there.'

Vasari's influential book carried the message to the North that the traditional method of meticulous care in the finish of paintings was only one of two possible approaches. In his didactic poem on the art of painting, which was written about 1600, Carel van Mander translated Vasari's account of Titian's two manners into a rhymed stanza and continued: 'And herewith, apprentices, I wanted to place before your eyes two perfect manners toward which you may now guide your path according to your bent, but I should still advise you to begin by applying yourselves to the neat manner . . . but whether you paint neat or rough, avoid too harsh highlights.'

The Dutch connoisseur who had read his van Mander would therefore know there was a place in the kingdom of art for both Dou [164], with his painstaking attention to smooth finish, and for Frans Hals [163] or the late Rembrandt. One of Rembrandt's few utterances about his art that have been preserved proclaims his adherence to the second manner. 'Don't poke your nose into my pictures,' he is reported to have said, 'the smell of paint will poison you.'

The biographer of Velázquez, Palomino, reports that the artist painted with especially long brushes to keep his distance from the canvas and adds that his portraits are unintelligible from close quarters but miraculous when seen from afar.

163. HALS: *Malle Babbe*. Detail.
About 1620

164. DOU: *Woman Reading*. Detail.
About 1630

The studio talk about the two manners is well summed up by the Venetian painter Boschini. In his poem of 1660 he contrasts the *diligente* with the *manieroso*, foreshadowing the difference between Canaletto [165] and Guardi [166].

'The work of industry can be achieved by any painter who has patience, love, and a good eye; but to achieve the manner or touch of Paolo, Bassano, Palma, Tintoretto, or Titian—by God, that is something to drive you mad.'

165. CANALETTO: *Campo San Zanipolo, Venice*. About 1740

The posthumous preface of one of Boschini's guidebooks enlarges upon the importance which an understanding of the styles of these masters has for the connoisseur and links the idea of the authentic touch with the traditional notion of *sprezzatura*.

'Even the painters who painted softly, particularly Titian, ended up with some brushstrokes in the highlights or shadows, setting down their work with bravura to remove the impression of the effort they had employed on the painting; hence when such brushstrokes cannot be discerned, especially in the heads, the work should be regarded as a copy, for he who imitates the work with much attention will produce a laboured thing.'

The connoisseur, therefore, is no longer advised simply to stand back. He should look at the painter's handiwork closely, admire his touch and the magic of his brush which thus conjure up an image. There is an increasing awareness of the fact that what we enjoy is not so much seeing these works from a distance as the very act of stepping back, as it were, and watching our imagination come into play, transforming the medley of colour into a finished image. The growing psychological interest of eighteenth-century critics made this idea more explicit. At the turn of the century we find Roger de Piles discussing this source of enjoyment in projection: 'As there are styles of thought, so there are also styles of execution . . . the firm style, and the polished. . . . The firm style gives life to work, and excuses for bad choice; and the polished finishes and brightens everything; it leaves no employment for the spectator's imagination, which pleases itself in discovering and finishing things which it ascribes to the artist *though in fact they proceed only from itself.*' (My emphasis.)

166. GUARDI: *Campo San Zanipolo, Venice.* 1782

With even greater shrewdness and acumen did that great French critic Count Caylus probe into the reasons why he and others preferred an unfinished and rapid sketch, a mere hint, to an explicit image: it is always flattering to feel 'in the know'.

We find thus emerging a psychological theory of painting that takes account of that interplay between the artist and the beholder which is our main concern in these chapters. It was Reynolds who gave it the finishing touches in his famous discourse in which he commemorated the art of his great rival Gainsborough.

Reynolds speaks of the odd scratches and
marks that are so often observable in
Gainsborough's pictures [167] and continues on the usual lines that 'this chaos,
this uncouth and shapeless appearance, by a
kind of magic, at a certain distance assumes
form, and all the parts seem to drop into
their proper place. . . . That Gainsborough
himself considered this peculiarity in his
manner, and the power it possesses of
exciting surprise, as a beauty in his works,
I think may be inferred from the eager
desire which we know he always expressed,
that his pictures, at the exhibition, should
be seen near, as well as at a distance. . . .
I have often imagined that this un-

167. GAINSBOROUGH: *Mrs. John Taylor*.
About 1780–1788

finished manner contributed even to that striking resemblance for which his
portraits are so remarkable. Though this opinion may be considered as fanciful,
yet I think a plausible reason may be given, why such a mode of painting should
have such an effect. It is presupposed that in this undetermined manner there is
the general effect; enough to remind the spectator of the original; the imagination
supplies the rest, and perhaps more satisfactorily to himself, if not more exactly,
than the artist, with all his care, could possibly have done. At the same time it
must be acknowledged there is one evil attending this mode: that if the portrait
were seen, previous to any knowledge of the original, different persons would form
different ideas, and all would be disappointed at not finding the original correspond
with their own conceptions, under the great latitude which indistinctness gives to
the imagination to assume almost what character or form it pleases.'

For Reynolds, Gainsborough's frequently unfinished and rather vague indications are little more than those schemata which serve as a support for our memory
images; in other words, they are screens onto which the sitter's relatives and
friends could project a beloved image, but which remain blank to those who
cannot contribute from their own experience. The role which projection plays,
and is intended to play, in works of this kind could not be brought out more
sharply.

As a matter of fact by the time Reynolds wrote, the pleasure in this game of
reading brushstrokes had become so popular that J. E. Liotard wrote his treatise
on painting mainly to combat the prejudice according to which 'all good painting
must be facile, freely painted and with fine touches'. He is prepared to admit that
such a painting will look better from afar, but better, he thinks, is in this case only

'less ugly'. To read his polemics against the loaded brush, written as it was in 1781, one wonders why the technique of the impressionists struck the public as such a daring innovation.

But impressionism demanded more than a reading of brushstrokes. It demanded, if one may so put it, a reading across brushstrokes. There were a good many painters among the fashionable virtuosos of the nineteenth century, men like Boldini and Sargent, who drew more or less with a loaded brush and made the game of projecting sufficiently easy to be attractive. Among the great masters, Daumier's technique is of this kind [28], the brush following the form firmly and boldly. It is the point of impressionist painting that the direction of the brushstroke is no longer an aid to the reading of forms. It is without any support from structure that the beholder must mobilize his memory of the visible world and project it into the mosaic of strokes and dabs on the canvas before him. It is here, therefore, that the principle of guided projection reaches its climax. The image, it might be said, has no firm anchorage left on the canvas [25]—it is only 'conjured up' in our minds. The willing beholder responds to the artist's suggestion because he enjoys the transformation that occurs in front of his eyes. It was in this enjoyment that a new function of art emerged gradually and all but unnoticed during the period we have discussed. The artist gives the beholder increasingly 'more to do', he draws him into the magic circle of creation and allows him to experience something of the thrill of 'making' which had once been the privilege of the artist. It is the turning point which leads to those visual conundrums of twentieth-century art that challenge our ingenuity and make us search our own minds for the unexpressed and inarticulate.

It may seem paradoxical to link impressionism with this appeal to subjectivity, for the advocates of impressionism talked otherwise. Impressionism was to them the triumph of objective truth. The implications of this claim will engage our attention in a subsequent chapter.

VII

Conditions of Illusion

> The mind, having received of sense a small beginning of remembrance, runneth on infinitely, remembring all what is to be remembered. Our senses therefore, which stand as it were at the entry of the mind, having received the beginning of anything, and having proffered it to the mind; the mind likewise receiveth this beginning, and goeth over all what followeth: the lower part of a long and slender pike being but slightly shaken, the motion runneth thorough the whole length of the pike, even to the speares-head . . . so does our mind need but a small beginning to the remembrance of the whole matter.
>
> After MAXIMUS TYRIUS as in FRANCISCUS JUNIUS,
> *The Painting of the Ancients*

I

THE EXAMPLES in the last chapter have confirmed the ideas which Philostratus attributes to his hero Apollonius of Tyana, the idea that 'those who look at works of painting and drawing must have the imitative faculty' and that 'no one could understand the painted horse or bull unless he knew what such creatures are like'. All representation relies to some extent on what we have called 'guided projection'. When we say that the blots and brushstrokes of the impressionist landscapes 'suddenly come to life', we mean we have been led to project a landscape into these dabs of pigment.

Psychologists class the problem of picture reading with what they call 'the perception of symbolic material'. It is a problem which has engaged the attention of all who investigate effective communication, the reading of texts or displays or the hearing of signals. The basic facts were described by William James with his usual lucidity in his *Talks to Teachers* before the turn of the century:

'When we listen to a person speaking or read a page of print, much of what we think we see or hear is supplied from our memory. We overlook misprints, imagining the right letters, though we see the wrong ones; and how little we actually hear, when we listen to speech, we realize when we go to a foreign theatre; for there what troubles us is not so much that we cannot understand what the actors say as that we cannot hear their words. The fact is that we hear quite as little under similar conditions at home, only our mind, being fuller of English verbal associations, supplies the requisite material for comprehension upon a much slighter auditory hint.'

It so happens I had an opportunity to study this aspect of perception in a severely practical context during the war. I was employed for six years by the

British Broadcasting Corporation in their 'Monitoring Service', or listening post, where we kept constant watch on radio transmissions from friend and foe. It was in this context that the importance of guided projection in our understanding of symbolic material was brought home to me. Some of the transmissions which interested us most were often barely audible, and it became quite an art, or even a sport, to interpret the few whiffs of speech sound that were all we really had on the wax cylinders on which these broadcasts had been recorded. It was then we learned to what an extent our knowledge and expectations influence our hearing. You had to know what might be said in order to hear what was said. More exactly, you selected from your knowledge of possibilities certain word combinations and tried projecting them into the noises heard. The problem then was a twofold one—to think of possibilities and to retain one's critical faculty. Anyone whose imagination ran away with him, who could hear any words—as Leonardo could in the sound of bells—could not play that game. You had to keep your projection flexible, to remain willing to try out fresh alternatives, and to admit the possibility of defeat. For this was the most striking experience of all: once your expectation was firmly set and your conviction settled, you ceased to be aware of your own activity, the noises appeared to fall into place and to be transformed into the expected words. So strong was this effect of suggestion that we made it a practice never to tell a colleague of our own interpretation if we wanted him to test it. Expectation created illusion.

While I was struggling with these practical tasks, I did not know that these problems of transmission and reception of communication—terms such as 'message' and 'noise'—were destined to become a most important, not to say fashionable, field of study under the name of 'Information Theory'. The technical and mathematical aspects of this science will always remain a closed book to me, but my experience enabled me to appreciate at least one of its basic concepts, the function of the message to select from an 'ensemble of possible states'. The knowledge of possibilities in the monitor is the knowledge of the language and the contexts in which it is used. If there is only one possibility, his receptor apparatus is likely to jump ahead and anticipate the result at what William James called the slightest 'auditory hint'. But it also follows from this theory that where there is only one such possibility the hint is in itself redundant and there is, in fact, no special message. The word we must expect in a given context will not add to our 'information'. We receive no message in the strict sense of the word when a friend enters a room and says 'good morning'. The word has no function to select from an ensemble of possible states, though situations are conceivable in which it would have.

The most interesting consequence of this way of looking at communication is the general conclusion that the greater the probability of a symbol's occurrence in any given situation, the smaller will be its information content. Where we can anticipate we need not listen. It is in this context that projection will do for perception.

The difficulty in distinguishing between the two in seeing as well as in hearing was well brought out in a fiendish experiment. The subjects were seated in the dark in front of a screen and were told their sensitivity to light was to be tested. At the request of the experimenter, the assistant projected a very faint light onto the screen and slowly increased its intensity, each person being asked to record exactly when he perceived it. But once in a while when the experimenter made the request no light was, in fact, shown. It was found that the subjects still saw it appearing. Their firm expectation of the sequence of events had actually led to a hallucination.

I suspect there is no class of people better able to bring about such phantom perceptions than conjurers. They set up a train of expectations, a semblance of familiar situations, which makes our imagination run ahead and complete it obligingly without knowing where we have been tricked. There are simple parlour tricks which show the problem in its most elementary form. Anyone who can handle a needle convincingly can make us see a thread which is not there. The conjuring trick is turned into art when a magician such as Charlie Chaplin performs a dance with a pair of forks and a couple of rolls that turn into nimble legs in front of our eyes.

II

TO THE STUDENT of the visual image, these experiences are of relevance because they show how the context of action creates conditions of illusion. When the hobby-horse leans in the corner, it is just a stick; as soon as it is ridden, it becomes the focus of the child's imagination and turns into a horse. The images of art, we remember, also once stood in a context of action. It must have been an uncanny sight to see the painting of a bison belaboured with spears in the darkness of the cave—if our ideas about these origins are right. What we do know is that the fetishes and cult images of early cultures stood in such contexts of action; they were bathed, anointed, clothed, and carried in procession. What wonder that illusion settled on them and that the faithful saw them smiling, frowning, or nodding behind the clouds of incense.

It was when art withdrew from the Pygmalion phase of action that it had to cast around for means to strengthen the illusion and to create the twilight realm of suspended disbelief which the Greeks first explored. But here, and ever since, illusion could turn into deception only when the context of action set up an expectation

168. PETO: *Old Scraps.* 1894

which reinforced the artist's handiwork. The most famous story of illusion in classical antiquity illustrates the point to perfection; it is the anecdote from Pliny, how Parrhasios trumped Zeuxis, who had painted grapes so deceptively that birds came to peck at them. He invited his rival to his studio to show him his own work, and when Zeuxis eagerly tried to lift the curtain from the panel, he found it was not real but painted, after which he had to concede the palm to Parrhasios, who had deceived not only irrational birds but an artist. In the cool light of reason, Parrhasios' feat is somewhat less admirable. Within the experience of poor Zeuxis, the probability of a curtain's being painted was surely nil. A few strokes of light and shade may therefore have been sufficient to make him 'see' the curtain he expected, all the more so as he was keyed up for the next phase, the picture he wanted to reveal. The *trompe l'œil* painters have ever since relied on the mutual reinforcement of illusion and expectation: the painted fly on the panel, the painted letters on the letter rack [168]; indeed the most successful *trompe l'œil* I have ever seen was on the level of Parrhasios' trick—painting simulating a broken glass pane in front of a picture.

169. *Monochrome wall painting from the house of Livia, Rome.* First century A.D.

Where these expectations cannot be controlled they have to be created. We read of one such attempt in classical antiquity to transcend the dream-reality of painting. The painter Theon revealed his painting of a soldier to the accompaniment of a blast of trumpets, and we are assured that the illusion was greatly increased. Those of us who still remember the first talking films can imagine something of the effect.

But whatever the eulogists of artists may have said, paintings and statues had no voice, and art had to be satisfied with working its wonders within its own medium and within its own isolated world. Even within this world of conscious make-believe, it was found, genuine illusion held its own: we have seen how the incomplete painting can arouse the beholder's imagination and project what is not there. Some of the history of this development was told in the last chapter; we have now to turn to its psychological interpretation. There are obviously two conditions that must be fulfilled if the mechanism of projection is to be set in motion. One is that the beholder must be left in no doubt about the way to close the gap; secondly, that he must be given a 'screen', an empty or ill-defined area onto which he can project the expected image.

The passage from Philostratus suggests that classical art understood these means of arousing our 'imitative faculty', and many of the illusionist paintings from Pompeii and Rome confirm this impression of sovereign mastery. The grisaille from the house of Livia [169], with its emphatic indications of form and its empty areas waiting to be filled in by our imagination, shows that these decorators could play this conjurer's trick with wonderful deftness.

But no tradition of art had a deeper understanding of what I have called the 'screen' than the art of the Far East. Chinese art theory discusses the power of expressing through *absence* of brush and ink. 'Figures, even though painted without eyes, must seem to look; without ears, must seem to listen. . . . There are things which ten hundred brushstrokes cannot depict but which can be captured by a few simple strokes if they are right. That is truly giving expression to the invisible.' [170]. The maxim into which these observations were condensed might serve as a motto of this chapter: '*i tao pi pu tao*—idea present, brush may be spared performance'.

Perhaps it is precisely the restricted visual language of Chinese art, with its kinship to calligraphy, that encouraged these appeals to the beholder to complete and project. The empty surface of the shining silk is as much a part of the image as are the strokes of the brush [171]. 'When the highest point of a pagoda reaches

170. *From the 'Mustard Seed Garden Manual of Painting'. 1679–1701*

the sky,' says another Chinese treatise, 'it is not necessary to show the main part of its structure. It should seem as if it is there, and yet is not there; as if it exists above and yet also exists below. Hillocks and earth mounds show only the half; the grass huts and thatched arbours should be represented only by their rough outlines.'

We do not know precisely how either the inhabitants of Pompeii or the Chinese art lover 'saw' these empty spaces. But it is easy to demonstrate that, given both conditions—familiarity and an empty screen—it really becomes as hard as it was for the listener to wartime broadcasts to distinguish the phantom from reality. Take the type of lettering known as Shadow Antiqua ('Granby Shadow'), in which the familiar forms of letters are only indicated by what would be the shaded side if they were formed of ribbons standing up [172]. The distance between the shades indicates there is a slight band along the thickness of the ribbon. There is no such band, but many observers see it running along the whole top of the letter. It is easy to destroy the illusion in two ways: either by isolating individual forms so that the familiar image of the letter disappears, or by destroying the 'screen'. Place the same shape on a strongly patterned background and the 'subjective contour', or phantom

171. UNKNOWN CHINESE ARTIST:
A Fisherman's Abode after the Rain.
Twelfth or thirteenth century.
Ink and tint on silk

ridge, will disappear. We see it only as long as nothing in our field of vision contradicts our most likely hypothesis.

ILLUSION
172

Those whose job it is to interpret images for the purpose of information have a story to tell of the tricks that these phantoms can play on perception. Intelligence officers intent on the reading of aerial reconnaissance photographs, X-ray specialists basing a diagnosis on the faintest of shadows visible in a tissue, learn in a hard school how often 'believing is seeing' and how important it therefore is to keep their hypothesis flexible. The art lover adopts the opposite mental set. Unless he is a restorer, he may go through life without ever realizing to what an extent the pictures he loves are crisscrossed by subjective contours of his own making. If he were ever to strip them of these projections, merely a meaningless armature might well be all that would remain.

III

IN A PREVIOUS CHAPTER we saw how much the artist of the Western tradition came to rely on the power of indeterminate forms. But this sophisticated appeal to our imagination is by no means the first and most elementary method of overcoming the limitations of the medium; these limitations are of a twofold kind. One concerns the necessary incompleteness of all two-dimensional representation. Some part of the motif will always be hidden from us, and there will always be some overlap. We have seen that this necessity for the naturalistic artist to sacrifice some of the naturalistic features that give the beholder the required information aroused the comment of ancient critics who admired the skill of Parrhasios to 'promise' what he cannot show 'and to reveal what he obscures'. The device of overlap caused similar admiration. In his description of a real or imaginary painting Philostratus commends the trick of the artist who surrounds the walls of Thebes with armed men 'so that some are seen in full figure, others with the legs hidden, others from the waist up, then only the busts of some, heads only, helmets only, and finally just spearpoints. All that, my boy, is analogy, for the eyes must be deceived as they travel back along with the relevant zones of the picture.'

It must have been this passage which inspired Shakespeare to describe in *The Rape of Lucrece* a painting of the fall of Troy:

For much imaginary work was there;
Conceit deceitful, so compact, so kind,
That for Achilles' image stood his spear,
Grip'd in an armed hand; himself behind,
Was left unseen, save to the eye of mind:
A hand, a foot, a face, a leg, a head,
Stood for the whole to be imagined.

It is important in this respect not to mix up inference or knowledge with that transformation of things seen that comes about through projection. A number of experiments by the great pioneers of Western naturalism illustrates this difference through their very failure to convince. There is a puzzling feature in Giotto's *Last Judgment* in the Arena Chapel in Padua [173] which exemplifies such a bold experiment at this turning point of art. Behind the cross held aloft by two angels in the centre of the wall, we discern two feet protruding, and as we look more carefully, we also discover the hands of the unseen body. They must belong to one of the souls aroused by the last trumpet who is seeking refuge behind the cross from the devils dragging the souls to hell. It is left to us whether we want to interpret this hidden figure as the soul of the donor, who kneels close by, or, perhaps, as that of the artist himself.

Some three generations later Jan van Eyck went further still in his expectation that we would and could complete his picture through intellectual inference. Looking at the panel with the music-making angels of the Ghent altarpiece, so familiar from many illustrations, we discover a curious feature which is almost lost in reproduction [174]. There is a glimpse of red and brown at the side of the organ, or rather behind it. You must know what organs are like to take the hint. It is the garment and hair of the angel working the bellows, which Jan van Eyck did not want to miss out. The illumination of a *Book of Hours* done scarcely ten years earlier in France elucidates Jan van Eyck's intention [175], though in this case it is the angel playing the manual who is half hidden from the beholder.

We might add to these examples the figure rushing out of the room, to the right on Donatello's Salome relief [176], of which only the legs are seen; the tail end of a bull on Dürer's print of *The Prodigal Son* [177], or many an experiment in incompleteness from impressionist paintings or those by Degas. On the whole, however, artists have come to accept the limits of these powers of suggestion through incompleteness. There is a famous visual joke attributed to the Carracci by their earliest biographer Malvasia that indicates their awareness of these limits [178]. These are picture puzzles intended to perplex the beholder. Three lines with a triangle on top 'represent' a Capuchin preacher asleep in his pulpit; the line with semicircle and triangle, the hat of a mason and his trowel on the other side of the

173. GIOTTO: *The Last Judgment.*
Detail. Arena Chapel,
Padua. About 1306

174. JAN VAN EYCK: *Music-making Angels.*
From the Ghent altarpiece.
About 1432

175. *From a French 'Book of Hours'.* About 1420

176. DONATELLO: *Herod's Banquet*. Baptistery, Siena, completed 1427

177. DÜRER: *The Prodigal Son*. About 1496

wall. This type of picture puzzle has lately gained some popularity under the name of 'droodle', but the droodle has not become an art form.

Yet one would only have to rummage through discarded snapshots to discover how often reality presents us with similar incomplete images, with puzzling droodles of all kinds when a 'slice of life' is arrested and transfixed at an accidental point. We rarely see these strange configurations because our own movement and that of the objects concerned will soon help us to clarify and identify those odd corners of objects that happen to arouse our attention. This vital difference between the stationary image with its confusions of overlap and the resources of life to sort them out was one of the themes of Adolf von Hildebrand's famous book on the problem of form to which I have referred in the Introduction.

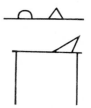

178. AFTER AN. CARRACCI: *Trick drawings*. About 1600

Trained as he was in classical ideals of clarity, Hildebrand insisted that the aims of his impressionist contemporaries to render an instantaneous moment would lead them into absurdities. It is the task of the artist to compensate for the absence of movement and space by giving his shapes the lucid completeness of a classical relief. Only thus can he avoid having to rely on the beholder's knowledge and power to guess.

The problem which Hildebrand raised is no doubt a genuine one, though it is hardly true that the impressionists disregarded it. Where they tease us with incomplete forms, they take good care to remain intelligible so that we can appreciate their concern with the transitory and elusive features of visual reality. And yet it is

179. MANET: *At the Races*. About 1875

180. FRITH: *Derby Day*. Detail. 1858

surely no accident that they limited themselves to the motifs and scenes of *la vie contemporaine,* where they could do precisely what Hildebrand objected to: rely on the beholder's knowledge.

Perhaps we shall become increasingly aware of this need to supplement their hints from our own experience as their period recedes from ours. Impressionist paintings are of less documentary value to the social historian than are the paintings of conventional realists. When horse racing becomes a dimly remembered ritual and the horse is as extinct as the dodo, Manet's spirited sketch of a race [179] certainly will tell the historian less about those bygone days than will that famous showpiece of Victorian realism, *Derby Day,* by Frith [180]. One is tempted to say that in contrast to Manet, Frith leaves nothing to the imagination, but in fact, as we have seen, there is no representation of which this can ever be true. It was Whistler who compared Frith's backgrounds with Manet's, and such a comparison is indeed instructive. Frith, it turns out, relies no less on our knowledge, on our faculty to project and to supplement what he has left indistinct. Taken in isolation, his treatment of the grandstand with its seething crowd is not more detailed than that by Manet—it is only less interesting pictorially. Into the Manet we can project the sparkle and movement of an excited mass of people. He uses the very ambiguity of his flickering forms to suggest a variety of readings and to compensate thereby for the absence of movement in the painting in a way Hildebrand never thought of.

There are worse ways of spending an afternoon in a gallery than in concentrating on this problem of abbreviation and information. We shall soon confirm the result of the last chapter, that the impressionists were by no means the first to discover and exploit the charm and challenge of incomplete representation as such. But where the earlier masters prepared the beholder for this artifice and facilitated the projection, the impressionists wanted him to enjoy the challenge of a visual shock. It is therefore no accident that twentieth-century art books like to show us details from the background of old paintings that startle us by the unexpected daring of these old masters. The daring, of course, is frequently that of their modern interpreters who present such images in isolation without that gradual transition which the earlier masters insisted upon.

Take the detail [182] from one of Altdorfer's paintings [181]. Nothing could be more daring than the way he reduces the shapes of angels to a series of luminous dots which we surely could not read without knowing their context. But how else could art suggest what is in fact unrepresentable, the idea of the infinite? In the context of his beautiful painting, the artist leads the willing beholder from the charming angels in the foreground to more and more indistinct shapes and thus makes him project a vision of infinite multitudes of the heavenly host into the sparkling dots that fade into the distance.

181. ALTDORFER: *The Virgin amidst Angels*. About 1525. Oil on wood

In Altdorfer's painting, infinitude acquires a special pathos and beauty through
its religious associations, but in principle, as Nietzsche knew, all claims to copy
nature must lead to the demand of representing the infinite. The amount of information reaching us from the visible world is incalculably large, and the artist's medium
is inevitably restricted and granular. Even the most meticulous realist can accom-
modate only a limited number of marks on his panel, and though he may try to
smooth out the transition between his dabs of paint beyond the threshold of

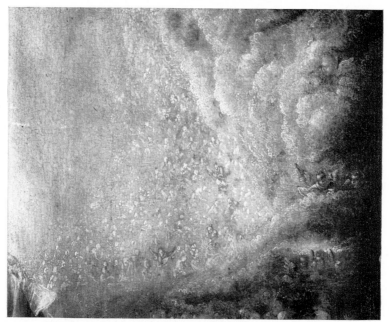

182. ALTDORFER: *The Virgin amidst Angels*. Detail (cf. 181)

183. JAN VAN EYCK: *Music-making Angel*. Detail (cf. 174)

184. *The Fraser spiral*

visibility, in the end he will always have to rely on suggestion when it comes to representing the infinitely small.

While standing in front of a painting by Jan van Eyck we fall under this very spell. We believe he succeeded in rendering the inexhaustible wealth of detail that belongs to the visible world. We have the impression that he painted every stitch of the golden damask, every hair of the angels, every fibre of the wood [183]. Yet he clearly could not have done that, however patiently he worked with a magnifying glass. Little though we may know about the secrets of such effects, they must be based on an illusion.

I believe that this illusion is assisted by what might be called the 'etc. principle', the assumption we tend to make that to see a few members of a series is to see them all. When we look at the trees in Constable's *Wivenhoe Park* [5], we take those farther back on trust because those near us are so convincingly articulated that the artist's painted 'etc.' hardly enters our awareness. Now it can be shown that this tendency of ours to take things as read can indeed lead to curious illusions when the mind is tricked into running ahead of the facts and expecting the continuation of a series that turns out to be less simple. The most famous illusion of this kind is the Fraser spiral [184], which is not a spiral at all but really a series of concentric circles. Only the tracing pencil will convince us that we are not confronted with a spiral moving toward the infinite. Pencil in hand we will also understand the illusion. There are innumerable movements toward the centre, and since we are baffled by the crisscross pattern of the background, we resort to the etc. principle and assume that the spiralling lines add up to a spiral. The illusion of a progression to infinitude that turns a painted panel into the semblance of fur or damask may well be based on similar reactions. In addition, the painter relies on those clues which give us the most reliable information about texture in real life: the way light behaves when it hits a surface and is either reflected, absorbed, or dissolved into innumerable light points. No one has done more to further our understanding of the way we react to texture than Professor J. J. Gibson in his book *The Perception of the Visual World*. In a footnote he refers to the fact that what the painter reproduced was 'the microstructure of the light reflected from these surfaces'. It may be an interaction of these various effects that makes a distribution of pigments 'stand for the whole to be imagined'. But the trick certainly could not work without our contribution to the illusion. Where we have no knowledge of the type of surface represented, our interpretation may still go very wrong. Writing of his experience when he came to England from South Africa, Roy Campbell says, 'The strange, crisp, salty consistency of snow was another puzzle. From paintings I had imagined it to be like wax, and snowflakes to be like shavings of candle grease.' Few artists who have painted snow scenes can have realized that they relied on what Philostratus called 'our imitative faculty', our knowledge of snow, for the illusion to work.

Once this fact is understood it may be easier to see why the amount of information packed into the picture may hinder the illusion as frequently as it helps it. The reason lies precisely in the limitations of the medium that may occasionally obtrude themselves and contradict the impression the painter wanted to conjure up. No wonder, therefore, that the greatest protagonist of naturalistic illusion in painting, Leonardo da Vinci, is also the inventor of the deliberately blurred image, the *sfumato*, or veiled form, that cuts down the information on the canvas and thereby stimulates the mechanism of projection. In describing this achievement of the 'perfect manner' in painting, Vasari praises those outlines 'hovering between the seen and the unseen'. In the same context, Titian's contemporary, Daniele Barbaro, adapts Pliny's praise of Parrhasios' outline to the technique of *sfumato* that leads us to 'understand what one does not see'. He speaks of 'the soft disappearance on the horizon of objects from our view which is and is not, and this can only be achieved by infinite practice, delighting those who do not understand it better and stunning those who do.'

We are back in the atmosphere and the period when the art lover discovered the joy of stepping back from the canvas to enjoy the sensation of visible brush-strokes disappearing behind the emergent illusion. Perhaps we can now describe this effect with a little more confidence. The distance from the canvas weakens the beholder's power of discrimination and creates a blur which mobilizes his projective faculty. The indistinct parts of the canvas become a screen, provided only that certain distinctive features stand out with sufficient force and that no contradictory messages reach the eye to spoil the impression.

IV

BUT AT THIS POINT the reader will want a question answered that may well have been in his mind for some time. Is it permissible to look at the reading of pictures in the same way we approach the hearing of speech? Are we not putting the cart before the horse when we thus concentrate on the beholder's share and neglect the painter's commerce, not with the public, but with nature herself? Is not the true reason why the painter blurs his image, particularly of distant objects, quite simply that this is how distant objects appear to his eye? Of course they do appear blurred. An early Chinese treatise already reminds the painter of the fact that 'distant men have no eyes, distant trees have no branches'. But though it is easy to specify what the eye cannot see in the distance, it is less easy to describe exactly what the eye does see. There is an amusing passage in Henry Peacham's book, *The Gentleman's Exercise*, that shows how seventeenth-century thinkers, trained in scholastic thought, still tried to tackle this problem in terms of Aristotelian philosophy:

'Have a regard, the farther your Landtskip goeth to those *universalia*, which, as Aristotle saith . . . (in respect of their particulars concealed from our senses) are *notiora*: as in discerning a Building ten or twelve miles off, I cannot tell whether it be Church, Castle, House, or the like: so that in drawing of it, I must expresse no particular sign, as Bell, Portculleis, etc. but shew it as weakly and as faintly as mine eye judgeth of it, because all those particulars are taken away by the greatnesse of the distance. I have seen a man painted coming down a Hill some mile and a half from me, as I judged by the Landtskip, yet might you have told all the buttons of his doublet: whether the Painter had a quick invention, or the Gentleman's buttons were as big as those in fashion, when Monseeur came into England, I will leave to my Reader's judgement.'

Peacham's passage may be one of the first to ridicule pictures that are too meticulously painted and to condemn the absurdity of these 'conceptual' methods in the name of visual truth. The criticism is undoubtedly justified in the sense that such paintings contradict every possible experience. We do not see buttons at a great distance. But when we ask ourselves exactly what it is that we do see, the question is far less easily answered. Oculists who test our eyesight know very well why they present us with random letters. Where we can guess, we cannot disentangle seeing from knowing, or rather, from expecting. Peacham unwittingly shows this dominance of 'conceptual' knowledge over the process of sight in his description of the generalizing tendencies of distance. It is no doubt true that as we travel away from a village we notice the loss of detail which he describes: first we can no longer read the clockface of the church steeple, then we lose the clock, and finally the distinctive features of the church become so blurred it might be any building. But it is a mistake to think the same process happens in reverse when we approach the village—at least it is by no means sure that the progression will be so orderly, so according to Aristotelian logic. In certain circumstances we may easily take a rock for a building and a building for a rock, and we may hold on to this wrong interpretation till it suddenly gives way to a different reading. Another seventeenth-century author has recaptured this experience more truly than Peacham.

There is an impressive description of these uncertainties and the activity they provoke in the searching mind in one of Calderón's plays, *The Constant Prince*. Relating the appearance of the hostile fleet during a voyage, one of Calderón's characters is reminded of the blurred distances of the subtle painter. The passage is so rich in beauty and insight that it warrants lengthy quotation even in translation.

> *For, as on the coloured canvas*
> *Subtle pencils softly blend*
> *Dark and light in such proportions*
> *That the dim perspectives end—*
> *Now perhaps like famous cities,*
> *Now like caves or misty capes,*
> *For remoteness ever formeth*
> *Monstrous or unreal shapes . . .*
> *So it was, while I alone,*
> *Saw their bulk and vast proportions*
> *But their form remained unknown.*
> *First they seemed to us uplifting*

High in heaven their pointed towers,
Clouds that to the sea descended,
To conceive in sapphire showers
What they would bring forth in crystal.
And this fancy seemed more true,
As from their untold abundance
They, methought, could drink the blue
Drop by drop. Again sea monsters
Seemed to us the wandering droves,
Which, to form the train of Neptune,
Issued from their green alcoves.
For the sails, when lightly shaken,
Fanned by zephyrs as by slaves,
Seemed to us like outspread pinions
Fluttering o'er the darkened waves;
Then the mass, approaching nearer,
Seemed a mighty Babylon,
With its hanging gardens pictured
By the streamers fluttering down.
But at last our certain vision
Undeceived, becoming true,
Showed it was a great armada
For I saw the prows cut through
Foam. . . .

V

THE PASSAGE repays study, for the poet succeeds where many psychologists have failed: in describing the panorama of illusions that may be evoked by the indeterminate. It is the power of expectation rather than the power of conceptual knowledge that moulds what we see in life no less than in art. Were we to voyage in the Mediterranean we would, alas, be unlikely to see the train of Neptune's suite so convincingly conjured up as did the seventeenth-century traveller steeped in the reading of the classics and the experience of mythological paintings. But since we all probe the distant and indeterminate for possible classifications, which we then test and elaborate in a game of projections, Calderón's beautiful text provides us with the desired justification for comparing the reading of indeterminate pictures with the reading of indeterminate scenery. The experience of the radio 'monitor' confronted with indistinct speech and that of the sailor confronted with indistinct shapes on the horizon are not incommensurate. We must always rely on guesses, on the assessment of probabilities, and on subsequent tests, and in this there is an even transition from the reading of symbolic material to our reaction in real life. When we wait at the bus stop and hope the Number Two is coming into sight, we probe the indistinct blot that appears in the distance for the possibility of projecting the number 'two' into it. When we are successful in this projection, we say we now see the number. This is a case of symbol reading. But is it different with the bus itself? Certainly not on a foggy night. Nor even in full daylight, if the distance is sufficiently great. Every time we scan the distance we somehow compare our expectation, our projection, with the incoming message. If we are too keyed up, as is well known, the slightest stimulus will produce an illusion. Here as always it remains our task to keep our guesses flexible, to revise them if reality appears to contradict, and to try again for a hypothesis that might fit the data. But it is always we who send out these tentacles into the world around us, who grope and probe, ready to withdraw our feelers for a new test.

As with the hypothesis of the monitor who listens to speech, so the fitting interpretation will inevitably transform the data beyond recognition. There are countless psychological experiments and observations that confirm this. A characteristic example is quoted from an article by G. K. Adams in M. D. Vernon's book *Visual Perception:*

'I was looking out of the window, watching for the street car, and I saw through the shrubs by the fence the brilliant red slats of the familiar truck; just patches of red, brilliant scarlet. As I looked, it occurred to me that what I was really seeing were dead leaves on a tree; instantly the scarlet changed to a dull chocolate brown. I could actually "see" the change, as one sees changes in a theatre with a shift of lighting. The scarlet seemed positively to fall off the leaves, and to leave behind it the dead brown. I tried to recover the red by imagining the truck, and found that I could redden the leaves somewhat; then I made them leaves again, and found that I could brown them somewhat; but I could not get either the original scarlet or the later dead chocolate. I went out to see what the colour "really" was, and found it to be a distinctly reddish brown. . . .'

Once more the effect experienced by the trained observer can be most conveniently imitated in the perception of images. It has been found in a well-known experiment that a familiar shape will induce the expected colour; if we cut out the shape of a leaf and of a donkey from identical material and ask observers to match their exact shade from a colour wheel, they will tend to select a greener shade of felt for the leaf and a greyer one for the donkey. We remember that the result of this experiment was anticipated by our ancient author Philostratus: 'Even if we drew one of these Indians with white chalk,' Apollonius concludes, 'he would seem black, for there would be his flat nose and stiff curly locks and prominent jaw . . .

185. G. D. TIEPOLO: *The Holy Family Passing near a Statue.* 1752. Etching

to make the picture black for all who can use their eyes.' He was right. Interpreting, classing a shape affects the way we see its colour. We need only analyse our own reactions when we look at black-and-white art to confirm these findings [185]. Objectively, the marble statue in Tiepolo's print is not whiter than the garment of St. Joseph, but it stands out in our minds as a luminous white against the dark foliage, while it is difficult even to remember the garments of the travellers as white. The print serves as a screen for a tentative projection which does not lead to illusion and yet 'colours' the way we see it. Perhaps the correct way to describe this experience would be to say we see the garment as potentially dark. The psychologist Hering spoke of 'memory colour'. Here we might speak of 'colour expectations'.

VI

WHAT WE CALLED 'mental set' may be precisely that state of readiness to start projecting, to thrust out the tentacles of phantom colours and phantom images which always flicker around our perceptions. And what we call 'reading' an image may perhaps be better described as testing it for its potentialities, trying out what fits. The activation of these phantoms has been most frequently tested in the many psychological experiments in which an image is flashed on the screen for a brief moment only. There are many accounts of the wide range of different things which subjects report to have 'seen', that is to say, of the images they were induced to project onto the screen by the clues presented to them just long enough to induce a hypothesis but not long enough to check it. A recent experiment has neatly demonstrated the persistence of these visual tentacles and their influence on subsequent fantasies. It appears that negative shapes, i.e., the accidental forms presented by the background, induced such fantasies if the picture was removed sufficiently fast. We may assume that such misreadings constantly flit through our minds but are usually discarded before we become aware of them because they are overlaid by the more consistent and more tenable hypothesis.

Once a projection, a reading, finds anchorage in the image in front of us, it becomes much more difficult to detach it. This is an experience familiar in the reading of puzzle pictures. Once they are solved, it is hard, or even impossible, to recover the impression they made on us while we were searching for the solution.

The possibility that all recognition of images is connected with projections and visual anticipations is strengthened by the results of recent experiments. It appears that if you show an observer the images of a pointing hand or arrow, he will tend to shift its location somehow in the direction of the movement. Without this tendency of ours to see potential movement in the form of anticipation, artists would never have been able to create the suggestion of speed in stationary images.

But here as always this projection needs a 'screen', an empty field in which nothing contradicts our anticipation. This is the reason why the impression of movement, and thereby of life, is so much more easily obtained with a few energetic strokes than through elaboration of detail. The fact is familiar, but the explanation that is usually given appeals too confidently to the visual experience we 'really have' in the presence of movement. The situation is similar to the blurring of perception with distance. In both instances it is easy to say what we cannot distinguish in such situations. The criticism of traditional methods of representation again took its starting point from this undeniable fact. In the same period when Peacham upbraided a painter who had painted the buttons of the doublet of a man miles away, the painter Philip Angel in Holland criticized his fellow artists for painting the spokes of a wheel when the carriage is supposed to be in motion: 'Whenever a cart wheel or a spinning wheel is turned with great force, you will notice that because of the rapid turning no spokes can really be seen but only an uncertain glimpse of them [*een twijfelachtige schemeringe derselves*], but though I have seen many cart wheels represented I have never yet seen this as it should appear because every spoke is always drawn as if the carriage did not appear to move.'

186. VELÁZQUEZ: *Hilanderas*. Detail. About 1660

Angel was of course right that the sight of these spokes destroys the illusion of movement, but there is no evidence that he found a remedy. It needed the imagination and skill of a Velázquez to invent a means of suggesting that 'uncertain glimpse' in the spinning wheel of the *Hilanderas* [186], which appears to catch the so-called 'stroboscopic effect', the streaking after-image that trails its path across the field of vision when an object is whizzing past.

The suggestion of this effect belongs now to the commonplace language of the cartoonist or comic-strip artist. There is hardly a picture narrative in which speed

187

is not conveniently rendered by a few strokes which act like negative arrows showing where the object has been a moment before [187]. Surely in such a case there can be no question of realism. By no stretch of imagination do figures chasing each other across a precipice look like Al Capp's heroes. But the success of this formula proves that while detail contradicts the illusion of movement, the strokes somehow confirm it. The pre-image, if one may coin this word for our anticipation of where the figure will be next, is confirmed by an anchorage for the after-image.

But the most important effect of these anticipatory probings which accompany the reading of images is that aura of space which appears to surround any naturalistic

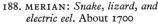

188. MERIAN: *Snake, lizard, and electric eel*. About 1700

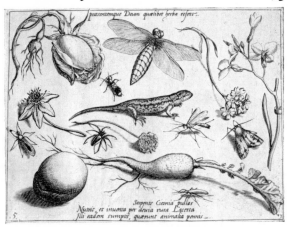

189. HOEFNAGEL: *From 'Archetypa studiaque'*. 1592

representation. The mere sign stands out as a figure against a neutral background, but this same ground recedes and assumes potential extension as soon as it forms part of the representation. It is an effect which can be observed with any picture or poster where letterpress is embodied. The caption on our Merian print of Notre Dame [46], for instance, does not appear to hover in space over Paris; it creates its own mental set, an aura of neutral ground around it, because we never probe letters for movement. The greater the suggestion of movement, or indeed of mobility—ours or that of the object—the more certain will be this effect which obliterates the ground from our awareness and turns it into a screen. Before we read Carracci's puzzle correctly, it looks like a flat diagram, or pattern [178]. As soon as we are guided to project the image of the mason into it, we also transform the ground above the line into a background space. But this suggestion will obviously be weak compared with the suggestion of depth in a print such as Tiepolo's [185], where we automatically transform the ground above the horizon into the infinite and indeterminate expanse of the sky.

We are so trained in assigning to each image its potential living space that we have no difficulty whatever in adjusting our reading to a configuration in which each figure is surrounded by its own particular aura. This happens every time a group of figures is assembled within one frame without being intended to share a common spatial setting. Once more we read such images by applying a rapid test of consistency. We understand without hesitation that the animals on the drawing by Maria Sibylla Merian [188] are to be read as individual specimens. Looking at J. Hoefnagel's plate [189] with its decorative assembly of plants and animals, we always supply the appropriate ground to the figure: the lizard sits on a slope, while some insects, throwing shadows, are imagined against a flat ground, and others are seen as flying. Without knowing it, we have carried out a rapid succession of tests

 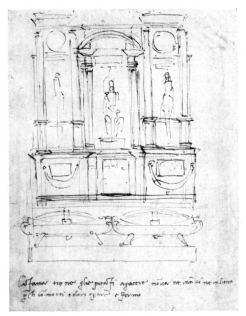

190. LEONARDO DA VINCI:
Sheet of studies. About 1480

191. MICHELANGELO:
Drawing for the Medici Tomb. 1521

for consistency and settled on those readings which make sense. Without such a test, even the images of traditional art may yield as variegated and fantastic a result as the proverbial shapes of clouds and inkblots. In a recent book, the rough brushwork of Rembrandt has been used as a screen for the projection of the most unexpected images and symbols. The author speaks of 'Rembrandts within Rembrandts', but the farmyard animals and grinning faces he discovered in folds of garments and in background shadows fail to live up to the consistency test which we must always use to discard our wrong guesses.

Where we do not find this consistency we immediately cast about for a frame of reference which will provide it, we revise our hypothesis about the type of 'message' which confronts us. Within the context of our culture we do this so automatically that we are hardly aware of the process itself. But this does not make our flexibility in these matters less interesting. When we look at a sketch, for instance, such as the sheet by Leonardo [190], we immediately take in the situation. We do not feel tempted for a moment to interpret its images literally, as if they were assembled in one space or the child had two left arms. We retranslate what we see into the context of action which gave rise to the image; we realize it is the record of various attempts, and we read it accordingly. We understand that certain lines are not to be interpreted strictly as representations but are intended as notes of the artist's intentions. Lines such as the rapid strokes indicating an alternative position of the Christ child's leg do not 'mean' so much a leg as the possible drawing of a leg.

VII

OF COURSE we employ the same faculty in our interpretation of speech in everyday life. Any recorded transcript of a real conversation shows how often a sentence is sketched before it is spoken and how tolerant we must be in our application of situational clues to 'make sense' of what is being said. We do so not by any conscious process of inference but through that faculty which was given us for understanding our fellow creatures, the faculty of empathy or identification. We first grope for the intention behind the communication, and the key to this intention lies largely in the way we feel we would react.

The idea of art, we have seen, has set up such a context of action within our culture and has taught us to interpret the images of art as records and indications of the artist's intention. To react adequately to the sketch, we instinctively identify ourselves with the artist. Our primary hypothesis is that what he does will make sense somewhere, and where one incomplete image does not give us the clues, we will place it in our minds in a series. The drawing by Michelangelo for the Medici tomb [191] would scarcely be intelligible. His rapid scrawls where he intended to indicate statues would not make sense by themselves, but they do in their context.

Sometimes, indeed, the process works the other way round, and a sketch elucidates for us the finished work of art. One of Constable's pencil notes for *Wivenhoe Park* [192] shows the motif of fishermen on the shore pulling in the net. To indicate the trees, the men, and the boat, Constable used only a few telling scribbles, but one thing he clearly marked—the net, or rather the floats from which the net hangs down into the water. It is through this indication that we are led to interpret the

192. CONSTABLE: *Pencil sketch for 'Wivenhoe Park'.* 1816

representation. In this particular case the sketch may even alert us to a more detailed interpretation of the final picture itself [5]. Without it one easily overlooks the tiny figures in the background who pull the net and thus link the boat with the distant shore.

It is doubtful whether Constable would have included such small details in the years of his full maturity. For then he came to rely increasingly on the artist's right to present his paintings less as records of the visible world than as indications of an artistic experience. The issue concerning the place of the sketch in Constable's work has been much debated, and we shall have to return to it. It has been claimed that in the paintings he exhibited he had to 'make concessions' to a public which was not prepared to read a sketch. But if concessions to vulgar taste are inartistic, those to understanding are not. All communication consists in 'making concessions' to the recipient's knowledge. It is dictated by the context and the awareness of possible alternative interpretations that have to be ruled out. The beholder's identification with the artist must find its counterpart in the artist's identification with the beholder.

We have seen some of the results of this give and take in the previous chapter— the admiration for the masterly touch, the seemingly careless brushstrokes; these allow us to experience vicariously the very process of creation, the virtuoso's control over his medium and that awareness of essentials which makes him cut out all redundancies because he can rely on a public that will play the game and knows how to take a hint. The social context in which this happens has hardly been investigated. The artist creates his own élite, and the élite its own artists.

It is well to remember, though, that this give and take is not confined to the sacred precincts of art. Wherever the image is used for communication, we can study that assessment of probable intention and the tests of consistency that lead to interpretation and illusion. We need think of nothing more solemn than the average comic strip, which presents quite a number of difficulties to those not familiar with its conventions. The public learns to know the recurrent characters and to recognize them at the merest hint. We are likewise trained by the poster artists to take in and assimilate the most baffling images. Thanks to their daring and inventiveness, we have learned how far the limits of our understanding of images can be extended beyond the indication of natural appearances. It is part of the function of the poster to attract attention by the improbable and to hold this attention by extending the process of reading. A study of the billboards on our way to work, or of advertising matter, will therefore teach us a good deal about those processes of interpretation we have been discussing in this chapter. For if we watch ourselves in our reactions, we are presented with a kind of slow-motion picture of the mechanism that jumps into action whenever we search for the meaning of an image.

193. ABRAM GAMES: *Poster.* 1953   194. ERWIN FABIAN: *Poster.* 1955

A few clues presented with sufficient boldness and clarity will make us find the solution of the puzzle which the image presents to us. Without asking more questions, we turn the rows of cigarettes in Abram Games's poster [193] into two flirting faces. Sometimes it is amusing to see what happens when we ask questions. We accept the chimney with the top hat as an industrialist who reads the *Financial Times* [194]. Where is his face? As soon as we ask, we notice we are scanning the poster, looking for indications where to anchor our projection. We find it somewhere along the line, and the faintest of phantom images settles on the chimney and transforms its visual character. True, it still remains a chimney, but it is also a face, according to the way we look at it. The character of the illusion is hard to describe and may vary from person to person. But if it did not exist to amuse and intrigue us, posters of this kind would scarcely be so popular.

The best opportunity to study this process of playful transformation through context and expectation is provided by the habit of advertisers in making use of stereotypes, identical symbols, that we are made to recognize in different settings.

For some decades now, the London Passenger Transport Board has provided the public with such an experiment in vision. It has adopted as its symbol the so-called 'bull's-eye' that originated as the standard frame used to set off the names of stations [195]. On one of the Board's posters by E. C. Tatum, the symbol discreetly functions as the button on the bridegroom's sleeve [199]. On another it appears on the distant hillside, enormous and mysterious, like those prehistoric images of horses cut out of the soil which puzzle the traveller through England [196]. But the most instructive, though not perhaps artistically the most rewarding, are the advertisements in which the emblem is used in a frankly representational context. The bull's-eye, for instance, has to function as a head [197]. Where the figure faces us, the transversal bar becomes a happy grin, and the protrusions ears.

195

Where the context makes us expect a profile, the grin disappears, and the frontal protrusion looks like a nose. It is not uninstructive to watch what happens in the less successful drawings where the context is just a trifle harder to take in [198]. It may take a fraction of a second to see how the boy is supposed to be standing, and only when we have understood his posture does he grow a convincing nose while the opposite protrusion of the bar shrinks from our awareness. We have projected a face onto the shape, and it then takes some effort to detach it again and recapture the frontal reading. The symbols behave like letters in reading that change their meaning with the total situation. Here, too, London Transport obliges with an example. On a book cover the bull's-eye is transfigured into an 'O', since we are set to classify it as a letter rather than as a representational shape [200].

What is interesting in this experience is not so much the flexibility of our interpretations as their exclusiveness. It is easy to see the bull's-eye as a head facing us, as a button, or as a letter. What is difficult—indeed impossible—is to see all these things at the same time. We are not aware of the ambiguity as such, but only of the various interpretations. It is through the act of 'switching' that we find out that different shapes can be projected into the same outline. We can train ourselves to switch more rapidly, indeed to oscillate between readings, but we cannot hold conflicting interpretations.

VIII

AMBIGUITY—rabbit or duck? [2]—is clearly the key to the whole problem of image reading. For as we have seen, it allows us to test the idea that such interpretation involves a tentative projection, a trial shot which transforms the image if it turns out to be a hit. It is just because we are so well trained in this game and miss so rarely that we are not often aware of this act of interpretation. Few people

196. SHEILA STRATTON: *London Transport poster*. Detail. 1954

197, 198. RAYMOND TOOBY: *London Transport advertisements*. 1954

199. E. C. TATUM: *London Transport poster*. 1954

200. ROBERT HARDING: *Cover of a history of London Transport posters*. 1949

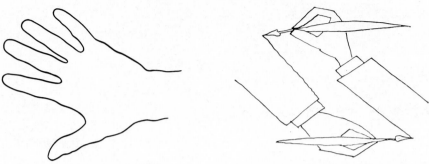

201   202. STEINBERG: *From "The Passport"*

realize that the outline drawing of a hand is ambiguous [201]. It is impossible to tell whether it is a left hand seen from the front or a right hand seen from the back. Yet confronted with such a drawing, we are startled by this unexpected lack of information. Such ambiguous hands are outside our range of experience and, more likely than not, we will have to use our own hands for guidance, trying to match them against the image and to project the alternatives until we are convinced of the ambiguity. It is only then we will come to realize that it was a matter of sheer accident which of the readings we adopted first. To detach the projection, once it was made, we must switch to the alternative one. There is no other way for us to see ambiguity.

The example demonstrates, I believe, what we mean by the 'test of consistency' —the possibility of classifying the whole of an image within a possible category of experience. If this sounds too abstract, let us see what happens where the artist has excluded such a reading. There is a charming little drawing by Saul Steinberg in which a drawing hand draws a drawing hand which draws it [202]. We have no clue as to which is meant to be the real and which the image; each interpretation is equally probable, but neither, as such, is consistent. If proof were needed of the

203. STEINBERG: *Drawing*

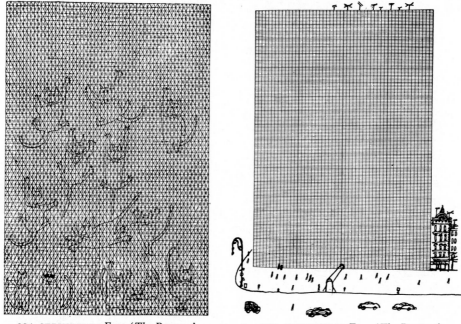

204. STEINBERG: *From 'The Passport'*   205. STEINBERG: *From 'The Passport'*

kinship between the language of art and the language of words, it could be found in this drawing. For the perplexing effect of this self-reference is very similar to the paradoxes beloved of philosophers: the Cretan who says all Cretans lie, or the simple blackboard with only one statement on it which runs, 'The only statement on this blackboard is untrue'. If it is true it is untrue and if untrue true. There is a limit to the information language can convey without introducing such devices as quotation marks that differentiate between what logicians call 'language' and 'meta-language'. There is a limit to what pictures can represent without differentiating between what belongs to the picture and what belongs to the intended reality.

© 1954 *The New Yorker Magazine, Inc.*

206. STEINBERG: *The Passport Photo*   207. STEINBERG: *From 'The Passport'*

It is no accident that this sophisticated example comes from the work of Saul Steinberg. There is perhaps no artist alive who knows more about the philosophy of representation than this humourist. He knows how the consistency test will make us transform any line according to context. In a recent drawing, he makes one straight line change its function and meaning in a series of situations from water level to washing line, from train track to sitting-room ceiling [203]. Or take his cats in a cage, from *The Passport* [204]. Normally we are set to ignore the ruled ground of a sheet of drawing-paper. But once we have understood the position of the cats, we see that the only hypothesis which fits the case is that they are clambering up a wire cage, and immediately the ruling is transformed for us into the picture of a cage. But a similar type of paper, such as is used in every architect's office, is turned into the image of a huge skyscraper [205] simply by adding a few minimum clues which inform us of its meaning and transform its visual character. After the many weighty tomes that have been written on how space is rendered in art, Steinberg's trick drawings serve as a welcome reminder that it is never space which is represented but familiar things in situations.

This formulation, though, requires an amendment which is also provided by Steinberg. Among the familiar things we can read into pictures, none may be more important than other pictures. The picture that provides the theme for Steinberg's *Passport* [206] is a fingerprint. We do not read it as a face so much as the photograph of a face; we file it not in terms of reality but as an existing type of representation. In another drawing [207], the fingerprint seems immensely enlarged by means of a few simple relational clues. Once more it stands for a picture the mannikin is painting. And if we look more closely, obediently responding with our projection, we discover the fingerprint can be read as a real landscape with a tree on the horizon and a

208. VAN GOGH: *Road with Cypresses.* 1889

ploughed-up field leading into space, a dark hedge showing gloomily against a weird spiralling sky. The fit is so close that no doubt is possible; the thumb print is an unmistakable van Gogh [208]. It is somewhat blasphemous to reproduce it side by side with the real thing because the very process of trained projection may lead us now to see van Gogh in terms of Steinberg—the purpose and effect of all parodies. But the comparison is not as frivolous as it may look. Steinberg here discovers that you can see a thumbprint as a thumbprint or as a van Gogh. Van Gogh's own discovery, of course, was immeasurably greater. He discovered that you can see the visible world as a vortex of lines. To many of us, stubble fields and cypresses have come to suggest van Gogh. Representation is always a two-way affair. It creates a link by teaching us how to switch from one reading to another.

VIII

Ambiguities of the Third Dimension

> The sense of sight discerns the difference of shapes, wherever they are . . . without delay or interruption, employing careful calculations with almost incredible skill, yet acting unnoticed because of its speed. . . . When the sense cannot see the object through its own mode of action, it recognizes it through the manifestations of other differences, sometimes perceiving truly and sometimes imagining incorrectly. . . .
>
> PTOLEMY, *Optics*

I

IN PROBING the illusions of art from various sides, we have come, in the last chapter, to stress increasingly the power of suggestion. In the reading of images, as in the hearing of speech, it is always hard to distinguish what is given to us from what we supplement in the process of projection which is triggered off by recognition. 'Recognition', though, is perhaps a misleading term in this connection. It was the 'guess' of the radio monitor, it will be remembered, that turned the medley of speech sounds into speech; it is the guess of the beholder that tests the medley of forms and colours for coherent meaning, crystallizing it into shape when a consistent interpretation has been found.

But the comparison between the hearing of speech and the reading of pictures, however useful it may have proved as a starting-point, is not without its pitfalls. The difficulties in identifying words, after all, are rather incidental. They become interesting only in abnormal conditions that blur those distinctive features that together make up the speech sign. In visual representation, signs stand for objects of the visible world, and these can never be 'given' as such. Any picture, by its very nature, remains an appeal to the visual imagination; it must be supplemented in order to be understood. This is only another way of saying that no image can represent more than certain aspects of its prototype; if it did it would be a double, and not even Pygmalion could make one. Unless we know the conventions, we have no means of guessing which aspect is presented to us. Even the famous glass models of flowers in the Harvard University museum would not tell a visitor from Mars very much about plants if he had never touched any. Which brings us back to the wisdom of Philostratus, who made his hero Apollonius say that no one can understand the painted horse or bull unless he knows what such creatures are like.

There is nothing paradoxical in this assertion. A picture of an unknown animal, or an unknown building, will tell us nothing of its size, for instance, unless some

204

209. HOGARTH: *False perspective.* 1754. Engraving

familiar object allows us to estimate the scale. Indeed, the point would hardly need elaboration were it not for the bearing it has on the most important trick in the armoury of illusionist art, the trick of perspective.

II

IN RECENT YEARS a great deal has been written on perspective and the rendering of space in art, but the beholder's share in the illusion of space is still somewhat incompletely understood. It is best illustrated by an amusing print by William Hogarth that was destined to be a title page for a textbook on perspective [209]. The picture is full of the illogicalities which, singly, are often found in the art of children and amateurs and which are said to have been perpetrated by a dilettante nobleman whom Hogarth wished to ridicule. The man on the distant hill looks as

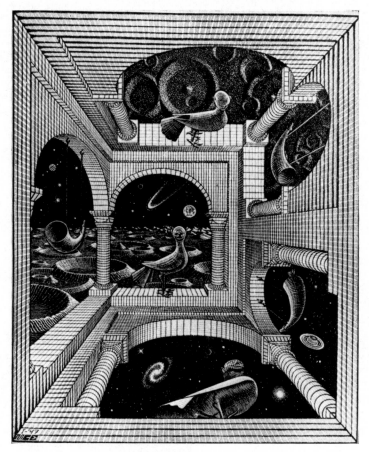

210. ESCHER: *Autre Monde.* 1947. Woodcut

large as the woman bending out of the window of the inn and can be seen to light his pipe at her candle. The trees on the hill appear to become larger the farther their distance from us, and yet some of them overlap the inn sign. Both ends of the church are clearly seen, and the bridge does not seem to span the river. The angler's lines interfere with each other, and the man in front must slide off the sloping pavement. Used as we are to the conventions of correct perspective, we interpret Hogarth's satire according to his intention. We see the print as an impossible picture. We rarely pause to think that it might also represent an impossible world, a world where the laws of gravity do not apply, where trees may grow to any height and arms to any length.

We are perhaps a little more aware of this possibility than Hogarth was, for our artists have accustomed us to the sight of impossible worlds. The print of the Dutch artist M. C. Escher [210] provides an instructive counterpart to Hogarth just because its perspective looks so correct. It is only when we come to look more

211. PIRANESI: '*Carceri*', pl. VII. Before 1750. Etching

closely that we see that such a structure cannot exist in our world and that the artist wants to transpose us into the giddy realms where terms such as 'up' and 'down' and 'right' and 'left' have lost their meaning. The print is an artist's meditation on space, but it is also a demonstration of the beholder's share; it is in trying to work out the intended relation of things and sights that we realize the paradoxes of his arrangement.

It is instructive to return from this extreme to a work of Hogarth's day that hovers on the fringe of the dream world. Piranesi, a master of perspective, used his skill in a series of prints of nightmare dungeons to conjure up an image of improbable and haunting scenery [211]. Is the perspective in Piranesi's print correct or false? As soon as we ask ourselves this question, we find that we must again set to work to sort out the things represented and to reconstruct the nightmare prison in our minds. The rope hanging from the pulley—where does it lead? How is the drawbridge tied up? What is the angle of the banister near the lower edge?

212. SALOMON KLEINER: *Riding school in Vienna.* About 1740

Watching ourselves trying to read the print in terms of a possible world, we gain some insight into the beholder's share in all reading of spatial arrangement. For it is always possible to stop the game and to baffle the search by a simple trick: transform the dungeon in your mind's eye into a stage design—for instance, the scenery for *Fidelio*, Act II—and your questions will have to sound very different. Where does the painted backdrop start, we would have to ask, and what shape should the stage props have to look like the design? Clearly there would be many answers possible to this question, indeed an infinite number of answers, and they all would depend on, among other things, the point of view from which the scene was to be looked at.

   If this experiment in imagination may be a little hard to perform, this is due only to the fact that twentieth-century artists and stage designers have come to spurn the tricks of illusion. We rarely get into situations where the eye is actually deceived, unless we visit the churches and monasteries of Austria or Bavaria decorated by travelling specialists in illusionist effects, the *quadratisti*, who made it their job to transform any old interior into a fairy palace by painting vistas of colonnades on the walls or grandiose cupolas on the ceiling. Entering such a hall we may often be uncertain what is painted and what is 'real', and it is interesting and amusing to watch the disappearance of the illusion when we trick the tricksters and view their work from an angle that was not intended.

Let us look at an engraving that does precisely this [212]. It represents a riding school in eighteenth-century Vienna which was obviously designed to appear much larger and more sumptuous than it really was. Standing, presumably, at the wrought-iron gate inside the garden, the visitor would see on his left a triumphal arch with an equestrian monument in the centre. On his right, he would see a colonnade seemingly extending far into the background and issuing into a rounded court with an obelisk in its centre. Turning round, he would behold the formal garden itself, giving a prospect that appeared to lead a considerable distance towards the boschetto. The strange and unexpected convolutions which these stage settings made for those actually riding in the court are hard to imagine.

Our engraving deliberately takes the illusion to pieces, but illusionist effects of this kind survive the processes of reproduction altogether badly. Alas, we have all come to see art too much through the falsifying media of photographs and slides; thus the old insight that it is naïve to demand that a painting should look real is gradually giving way to the conviction that it is naïve to believe any painting can ever look real.

This conviction has been strengthened by certain muddles in the philosophy and psychology of perception that have led to a rumour of some mysterious flaw in perspective. 'We do not always realize,' writes Sir Herbert Read, 'that the theory of perspective developed in the fifteenth century is a scientific convention; it is merely one way of describing space and has no absolute validity.'

III

IT MAY BE LUCKY, therefore, that precisely at this juncture, when critics and art historians have somewhat lost their bearings in these matters, psychology has taken over the investigation of illusion with scientific precision. It was Adelbert Ames, Jr., in particular who, starting as a practising artist, invented a number of ingenious examples of *trompe l'œil* for the laboratory, which may help to explain why the theory of perspective is in fact perfectly valid though the perspective image demands our collaboration.

Most of these demonstrations are arranged in the form of peep shows. One of them which can be fairly successfully illustrated [213] makes use of three peepholes through which we can look with one eye at each of three objects displayed in the distance. Each time the object looks like a tubular chair. But when we go round and look at the three objects from another angle, we discover that only one of them is a chair of normal shape. The right-hand one is really a distorted, skewy object which only assumes the appearance of a chair from the one angle at which we first looked at it; the middle one presents an even greater surprise: it is not even one

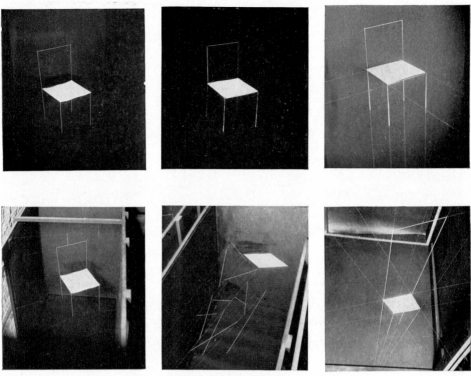

213. *The Ames chair demonstrations*

coherent object but a variety of wires extended in front of a backdrop on which is painted what we took to be the seat of the chair. One of the three chairs we saw was real, the other two illusions. So much is easy to infer from the photograph. What is hard to imagine is the tenacity of the illusion, the hold it maintains on us even after we have been undeceived. We return to the three peepholes and, whether we want it or not, the illusion is there.

It is important to be quite clear at this point wherein the illusion consists. It consists, I believe, in the conviction that there is only one way of interpreting the visual pattern in front of us. We are blind to the other possible configurations because we literally 'cannot imagine' these unlikely objects. They have no name and no habitation in the universe of our experience. Of chairs we know, of the crisscross tangle we do not. Perhaps a man from Mars whose furniture was of that unlikely kind would react differently. To him the chair would always present the illusion that he had the familiar crisscross in front of his eye.

One of the facts that Ames and his associates want to drive home with these demonstrations is, as they put it, that 'perceptions are not disclosures'. What we can see through the peephole does not directly and immediately reveal to us 'what is there'; in fact, we cannot possibly tell 'what is there'; we can only guess, and our guess will be influenced by our expectations. Since we know chairs but have no experience of those crisscross tangles which also 'look like' chairs from one point, we cannot imagine, or see, the chair as a crisscross tangle but will always select from the various possible forms the one we know.

The example illustrates the inherent ambiguity of all images and also reminds us of the reasons why we are so rarely aware of them. Ambiguity, as we observed in the last chapter, can never be seen as such. We notice it only by learning to switch from one reading to another and by realizing that both interpretations fit the image equally well.

That is the reason why people are generally puzzled if they are told that any correct rendering of perspective may stand for an infinity of shapes in space: it strikes them as perverse to insist that, say, the houses in Canaletto's view of Venice [165] might be imagined as standing at any angle and distance from the beholder, provided we give up the idea that they are houses of a familiar type. It is quite possible that only a stage designer, or at least a person accustomed to moving on an illusionist stage, would be able to perform the necessary switches and really 'see' the ambiguity.

Let us remember that the need for the beholder's collaboration in the reading of perspective images, so dramatically confirmed in the Ames demonstrations, does not contradict the contention that perspective is in fact a valid method of constructing images designed to create illusion. On the contrary, Ames constructed his exhibits entirely on the basis of perspective theory and proved, if proof was ever needed, that this theory suffices to 'deceive the eye'.

IV

NOW perspective may be a difficult skill, but its basis, as has been said, rests on a simple and incontrovertible fact of experience, the fact that we cannot look round a corner. It is due to this unfortunate inability of ours that as long as we look with one stationary eye, we see objects only from one side and have to guess, or imagine, what lies behind. We see only one aspect of an object, and it is not very hard to work out exactly what this aspect will be from any given point. All you have to do is to draw straight lines to that point from any part of the object's surface. Those that will lie behind an opaque body will be hidden, those that have free passage will be seen. Moreover, the fact that we see only along straight lines is also sufficient to account for the diminution of the aspect at a distance. The whole rationale of the process is illustrated with masterly simplicity in Dürer's famous woodcut [214]. He represents the straight line of sight by a string and shows how the lute will appear in the frame from the point of the painter's eye, which must be imagined

214. DÜRER: *From 'Unterweisung der Messung'*. 1525

to be where the string is attached to the wall. It also follows from Dürer's demonstration that any number of objects can be constructed that will result in the
identical aspect from the peephole.

Perhaps the easiest way to get that point clear is to imagine all these objects as
constructions of wire (as some of Ames's indeed are), or as a sequence of wire-
screen gates [215]. Our diagram shows that with the help of taut strings, real or

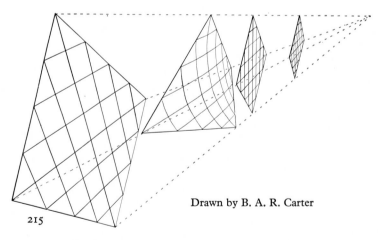

Drawn by B. A. R. Carter

215

imagined, radiating from one point, we can devise and arrange any number of such
gates which will appear to be superimposed upon one another from that point so
that all but the nearest will be hidden from sight. The geometry of similar triangles

tells us that all the gates parallel to each other will differ in scale but not in proportion. If one has a series of identical squares, all the others will have, too. It will be well for the reader to keep this fact in mind, for much of our later argument will hinge on it. But our demonstration also makes it clear that such gates would not have to be parallel to each other or at right angles to the central line of sight. If we are free to change their proportions, we can construct them for any oblique or curved arrangement while taking care that all their nodal points (where the wires cross) remain located on the same straight 'strings'. All these skewy configurations would still present from one point of view the same aspect as the straight ones. The geometry needed for our construction is called the 'art of perspective', and the technical term for oblique or curved images that fulfil this condition is 'anamorphosis'.

The sixteenth-century portrait of Edward VI [216] is such an 'anamorphosis'. Seen from in front it presents a weird appearance, but seen from very close to the edge, the distortion is rectified, and we see the head transposed into the normal view. This display of the magic skill of perspective yields an unexpected bonus: in the original peep show, the head will look surprisingly plastic, as if protruding from the oblique panel. The reason is the same that makes us 'see' the chair in the Ames

216. UNKNOWN ARTIST: *Anamorphic portrait of Edward VI, from front and side.*
1546 (after Holbein, 1543)

demonstrations rather than a crisscross of wires. Having difficulty even in imagining the shape of the distorted profile that is equivalent to the normal view, we interpret what we see as a configuration parallel to our eyes, a kind of phantom arising from the picture. Ames, in fact, has employed this age-old device of anamorphosis, and his demonstrations prove that there is nothing wrong with the theory of perspective as illustrated by Dürer. From a fixed viewpoint, any distortion in perspective can be made indistinguishable from the normal image. Why, then, do we call it a distortion? Clearly because it is not a relational model. We remember Plato's protest at the trickery of sculptors, who lengthened the proportions of statues destined to be seen from below, because they failed to represent things as they 'really are'. Like Plato, we are tempted to reserve this description for a correct relational model of three-dimensional objects.

We have all seen scale models of buildings such as the Parthenon, some with little toy mannikins dotted around. Now it is obvious that if we bend down to the point where these toy mannikins stand, the aspect of the building will appear the same as it would from the corresponding position on the Acropolis. Film producers make use of this fact when they have to represent disasters such as earthquakes. A scale model of a burning house, or a collapsing bridge, can be made to look indistinguishable from the 'real thing' if all standards of comparison are eliminated.

A picture on a flat surface, of course, can never be such a scale model. It can only represent identical relationships in two dimensions and not in three. Would it therefore be useless for the film trick? Not necessarily. A flat picture of a façade for instance, would serve its purpose. If it were drawn to scale, let us say 1 inch to a yard, it would clearly result in the same image from a distance of 100 inches as the real building from 100 yards. There is nothing 'conventional' in this fact, which follows from elementary geometry. The belief that perspective rests on a convention arises from confusion between relational models and images. What is a convention, though a convenient one, is that we like to paint on flat surfaces and can therefore present only relational models of two dimensions. If we wanted to draw a relational model of a curved façade, say of a crescent in the city of Bath, it might indeed be convenient to abandon the convention of the flat drawing surface and select a curved one.

This convenience should not be confused with the power of a curved surface to create that illusion of reality we experience in the circular panorama painting beloved of the nineteenth century, or under the vaulted dome of the Zeiss Planetarium, beloved of the twentieth. Here there are two illusions interacting which must be carefully separated. The first is the illusion that the real sky is vaulted or even (though less obviously so) that a real panorama from a mountain-top is circular. What is real in such life situations is our freedom to turn round and to assign imaginary equal distances to all remote objects in our field of vision. Enjoying the same freedom of movement in the panorama or planetarium, we experience the second illusion that even to the arrested gaze the curved picture will be more truthful than the flat one. This is not so. In fact the method of the planetarium can be used to demonstrate the equal validity of perspective projection on a flat surface.

The light points on its vaults are real 'projections'. They are thrown there by a powerful lamp in the centre in which the stars are 'represented' by so many search-light beams. Now to the stationary eye close to that apparatus it can make no difference whether these beams strike a flat or a curved surface. Naturally the objective relationship of the lightpoints will change, but to the stationary beholder their pattern must look the same. He can no more tell in the dark what their real relationships are 'up there' on the ceiling than he can tell this of the stars in outer space. Both are infinitely ambiguous. All he knows is that nothing prevents him from reading (and seeing) them in the same way as he reads (and therefore sees) the night sky.

This is all perspective can and does claim. Following as it does from our inability to look round corners, a perspective picture cannot exist in its own right, as a three-dimensional model can. Even our two eyes, since they view it from two different points, can in fact look round a corner and must therefore find fault with the panel designed for a peep show. To ask for it, finally, to be hung on a wall and viewed from any part of the room while still preserving the illusion is to ask for an absurdity. Perhaps the demand still hides the Pygmalion wish that a picture be more than a shadow, a little world independent of the beholder.

Here perhaps are the inarticulate roots of the idea that perspective is merely a convention and does not represent the world as it looks. Perhaps, also, a wish was father to the thought: the wish for a stick with which to beat the Philistine who wants to have his picture 'correct'. Moreover, certain facts could be cited to show that perspective theory leads occasionally to paradoxical results. One of these was discussed by Piero della Francesca and Leonardo, who showed that if we paint a picture of a row of columns, such as a temple façade, seen from the front, the columns on the side will come out wider in the construction than those directly in front [217]. The reason for this paradox, however, is not that the laws of perspective are inexact but that the ordinary results of geometrical projection sometimes take us by surprise. Columns, of course, extend both in width and in depth, and it is this extension away from the frontal plane of the elevation that causes the slight anomaly. That point becomes clearer if we imagine square pillars instead of columns and still clearer if we imagine those pillars painted red along the façade but green on the sides. Now perspective shows that in such a case the identical red fronts of the pillars will appear as identical red rectangles on the projective plane, but while the pillar in the centre—right in front of us—will disclose no green side, we will see an increasing amount of green as more and more of the sides of the pillars become visible. It is this addition of the sides, which project in ever greater width, that accounts for the apparent thickness of the pillars. If we replace the pillars by columns, we have to contend with additional consequences of projective geometry. With one eye, as the diagram shows, we never see the full width of a

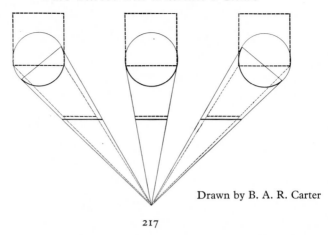

Drawn by B. A. R. Carter

217

column, since the tangents formed by the straight lines of sight touch the circum-
ference nearer to each other the nearer we stand. Conversely, we see slightly more
of the surface of the column that is farther away from us. At very close range, this
small unexpected increase in the area taken in by our eye when we step back partly
compensates for the decrease in size due to the greater distance. All this is no
doubt a little confusing; if it is a consolation to the reader, let me state my conviction that many writers on perspective have also become confused at this point, not
excluding myself, of course. But I believe that basically the column paradox is very
simple: it is caused by the beholder's difficulty in interpreting the projection of a
shape extending in depth that offers no clues as to its orientation. Columns or
spheres look the same from any angle, and it is this special case of ambiguity that
creates the painter's difficulty in coping with such undifferentiated shapes.

These facts, then, may for once really be described as the 'exceptions which
prove the rule', for the rule postulates that perspective is the theory of indistinguishable aspects from one point. There is another chain of arguments that presents
greater difficulties. If it is true, the argument runs, that things of equal size will
look smaller when farther away, it cannot also be true that a scale drawing of, say,
a palace façade will represent its real appearance. After all, the windows of the
wings will be farther away from us than those in the centre. The height of the
palace, too, must appear to shrink as the wings extend farther to the right and left.
Does this not suggest that a correct picture should have slowly and slightly converging curves ? This argument is usually countered by a reminder that what goes
for the palace will go for its picture. If the one looks foreshortened and perhaps
curved, the other, which we see from the same angle and which will therefore look
identical, will also share this appearance. The peep-show arrangement could
therefore look right while the world of our visual experience would still be subtly
different, non-Euclidian, and curved (as has been claimed), like Einstein's universe.

But as a matter of fact this argument, too, is somewhat unrealistic. Sitting in front of that long-stretched façade and looking at its centre, the painter would not see much of the wings, for the angle of vision which allows us to discriminate clearly is very small. He would therefore scan the view by moving his head, and as soon as he did that, the whole situation would change. Naturally, as he turns right, the façade will appear to converge in one way, and as he turns left in another; but if he wanted to paint these aspects, he would quite instinctively shift his easel so as to stand obliquely to the façade, and in this changed situation ordinary perspective demands a converging image. While he turns, in other words, he is aware of a succession of aspects which swing round with him. What we call 'appearance' is always composed of such a succession of aspects, a melody, as it were, which allows us to estimate distance and size; it is obvious that this melody can be imitated by the movie camera but not by the painter with his easel. It is understandable if painters feel that the curve will suggest the movement of lines more convincingly than the straight projection, but this curve is a compromise that does not represent one aspect but many. Neither this nor any other system can claim that it represents the world 'as it appears', but within the orthodox perspective arrangement, we deal with tangible, measurable relationships. Provided our wire-screen gates or grills [215] are parallel to one another, they will be identical in patterns and relationships and will be super-imposed on one another from one point. Remembering the Ames demonstrations, it is really up to us in such a case to say which of these shapes, classified and arranged in a sequence of progressive diminution, we call the 'real' gate and which 'the image', though for obvious reasons we have become used to thinking of the outermost as the 'motif' and of all the others as its 'representations' from a given point of view.

One cannot insist enough that the art of perspective aims at a correct equation: it wants the image to appear like the object and the object like the image. Having achieved this aim, it makes its bow and retires. It does not claim to show how things appear to us, for it is hard to see what such a claim should mean. If two gates are indeed indistinguishable from one point, the same is true of all others which answer the same condition. If the lines of one are straight, so will all the others be. There is no room in this arrangement for some ultimate gate which gives us the shape in which all the others 'appear to us'.

It is tempting to identify this ultimate gate with what is called the 'stimulus pattern', the actual relationships of the lines on the retina, and the fact that the retina is curved has indeed been brought into this discussion. But psychology warns us increasingly not to be too rash with this identification. We can never see our own retinas.

V

IT IS for this reason, I believe, that the psychology of vision and even phenomeno-
logical introspection have proved a will-o'-the-wisp for the student of art. It may
well be, for instance, that a taut string held very close to our eyes 'appears curved',
but the only meaning we could attach to this statement, as to all descriptions of
illusions, is the literal meaning that it 'looks like a curved string'. With strings held
very close to our eye, judgment becomes uncertain and we may make mistakes.
But to say that all straight lines in our field of vision look curved seems to me a much
more doubtful statement. It would imply that all straight strings look like curved
strings, and that is manifestly not the case. It is perhaps significant that the prime
argument for this claim of a curvilinear world is taken from architecture and not
from painting. The Greeks allegedly introduced the so-called 'refinements' of
deviation from rectangularity in their temples to correct the distortions of vision.
But if we can see the difference between a curved building and a straight one, the
argument falls to the ground. In any case, it would not touch the painter, for if he
painted the curves we would only see them more curved.

    Leonardo called the mirror 'the painter's master', and the mirror can indeed
help us to clarify this much-debated issue. Take any rectangular pocket mirror and
hold it so that the straight lines of a building, whether roof or wall, are reflected
in it very close to the mirror's straight edge. It will be easy to make the two parallel,
and the building will be seen to run true with the straight mirror side. Now it is
certainly possible to say that this effect is due to our seeing both the mirror and the
building curved. But we may now see why this is not a helpful description. Perceiving from the standpoint of experience, as has been said, 'is synonymous with
observing differences, relationships, organizations, and meanings'. The idea that
our world is really curved and should be so painted is little better than the old
argument that we 'really' see the world double and upside down.

VI

PERHAPS the reader will feel, by a sense of approaching giddiness, that we are here
moving towards the unfathomed abyss that threatens to swallow up psychological
and philosophical inquiries into the 'really real'. But if we hold fast to the railing of
our subject—the beholder's share in the reading and interpretation of visual images
—we may perhaps peer down for a moment.

    It will be remembered that the digression on perspective aimed at sorting out
various spurious problems from that of ambiguity. Ames showed that perspective
'works' but that it cannot explain why we select one of the possible configurations
as the 'real' one.

The nature of this problem is best demonstrated on the basis of the best-known visual ambiguity, the so-called 'size-distance relationship'. It is a fact that was known to the Greeks and the Arabs, and must have been observed by many a sailor and hunter, that where we lack other clues we cannot judge the size of an object unless we know its distance, and *vice versa*. This uncertainty was dramatically illustrated quite recently when a party of explorers diving in a bathyscaphe declared themselves unable to judge the size of the unknown creatures they had seen in the deep.

Ames has made use of this interdependence of knowledge and the estimation of distance by making his subjects look through a peephole at the enlarged or diminished images of familiar objects, such as wrist watches or playing-cards. The expected reactions happened: the large wrist-watch was judged to be of normal size but nearer; the diminutive one was estimated to be farther away than it really was. What is interesting in this experience is not that one is easily deceived, but that even an awareness of the ambiguity will not prevent one from making a guess. On the contrary, the habit, or compulsion, of jumping to a conclusion will always have the better of us when we look through the peephole. We will always see an object at a distance, never an appearance of uncertain meaning. The best we can achieve is a switch from one reading to another, a trying-out of various interpretations, but the demonstration confirms the conclusion of our preceding chapter, that ambiguity as such cannot be perceived. The disciples of Ames refer to this fact as the 'thereness-thatness' experience; to perceive means to guess at something somewhere, and this need will persist even when we are presented with some abstract configuration where we lack the guidance of previous experience. Presented with a circular disk, for instance, we are well aware of the fact that it might be fairly large and far away, or small and close by. We also may remember intellectually that it might be a tilted ellipse, or a number of other shapes, but we cannot possibly see these infinite possibilities; the disc will appear to us as an object out there, even though we may realize, as students of perception, that another person may guess differently.

One must have experienced these effects to realize how elusive they make the idea of 'appearance' as distinct from the object itself. The stimulus school of psychology and the phenomenalists talked as if the 'appearance' of the disk, the stimulus pattern, were the only thing really 'experienced' while all the rest was inference, interpretation. It sounds like a plausible description of vision, but it is untrue to our actual experience. We do not observe the appearance of colour patches and then proceed to interpret their meaning. Perception as such, as has been said, has a subject-predicate character. To see is to see 'something out there'. Even where the retina is really the only agent, in after-images and the like, we still project the colour patches into space.

This fact, as we shall see, also helps to account for the difficulty in the demand for fixing 'appearances' on to a canvas. Phrased in this general way, it is an impossible demand. What we can do is to set up an easel and submit to the concrete problem of making the image out there look like a given object in the distance, knowing full well (but not caring at all) that in doing so it must of necessity also look like any number of unreal objects. No wonder we need a starting-point for this matching process, something man-made with which to compare the object and which can then be modified and approximated within the terms of the equation. The statement, 'From where I stand this picture here looks like the castle there', is manageable and sometimes even testable. The general statement, 'This picture represents reality as it appears to me', may undoubtedly be sincere, but strictly speaking, it makes no sense. It is about as profitable as the quarrel whether the moon looks like a sixpence or a half-crown. The difficulty in answering this poser has never prevented a child from drawing the moon. As long as it is recognizable within the universe of its picture, no problem can arise. All I need to interpret the picture are those contextual aids that will make me think of the moon as the appropriate guess.

218. GIOVANNI DI PAOLO: *The Annunciation.* About 1440–1445

VII

WE HAVE come back, so it seems, to where we were at the end of the last chapter. The illusions of art presuppose recognition; to repeat the phrase from Philostratus, 'No one can understand the painted horse or bull unless he knows what such creatures are like.' The mistake which has led so much theorizing on art into the bog is in thinking that there must be means of representing 'appearances' or even 'space' as such.

It is our knowledge, or more precisely our guess, that makes us interpret the small horse or bull in many a picture as a distant horse or bull. It is not for nothing, therefore, that perspective creates its most compelling illusion where it can rely on certain ingrained expectations and assumptions on the part of the beholder. The Baroque decorator's illusion of painted ceilings or architecture works so well because these paintings represent what might, after all, be real. Every care is taken to blur the transition between the solidly built and the flatly painted, and we continue to interpret the one in terms of the other. It is for similar reasons that Renaissance painters liked to suggest depth through the rendering of tiled pavements [218]. Assuming as we must that the pavements are flat and the tiles identical units, we are compelled to read their progressive diminution as recession. But here, as always, the impression of depth is entirely due to our share, our assumption, of which we are rarely aware. In a similar way, modern poster artists often rely on our expectation of the normal letter form to give us the impression of letters or words arranged in depth or coming toward us with aggressive force [219]. It is an effect which would be lost on someone who did not know the conventions of lettering.

219

At this point the reader should be warned that the argument here developed would not be accepted by all schools of psychology. The Gestalt school would have none of it. The pioneers of this important movement want to minimize the role of learning and experience in perception. They think that our compulsion to see the

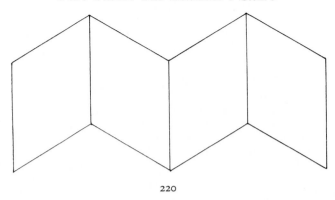

220

tiled floor, or the letters, not as irregular units in the plane but as regular units arranged in depth is far too universal and too compelling to be attributed to learning. Instead they postulate an inborn tendency of our brain. Their theory centres on the electrical forces which come into play in the cortex during the process of vision. It is these forces, they claim, that tend toward simplicity and balance, and make our perception always weighted, as it were, in favour of geometrical simplicity and cohesion. A flat, regularly tiled floor is simpler than the complex pattern of rhomboids in the plane, hence it is a flat, regularly tiled floor we actually see.

To support this view, the Gestalt psychologists are fond of demonstrating that we select the simple configuration even where there is no question of our knowing such shapes from experience. The most obvious example is a pattern of rhomboids [220]. Most of us will see it as a zigzagging band of regular rectangles rather than as a chain of rhomboids. Moreover, there are two possible readings of the regular band in space, and both are indeed adopted almost at random. We can see it starting from behind or from in front. We can even make it switch round from one position to the other with little effort. What we cannot do even with the greatest effort is to see or imagine the various irregular shapes the rhomboids would have to make to fit any in-between position, though reason and mathematics assure us that an infinite number of such irregular shapes must exist and can be construed.

At first glance, these findings would seem to apply remarkably well to the reading of pictures. Take one of Klee's fantasies, his *Old Steamer* [221]. We have never seen a craft of this kind and have no experience to guide us in the reading of such an image. Yet we will surely see it as a three-dimensional construction. It is only when we ask ourselves how we are to imagine the rickety vessel that we notice the possibility of several readings. The plank on top of the wheel may be imagined as going backward or upward, and it is this ambiguity that adds to the impression of rocking instability that Klee, the great explorer of forms, certainly aimed at.

The example shows, I hope, that the issue raised by the Gestalt psychologists is of much more than theoretical interest in relation to art. Since art has begun to cut

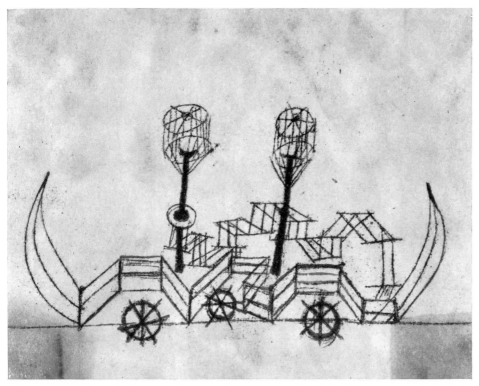

221. KLEE: *Old Steamer*. 1922. Water colour

itself loose from anchorage in the visible world, the question how to suggest one reading rather than another of any arrangement of forms has become of crucial importance. It is true that artists and critics are rarely aware of what is at stake. It is so easy to talk at cross-purposes about these matters. Our inability to see ambiguity often protects us from the knowledge that 'pure' shapes allow of an infinity of spatial readings. Even so, the dynamics of form and colour as such have naturally aroused increasing interest, and it would be comforting to know that three-dimensional forms can still be suggested unambiguously in a non-representational context. But what is comforting is not necessarily true, and I feel that much more research is needed to confirm or refute the artist's subjective feeling that he has 'represented' an abstract three-dimensional shape. For though the simplicity criterion certainly guides our reading in certain cases that happen to be simple, it is easy to show that its application is limited. We need not go to abstract art to make this demonstration. Any picture of a tree will demonstrate the dilemma more or less. Turn back to Hobbema's *Village with Watermill* [33]. How much can we tell about the spatial relations of its tree branches? And yet, I contend, we do not see the distant trees as a flat silhouette—rather we accept any one reading that would fit the image and rarely even notice its ambiguities. One would have to ask a number

222. LESTER BEALE: *Poster*. 1952   223. ALICK KNIGHT: *Poster*. 1952

of observers to make a wire model of the trees concerned to bring out the different readings of the same image.

A series of simple posters may serve to bring these conflicting views into focus. Take the effective design for the United States Lines [222]. Though nobody has ever seen such a sight, most people, I find, confidently read it as an arrow pointing obliquely backward across the Atlantic. This reading conforms to the expectations of the Gestalt psychologists, for it tallies with the simplicity criterion. We take the stripes on the arrow to be parallel and therefore read their convergence as recession. We are told this reaction is so basic that it cannot be put down to assumptions and interpretations. And yet the explanation breaks down in another simple poster for the *Post Office Guide* [223]. The simplicity criterion would compel us to accept the lettering on the arrows as uniform and therefore to see the arrows as lying parallel to the book. I doubt if many readers will see the arrangement this way. The situation indicates too strongly that the arrows are meant to point toward the book, much as the arrow in the previous poster pointed across the ocean. But as soon as we adopt this reading, we have here no clue as to the exact angles in which the arrows are supposed to be pointing. They are obviously to be imagined as tapering off towards the arrowhead, and therefore the simplicity criterion lets us down. Yet here, as always, we will not leave the picture uninterpreted; rather we will adopt at random any reading that is not inconsistent with the situational clues and be satisfied with some image of cardboard arrows in a window display. Few of those who have seen the poster are likely ever to compare notes and discover that their illusions differed because each of them contributed a different share of 'space' to the arrangement.

VIII

WHY IS IT DIFFERENT with the Graz trade fair poster [224], which also represents a tapering shape none of us has seen? Merely to ask this question is to remind the reader at last of the gigantic over-simplification that lies in discussing the rendering of space without reference to modelling, that is, the rendering of light and shade.

In light and shade Western artists have discovered a means of vastly reducing the ambiguity of shapes as seen from one side. Hogarth, the great empiricist who so wittily worked out the effects of 'false perspective', explained with admirable lucidity what he meant by 'the retiring shade': 'It is equally instrumental with converging lines, in showing how much objects, or any parts of them, retire or recede from the eye; without which, a floor, or horizontal-plane, would often seem to stand upright like a wall. And notwithstanding all the other ways by

224. WALTER HOFMANN: *Poster.* 1951

which we learn to know at what distances things are from us, frequent deceptions happen to the eye on account of deficiencies in this shade: for if the light chances to be so disposed on objects as not to give this shade its true gradating appearance, not only spaces are confounded, but round things appear flat, and flat ones round.'

Hogarth knew that shade had a defining character only where it is used to plot a foreshortening, 'thus mutually compleating the idea of those recessions which neither of them alone could do'. But he also knew that in given situations even these two clues together will not rule out ambiguity unless a third, 'reflection', completes the definition: 'As an instance that convex and concave would appear the same, if the former were to have no reflection thrown upon it, observe the ovolo and cavetto, or channel, in a cornice, placed near together, and seen by a front light, when they will each of them, by turns, appear either concave, or convex, as fancy shall direct.'

It is possible that Plato referred to the same ambiguity when he said that 'the same things appear bent and straight to those who view them in water and out, or concave and convex, owing to similar errors of vision about colours, and there is obviously every confusion of this sort in our souls'. At any rate, the decorators of classical antiquity must have known of our ability to switch between various readings, even of shaded objects, 'as fancy directs' for they used the most striking

225. Mosaic from Antioch   226

pattern of this kind, the reversible cubes, on walls and pavements [225]. We can read each of these units as a solid cube lighted from above or as a hollow cube lighted from below.

It is possible to imitate these conditions in a photograph of a staircase [226]. If the reader has sufficient patience, he will discover that the photograph can be read in three different ways. The one is the obvious (and correct) version which makes him imagine he is walking up the stairs to the attic, with his left hand on the railing and the light coming down from above onto the dark patches of linoleum which protect the steps in the centre. But if he turns the book round and manages to forget his previous reading, he can see the stairs leading upward once more, with the light again falling in from the top and the linoleum ready to be stepped upon. But there is a third possibility: we see the linoleum as upright and the shadowed intervals as the steps onto which we look from high above with the light coming from below. Covering up the railings and looking only at a section of the picture helps greatly in the task of switching between various readings. It is clear why: the more evidence of the spatial situation is taken in, the less possible will it be to accept the alternative reading. The consistency test will be put to increasing strain. We are reminded of our efforts to sort out the complex spatial arrangement of Piranesi's print and to judge our interpretation against our experience of 'possible worlds'. We begin to see a little more clearly that these tests rely on what Hogarth called the 'mutual compleating of ideas', the consistent interaction of clues.

IX

IT IS IMPORTANT to recall these elementary facts from the psychology of perception if we, as historians, are to understand what is involved in the invention of illusionist art. Neither the invention of perspective nor the development of shading by itself would be enough to create an unambiguous, easily readable image of the visual world. Used as we are to the reading of naturalistic images, we are rarely aware of this need for interaction; we are well satisfied with outline drawings which we read correctly by means of the simplicity criterion alone. But reports of the difficulty encountered by beholders brought up in a different tradition may make us pause before we declare our reading as automatic.

Early in this century, a Japanese artist, Yoshio Markino, came to Europe. In his childhood reminiscences (which his publishers rather cruelly printed in the author's own idiom) he writes:

'About the perspective, I have some story of my own father. When I got a book of the drawing lessons at my grammar school there was a drawing of a square box in the correct perspective. My father saw it and said, "What? This box is surely not square, it seems to me very much crooked." About nine years later he was looking at the same book and he called me and said, "How strange it is! You know I used to think this square box looked crooked, but now I see this is perfectly right." . . . This example shows you that if one is ignorant of the law of nature, a quite correct thing looks to him quite wrong. That is why I say that you must have the scientific training, although it may make you feel disagreeable, and you must not rely upon only your Human Sense, which is very dangerous.' We have seen that actually 'scientific training' says otherwise. The unshaded perspective drawing of a box which the artist's father probably saw in his son's drawing-book was, no doubt, the correct projection of a rectangular shape [227]. It therefore can suggest such a shape, but it need not. For as we have seen in the discussion of Ames and of the theory of perspective, there are also an infinite number of skewy boxes which will result in the same aspect. And so Markino's father was right both times: when, as a Japanese, he judged the drawing to represent a crooked box, and later, when he had trained himself to exclude such an unlikely reading of a well-intentioned drawing-book.

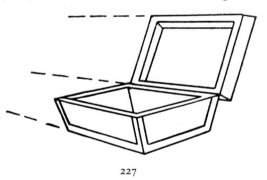

227

The correct interpretation of such traffic accidents on the way between artist and beholder is clearly of crucial importance for the whole issue of the changing

228. CATLIN: *Little Bear*. About 1838

conventions of art. In common with all nineteenth-century writers, Ruskin used these difficulties as evidence that 'the truth of nature is not to be discerned by the uneducated senses'.

'The Chinese, children in all things, suppose a good perspective drawing to be as false as we feel their plate patterns to be, or wonder at the strange buildings which come to a point at the end. And all the early works, whether of nations or of men, show, by their want of *shade*, how little the eye, without knowledge, is to be depended upon to discover truth. The eye of a Red Indian, keen enough to find the trace of his enemy or his prey, even in the unnatural turn of a trodden leaf, is yet so blunt to the impressions of shade, that Mr. Catlin mentions his once having been in great danger from having painted a portrait with the face in half light, which the untutored observers imagined and affirmed to be the painting of half a face.'

Neither Catlin's own account nor the painting to which he refers and which still exists in the Smithsonian Institution [228] quite bear out Ruskin's words. It is true that a quarrel broke out among the Indians which ended badly for Catlin's sitter, 'Little Bear', one of the Indians having remarked that the white man's painting showed 'but half a man', but the remark was obviously intended as a provocation. Catlin's memoirs certainly confirm, as do many other stories of painters who worked among primitives, that his activities were regarded with much suspicion and little understanding. But we have come to see that there need be no contradiction between this failure to read naturalistic images as they are meant to be read and that keenness of eye which Ruskin rightly admired. For not only is it perfectly true that a half-shaded face might represent but half a face, but such an interpretation might not even look improbable to a beholder who is used to the idea of a world peopled with spirits and monsters.

There is an old Chinese treatise about art which throws light on this difference: 'Everyone is acquainted with dogs and horses since they are seen daily. To reproduce their likeness is very difficult. On the other hand, since demons and spiritual beings have no definite form and since no one has ever seen them they are easy to execute.'

229

The passage of course refers to the painter who can indulge in all kinds of improbabilities where he represents things no human eye ever saw. In our context we are more interested in the corollary that what would make art easy for the painter would make it impossible for the beholder.

If nothing were too improbable to make a picture, paintings could not be read. It is easy to show that we would all make the kind of mistakes which so surprised Ruskin if we lacked the relevant clues for a better hypothesis. A sufficiently small detail of any picture will be infinitely ambiguous. Isolate the hand of 'Little Bear', and it might be mutilated. Take his neck alone, and the shadow might be a black smudge.

For shadow, as Hogarth knew, is only an indication of form as long as we know where the light comes from. If we do not know, we have to guess. Psychologists have found that in the absence of other clues, Western observers have settled for the probability that the light falls from high up and from the left-hand side. It is the position most convenient for drawing and writing with the right hand, and it therefore applies to most paintings. To most observers, therefore, the form in [229] will appear as part of a sphere. As a matter of fact, it is the conch from Crivelli's picture of the Virgin [230], isolated and turned upside down. When it is viewed in context, the ambiguity disappears from our awareness, because, seeing the throne, we understand the motif that the painter intended to represent, and everything falls into place.

The method of isolation and guessing is not merely a frivolous game. It reminds us of the tremendous gulf that separates the reading of pictures from the sight of the visible world. Simply to equate the one with the other, as Ruskin did, in

230. CRIVELLI: *Madonna and Child Enthroned with Donor*. About 1470

common with so many nineteenth-century critics, is to bar one's way to the understanding of representation. But if we remain aware of the difference between the
reading of pictures and the reading of situations, the game of isolation may yet
prove of value for the understanding of both processes.

X

RUSKIN MARVELLED that an eye keen enough to find a trace of an enemy or prey
even in the unnatural turn of a trodden leaf should be so blunt as to misinterpret
the isolated clues of Catlin's picture. But the true marvel of the eye is precisely the
speed and assurance with which it interprets the interaction of an infinite number
of clues. The psychologist in his laboratory has this in common with the artist,
that he will test our reactions to isolated clues. We remember Ames's confirmation
of the size-distance relationship in such isolation. Show the Red Indian a leaf of
which he knows neither the size nor the distance in a peephole and his guess
cannot, in the nature of things, be better or keener than anybody else's. It is the
same with movement. We cannot tell whether what we see, in the absence of other
clues, is a sphere approaching or a balloon being blown up. Nor will isolation
allow us to perform that strange feat at which we have become so expert – separat-
ing the permanent colour of things from the degree and hue of illumination. Taken
in isolation, therefore, Ruskin's Red Indian might well interpret the upturned leaf
swaying in the wind as a queer creature, changing shape and colour in rhythmic
succession. He will not do so, not because his eyesight is keen, but because he
knows the type of world he lives in and has learned to make and test assumptions.
It is particularly the assumption of the constancy of things which has proved its
worth to animal and man. We look out into the world with the confidence that this
thing out there will be more likely to change its place than its shape and that its
illumination will vary more easily than its inherent colour. This confidence in the
stability of things in a changeable world is deeply ingrained in the structure of our
language and has formed the basis of man's philosophy. The Aristotelian distinction between 'substance' and 'accident' is nothing but the codification of this faith
in a stable world, modified by such accidents as the angle of vision, the reflection
of light, or the change of distance.

It is easy to show that our reading of images and our reading of natural situations
really proceed from substance to accident. We could not make sense of Constable's
Wivenhoe Park [5] without the well-proven assumption that grass is as a rule
sufficiently uniform in colour for us to recognize the modifications due to light and
shade, that Lilliputians rarely populate the English landscape and that therefore

the small mannikins are far away, and that even fences are generally built fairly even in height so that the tapering off must indicate increasing distance – all these interpretations are found to dovetail and support one another so that a coherent picture emerges.

It might be said, therefore, that the very process of perception is based on the same rhythm that we found governing the process of representation: the rhythm of schema and correction. It is a rhythm which presupposes constant activity on our part in making guesses and modifying them in the light of our experience. Wherever this test meets with an obstacle, we abandon the guess and try again, much in the way we proceeded in reading such complex pictures as Piranesi's *Carceri* [211].

In this emphasis on elimination of false guesses, on trial and error in all acquisition of knowledge 'from the amoeba to Einstein', I am following K. R. Popper. It would be tempting to take up the problems of Gestalt psychology from this angle, for Popper emphasizes that the assumption of regularity is of the utmost biological value. A world in which all our expectations were constantly belied would be a lethal world. Now in looking for regularities, for a framework or *schema* on which we can at least provisionally rely (though we may have to modify it for ever), the only possible strategy is to proceed from simple assumptions. Popper has shown that paradoxically this is not due to the fact that a simple assumption is more probably right but because it is most easily refuted and modified. Take the history of man's grandiose attempt to find the regularities behind the bewildering movement of the planets in the sky. Ptolemy's complex system of cycles and epicycles could always be amended to 'save the phenomena', but what appeared to be its strength was indeed its fatal flaw. Copernicus' inspired guess, according to which the planets moved in circles round the sun, was easily disproved by Kepler, but it was capable of an amendment which gave a coherent picture of the solar system and paved the way for Newton.

Without some initial system, without a first guess to which we can stick unless it is disproved, we could indeed make no 'sense' of the milliards of ambiguous stimuli that reach us from our environment. In order to learn, we must make mistakes, and the most fruitful mistake which nature could have implanted in us would be the assumption of even greater simplicities than we are likely to meet with in this bewildering world of ours. Whatever the fate of the Gestalt school may be in the field of neurology, it may still prove logically right in insisting that the simplicity hypothesis cannot be learned. It is, indeed, the only condition under which we could learn at all. To probe a hole we first use a straight stick to see how far it takes us. To probe the visible world we use the assumption that things are simple until they prove to be otherwise.

In his perceptive book *Scenery and the Sense of Sight*, V. Cornish records his discovery that we 'instinctively regard an object as extended in the plane at right angles to the line joining the object to the eye'. He seeks the reason for this tendency in the shape of the retina, but it is more likely due to the need for some initial assumption, a lump of unarticulated hypothesis from which we start paring away till the image of our world emerges from it. The apparent vault of heaven must be a case in point.

It is hardly necessary to stress how immeasurably richer is the information we have at our disposal in this process of trial and error when we move around in the real world, compared with the interpretation of representations. The philosophers and psychologists from Berkeley's time onwards were certainly right when they stressed the importance of touch for our confidence in a solid, permanent world. But we now know that touch is only one of a whole battery of cross checks at our disposal. Texture, for instance, as Gibson has recently shown, is a further important one. Assuming that the texture of individual substances will be constant, we can estimate the effect of recession by the same token that we use in perspective. Even in Escher's impossible world [210] this permanency of texture is not affected: as we see the hatching increase in density, we feel the effect of recession on one individual substance. The clue of texture, therefore, is basically also a clue of regularity and one which proves so reliable because the microstructure of things is least affected by accidents. Looking over a sandy plain, we have a right to start with the assumption that there will be no real, steady decrease in the size of the grains as they recede from our eye.

But all these clues, we may be sure, are subsidiary to the test of movement. Whenever we do not quite trust our eyes or want additional information, we shift our head slightly and watch the relative change of position. It is this test, of course, which is excluded by the peephole in the Ames demonstrations. With its aid, any false guess concerning the distance of a flat object seen against a background can be immediately eliminated, and the true shape of a three-dimensional configuration begins to emerge when we start 'looking round a corner'. Learning to 'see' may have much to do with the acquisition of expectations of serial orders, the sequence of shapes a chair or a table will project onto our retina as we move our head. It is this Ames had in mind when he stressed that perceptions are not disclosures but are essentially prognostic in character. The prognosis is of the shape that will appear if and when we move.

But granted the role of our expectations and anticipations in perception, which has even led one psychologist to talk of the unity between movement and perception, does not this insight militate against any comparison between the reading of paintings and the sight of the world in life situations? In a way it does. The world never presents a neutral picture to us; to become aware of it means to become aware of possible situations that we can try out and test for their validity. It is one of the miracles of art that it can compel us to apply this attitude, this test, to an imitation of nature, a stationary image. We have seen in the last chapter that such an imitation does indeed stimulate us to probe and anticipate, to project our expectations, and thus to build up an imaginary world of illusion.

The fact that this is possible suggests that in these discussions the resources of the stationary eye have sometimes been somewhat underrated. Like all good communication services, our senses rarely take chances with one signal alone. They make use of what engineers call 'redundancies', the mutual confirmation of messages by repetition and cross reference. Though I have stressed in this chapter how ambiguous are the stimuli which, singly, have to be used by the stationary eye, their interaction even without the test of movement proves a very strong instrument to weed out false guesses.

In the course of time, artists have in fact succeeded in simulating one after the other of these clues on which we mainly rely in stationary one-eyed vision, and the result is that mastery of *trompe l'oeil* illusion in which painting beat the mechanical means of photography by a few generations.

XI

WE MAY NOW BE in a somewhat better position to describe the character of that illusion. It implies, I think, that in certain circumstances we would be unable to *disprove* that a *trompe l'œil* is 'real'—unless, that is, we could apply some movement test either by touching it or by shifting our position. Take a painting such as Fantin-Latour's *Still Life* in Washington [231]. One could probably imagine an arrangement of two boxes with peepholes, one of which would show the painting, another a reconstruction of the motif. Under suitable lighting conditions, it might then become hard to decide which of the two peepholes opens on the painting, which on a real table with flowers and fruit. But remembering a similar experience in the laboratories set up by Ames and his pupils, we would have to add that these are not the only two alternatives between which we would have to decide. After all, there might be any number of combinations and permutations of real lemons and false flowers, flat or skewy oblique cardboard models of the cup or the book, all of which would result in the same stimulus pattern to the stationary eye. They would all be first and readily interpreted in terms of the real 'possible' world of our experience, and there would be no jarring contradiction to prevent the illusion. From this point of view, the successful *trompe l'œil* might be described as the height of visual ambiguity. It is a multi-coloured canvas that we can interpret as a dining-table.

That such illusions are rarely complete goes without saying. After all, we do not generally display pictures in peep shows, and as soon as we move, the illusion must disappear, since the objects in the still life will not shift in relation to each other. The painter of a real *trompe l'œil*, therefore, will have to be content with a shallow arrangement, such as a letter-rack [168], or a flat relief where this failure of internal movement is less noticeable. The wonder is only that this handicap is not more serious than it is. It appears that once again we contribute some of the imagined movement from the store of our own expectations. I believe that some of this effect is even noticeable when we look at the Fantin-Latour from various sides, but the most instructive instances are those posters and pictures where a pointing finger or gun always seems to aim at us [83], or the portraits—already mentioned— which 'follow us with their eyes'. In a sense, I believe, all portraits do this when they do not clearly *look elsewhere*, as the reader may test by turning back to the portrait by Reynolds [29]. Here again we come up against the importance of the negative test. In our perceptions we are completely self-centred, and for good reason: we constantly scan the world for things which may concern us directly; we will assume that an eye looks at us, or a gun points at us, unless we have good evidence to the contrary. If the picture does not supply this contrary evidence and our projective tests fail to find it, we will succumb to the illusion. There are geo-metrical reasons why the eye, or the muzzle of the gun, will fail to respond to our movement test. A real gun when seen at an increasing angle would show less and less of the muzzle. The painted round of the muzzle threateningly fails to do so— the imagination supplies the rest. The same is true of the eyes, particularly if we are subject to the verbal suggestions of a guide who appeals to our Pygmalion wishes.

These are extreme cases between illusion and suggestion, but they help to explain, I believe, why we still experience some kind of illusion when we see a picture on a wall or in a book—from a point, that is, where the perspective should go wrong. Here as always we first read the picture for consistency, and this consis-tency, the interaction of clues, is not wholly upset by our changing viewpoint. The painting may cease to be consistent with the world around it, but it remains closely knit within its own system of references. The frame sets off what Leonardo called a microcosm, and if this microcosm contains no jarring refutations of our attempted reading, we will read it *as if* we saw it from where the artist stood. We have had occasion before to recall the experience at the cinema when we see the screen at an angle. We soon cease to notice the distortion, and when the actor speaks to the public, he also speaks to us. We can now perhaps explain this experience a little better: there is nothing in this one-way distortion which would contradict or eliminate a consistent reading.

Only in extreme cases, therefore, are the illusions of art illusions about our real environment. But they are illusions all the same, and as such they result in some

231. FANTIN-LATOUR: *Still Life*. 1866

unexpected and unintended consequences. We have seen in many instances that to interpret is to transform. We suspected, in the last chapter, that what is known as 'mental set' is a state of readiness for certain tests. We have observed how these anticipated projections flicker round the image, completing the process that has been started off. The most famous description of this continued activity is Berenson's account of what he calls 'ideated sensations' in front of paintings which stimulate his 'tactile sense' and change the tonus of his muscles. He is set, we may say, to test the illusion of solidity. Earlier literature liked to dwell on other states of readiness. The one which has developed into a commonplace of rhetorical description is the illusion that we seem to hear what is going on. 'It only lacks the voice' is the standard form of praise for a portrait in eulogistic poetry. This form of praise deserves a moment's attention. It implies that the image looks so lifelike that we get ready for an additional test; having exhausted the resources of vision, we turn to touch or hearing. Here, as so often, Dante has revivified an ancient commonplace and restored it to its original immediacy when he describes the effect of the reliefs in Purgatory, reminding the expiating proud souls of such examples of humility as David dancing before the ark of the covenant:

> *In front there was a throng of seven choirs*
> *Depicted, causing strife between two senses,*
> *One saying 'no', the other 'yes', they sing,*
> *So with the clouds of incense, that were rendered*
> *So that my vision and my sense of smell*
> *Came into conflict over 'yes' and 'no'.*

In Dante no less than in Berenson these ideated sensations are exalted as a triumph of art, and it is easy to see why. What is less often realized is the reason which makes them prove irksome to the artist. In a sense, Dante's description implies that reason. A conflict is set up which is far from pleasurable. What Dante could not know, because he had never seen really illusionist pictures, is that this conflict might extend into the sphere of vision itself. I believe we have here the reason why the perfection of illusion was also the hour of disillusionment.

XII

WE HAVE SEEN that we enjoy nothing more than the demand made on us to exercise our own 'imitative faculty', our imagination, and thus to share in the creative adventure of the artist. But if this pleasure is to be felt, the transformation must not be so easy as to be automatic. The further illusionist skill advanced, the more frequently we therefore hear of the difference between a work of art and the mere trick of deception. In 1823 the great neoclassical critic, Quatremère de Quincy, devoted a whole book to this important distinction. Our pleasure in illusion, he insisted, rests precisely in the mind's effort in bridging the difference between art and reality. This very pleasure is destroyed when the illusion is too complete. 'When the painter packs a vast expanse into a narrow space, when he leads me across the depths of the infinite on a flat surface, and makes the air circulate . . . I love to abandon myself to his illusions, but I want the frame to be there, I want to know that what I see is actually nothing but a canvas or a simple plane.'

These demands have been echoed ever since in French art criticism. They formed the basis of the aesthetics of Puvis de Chavannes and his Swiss follower Hodler and were given their most famous formulation in the injunction by Maurice Denis to the *Nabis*: 'Remember that a picture, before being a battle horse, a nude woman, or some anecdote, is essentially a plane surface covered with paint in a certain arrangement.'

It is a fact not very difficult to remember for those who are engaged in storing paintings or packing them into trunks. But is it possible to 'see' both the plane surface and the battle horse at the same time? If we have been right so far, the demand is for the impossible. To understand the battle horse is for a moment to disregard the plane surface. We cannot have it both ways.

I am well aware that at this point many a reader will tend to disagree, or will at least suspect me of quibbling with very subtle and unreal distinctions. If he has this suspicion, I would like him to produce a real illusionist image to test my assertion: I would ask him to revert to that experiment I urged him to make in the Introduction and look at his

232

image in the mirror. The fact that the area of the mirror that reflects the face is always exactly half the size of the face is so startling as to meet with scepticism on the part of most people who have looked into mirrors all their lives. Obviously, therefore, that is not what they see. They see the face in the distance behind the mirror surface, and thus they see it correspondingly larger. Now the mirror, because of the perfection of the illusion, may be a special case, an extreme, but one which it is useful to keep in mind, because it seems that the better the illusion, the more we see a picture as if it were a mirror. Psychologists have long recognized that our reaction to images also transforms what we 'see' in a much more radical way than we usually notice.

There is an uncanny black man who stalks through the pages of our psychology books to remind us of this basic fact [232]. As he walks into the depth, he appears to increase in size. Our experience of the size-distance relationship suggests to us that a man farther off must be very tall to present the identical aspect of an ordinary man nearby. We are right in this conclusion, and if the picture contains no contrary clue, we will therefore see a larger man, regardless of the fact that as a pattern on the plane surface the three images take up the same size. Most of us must have recourse to actual measurement to fight down the movements of anticipation and conviction that transform the image before our very eyes. It is said that children— less trained in the interpretation of paintings in terms of an imagined reality—are less subject to this curious illusion. That may be so. But then they see the picture still as a flat surface covered with a pictogram. We can all achieve this with more or less effort; we may even train ourselves to oscillate between the two readings, but I doubt whether we can hold them both.

This unexpected effect of illusion must be disconcerting to any artist who wishes to remain in control of the architecture of his canvas. To create a harmonious pattern in the plane, he must be able to rely on identical shapes remaining identical and steps in hue remaining independent of the beholder's imagination. In illusionist painting, neither is the case. The ambiguity of the canvas destroys the artist's control over his elements. I believe this is the real explanation for the revulsion against illusionism that set in at the very time when its means were perfected. They were found to be inartistic, they militated against visual harmonies.

At the beginning of this century, at the time when these issues were still in the balance, the German critic Konrad Lange wrote a long book on the aesthetics of illusion. He saw, correctly I believe, that all reading of images demands what Coleridge calls a 'willing suspension of disbelief'. To him all aesthetic pleasure in art was rooted in our oscillation between two series of associations, those of reality and those of art. The terminology and the examples of the book sound curiously old-fashioned, and its aesthetic bias is no longer ours. But his psychological insights enabled Lange to diagnose the tendencies of his time pretty shrewdly:

'Following the over-emphasis of the idea of nature for a time, we now have the stressing of the idea of art. Elements which impede illusion gain in interest. . . . A painting must not be natural but must aim at 'decorative' effects. . . . If previously painting strove passionately . . . after the illusion of depth, artists now strive with equal passion to emphasize the plane. . . . If previously geometric schematization was rejected as inartistic, artists now wallow in canonic proportions, the golden section, the equilateral triangle. . . . If previously glazes were used to give luminosity to colours and to increase the sense of distance, colours are now spread in a dull mat medium that is seen mainly as pigment. . . . If previously technical skill was overrated, it is now held in contempt. . . .'

XIII

ALL THIS was written before the last desperate revolt against illusion and the peep-show picture, the rise of cubism. Cubism, I believe, is the most radical attempt to stamp out ambiguity and to enforce one reading of the picture—that of a man-made construction, a coloured canvas. If illusion is due to the interaction of clues and the absence of contradictory evidence, the only way to fight its transforming influence is to make the clues contradict each other and to prevent a coherent image of reality from destroying the pattern in the plane. Unlike the Fantin-Latour, a still life by Braque [233] will marshal all the forces of perspective, texture, and shading, not to work in harmony, but to clash in virtual deadlock. Perhaps the most telling of these contradictions is Braque's treatment of light.

233. BRAQUE: *Still Life: The Table.* 1928

There are black patches on the apples where Fantin-Latour painted highlights. In thus inverting the relationships, the painter drives home the message that this is an exercise in painting, not in illusion.

Cubism has sometimes been explained as an extreme attempt in compensation for the shortcomings of one-eyed vision. The picture embodies clues of which we could become aware only through movement or touch. We are made to see the outline of the table even under and behind the objects, and it can be claimed that this corresponds to our actual experience in life, where we always remain aware of the continued existence of objects half hidden by overlap. I am inclined to suspect that the problems raised by Hildebrand, which so excited the world of art at the turn of the century, had their share in the creation of cubism and particularly in its success. The idea that the visible world of our experience is a construct made up of memories of movement, touch, and sight justified the experiment to do away with the peep-show convention and even to show various aspects of one object in the same painting.

But whatever the theories of the cubists may have been and whatever whiffs of conversations may have reached them from the discussions of the critics, they were, after all, artists and not psychologists. The main impulse behind cubism must have been an artistic one. It is hardly just to look at cubism mainly as a device to increase our awareness of space. If that was its aim, it should be pronounced a failure. Where it succeeds is in countering the transforming effects of an illusionist reading. It does so by the introduction of contrary clues which will

234. PICASSO: *Still Life.* 1918

resist all attempts to apply the test of consistency. Try as we may to see the guitar
or the jug suggested to us as a three-dimensional object and thereby to transform
it [233, 234], we will always come across a contradiction somewhere which compels
us to start afresh.

The result is exactly the opposite of the experience I described as the sorting
out of clues in Piranesi's *Carceri*. There we tried out various interpretations until
we found the one which fitted a possible world, however fantastic. It is a point of
cubism, I believe, that we are constantly teased and tempted into doing this but
that each hypothesis we assume will be knocked out by a contradiction elsewhere,
so that our interpretation can never come to rest and our 'imitative faculty' will be
kept busy as long as we join in the game.

Some of the effects exploited by the cubists were known to art for a long time,
though they remained in comparative obscurity as decorative devices. The mosaicists of the ancient world were fond of the *trompe l'œil* [16], but they also knew how
to tease the eye with ambiguities. We have seen that they knew ambiguous patterns
of the type discussed by the Gestalt psychologists [225]. But the mosaicists of
Antioch and Rome may have been as eager to counteract a purely spatial reading as
were the cubists two thousand years later. The pattern of mosaic [235] will suggest
a spatial reading in every detail but tends to resist the effort to complete it consistently so that we are driven round and round. Experimental psychology is

235. *Mosaic from Antioch*   236. *Mosaic from Rome*

familiar with this effect from the configuration called 'Thiéry's figure' [237]. It is practically impossible to keep this figure fixed because it presents contradictory clues. The result is that the frequent reversals force our attention to the plane.

Thiéry's figure, I believe, presents the quintessence of cubism. But this device of artful contrariety is supplemented by other methods designed to prevent a consistent reading. Again we may go back to classical mosaics to find the first prototypes of these visual teasers. The whirling pattern from a floor in Rome [236] will set us searching for a point of rest from which to start interpreting. We cannot find it, and so we have no means of telling which of the overlapping arcs is supposed to lie on top and which below. An analysis of cubist painting would reveal a great number of such devices to baffle our perception by the scrambling of clues. To see them in isolation, we had better return to the methods of commercial artists who have profited from these experiments. The most familiar is the divergence between outline and silhouette that results in the feeling that two images have been superimposed on each other. But the word 'superimposed' somehow begs the question. It is precisely the point of these devices that it is often impossible to tell which of the shapes is meant to lie at the top and which below [234].

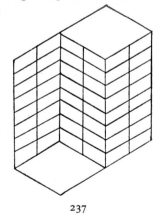

237

A more complex device results in the impression of transparent forms piled one upon the other but with the same ambiguity as to their sequence. The cubists discovered that we can read and interpret familiar shapes even across a complete change of colour and outline. In earlier art the figure had to stand out unambiguously against the ground. In many contemporary posters, even letters or symbols

238. *London Transport sign*

are no longer formed of positive shapes. Relationships are reversed and still remain readable [238]. These simple methods give the artist one extra dimension for the arrangement of forms without at the same time committing him or us to any one special reading. This type of ambiguity is cleverly exploited in a poster by McKnight Kauffer [239]. We can read it in any number of ways for we cannot tell which of the 'early birds' is actually leading, and though we may not be aware of it, his checkerboard shapes contribute to the impression of rapid flight, just as the Roman artist's whirl resulted in a feeling of movement. The device recalls Fraser's spiral [184], but the effect is the opposite. There our baffled perception finds refuge in an illusionary cohesion of forms. In cubism even coherent forms are made to play hide-and-seek in the elusive tangle of unresolved ambiguities.

XIV

IT IS IMPORTANT to distinguish these contradictions from non-figurative art. A painting such as Jacques Villon's *Abstraction*, from the Arensberg collection [240],

239. E. MCKNIGHT KAUFFER: *The Early Bird. Poster.* Detail. 1916

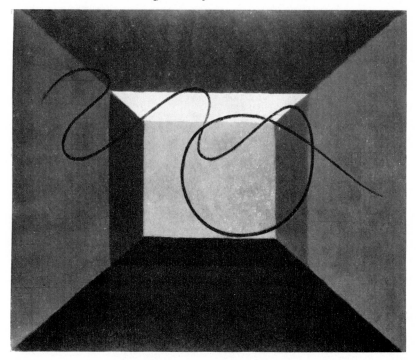

240. VILLON: *Abstraction*. 1932

can be read as a pyramid protruding towards us with a wavy line hovering in front, or as the interior of a box. There are various other readings, all of which fit, and still the picture lacks that tension which the cubists achieved by similar means. We now see why. There is no possible test by which we can decide which reading to adopt. The example reminds us of one of the intrinsic problems of abstract art that are too rarely discussed: its overt ambiguity. The function of representational clues in cubist paintings is not to inform us about guitars and apples, nor to stimulate our tactile sensations. It is to narrow down the range of possible interpretations till we are forced to accept the flat pattern with all its tensions.

Even non-objective art derives some of its meaning and effects from the habits and mental sets we acquired in learning to read representations. Indeed, we have seen that any three-dimensional shape on the canvas would be illegible or, which is the same, infinitely ambiguous without some assumptions of probabilities that we must bring to it and test against it.

The painter who wants to wean us from these assumptions has perhaps only one way open to him. He must try to prevent us from interpreting his marks on the canvas as representations of any kind by compelling us to switch over to that alternative which we have observed in the interpretation of drawings; he must make us read his brushmarks as traces of his gestures and actions [241]. This, I

241. JACKSON POLLOCK: *Number 12.* 1952

take it, is what the 'action painter' aims at. He wants to achieve an identification of the beholder with his Platonic frenzy of creation, or rather with his creation of a Platonic frenzy. It is quite consistent that these painters must counteract all semblance of familiar objects or even of patterns in space. But few of them appear to realize that they can drive into the desired identification only those who know how to apply the various traditional consistency tests and thereby discover the absence of any meaning except the highly ambiguous meaning of traces. If this game has a function in our society, it may be that it helps us to 'humanize' the intricate and ugly shapes with which industrial civilization surrounds us. We even learn to see twisted wires or complex machinery as the product of human action. We are trained in a new visual classification. The deserts of city and factory are turned into tanglewoods. Making results in matching.

Part Four

INVENTION AND DISCOVERY

IX

The Analysis of Vision in Art

> The more closely the artist's hieroglyphs approximate the sense impressions from nature—and all art is but hieroglyphics—the more imaginative effort was needed to invent them.
>
> MAX LIEBERMANN, *Die Phantasie in der Malerei*

I

IN OUR study of the language of art we have come increasingly to stress one fact—the power of interpretation. We saw it at work in the last three chapters, which probed the beholder's share in the readings of images, his capacity, that is, to collaborate with the artist and to transform a piece of coloured canvas into a likeness of the visible world. We had seen it in earlier chapters, where it was the artist who interpreted the world in terms of the schemata he made and knew.

I believe it is only by considering these psychological aspects of image making and image reading that we may come closer to an understanding of the central problem of the history of art that I set out in the Introduction—the problem, that is, why representation should have a history; why it should have taken mankind so long to arrive at a plausible rendering of visual effects that create the illusion of life-likeness; and why artists such as John Constable, who strove to be true to his vision, still had to admit that no art is ever free of convention or of what Constable called 'manner'. It is these conventions, we remember, which enable the art historian to date a work such as Constable's *Wivenhoe Park* [5] despite its apparent truthfulness; it is their totality which makes up what we call 'style' in painting.

In returning to this problem, we cannot do better than to consider a passage from Roger Fry's *Reflections on British Painting* which is concerned with Constable's place in history.

'From one point of view the whole history of art may be summed up as the history of the gradual discovery of appearances. Primitive art starts, like that of children, with symbols of concepts. In a child's drawing of a face a circle symbolizes the mask, two dots the eyes, and two lines the nose and mouth. Gradually the symbolism approximates more and more to actual appearance, but the conceptual habits, necessary to life, make it very difficult, even for artists, to discover what things look like to an unbiassed eye. Indeed, it has taken from Neolithic times till the nineteenth century to perfect this discovery. European art from the time of Giotto progressed more or less continuously in this direction, in which the discovery of linear perspective marks an important stage, whilst the full exploration of atmospheric colour and colour perspective had to await the work of the French Impressionists. In that age-long process Constable occupies an important place.'

Roger Fry's explanation of the sway of conventions in art is based on the old distinction between 'seeing' and 'knowing' which can be traced back to classical antiquity. It is a distinction which would not have retained its popularity with artists, critics, and teachers had it not proved extremely handy to all those who want to discuss the problems of representation and the mistakes beginners are likely to make. In this terminology the image which relies on 'knowledge' only is 'purely conceptual', and the history of art, as we have seen, becomes the history of the expulsion of this intruder.

The reader who has arrived at this chapter along the devious road we have taken will be prepared for the objection that the truth can hardly be as simple as that. The equation of the way things are represented with the way things are 'seen' is surely misleading. No child sees its mother in terms of those crude schemata it draws. But there are other flaws in this tidy story. The one most frequently discussed is the awkward fact that prehistoric artists knew how to render animals very convincingly—at least to us who are rarely well acquainted with bison. But we have seen that in all styles the artist has to rely on a vocabulary of forms and that it is the knowledge of this vocabulary rather than a knowledge of things that distinguishes the skilled from the unskilled artist. This need for such schemata was demonstrated in the 'pathology of portrayal' in our Chapter II. What accounts for the ease or difficulty in rendering a given building or landscape is not so much the intrusion of knowledge as the lack of schemata.

But this criticism should not obscure the value of the traditional distinction, for however we interpret the facts, it remains true that all representations can be somehow arranged along a scale which extends from the schematic to the impressionist. What is more, it remains important that there exists a natural pull toward the schematic which artists such as Giotto or Constable succeeded in overcoming. Because of this gravitation toward the schematic or 'conceptual', we have a right to speak of 'primitive' modes of representation, modes, that is, which assert themselves unless they are deliberately counteracted.

It is easy to show that these modes have their permanent and roughly predictable features which distinguish them from Constable's approach. I have asked a child of eleven to copy a reproduction of Constable's *Wivenhoe Park* [244]. As expected, the child translated the picture into a simpler language of pictorial symbols. The copy is really a tidy enumeration of the principal items of the picture, particularly those which would interest a child—the cows, the trees, the swans

242. SASSETTA: *The Meeting of St. Anthony and St. Paul.* About 1445

243. DUCCIO: *The Calling of the Apostles Peter and Andrew.* 1308–1311

on the lake, the fence, the house behind the lake. What has been missed, or much underrated, are the modifications which these classes of things undergo when seen from different angles or in different light. The house, therefore, is much larger than in Constable's picture, and the swans are gigantic. The boat and the bridge are seen from above in that 'conceptual' maplike mode which brings out the characteristic features. The trees all have their trunks, the fence runs parallel to the edge and then turns back in an uneasy compromise between a scale model of a fence and a perspective rendering. Each object has its own and proper colour, the lake is dark blue, the lawn green, and such modifications as there are are due to impatience and accident rather than intention.

If we leave out all considerations of manual skill and, needless to say, of artistic merit, our little experiment tends indeed to confirm Roger Fry's placing of Constable at the end of a long evolution that led away from conceptual modes. It is undoubtedly true, for instance, that the child's method of drawing trees resembles more closely the methods of Sassetta [242], which she did not know than those of Constable, whose picture she had before her eyes. In the same way, her boat resembles the boat in Duccio's Biblical narrative [243] more closely than the one she was asked to copy. The question is only how we should interpret this similarity. One thing we can be sure of: neither Duccio nor Sassetta had a childish, undeveloped mentality. Perhaps we come closer to an explanation if we remember the dominance of making over matching: The medieval artist, like the child, relies on the minimum schema needed to 'make' a house, a tree, a boat that can function in the narrative. When we say these schemata look somewhat like toy trees or toy boats, we are presumably closer to an explanation of the essentials of 'primitive'

244. A child's copy after Constable's 'Wivenhoe Park'

art. The child's rendering of Wivenhoe Park could easily be turned into a 'cutout' game and propped up to make a park on the nursery floor. Constable's picture would resist this translation, because here the artist made allowance for the transformations which shapes and colours undergo through the accident of the position

245. TURNER: *Approach to Venice*. About 1843

from which he viewed the scene. Taking their real shape for granted, he modified them even at the risk of sacrificing functional clarity in order to match the here and now of their appearance at a given moment.

But in giving us more information about that moment of time, Constable did in fact have to take other things for granted. He had to rely on our reading capacity to a much larger degree than Duccio did. From Duccio's painting we could infer some essential structures of wooden boats even if other information were lost. From Constable's, hardly. And when we come to the paintings of Constable's great rival Turner [245], the structure of objects is often quite swallowed up by the modifications of the moment—mist, light, and dazzle. Matching wins over making. There is some justification in the idea that he suppressed what he knew of the world and concentrated only on what he saw.

II

IT WAS, in fact, in these terms that Turner's great friend and champion John Ruskin posed the problem of painting, and it was this theory that made Roger Fry hail impressionism as the final discovery of appearances. To Ruskin, as to Roger Fry, it is our knowledge of the visible world that lies at the root of all the difficulties of art. If we could only manage to forget it all, the problem of painting would become easy—the problem, that is, of rendering a three-dimensional world on a flat canvas. In reality, Ruskin thought, we do not even see the third dimension. What we really see is only a medley of coloured patches such as Turner paints.

Ruskin's presentation of this theory, written in 1856, anticipates the doctrine of the impressionists:

'The perception of solid Form is entirely a matter of experience. We *see* nothing but flat colours; and it is only by a series of experiments that we find out that a stain of black or grey indicates the dark side of a solid substance, or that a feint hue indicates that the object in which it appears is far away. The whole technical power of painting depends on our recovery of what may be called the *innocence of the eye;* that is to say, of a sort of childish perception of these flat stains of colour, merely as such, without consciousness of what they signify—as a blind man would see them if suddenly gifted with sight.

'For instance: when grass is lighted strongly by the sun in certain directions, it is turned from green into a peculiar and somewhat dusty-looking yellow. If we had been born blind, and were suddenly endowed with sight on a piece of grass thus lighted in some parts by the sun, it would appear to us that part of the grass was green, and part a dusty yellow (very nearly of the colour of primroses): and if there were primroses near, we should think that the sunlighted grass was another

mass of plants of the same sulphur-yellow colour. We should try to gather some
of them, and then find that the colour went away from the grass when we stood
between it and the sun, but not from the primroses; and by a series of experiments
we should find out that the sun was really the cause of the colour in the one,—not
in the other. We go through such processes of experiment unconsciously in childhood; and having come to conclusions touching the signification of certain colours,
we always suppose that we *see* what we only know, and have hardly any consciousness of the real aspect of the signs we have learned to interpret. Very few people
have any idea that sunlighted grass is yellow. . . .'

could be further generalised

We remember that the ideas about perception on which Ruskin built with such
confidence, and artistically with such success, had been propounded more than a
century earlier by Bishop Berkeley in his *New Theory of Vision* in which a long
tradition had come to fruition: The world as we see it is a construct, slowly built
up by every one of us in years of experimentation. Our eyes merely undergo stimu-
lations on the retina which result in so-called 'sensations of colour'. It is our mind
that weaves these sensations into perceptions, the elements of our conscious picture
of the world that is grounded on experience, on knowledge.

Given this theory, which was accepted by nearly all nineteenth-century psychologists and which still has its place in handbooks, Ruskin's conclusions appear to be
unimpeachable. Painting is concerned with light and colour only, as they are
imaged on our retina. To reproduce this image correctly, therefore, the painter
must clear his mind of all he knows about the object he sees, wipe the slate clean,
and make nature write her own story—as Cézanne said of Monet: '*Monet n'est
qu'un oeil—mais quel oeil !*'

III

BUT THOUGH we can accept much of Berkeley's account, we must doubt all the
more whether such an achievement of innocent passivity is at all possible to the
human mind. Whenever we receive a visual impression, we react by docketing it,
filing it, grouping it in one way or another, even if the impression is only that of
an inkblot or a fingerprint. Roger Fry and the impressionists talked of the difficulty
of finding out what things looked like to an unbiassed eye because of what they
called the 'conceptual habits' necessary to life. But if these habits are necessary
to life, the postulate of an unbiassed eye demands the impossible. It is the business
of the living organism to organize, for where there is life there is not only hope,
as the proverb says, but also fears, guesses, expectations which sort and model the
incoming messages, testing and transforming and testing again. The innocent eye
is a myth. That blind man of Ruskin's who suddenly gains sight does not see the
world as a painting by Turner or Monet—even Berkeley knew that he could only

experience a smarting chaos which he has to learn to sort out in an arduous apprenticeship. Indeed, some of these unfortunates give up and never learn it at all. For
seeing is never just registering. It is the reaction of the whole organism to the
patterns of light that stimulate the back of our eyes; in fact, the retina itself has
recently been described by J. J. Gibson as an organ that does not react to individual
stimuli of light, such as were postulated by Berkeley, but to their relationship, or
gradients. We have seen that even newly hatched chickens classify their impressions
according to relationships. The whole distinction between sensation and perception,
plausible as it was, had to be given up in the face of the evidence from experiments
with human beings and animals. Nobody has ever seen a visual sensation, not even
the impressionists, however ingenuously they stalked their prey.

We seem to have arrived at an impasse. On the one hand, Roger Fry's and
Ruskin's accounts of painting do somehow correspond with the facts. Representation really does seem to advance through the suppression of conceptual knowledge. On the other, no such suppression appears to be possible. It is an impasse
which has led to a certain amount of confusion in writing on art. The easiest way
out is to deny the traditional reading of the historical facts altogether. If there is
no unbiassed eye, Roger Fry's account of the discovery of what things look like to
such an unbiassed eye must be false. The reaction against impressionism which we
witnessed in the twentieth century increased the appeal of such a conclusion. Here
was another convenient stick with which to beat the Philistine who wanted paintings to look like nature. The demand was nonsense. If all seeing is interpreting, all
modes of interpretation could be argued to be equally valid.

I have myself in these pages often stressed the conventional element in many
modes of representation. But it is for this very reason that I cannot accept this easy
way out of the impasse. For obviously it is also nonsense. Granted, as I have tried
to show in the first chapter, that Constable's painting of Wivenhoe Park is not a
mere transcript of nature but a transposition of light into paint, it still remains
true that it is a closer rendering of the motif than is that of the child. I have also
attempted to define a little more explicitly what may be meant by such a statement.
It means, I suspect, that we can, and almost must, interpret Constable's paintings
in terms of a possible visible world; if we accept the truth of the label that the
painting represents Wivenhoe Park, we will also be confident that this interpretation will tell us a good many facts about that country-seat in 1816 which we would
have gathered if we had stood by Constable's side. Of course, both he and we
would have seen much more than can be translated into the cryptograms of paint,
but to those who can read the code, it would at least give no false information.
This formulation, I know, may sound chilling and pedantic, but it has one advantage. It eliminates the 'image on Constable's retina' and, indeed, the whole idea of
appearances that has proved such a will-o'-the-wisp to aesthetics.

IV

WHEN A DISCUSSION has become tangled, it is always useful to trace one's steps back to its origins and see where the misunderstanding occurred. The theoretical origins of pictorial illusionism are to be found among the Renaissance champions of perspective. It was Alberti who first suggested the idea of considering a painting as a window through which we look at the visible world. It was Leonardo da Vinci who gave substance to this idea by suggesting that 'perspective is nothing else than seeing a place behind a pane of glass, quite transparent, on the surface of which the objects behind the glass are to be drawn'.

Accepting these conditions, it is of course quite easy to agree that if we looked at Wivenhoe Park through such a window from roughly where Constable stood, the tracing would resemble his painting more than it would resemble the child's copy. It is only when the claim is made that the view we trace on the window is precisely what we see 'out there' in the park that we must be careful before we accept this harmless-looking step. The reader who has followed my advice and traced his face on the mirror surface will be prepared for surprises here. If he steps to the nearest window and repeats Leonardo's experiment, he will have more to puzzle over. The first thing he will discover—unless he has had training in art—will be that the house in the distance makes a startlingly tiny image on the pane. We all know that distant objects 'look small', but we are rarely prepared for the real relationship of objects projected onto a plane. By forcing us to attend only to these relative sizes within our field of vision, the window experiment breaks down the so-called 'constancies' that make for a stable world.
We have met with these constancies before, when we hailed them as friends of art. The real extent of illumination, we saw, could never be rendered in conventional media such as oil painting unless we had this inbuilt mechanism that minimizes these changes. Without such a stabilizer, we would see a man who approaches us double in size after a few steps, and when he extends his right hand in greeting, it would loom enormously in our field of vision. We know how unexpected photographs which

246. Photo by G. Tenney, "Life", 1958

register these facts of perspective can look [246]. Yet the window or the mirror will confirm them. It is understandable that in the flush of these discoveries, artists thought that now at last they had a means of demonstrating what we 'really see' as distinct from what we 'know to be there'. The flat image on the window was identified—as Ruskin implies—with the patchwork of flat colour that is all we really register through our 'innocent' eyes. But a moment's reflection (or several moments) will show that this identification is quite mistaken. For while it is true that the distant house projects as a small patch on the window, it is demonstrably untrue that I therefore 'see it' as a small patch. The idea of a patch implies a given size and location, and the innocent eye, almost by definition, cannot perceive size. Let us return to our window to clarify this vital point. Clearly the size which the distant house will assume on the window-pane will depend not only on its distance from me but also on my distance from the pane. And while the view through the window will remain nearly the same while I move, its projection on the window will vary dramatically, shrinking as I approach and growing as I step back. (If the reader thinks it must be the other way round, he must think again!) Now which of these different projections shows us what we 'really see'? The answer is, none of them. We really see through the window into the distance. We really see a house and not a patch unless we are mistaken in our guess, and what we take to be a house in the distance is in fact a patch on the window. To 'see' means to guess at something 'out there', what Ames called the 'thereness-thatness experience'. The pure patch without extension and location can certainly not be painted; I doubt whether it can be thought of.

All thinking is sorting, classifying. All perceiving relates to expectations and therefore to comparisons. When we say that from the air houses appear like toys to us, or human beings like ants, we mean, I suggest, that we are startled by the unfamiliar sight of a house that compares to the familiar sight of a toy on the nursery floor. We feel that but for our knowledge we might have been deceived and have almost mistaken the one for the other. Our guesses and methods of testing them have become somewhat unsettled, and we try to describe the experience by indicating possibilities which flitted through our minds. But, to repeat, there is no 'objective' sense in which a human being can look 'the size of an ant' simply because an ant crawling on our pillow will look gigantic in comparison with a man in the distance. In Professor E. G. Boring's words, 'Phenomenal size, like physical size is relative and has no meaning except as a relation between objects.'

V

IF THIS is true—and it can hardly be gainsaid—the problem of illusionist art is not that of forgetting what we know about the world. It is rather that of inventing comparisons which work; in our instance, crudely speaking, of finding the patch on the window that might be mistaken for a house in the distance when viewed from a given spot. Once the problem is put in this roundabout way, the difficulty of selecting this patch looks much less surprising. In fact it has been shown that, taken in isolation, it is a task beyond even the capacity of the trained painter. We must look at this demonstration because it has been used in this very debate on whether the traditional methods of illusionist art reproduce the world as we see it. It was Sir Herbert Read, whose criticism of perspective we have encountered before, who drew attention in his book *Art Now* to a fascinating experiment by Professor Thouless of Cambridge that was designed to show we do not really see things as their projection would suggest. The experiment once more concerns the constancy of shape. It shows that when we look sideways at a penny or a dinner plate we tend to underrate the degree to which it is foreshortened.

The fact as such was known to the medieval students of optics, who already used it as an argument against the geometry of visual rays. But Thouless was the first to devise a method by which this degree of under-estimation could be measured. Fixing a viewing point at which the round objects are to be seen, he asked his subjects to select from a graded series of ovals the one which corresponded most nearly to what they saw. Comparing this choice with the mathematical results of perspective, he found that even painters tend to see the penny as somewhat rounder than they can have seen it from where they stood. Thouless has termed this phenomenon 'regression towards the real object'. It is a more sophisticated, because measurable, version of the old idea we found in Ruskin and Roger Fry, the idea that knowledge will influence the way we see things. The stimulus patterns on the retina are not alone in determining our picture of the visual world. Its messages are modified by what we know about the 'real' shape of objects.

The results of Professor Thouless' experiment are not in doubt, but their interpretation is open to question. In speaking of the 'real' object he has somewhat prejudged the issue.

A penny is not more real when seen from above than when looked upon sideways. But the frontal view happens to be the one which gives us most information. It is this aspect which we call the 'characteristic shape' of the object, the one (or sometimes two) which exhibits most of those distinctive features by which we classify and name the things of our world. It is on these distinctive features, as we have seen, that primitive art will concentrate, not because it draws on knowledge rather than sight, but because it insists on clear classification.

Now, this same insistence on distinctive features also influences our reactions in real life whenever we are confronted with an uncertainty. It is therefore inexact to speak of our knowledge which influences our perception of the oblique penny. Rather is it our search for knowledge, our effort after meaning, to use Bartlett's term. In the terminology of this book, we would have to speak of expectations, guesses, hypotheses which influence our experience. We have frequently seen that these expectations can become so strong that our experience runs ahead of the stimulus situation. Perception, in other words, is a process in which the next phase of what will appear when we test our interpretation is all but anticipated. To experience the sight of a penny or dinner plate and to read it as such is to experience the anticipation that the shape will become rounder in a predictable way if we crane our neck a little and look at it from higher up.

But is it different with the so-called 'constancy of size'? We have seen that the stimulus pattern of the house or the penny alone can suggest no size because it might stand for an infinite number of objects 'out there'. If we still assign a size in our mind to images of pennies or houses this is due to the same habit, as Professor Osgood has suggested, of thinking of things in some standard situation in which we usually inspect them. We compare the penny in the hand with the house across the road. It is this imaginary standard distance which will influence the scale at which a child draws such objects and which will also determine our descriptions of ants and men. The notorious question whether the moon looks as large as a sixpence or a half-crown, to which I have alluded before, may not allow of a clear-cut answer, but most of us would protest if anyone suggested that it looks like a pinhead or an ocean steamer, easy though it would be to devise a situation where these statements would be true.

VI

BUT strangely enough these vagaries of our perceptive expectations and the influence they have on our picture of the world do not invalidate the windowpane experiment. For it is just the point that once these various patches or tracings are placed in position they will produce the illusion that they are not here but there, not flat but round, not small but large. If we can indeed build up a peep-show in which Fantin-Latour's *Still Life* [231] looks indistinguishable from a real breakfast table, it follows that the Thouless experiment on both the real and the painted plate or cup would result in the same errors of estimate. In fact, to say that we see Fantin-Latour's cup 'in the round' means probably no more than that it induces those expectations that transform the image. The child's copy of Constable's *Wivenhoe Park* suggests a similar interpretation, and since Constable spoke of his own paintings as scientific experiments, it may be permissible to perform yet another experiment with his portrayal of the visible world. I have slightly rearranged his world by shifting the house from the background to the lawn in the right-hand corner and by repeating the last section of the fence once more in front of the first section on the left [247]. The effect is surprising, more surprising perhaps than the opposite illusion of the black man's walking into the background [232] considered in the last chapter. The house looks diminutive, so much so that

247. *Montage of Constable's 'Wivenhoe Park'*

we can hardly believe its size is unchanged. But if we superimpose a regular grid on the painting [248], we become aware of those objective relationships within the picture that our reading ignores. This is indeed what a painter would do if he wanted to make a facsimile of Constable's painting in order to overcome the pull towards interpretation which is exemplified in the child's copy [244].

The grid with its easily perceived units of measurement allows him to halt that movement of interpretation that goes with the testing and understanding of forms. Instead of a picture of a house, he will see squares filled with white and grey paint.

248

VII

BUT IS NOT THIS precisely what Ruskin wants the artist to do in front of his motif? To empty the prospect of meaning in order to see it for what it is? In a sense it is. But this process can never be one of innocence and passivity. Ruskin's description itself indicates that the painter can achieve the feat of looking at the visible world while ignoring its meaning only by expelling one interpretation through another. His artist introduces an alternative meaning which is so obvious that it easily eludes description. He sees the meadow, not like an innocent child in terms of light and shade, but like a painter in terms of pigments, green and sulphur yellow.

As a bald statement this amendment may sound little better than a quibble. Of course the painter must interpret nature in terms of paint, for how else could he get it on the canvas? But when we say that he must also learn to see it in terms of paint, this may have some interesting consequences that may help us to see the story of visual discoveries in a fresh light.

Here, I think, I can appeal to an experience most of us have had. We go to a picture gallery, and when we leave it after some time, the familiar scene outside, the road and the bustle, often look transformed and transfigured. Having seen so many pictures in terms of the world, we can now switch over and see the world in terms of pictures. For a brief moment, that is, we look at things a little with a painter's eye, or, more technically speaking, with a painter's mental set, scanning the motif to look for those aspects he can build up in paint on his canvas.

Those who teach the art student that he must train this faculty are certainly right. They are also right when they insist that he must find means of battling down his knowledge of the familiar meaning of things and look only at shapes and tones projected onto an imaginary plane. We have seen that he can break down the constancies only if he ceases to attend to the meanings of things. The need for the artist to become detached, to introduce an entirely different set of meanings, could scarcely be more drastically illustrated than in Dürer's woodcut of the painter and his frame [249]. But even Alain's imaginary Egyptians [1] who measure the model against the brush in the outstretched hand will succeed in this.

If these are somewhat mechanical devices, all artists know of more psychological methods to increase their awareness of pure shapes and relationships—for instance, half closing the eye, or switching attention from the meaningful objects to the shapes they leave empty against the background, a device which Sickert, for instance, taught his students. These negative shapes, which have no meaning in terms of things, form an admirable check for the correction of the first scheme.

Cézanne's much-quoted advice to Bernard to look at nature in terms of simple

249. DÜRER: *Woodcut*. About 1527

shapes of known property, that is, in terms of cylinders, cones, and spheres, aims at exactly the same type of reclassification. It surely has nothing to do with cubism but rather with the type of art teaching in French schools which was current at the time Cézanne was young and which he wished to pass on to his young admirer.

Art teaching, then, like that of most painters' manuals, still proceeds on the basis of what may be called a 'common-sense version' of traditional Western philosophy. The world consists of substances which have sensory qualities of varying permanence. Beech leaves 'are' small, lozenge-shaped, and bright green, distant mountains 'look' blue. The artist's business is simply to analyse appearances down into these qualities and to match those he can in his medium.

There is no essential difference, in this view, between the artist who paints a landscape and another who copies a picture. Both are concerned with piecemeal matching, much as a mosaicist would be who works from a cartoon and selects one stone after another that comes as close as possible to the corresponding hue of his prototype, arranging them in the shapes he sees in front of him.

VIII

NOW the facsimile, like the photograph, has mainly served the aestheticians as a foil to stress the creative element necessary to art. One may admit that the creation of indistinguishable duplicates is of greater interest to the forgers of banknotes than the artists, but we have seen, I hope, that psychologically the making of any likeness is far from being a trivial achievement. In a previous chapter we have discussed the approach by the copyist through schema and correction, his choice of a vocabulary that is subsequently adjusted to correspond to his prototype. We may now ask why it is that such schemata are needed if all the artist has to do is to match what he sees, area by area? The answer is, I believe, that there are greater obstacles in the way of such a mosaic approach than merely the difficulty of forgetting our knowledge of meanings. Even pure shapes and patterns have a way of

transforming themselves
before our very eyes. It
almost looks as if the eye
knew of meanings of
which the mind knows
nothing. The juxtaposi-
tion of shapes and colours

250

plays us the most unexpected tricks, the tricks
known as 'optical illusions'.

Parallel lines when crossed look as if they
were bent; an upright line looks longer than
the same line tilted [250]. These illusions, of
which the psychology books are full, used to be considered mere freaks, slight flaws
in our perceptive apparatus. Today they are looked upon with a little more
respect. We have come to see that they do not represent exceptions but the
rule. 'Strictly speaking,' writes Professor Edwin Boring, 'the concept of illusion has
no place in psychology because no experience actually copies reality.' Those who
want to produce such copies, therefore, cannot rely on their visual experience alone.

The most striking instance of this source of difficulty is the so-called 'spreading
effect' [251]. Only two colours are used, one tone of red and one of blue. If they
look different in combination with different patterns of black and white, this is
due to their mutual influence, which no one claims to understand completely: we
obviously do not see the ground in isolation; we see the whole pattern as one and
attribute its total brightness or darkness to its elements. There is only one way of
convincing ourselves that it is only the proximity of white which makes for the
impression of a brighter background while the proximity of black casts a shadow
over its surroundings. We must follow with the eye the stripes of colour that lead
from the gloomy part to the bright region. There is no break.

This example seems to me specially instructive because it shows both the power
of artificial isolation and comparison and also its limits. By means of such juxtaposition we can rationally classify the colour as a certain red of known quality. But
even this correct classification will not convince us that the sensory qualities of the
two areas are identical. Nor are they. We really see a bright red here, a dark red
there. If such areas occurred in a motif we had to paint, all we could do would be
first to take a bright red for the bright strip and then tone it down after we had
discovered the effect of the superimposed colour. We could only find it, that is, by
trial and error guided by long experience in the ways of paint.

Nobody knew this better than Ruskin, the propagator of the theory of the
innocent eye. Indeed I know of no clearer analysis of what is here involved in the
painter's art than another paragraph from Ruskin's little manual.

251. The 'spreading effect'

'While form is absolute, so that you can say at the moment you draw any line that it is either right or wrong, colour is wholly *relative*. Every hue throughout your work is altered by every touch that you add in other places; so that what was warm a minute ago, becomes cold when you have put a hotter colour in another place, and what was in harmony when you left it, becomes discordant as you set other colours beside it; so that every touch must be laid, not with a view to its effect at the time, but with a view to its effect in futurity, the result upon it of all that is afterwards to be done being previously considered. You may easily understand that, this being so, nothing but the devotion of life, and great genius besides, can make a colourist.'

In stressing this need for the imitator of nature to hold the effect of all elements upon each other simultaneously in his mind, Ruskin has, without realizing it, amended his own theory of childlike vision. For this mental act rests on knowledge of how colours will affect each other. In fact, it demands a willingness to use a pigment which in isolation still looks unlike the area to be matched in order that it may look like it in the end.

This power, I believe, is not only independent of the eye, or the image on the retina, it has also very little to do with visual memory. There are psychological types, we are told, who can hold a visual impression for quite some time after it has vanished from their eyes. They keep something like a colour photograph in their minds, even when closing their eyes. Obviously such a faculty may be useful for a painter who wants to memorize a scene and who can devote more time to painting than to looking. But the claims that have been made for this so-called 'eidetic faculty' in relation to art seem to me as unfounded as are those for the innocent eye. For we have seen that even the humble task of copying nature facsimilewise presents difficulties of a much higher order than those of remembering. Whether the artist has his prototype in front of him or 'in his mind' can make little difference here. That power of holding on to an image that Ruskin describes so admirably is not the power of the eidetic; it is that faculty of keeping a large number of relationships present in one's mind that distinguishes all mental achievement, be it that of the chess player, the composer, or the great artist.

We need not even climb these heights to get a glimpse of the psychological problem. Every woman knows that you can no more predict the effect of forms and colours on one another without experimenting than you can know the exact effect of ingredients in a dish without tasting. Both are 'global' impressions that result from the interaction of innumerable stimuli. Even the most clothes-conscious woman would not, therefore, claim she can predict how a hat will suit her without having tried it on in front of a mirror, for any line or tone may change the *Gestalt* of her physiognomy in the most unexpected way.

It is true that in this act of choice the lady of fashion does not aim at modelling her image after any prototype, except, perhaps, the ideals of fashion created for the purpose of imitation and emulation. But any maker of facsimiles has a story to tell of the unexpected behaviour of his elements when placed in juxtaposition. It turns out, in fact, that we can speak of a real facsimile only when the copy is of the same size as the original. For size affects tone, as is also known to all women who have learned to make allowance for this change when selecting material from a book of small samples. Since the same colour will look different when the size of the area changes, a facsimile reduced in scale will look false when all colours are identical with the original. One may well doubt whether this handicap can ever be overcome by those who make colour reproductions of paintings for books. All the technician can do is to grope his way by trial and error toward relationships that he feels to be equivalent to those of the original. There are no scientific standards or measurements to which he can appeal in this delicate adjustment.

There is one type of scientific illustration in which this effect of scale on impression is acknowledged officially, as it were. Geographers who draw sections of mountain ranges will exaggerate the relation of height to width according to a stated proportion. They have found that a true rendering of vertical relationship looks false. Our mind refuses to accept the fact that the distance of 29,000 feet to which Mount Everest soars from sea level is no more than the distance of just over five miles which a car traverses in a matter of minutes.

IX

HERE IS ONE of the reasons why a comparison between Cézanne's *Mont Ste.-Victoire* and photographs of the mountain [38, 39] can be somewhat misleading if it is used for aesthetic analysis. The fact, for instance, that Cézanne exaggerated the steepness of the silhouette is trivial. The question whether the photograph in this respect looks more 'like' the mountain or less so would have to be reformulated rather carefully to make sense. Some photographs, like some paintings, do look convincing; others do not. Their scale, the proximity of the mountain to the edge, even their mounting or frame may influence the general impression in the most unpredictable way. The same is true of topographical views, but these questions are still far removed from the problems which an artist of Cézanne's stature wrestles with.

These problems came to the fore when complete fidelity to visual experience had become both a moral and an aesthetic imperative. For the impressionists, the contradictions of this demand were still hidden in the coloured haze of their flickering canvases. But Cézanne's uncompromising honesty and his interest in clarity and structure made it manifest that if you were really faithful to your vision in every detail the equation would not work out: the elements will not fuse in the end into a convincing whole. This spelled the end of the mosaic theory of representation. New principles of organization had to be groped for. But Cézanne, if anyone, knew that you cannot plan these organizations because you cannot predict the mutual effect of all the elements of a picture. Paradoxically, the agonies and triumphs of his struggle have become somewhat obscured for us by the very pleasure which even his failures give us; but there is no doubt that many canvases he left unfinished were to him experiments that had not come off, trial pieces which made him retrace his steps and start again on the road into the unknown that would enable him to 'redo Poussin from Nature' through exploring alternative methods for suggesting a solid organized world.

The cubists took the opposite path. They kicked aside the whole tradition of faithful vision and tried to start again from the 'real object' which they squashed against the picture plane. One can enjoy the resulting confusion of telescoped images as a commentary on the unresolved complexities of vision without accepting the claim that they represent reality more really than a picture based on projective geometry.

We have seen before that science is always a double-edged weapon to defend or attack any artistic procedure. It can probe a little into the mysteries of vision; it cannot tell the artist what conclusions to draw from his findings. And so the observable fact that looking at the elements in our field of vision will result in a picture which will not create an illusion can be adduced to prove that traditional methods are false, or conversely, that they are indispensable.

We have no right to assume that the upholders of the academic tradition were ignorant of this dilemma. It is formulated quite explicitly in the charter of academic theory, *Idée de la perfection de la peinture* by Roland Fréart de Chambray, one of the patrons of Poussin, published in Le Mans in 1662:

'Whenever the painter claims that he imitates things as he sees them he is sure to see them wrongly. He will represent them according to his faulty imagination and produce a bad painting. Before he takes up his pencil or brush he must therefore adjust his eye to reasoning according to the principles of art which teach how to see things not only as they are in themselves but also how they should be represented. For it would often be a grave mistake to paint them exactly as the eye sees them, however much this may look like a paradox.'

It is this paradox, I believe, which accounts for the fact that illusionist art grew out of a long tradition and that it collapsed as soon as the value of this tradition was questioned by those who relied on the innocent eye.

Some of the historical facts supporting this contention have been discussed in preceding chapters. All representations are grounded on schemata which the artist learns to use. But we may now see more clearly why he is so dependent on tradition. The injunction to 'copy appearances' is really meaningless unless the artist is first given something which is to be made like something else. Without making there can be no matching. Without some example of relationships and the way visual elements interact, he could never start on the difficult path of adjusting the 'patch' of 'sulphur yellow' till it might not only be taken for primroses (to remain with Ruskin's example) but might also suggest, in the right juxtaposition with green, a sunlit lawn. In fact, the achievement of the innocent eye, what modern authorities call 'stimulus concentration', turned out to be not only psychologically difficult but logically impossible. The stimulus, as we know, is of infinite ambiguity, and ambiguity as such, to return to the theme song of this book, cannot be seen—it can only be inferred by trying different readings that fit the same configuration. I believe, indeed, that the artist's gift is of this order. He is the man who has learned to look critically, to probe his perceptions by trying alternative interpretations both in play and in earnest. Long before painting achieved the means of illusion, man was aware of ambiguities in the visual field and had learned to describe them in language. Similes, metaphors, the stuff of poetry no less than of myth, testify to the powers of the creative mind to create and dissolve new classifications. It is the unpractical man, the dreamer whose response may be less rigid and less sure than that of his more efficient fellow, who taught us the possibility of seeing a rock as a bull and perhaps a bull as a rock. An artist of our own day, Georges Braque, has recently spoken of the thrill and awe with which he discovered the fluidity of our categories, the ease with which a file can become a shoehorn, a bucket a brazier. We have seen that this faculty for finding and making underlies the child's discoveries no less than the artist's. Finding, indeed, even precedes making, but it is only in making things and trying to make them like something else that man can extend his awareness of the visible world. It was Konrad Fiedler who constantly stressed this aspect of human creativity, but even he, perhaps, underrated the difficulty of extending our knowledge, the achievement in the 'discovery of appearances' that is really the discovery of the ambiguities of vision.

X

IT IS in these facts that we must see the ultimate reason why representational art has a history, and a history of such length and complexity. To read the artist's picture is to mobilize our memories and our experience of the visible world and to test his image through tentative projections. To read the visible world as art we must do the opposite. We must mobilize our memories and experience of pictures we have seen and test the motif again by projecting them tentatively onto a framed view.

Sir Winston Churchill appealed to psychology to elucidate the part which memory plays in painting, or what he calls the 'post office' that turns the message of light into the code of paint. The conclusion seems to me inescapable that the memory that performs this miracle is very much a memory of pictures seen. We have come to the paradoxical result that only a picture painted can account for a picture seen in nature. But we have seen a good deal of evidence to support this paradox. Indeed, the argument of this book was designed mainly to account for these phenomena and to lead up to this conclusion; yet if it were to be taken literally, it would also end in an impasse. If only those who had experience of reading pictures in terms of nature could turn round and see nature in terms of pictures, the process would never have started and the first picture would never have been painted. But after all, we have seen that the first picture was not intended as a likeness. There are few civilizations that even made the change from making to matching, and only where the image has been developed to a high degree of articulation does that systematic process of comparison set in which results in illusionist art. But even then the imitation of nature remains selective. Not every motif invites the artist. Even after the development of naturalistic art, the vocabulary of representation shows a tenacity, a resistance to change, as if only a picture seen could account for a picture painted. The stability of styles in art is sufficiently striking to demand some such hypothesis of self-reinforcement.

It was in the field of landscape painting, where sight counts for so much more than calculation, that these psychological facts were first discovered and discussed. Eleven years after Fréart de Chambray had told his *Poussinist* friends of the 'paradox' that the good artist must never trust to his vision, the leader of the emergent *Rubeniste* party, Roger de Piles, pointed to the other side of the case in his *Dialogue sur le Coloris* (1673). The bad habits of painters, he says, 'even affect their organs, so that their eyes see the objects of nature coloured as they are used to painting them'. We have seen the effect of this mutual induction both in the 'pathology' of topographic portrayal and in its transformation into an art. For there is always the credit side to be remembered: nature could never have become 'picturesque' for us unless we, too, had acquired the habit of seeing it in pictorial terms. Richard Payne Knight, a clear-sighted art lover of the eighteenth century, knew very well that the search for picturesque beauty that sent poets

252. CONSTABLE: *Sketch of Borrowdale.* 1806, water colour

and painters to the Lakeland was a search for motifs that reminded the art lover of paintings, preferably those of Claude and Poussin.

We are back at the problem of Constable's achievement, the exact character of those visual discoveries that were characterized by Roger Fry as an 'advance towards appearances'. There is no doubt that Constable saw his work in this light. He rebelled against a public that 'looked upon pictures as standards by which nature is to be judged rather than the reverse'. But the very violence of his reaction would be unintelligible if it were not for that inevitable pull which the memory of pictures seen also exercised on his sensitive mind. The Victoria and Albert Museum possesses a fine study by Constable of Borrowdale in the

253. CONSTABLE: *Motif in Wivenhoe Park.* 1817, crayon

254. GAINSBOROUGH: *The Watering Place.* 1777

Lakeland which he made at the age of twenty-two [252]. On the reverse he wrote the following note to aid his memory: 'Fine, blowing day, tone very mellow, like the mildest of Gaspar Poussin and Sir George Beaumont, on the whole deeper toned than this drawing.'

We can observe how a comparison immediately arises in the painter's mind in front of his motif. He thinks of Gaspar Poussin, whose grandiose mountain scenes had taught the eighteenth century to see the Lakeland in terms of the picturesque. Sir George Beaumont we remember as that representative of the academic tradition who figures in the anecdote about the brown fiddle.

But even when he renounces the picturesque, it is still in terms of pictures that Constable thinks. Of his native Suffolk he writes: 'It is a most delightful landscape for a painter. I fancy I see Gainsborough in every hedge and hollow tree.' And indeed, it is not hard to show that the vocabulary which Constable used for the portrayal of these East Anglian scenes comes from Gainsborough. We have seen one of Constable's preliminary sketches [192] for his painting of Wivenhoe Park. On a later drawing [253] we see him groping for a paintable picturesque motif on the estate of his patron. What did he select? A group such as he must often have seen in Gainsborough's idyllic compositions—the *Watering Place* [254], for example, with its woodland pastoral. He saw the scene in terms of Gainsborough.

255. GAINSBOROUGH: *Drawing after Ruisdael*. About 1748

But if this is true, are we not led into what philosophers call an infinite regress, the explanation of one thing in terms of an earlier which again needs the same type of explanation? If Constable saw the English landscape in terms of Gainsborough's paintings, what about Gainsborough himself? We can answer this. Gainsborough saw the lowland scenery of East Anglia in terms of Dutch paintings which he arduously studied and copied. We have his drawing [255] after Ruisdael [256], and we know that it was this vocabulary which he applied to the rendering of his own idyllic woodland scenes [257]. And where did the Dutch get their vocabulary? The answer to this type of question is precisely what is known as the 'history of art'. All paintings, as Wölfflin said, owe more to other paintings than they owe to direct observation.

That the artist can learn from tradition how to render nature it never entered Constable's mind to doubt. Ruskin having repeated the legend of Constable's unwillingness to learn from others, Leslie reminded the readers of his *Handbook for Young Painters* that 'Constable's first-known attempts in Art were pen-and-ink copies of the prints from Raphael's Cartoons; his next, copies of the etchings of Ruysdael; and that, later in life . . . he made careful copies of Wilson, of Ruysdael, Rubens, Teniers, and Claude. . . . His walls also were covered with pictures, drawings and prints, of the great landscape and other painters.' We have seen him copying the drawing-book of Alexander Cozens, and even toward the end of his life he wrote to the father of a young painter-friend who had recently died, 'If you can lend me two or three of poor John's studies of the ashes in the town meadow . . .

256. RUISDAEL: *The Forest*. About 1660

257. GAINSBOROUGH: *Cornard Wood*. 1748

258. CUYP: *Dordrecht in a Storm.* About 1650

259. CONSTABLE: *Salisbury Cathedral from the Meadow.* 1831

I will take great care of them . . . I am about an ash or two now.' In the same period, we find him writing about the collection of Ham House: 'There is there a truly sublime Cuyp [258], still and tranquil, the town of Dort is seen with its towers and windmills under the insidious gleam of a feint watery sun, while a horrid rent in the sky almost frightens one, and the lightning descends to the earth over some poor cottages with a glide that is so much like nature that I wish I had seen it before I sent away my "Salisbury" [259].'

Constable was convinced Cuyp had made a valid discovery. He had examined Cuyp's rendering of lightning and found it like nature. Not a transcript, of course —who could transcribe a flash of lightning, and that in oil paint?—but a con-figuration which, in the context, became the valid cryptogram for that unpaintable glare. On that point, then, there was no need to experiment any more.

For I think we may now be a little better equipped to appreciate Constable's description of landscape paintings as experiments in what he calls 'natural philo-sophy', that is, in science. He thought, and rightly, that only experimentation can show the artist a way out of the prison of style toward a greater truth. Only through trying out new effects never seen before in paint could he learn about nature. Making still comes before matching.

XI

THE REVISION I advocate in the story of visual discoveries, in fact, can be paral-leled with the revision that has been demanded for the history of science. Here, too, the nineteenth century believed in passive recording, in unbiassed observation of uninterpreted facts. The technical term for this outlook is the belief in induction, the belief that the patient collection of one instance after the other will gradually build up into a correct image of nature, provided always that no observation is ever coloured by subjective bias. In this view nothing is more harmful to the scientist than a preconceived notion, a hypothesis, or an expectation which may adulterate his results. Science is a record of facts, and all knowledge is trustworthy only in so far as it stems directly from sensory data.

This inductivist ideal of pure observation has proved a mirage in science no less than in art. The very idea that it should be possible to observe without expectation, that you can make your mind an innocent blank on which nature will record its secrets, has come in for strong criticism. Every observation, as Karl Popper has stressed, is a result of a question we ask nature, and every question implies a tentative hypothesis. We look for something because our hypothesis makes us expect certain results. Let us see if they follow. If not, we must revise our hypo-thesis and try again to test it against observation as rigorously as we can; we do that by trying to disprove it, and the hypothesis that survives that winnowing process is the one we feel entitled to hold, *pro tempore*.

This description of the way science works is eminently applicable to the story of visual discoveries in art. Our formula of schema and correction, in fact, illustrates this very procedure. You must have a starting point, a standard of comparison, in order to begin that process of making and matching and remaking which finally becomes embodied in the finished image. The artist cannot start from scratch but he can criticize his forerunners.

There is an interesting pamphlet by a minor painter called Henry Richter, published in 1817—the year Constable exhibited Wivenhoe Park—which well illustrates the spirit of creative research that animated the young painters of the nineteenth century. It is called *Daylight: A Recent Discovery in the Art of Painting*. In this amusing dialogue the painter challenges the Dutch seventeenth-century masters, or rather their ghosts assembled at an exhibition, with the question: 'Was there no clear sky in your day, and did not the broad blue light of the atmosphere shine then, as it does now . . . ? I find it is this which gives the chief splendour of sunshine by contrasting the golden with the azure lights. . . .'

Like Constable, Richter scrutinized the traditional formula handed down in the science of painting and found that if you tested pictures painted in that way they did not look like scenes in daylight. He therefore advocated the addition of more blue in contrast to yellow in order to achieve that equivalence to daylight which had hitherto eluded art.

260. MANET: *Le Déjeuner sur l'herbe*. 1863

Richter's criticism was right, but he does not appear to have succeeded in producing a satisfactory alternative. Perhaps he was not inventive enough to put his hypothesis to the test of a successful painting, perhaps he lacked the stamina for trying again and again, and so he disappeared into the oblivion of a tame and uninspired

Victorian illustrator while Constable went on experimenting till he found those brighter and cooler harmonies which, indeed, took painting nearer to the *plein air*.

But the evidence of history suggests that all such discoveries involve the systematic comparison of past achievements and present motifs, in other words, the tentative projection of works of art into nature, experiments as to how far nature can in fact be seen in such terms. One of the most influential teachers of art in nineteenth-century France, Lecoq de Boisbaudran, who was an ardent reformer and advocate of memory training, provides another instance of this interaction. Critical of accepted life-class routines and eager to guide the student toward 'the immense field, almost unexplored, of living action, of changing, fugitive effects', he obtained permission to let models pose in the open air and made them move freely, as Rodin was to do: 'Once our admiration rose to the height of enthusiasm. One of our models, a man of splendid stature with a great sweeping beard, lay at rest upon the bank of the pond, close to a group of rushes, in an attitude at once easy and beautiful. The illusion was complete—mythology made true lived before our eyes, for there, before us, was a river god of old, ruling in quiet dignity over the course of his waters. . . .'

What an opportunity, we may infer, to test tradition and improve upon it. It is examples such as these which explain the gradual nature of all artistic changes, for variations can be controlled and checked only against a set of invariants.

261. MARCANTONIO RAIMONDI: *The Judgment of Paris.*
About 1515, engraving

Does not the experience of Lecoq de Boisbaudran suggest the revolutionary work of a much greater innovator, Manet's *Déjeuner sur l'herbe* [260]? It is well known that this daring exploit of naturalism was based, not on an incident in the environs of Paris as the scandalized public believed, but on a print from Raphael's circle [261] which none other than Fréart de Chambray had extolled as a

262. PISSARRO: *Boulevard des Italiens, Morning, Sunlight.* 1897

masterpiece of composition. Seen from our point of view this borrowing loses much
of its puzzling nature. The systematic explorer can afford less than any one else to
rely on random actions. He cannot just splash colours about to see what happens, for
even if he should like the effect he could never repeat it. The naturalistic image, as
we have seen, is a very closely knit configuration of relationships which cannot be
varied beyond certain limits without becoming unintelligible to artist and public
alike. Manet's action in modifying a compositional schema of Raphael's shows that
he knew the value of the adage 'One thing at a time'. Language grows by introducing new words, but a language consisting only of new words and a new syntax
would be indistinguishable from gibberish.

These considerations must surely increase our respect for the achievement of the
successful innovator. More is needed than a rejection of tradition, more also than
an 'innocent eye'. Art itself becomes the innovator's instrument for probing reality.
He cannot simply battle down that mental set which makes him see the motif in
terms of known pictures; he must actively try that interpretation, but try it critically, varying here and there to see whether a better match could not be achieved.
He must step back from the canvas and be his own merciless critic, intolerant of
all easy effects and all short-cut methods. And his reward might easily be the

public's finding his equivalent hard to read and hard to accept because it has not yet been trained to interpret these new combinations in terms of the visible world.

No wonder the boldest of these experiments led to the conviction that the artist's vision is entirely subjective. With impressionism the popular notion of the painter became that of the man who paints blue trees and red lawns and who answers every criticism with a proud 'That is how I see it.' This is one part of the story but not, I believe, the whole. This assertion of subjectivity can also be overdone. There is such a thing as a real visual discovery, and there is a way of testing it despite the fact we may never know what the artist himself saw at a certain moment. Whatever

263. WHISTLER: *Chelsea Wharf; Gray and Silver.* Probably 1875

the initial resistance to impressionist paintings, when the first shock had worn off, people learned to read them. And having learned this language, they went into the fields and woods, or looked out of their window onto the Paris boulevards [262], and found to their delight that the visible world *could* after all be seen in terms of these bright patches and dabs of paint. The transposition worked. The impressionists had taught them, not, indeed, to see nature with an innocent eye, but to explore an unexpected alternative that turned out to fit certain experiences better than did any earlier paintings. The artists convinced art lovers so thoroughly that the *bon mot* 'nature imitates art' became current. As Oscar Wilde said, there was no fog in London before Whistler painted it [263].

XII

THOSE WHO HAVE EXPERIENCED the thrill of such visual discoveries have generally expressed their gratitude in the words that only art has taught them to *see*. Even in classical antiquity Cicero had marvelled at the many things painters saw in shade and light that we ordinary mortals do not see. No doubt this is true, and yet it is not the whole truth. Seeing in itself is so complex and miraculous a process of interaction and integration that not even art could teach us that. The current idea that we look lazily into the world only as far as our practical needs demand it while the artist removes this veil of habits scarcely does justice to the marvels of everyday vision. I believe that André Malraux here came much nearer to the truth when he stressed that all seeing is a purposeful activity, the artist's purpose being painting. In thus looking for possible alternatives the artist does not necessarily see more than the layman. In a certain sense he sees even less (as he shows when he half closes his eyes). And yet he enriches our experience because he offers us an equivalence within his medium that may also 'work' for us. The layman who looks at his painting and says, after an honest try, 'I am afraid I cannot see it like that' is not the artist's enemy, he is his partner in the game of equivalences. Admittedly there are other games in art, but it is not always the layman who is a little muddled about what game is actually being played at a certain moment.

I believe it is necessary to stress this partnership and the act of acceptance, not because we need worship success and popularity in art, but because we cannot speak of experiments without some standard by which to judge their success or failure.

The history of naturalism in art from the Greeks to the impressionists is the history of a most successful experiment, the real discovery of appearances, as Roger Fry described it. The only question mark we are forced to make after his account concerns the term 'discovery'. You can only discover what was always there. The term implies the idea of the innocent eye, the idea, that is, that we really 'ought' to see those coloured patches of which Berkeley spoke and that there is a kind of original sin that has made us transform and corrupt the beauty which was given us to contemplate.

I believe this reading of mankind's development is in increasing contradiction to the findings of psychology. Only recently, J. J. Gibson made an eloquent case for the opposite reading of the facts. He argues that we are born with the capacity to interpret our visual impressions in terms of a possible world, that is, in terms of space and light. His wartime work on such problems as how pilots estimate speed and distance when they land on an aircraft carrier has given him a sound respect for the efficiency of our visual endowment. Would such feats be possible if we really had to learn about space through a series of experiments? Indeed, could a squirrel ever jump from branch to branch if all it 'really' saw were black streaks which 'stand for' branches in the distance?

Luckily for our purpose we need not await the final answer to this question that has divided psychologists for centuries into 'nativists' and 'empiricists'. For, whether by endowment or by early learning, we are certainly equipped with a miraculous capacity for interpreting the clues which rush in on us from the outside world and for testing their consistency in terms of possible configurations in space and light.

This does not mean, as we have seen, that these interpretations are always right or, as the technical term has it, 'veridical'. If they were, accidents could not happen. On the contrary, our first hypothesis is often mistaken and remains so if we lack adequate clues for eliminating false guesses. We have seen that it is in the work of elimination that such cross checks as touching things and, most of all, movement play a vital part. Though they may not teach us to learn the skill of interpreting visual impressions as such, they do teach us how to decide between alternative interpretations and possible reactions.

XIII

FOR THIS, to sum up, seems to be the decisive matter of which the historian should take cognizance: that all organisms to some extent, but human beings to a marvellous extent, are equipped to probe and learn by trial and error, by switching from one hypothesis to another till one is found that ensures our survival.

One of Bernard Berenson's most brilliant essays, in which he restates the theory of 'seeing and knowing' that I have been trying to amend, opens with a description of the Palio in Siena, with the surging crowd on the piazza looking to the sensitive beholder like a field of flowers. It is only his knowledge, Berenson concludes, that makes him see people and not flowers. I would rather say that it is only his knowledge that allows him to decide between these two interpretations by testing them against the situation. It is true that for him there is always that other possibility in the background: he can interpret what he sees in terms of mere coloured patches; but this, I submit, is not because he is aware of his visual sensations but because once more he interprets what he sees in terms of something he probably knows even better than people and flowers, I mean in terms of paintings.

It was again J. J. Gibson who drew the most radical conclusion from this experience, albeit only as an aside in the context of a discussion when E. G. Boring had challenged the whole distinction between the visual world (the world of things) and the visual field (the experience of colour patches) on which Gibson's book had been based.

'The visual field, I think,' wrote Gibson, 'is simply the pictorial mode of visual perception, and it depends in the last analysis not on conditions of stimulation but on conditions of attitude. The visual field is the product of the chronic habit of civilized men of seeing the world as a picture. . . . So far from being the basis, it is a kind of *alternative* to ordinary perception.'

If this analysis should prove correct, a good deal would follow for the student of art. In fact, it is one of the points where the psychologist might with profit test his theories against the material offered by the historian. He might find, I believe, that the 'chronic habit of civilized men' is not sufficient for most of them to adopt the attitude necessary to paint without training. But the very difficulties encountered in presenting the alternative to ordinary perception confirms, I believe, this bold reversal of the traditional way of putting things.

It is even harder to see the visible world as a two-dimensional field than it is to see one's own image on the mirror's surface. Our belief that we can ever make the world dissolve into such a flat patchwork of colours rests in itself on an illusion, connected, maybe, with the same urge for simplicity that makes us see the indeterminate sky as the vault of heaven. It is to the three-dimensional world that our organism is attuned, where it learns to test its anticipations against the flow of incoming stimuli, weeding out or confirming the predictable melodies of transformation that result from movement. The relationships in the plane that the illusionist painter has learned to attend to are of no biological relevance. They are studied in the highly artificial situation of one-eyed stationary vision. Now, under this constraint, as we remember from the Ames demonstrations [213], the stimulus pattern on the retina must of necessity allow of an infinite number of interpretations, none of which can be further confirmed or refuted except on grounds of probability. Neither logic nor psychology, therefore, allows us to say that any flat intersection of the visual cone represents more 'really' what we see than any other. Distant ones and near ones, oblique ones and curved ones, must be equivalent, and none can be privileged. Yet, we remember from the last chapter, our mind will still react to the challenge of this conundrum by throwing out a random answer, making ready to test it in terms of consistent possible worlds. It is these answers that will transform the ambiguous stimulus pattern into the image of something 'out there'.

What Constable 'really' saw in Wivenhoe Park was surely a house across a lake. What he had learned to paint was a flat patch that allowed of any number of readings, including the correct one. Ambiguity cannot be seen, and so we rightly ignore the innumerable weird interpretations that must also lurk behind the serene surface of the painting. For as we scan the flat pigments for answers about the motif 'out there', the consistent reading suggests itself and illusion takes over. Not, be it said, because the world really looks like a flat picture, but because some flat pictures really look like the world.

By its very function and intention naturalistic art was driven to search for alternatives which could be developed in the media of painting. One by one it eliminated the memories and anticipations of movement and separated out those clues which fuse into a convincing semblance of the visible world. Long before experimental psychology was ever thought of, the artist had devised this experiment in reduction and found that the elements of the visual experience could be taken to pieces and put together again to the point of illusion. Ultimately we owe it to this invention that we can now discover for ourselves that the world can be contemplated as pure appearance and as a thing of beauty.

X

The Experiment of Caricature

I

THE LAST chapter has led this inquiry back to the old truth that the discovery
of appearances was due not so much to a careful observation of nature as
to the invention of pictorial effects. I believe indeed that the ancient writers
who were still filled with a sense of wonder at man's capacity to fool the eye came
closer to an understanding of this achievement than many later critics. We have
seen that to Pliny every step on the road towards mimesis was an invention which
he attributed to a *heuretes*, a finder. Vasari, too, still remembered this ancient
truth and understood, as we have seen, that this invention can only progress
piecemeal, building up through gradual improvement on past achievements. I
trust that if we take this view more seriously again, the history of Western art will
yield fresh and interesting aspects which have been somewhat obscured by the
belief that the imitation of nature was always there for the picking. As far as I
can see, only one aspect of mimesis has never ceased to be seen in the light of a
real scientific invention, the rendering of space and the development of 'artificial
perspective' by Brunelleschi and his followers. Perhaps it is for this reason
that this aspect has attracted so much attention on the part of art historians.
I do not deny for a moment that the suggestion of space is an interesting achievement, but if we discard Berkeley's theory of vision, according to which we
'see' a flat field but 'construct' a tactile space, we can perhaps rid art history
of its obsession with space and bring other achievements into focus, the
suggestion of light and of texture, for instance, or the mastery of physiognomic
expression.

In all these cases there is the same need to proceed by experiment, and for the
same reason: The filing system of our minds works so differently from the measurements of science. Things objectively unlike can strike us as very similar, and
things objectively rather similar can strike us as hopelessly unlike. There is no
way of finding out except by trial and error, in other words, through painting. I
believe that the student of these inventions will generally find a double rhythm

264. REMBRANDT: *Artemisia or Sophonisba.*
Detail. 1634

265. *Detail of gold braid*

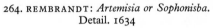

which is familiar from the history of technical progress but which has never yet been described in detail in the history of art—I mean the rhythm of lumbering advance and subsequent simplification. Most technical inventions carry with them a number of superstitions, unnecessary detours which are gradually eliminated through short cuts and a refinement of means. In the history of art we know this process mainly in the work of the great masters. Even the greatest of them—maybe the greatest most of all—began their careers with a very circumspect and even heavy technique, leaving nothing to chance. We have read Vasari's comment on the distinction between Titian's early manner and the loose brushwork of his later masterpieces. Such sublime simplification is only possible on the basis of earlier complexities. Take Rembrandt's development: he had to learn to build up the image of sparkling gold braid in all its detail [264, 265] before he could find out how much could be omitted for the beholder ready to meet him halfway. In his portrait of his enlightened patron Jan Six, one brush-stroke is really all that is needed to conjure up the gold braid [266, 267]—but how many such effects did he have to explore before he could thus reduce them to this magic simplicity!

We would not call it magic, though, if it did not work better than the laborious method. There is less paint there to explain and disturb. We remember the Chinese formula: 'Ideas present, brush may be spared performance'—and the idea is more truly present the less there is to contradict our projection.

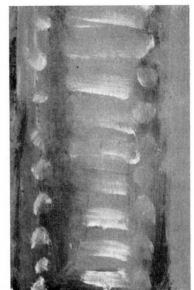

266. REMBRANDT: *Portrait of Jan Six*. 1654

267. *Detail of gold braid*

Such sublime wizardry eludes the history of styles, but the rhythm of invention and simplification is similar, with the beholder playing the willing partner in the game of equivalences. The laborious constructions of Uccello and Piero della Francesca soon ceased to be necessary for the suggestion of space and solidity when the public was prepared to 'take them as read'. It was found, moreover, that once the requisite mental set was established among the beholders, the careful observation of all clues was not only redundant but something of a hindrance. One effect could do the work of many, provided again there was no blatant contradiction in the work which hindered the illusion from taking shape.

The rendering of texture also provides an illustration of this collective, or 'stylistic', development. Jan van Eyck still rendered 'every stitch'—or so we are led to believe. But soon it turned out that this labour was unnecessary if the light was skilfully disposed. You do not have to be a Rembrandt to achieve some such effect. More than one amateur has blessed the invention of highlights which gave his painted jug a plausibility which it did not, strictly speaking, 'deserve'. This is an old observation: 'Wee finde many painters,' says Lomazzo, in Haydock's lively translation, 'who being ignorant of the arte of proportions, onely by a little practize in disposing their lights in some tolerable sorte, have notwithstanding bin reputed good workemen.'

It would be interesting to speculate on the reasons for this dominance of light over form. Somehow, I believe, these equivalences of texture touch a deeper layer of our awareness. We instinctively feel that glitter means, if not gold, at least smoothness, brightness, a sensual quality to which we respond with greater immediacy than we respond to outline and which is therefore less easily analysed. What we see when we respond to moistness or smoothness is the 'global' quality itself, not the elements of local colour and reflection—hence the intriguing and compelling effect of the pictorial illusion.

But if there is one effect more difficult to analyse than the impression of texture it is that of physiognomic impression. Here we are even more deeply involved. We hardly know how we take it in—it is there, and we respond. No wonder, therefore, that the rendering of facial expression in art is far from being an obvious problem. In the earliest treatise on painting, Alberti's *Della Pittura*, we read that it is hard for the painter to distinguish a laughing from a weeping face. Even today the rendering of the exact nuance of facial expression is notoriously difficult. Portrait painters know those tiresome relatives of their sitters who 'can't see him like that' and complain that there is something around the mouth which is not quite right. Nor does this difficulty apply only to a copy from life. Max Friedländer tells the revealing story of the bank official who insisted that German bank notes should retain a portrait head in their design. Nothing, he said, was harder for the forger to imitate than precisely the right expression of these artistically quite insignificant heads, nor was there a quicker way of discovering a suspect note than simply observing the way these faces look at you. I believe the same is true of forged paintings. They look at you with a 'modern' look, which for those who like to converse with the figures of the past, is easy to spot but extremely hard to analyse. The reason is plain. We respond to a face as a whole: we see a friendly, dignified, or eager face, sad or sardonic, long before we can tell what exact features or relationships account for this intuitive impression. I doubt if we could ever become aware of the exact changes that make a face light up in a smile or cloud over in a pensive mood simply by observing the people around us. For, as in our previous examples, what is given us is the global impression and our reaction to it; we 'really' see distance, not changes in size; we 'really' see light, not modifications of tone; and most of all we really see a brighter face and not a change in muscular contractions. The very immediacy of the impression stands in the way of analysis, and so the discovery and simplification of facial expression provide the best example of the course taken by an artistic invention. It is also an example of an invention the history of which has not been attempted. I dare say to write it seriously would present great difficulties, precisely for the reasons alluded to. Expression is hard to analyse and harder to describe unequivocally. It is a curious fact, moreover, that our immediate reaction results in firm convictions, but convictions which are rarely shared by all—witness the pages of interpretation that have been devoted to Mona Lisa's smile.

II

IT MAY be better, therefore, to start at the end and to demonstrate the final distillation of expression in the simple works of illustrators or of designers of children's books, for instance, a drawing by the lovable creator of the Babar stories, Jean de Brunhoff. Brunhoff with a few hooks and dots could impart whatever expression he desired even to the face of an elephant [268], and he could make his figures almost speak merely by shifting those conventional signs which do duty for eyes in children's books. Al Capp's Shmoo of happy memory [269] receives the law of its blissful being from a mere shapeless form endowed with a speaking expression.

268. JEAN DE BRUNHOFF: *From 'The Story of Babar'.* 1937

269. AL CAPP: *The Shmoo*

270. WALT DISNEY: *Dumbo*

And how could Disney have enchanted us if he and his team had not probed into the secret of expression and physiognomy that allowed them to perform that true magic of animation which created a Mickey Mouse, a Donald Duck, a Dumbo [270], even before animation through movement began?

I believe there are two conditions which account for this success in the illusion of life which can do without any illusion of reality: one is the experience of generations of artists with the effect of pictures, another the willingness of the public to accept the grotesque and simplified partly because its lack of elaboration guarantees the absence of contradictory clues. If this sounds chilling, it is perhaps lucky that these points about the discovery of the springs of expression within the context of pictorial entertainment have been anticipated by an artist who did not have my particular psychological axe to grind: I am referring to a pamphlet on physiognomics published in 1845 by the humourist and draughtsman Rodolphe Töpffer of Geneva.

It is no accident that we should be led back from Disney, Al Capp, and Brunhoff to that half-forgotten artist and thinker, for to Töpffer belongs the credit, if we want to call it so, of having invented and propagated the picture story, the comic strip.

Töpffer's humorous picture novels, the first of which Goethe admired and encouraged him to publish, are the innocent ancestors of today's manufactured dreams. We find everything in them, albeit still in genuinely comic garb. There is violence, as in the sequence [271] where the miller thrashes his wife for having seen nothing and she thrashes the boy for having said he saw something and the boy thrashes the donkey who was the cause of that particular episode. There is also space travel, though not intentional: Töpffer's scientists were hurled into outer space [272] by an explosion while their telescope was transported on a steamer. Everywhere in these countless episodes of almost surrealist inconsequence we find a mastery of physiognomic characterization [273] which sets the standard for such influential humorous draughtsmen of the nineteenth century as Wilhelm Busch in Germany.

As so often in the history of art, a personal and a technical factor conspired to produce this invention. Töpffer, the son of a well-known painter of landscapes and genre pieces, had himself become a painter in a similar vein, but he had trouble with his eyes and turned to writing—some of his short stories and idylls are among the gems of Swiss literature. Though his eyes could not take the strain of a meticulous technique he did feel the urge to continue as an artist, and here the invention of new graphic techniques stood him in good stead. Lithography enabled him to draw without encumbrance, and to have his light and unpretentious line drawings reproduced cheaply.

In view of what has happened during the last decades, Töpffer's little treatise on physiognomics sounds prophetic. 'There are two ways of writing stories, one in chapters, lines, and words, and that we call "literature", or alternatively by a succession of illustrations, and that we call the "picture story".' The advantage of this second method over the first was put to the test by Hogarth, whose short

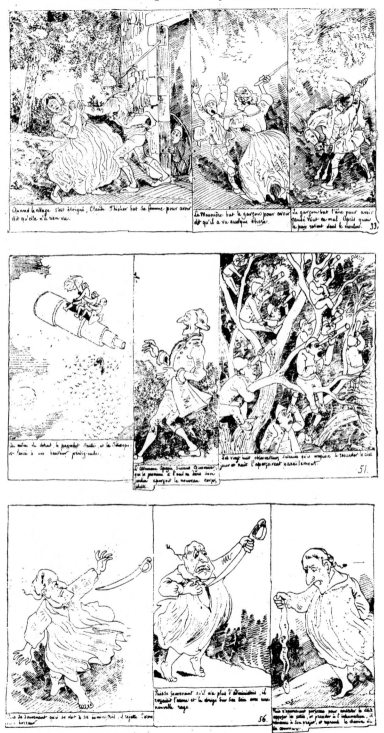

271–273. TÖPFFER: *From 'Le Docteur Festus'*. Drawn in 1829

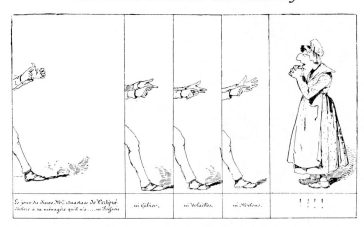

274. CHAM: *M. de Vertpré* (1840)

sequence of pictures *Marriage à la Mode* is equivalent to at least two volumes of Richardson's novels. 'The picture story to which the criticism of art pays no attention and which rarely worries the learned,' Töpffer goes on, 'has always exercised a great appeal. More, indeed, than literature itself, for besides the fact that there are more people who look than who can read, it appeals particularly to children and to the masses, the sections of the public which are particularly easily perverted and which it would be particularly desirable to raise. With its dual advantages of greater conciseness and greater relative clarity, the picture story, all things being equal, should squeeze out the other because it would address itself with greater liveliness to a greater number of minds, and also because in any contest he who uses such a direct method will have the advantage over those who talk in chapters.'

Töpffer thought there must be a great power for good in so potent a weapon, and so he deplored the fact that artists, on the whole, work for art and not for morals. Luckily, so he thought, little artistic skill is needed for telling a story in pictures; his own idle fancies had been so well received he regretted not having embodied some useful or moral idea in his picture stories.

To recommend the medium to well-meaning but untrained educators, Töpffer comes out with his psychological discovery—you can evolve a pictorial language without any reference to nature, without learning to draw from a model. The line drawing, he says, is purely conventional symbolism. For that very reason it is immediately intelligible to a child, who might have difficulty in disentangling a naturalistic painting. Moreover, the artist who uses such an abbreviatory style can always rely on the beholder to supplement what he omits. In a skilled and complete painting, any gap will be disturbing; in the idiom of Töpffer and his imitators these elliptic expressions are read as part of the narrative [274].

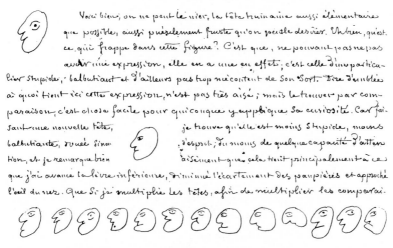

275. TÖPFFER: *From the 'Essay de physiognomie'.* 1845

One thing only is needed for the pictorial narrator—a knowledge of physiognomics and human expression. After all, he must create a convincing hero and characterize the people he comes into contact with; he must convey their reaction and let the story unfold in terms of readable expressions. Does this not need a skilled artist who has spent years drawing from plaster casts, who has drawn those eyes, ears, noses which, as Töpffer says, are the pleasant exercises which art schools impose on budding artists? For Töpffer all this is waste of time. The practical physiognomics needed for a picture story could be learned by a recluse who never sets eyes on any human being. All he needs is drawing material and some perseverance. For any drawing of a human face, however inept, however childish, possesses, by the very fact that it has been drawn, a character and an expression. This being so, and being quite independent of knowledge and of art, anybody who wants to try should be able to find out the traits in which this expression resides. All he must do is to vary his scrawl systematically. If his first mannikin [275] looks stupid and smug, another with the eyes a little closer to the nose may look less so. By a simple reshuffle of these primitive traits, our lonely hermit will find out how these elements and their combinations affect him and us. Thus a little experimentation with noses or mouths will teach us the elementary symptoms, and from here we can proceed, simply by doodling, to create characters. Töpffer maintains that the heroes of his stories thus arose out of his pen-plays. Only one more step is needed for the picture story. We must learn to distinguish between what Töpffer calls the 'permanent traits' indicating character and the 'impermanent ones' indicating emotion. As to the permanent ones, Töpffer makes fun of the phrenologists of his time who sought the root of character in certain isolated signs. All of a dozen profiles [276], he maintains, have the same forehead, that of the Apollo

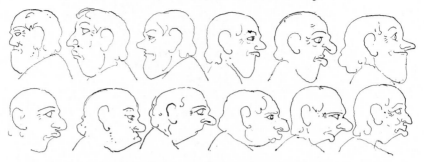

276. TÖPFFER: *From the 'Essay de physiognomie'*

Belvedere. But look at the difference in the *Gestalt*! The 'impermanent traits' can also be found by similar methods of trial and error. We will soon be able to draw Johnny laughing and Johnny weeping [277] and isolate the features which make the expression. We cannot follow Töpffer here into all his subtle observations, his attempts, for instance, to combine laughing eyes and a weeping mouth and his comments on the resulting character [278]. What matters to us is the principle he established with these light-hearted experiments. Perhaps we should say the principle *of* experiments, which we know from Constable who was a child of the same generation. We have here a further shift, compared with Constable, from the idea of imitation and observation of the visible world to that of an exploration of our own imitative faculty. Töpffer looks for what psychologists would call the 'minimum clues' of expression to which we respond whether we meet them in reality or in art. In trying to find out what happens, not to the doodle but to himself, when these clues are systematically varied, Töpffer uses them as a tool to probe into the secrets of physiognomic perception.

277, 278. TÖPFFER: *From the 'Essay'*

In a previous chapter we have met with this very principle of systematic variation in the psychologist's laboratory—in those experiments designed to test inborn release mechanisms of the lower species [71]. I mentioned the possibility that even man shows traces of such inborn responses, that, in particular, our reaction to faces and physiognomic expression may not be wholly due to learning, and that the

279. GUY BARA: *From 'Tom the Traveller'*. 1957

mental set which makes us read faces into blots, rocks, or wallpapers may be biologically conditioned.

The most astonishing fact about these clues of expression is surely that they may transform almost any shape into the semblance of a living being. Discover expression in the staring eye or gaping jaw of a lifeless form, and what might be called 'Töpffer's law' will come into operation—it will not be classed just as a face but will acquire a definite character and expression, will be endowed with life, with a presence. If there is a hierarchy of clues to which we react instinctively, expression will surely trump light. I believe it needed Töpffer's method of a prior construction to bring about an easy mastery of that aspect of representation and that art here, as always, actually went that way. But why, we may still ask, did this method not develop much earlier? Questions of why are dangerous in history. But may it not be that its very power held it in check? It needs the detachment of an enlightened nineteenth-century humourist to play with the magic of creation, to make up these playful doodles, and to question them for their character and soul as if they were real creatures. To the humble craftsman of earlier periods, the experience may not have been free from half-conscious or unconscious fears. One of Töpffer's later successors has summed them up in a witty strip [279]. The very laws of proportion and style that held the schemata of beauty together in past centuries may have served this additional aim of preventing too much life from entering the artist's creations.

III

THESE SPECULATIONS were particularly suggested to me by researches into the history of caricature which I was privileged to undertake with my friend Ernst Kris. Our starting-point at the time was the question of why portrait caricature, the playful distortion of a victim's face, makes only so late an appearance in Western art. The word and the institution of caricature date only from the last years of the

280. AGOSTINO CARRACCI:
Caricatures. About 1600

281. BERNINI:
Caricature. About 1650

sixteenth century, and the inventors of the art were not the pictorial propagandists who existed in one form or another for centuries before but those most sophisticated and refined of artists, the brothers Carracci. Few of their caricatures have been identified [280], but according to literary sources which we have no reason to doubt, they also invented the joke of transforming a victim's face into that of an animal, or even a lifeless implement, which caricaturists have practised ever since.

We thought at the time that it was the fear of image magic, the reluctance to do as a joke what the unconscious means very much in earnest, which delayed the coming of that visual game. I still believe these motives may have played their part, but the theory might be generalized. The invention of portrait caricature presupposes the theoretical discovery of the difference between likeness and equivalence. This is how the great seventeenth-century critic Filippo Baldinucci defines the art of mock portraiture: 'Among painters and sculptors,' he explains in his dictionary of artistic terms, which came out in 1681, 'the word signifies a method of making portraits, in which they aim at the greatest resemblance of the whole of the person portrayed, while yet, for the purpose of fun, and sometimes of mockery, they disproportionately increase and emphasize the defects of the features they copy, so that the portrait as a whole appears to be the sitter himself, while its components are changed.' The caricatures Baldinucci had in mind were those by Bernini [281], the great sculptor who had mastered the skill of physiognomic reduction to perfection. But the *locus classicus* for a demonstration of this discovery of like in unlike is the *Poire* [282], the pear into which Daumier's employer, Philipon, transformed the head of the *Roi Bourgeois*, Louis Philippe. *Poire* means a 'fathead', and when Philipon's satirical papers continuously pilloried the King as a *poire*, the editor was finally summoned and a heavy fine was imposed. The famous sequence, a kind of slow-motion analysis of the process of caricaturing, was published in his paper as his defence. It rests on the plea of equivalence. For which step, it asks, am I to be punished? Is it a crime to substitute this likeness for that? Or then the next? And if not that, why not the pear? And indeed we feel that despite the change of each individual feature, the whole remains remarkably similar. We accept it as a possible alternative mode of seeing the King's face. For this is the secret of a good caricature—it offers a visual interpretation of a physiognomy which we can never forget and which the victim will always seem to carry around with him like a man bewitched.

LES POIRES,

Faites à la cour d'assises de Paris par le directeur de la CARICATURE.

Vendues pour payer les 6,000 fr. d'amende du journal le *Charivari*.

(CHEZ AUBERT, GALERIE VÉRO-DODAT)

Si, pour reconnaître le monarque dans une caricature, vous n'attendez pas qu'il soit designé autrement que par la ressemblance, vous tomberez dans l'absurde. Voyez ces croquis informes, auxquels j'aurais peut-être dû borner ma defense :

Ce croquis ressemble à Louis-Philippe, vous condamnerez donc ?

Alors il faudra condamner celui-ci, qui ressemble au premier.

Fait condamner cet autre, qui ressemble au second.

Et enfin, si vous êtes conséquens, vous ne sauriez absoudre cette poire, qui ressemble aux croquis précédens.

Ainsi, pour une poire, pour une brioche, et pour toutes les têtes grotesques dans lesquelles le hasard ou la malice aura placé cette triste ressemblance, vous pourrez infliger à l'auteur cinq ans de prison et cinq mille francs d'amende!! Avouez, Messieurs, que c'est là une singuliere liberté de la presse!!

282. PHILIPON: *From 'Le Charivari'.* 1834

IV

IN THIS FORMULATION caricature becomes only a special case of what I have attempted to describe as the artist's test of success. All artistic discoveries are discoveries not of likenesses but of equivalences which enable us to see reality in terms of an image and an image in terms of reality. And this equivalence never rests on the likeness of elements so much as on the identity of responses to certain relationships. We respond to a white blob on the black silhouette of a jug as if it were a highlight; we respond to the pear with these crisscross lines as if it were Louis Philippe's head.

It is precisely because these identities do not depend on the imitation of individual features so much as on configurations of clues that they are so difficult to find by mere looking. What we experience as a good likeness in a caricature, or even in a portrait, is not necessarily a replica of anything seen. If it were, every snapshot would have a greater chance of impressing us as a satisfactory representation of a person we know. In fact only a few snapshots will so satisfy us. We dismiss the majority as odd, uncharacteristic, strange, not because the camera distorts, but because it caught a constellation of features from the melody of expression which, when arrested and frozen, fails to strike us in the same way the sitter does. For expression in life and physiognomic impression rest on movement no less than on static symptoms, and art has to compensate for the loss of the time dimension by concentrating all required information into one arrested image.

Put in this form, the problem may sound somewhat forbiddingly abstract, but its practical consequences were well known to the guardians of the academic tradition. One of them, Arnold Houbraken, who in the early eighteenth century wrote the biographies of the Dutch masters, discusses this issue, not without some asperity, in the chapter he devotes to Rembrandt. Rembrandt, Houbraken maintains, rejected the road to perfection offered by the academic method, the road of tradition, insisting that the artist should only imitate nature. Houbraken denies that this can ever be desirable. Nature in the raw lacks that decorum and beauty which secure the dignity of art and which Rembrandt so often violated. But quite apart from being undesirable, Houbraken argues, Rembrandt's programme demands the impossible. You may be able to paint a still life from nature. But how are you to copy rapid movement, running, flying, jumping? These will be over before you ever put pen to paper. But worse still, how are you to copy what he calls the 'expression of human passions'? It is true that you might ask a model to feign laughing or weeping, but you will not get more than a grimace, for genuine expression must be genuinely felt, and—most of all—it, too, happens in time.

283. *The Disciples at Emmaus, after a lost drawing by Rembrandt.* 1753

284. REMBRANDT: *Study for 'The Disciples at Emmaus'.* About 1632

At this point in the argument Houbraken must ask himself whether he has not proved too much. For though he found much to censure in Rembrandt's outlook, he granted him unrivalled knowledge of the human heart, a complete understanding of gesture and expression. As an example of Rembrandt's mastery in this sphere, he includes, for the benefit of aspiring art students, a print after a drawing by Rembrandt [283], now lost, which shows the disciples at Emmaus in fear and awe at the sudden disappearance of the companion in whom they had just recognized Christ. In comparison with the master's still extant drawings [284] for the same subject, the copyist has coarsened and overdramatized Rembrandt's mysteriously subtle art. I know few more moving illustrations of a conflicting emotion than the rapid study for one of the disciples in whom fear is just giving way to the joy of recognition.

To account for this miracle in Rembrandt's art, the eighteenth-century critic attributes to Rembrandt an unusual visual memory—a memory so retentive it could hold any phase of any movement and use it in his art. We must agree with Houbraken that Rembrandt was not like ordinary mortals, but the explanation he gives is still unconvincing. We possess a mechanical device which does exactly what Rembrandt was supposed to do—the snapshot which arrests movement and fixes it for ever. We also know, therefore, how unlike Rembrandt's drawing is to such a snapshot. It is true that Otto Benesch in his great work on Rembrandt's drawings calls our sketch a 'study from life'. But even if it is, it is invented in the highest sense of the term. Houbraken was certainly right when he argued that such things cannot be a transcript of things seen. But they cannot be a transcript of things remembered either. There is no difference in principle between representing a thing seen and a thing remembered—neither of them can be transcribed

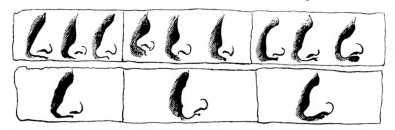

285. LEONARDO DA VINCI: *From the 'Treatise on Painting'*

as such without a language, in this case without that command of expression which Rembrandt had made his own in and through his art. Here as always the memory of successful solutions, the artist's own and those of tradition, is as important as the memory of observations.

This great truth, like so many others, was well known to Leonardo da Vinci. When he discusses a memory for physiognomics in his *Treatise on Painting*, Leonardo advises the artist to hold in readiness a system of classifications—divide the face for this purpose into four parts: the forehead, the nose, the mouth, and the chin—and study the possible forms they can take. Our illustration [285] shows the categories for noses he admits. Once you have these elements of the human countenance firmly engraved on your mind, you can analyse and retain a face at a single glance.

Leonardo here speaks of what Töpffer called the 'permanent traits' of physiognomics, their structure. Like Töpffer, he was fond of experimenting with what happens to such faces if you vary the elements to their extremes in doodles and caricatures [67]. The systematic investigation of the changing traits—that is to say, of the passing emotions—had to wait for the next century. In discussing the difficulties of rendering these fleeting emotions, Rembrandt's critic Houbraken referred

286. LE BRUN: *From 'Le Méthode pour apprendre à dessiner les passions'*. 1696

his readers to a work which might help them to enrich their knowledge of expression. It was the treatise by the head of the French Academy in the *Grand Siècle*, Charles Le Brun.

The method used by Le Brun is all the more interesting in our context because it, too, is based on the study of art rather than on the observation of living expression. Le Brun compiled a patternbook of typical heads [286] in the grand manner —the fierce soldier, the simpering maiden—and then proceeded to analyse these heads in order to find out what it was that made them expressive. His treatise includes a series of schematic heads exhibiting the decisive clues indicative of the 'passions of the mind'.

These are the diagrams which were recommended as a substitute for that incredible visual memory to which Houbraken had attributed Rembrandt's success in the rendering of emotions. Intended to enable ordinary mortals to master human expressions, they were spread all over Europe in many handbooks and drawing books. I believe they did in fact contribute to the store of visual knowledge, though not, at first, in Great Art. There that other shibboleth of academic creeds, decorum, militated against experimenting with all varieties of human types and emotions. The noble neither laugh nor cry. Thus humorous art was left to become the testing ground of these discoveries.

V

AMONG THE eighteenth-century artists who mention Le Brun in their writings, none is more interesting in this respect than William Hogarth [287]. His autobiographical notes show that he, too, was much concerned with the problem of acquiring a retentive memory for physiognomies and expressions. And he, too, doubted whether copying from nature would really be of use to the artist in this respect. The gist of his doctrine is found in a remark that he attributes to an 'arch brother of the pencil' who turned Hogarth's fulminations against prevalent teachings into the paradox that 'the only way to learn to draw well is never to draw at all'. Copying the model in the academies was mostly a waste of time. The artist should 'learn the language' of objects and 'if possible find a grammar to them'. In other words, he should stock his mind well with what we called 'schemata', and among those Hogarth certainly gave pride of place to schemata for 'character' and 'expression' [288].

In our story, therefore, Hogarth stands somewhere in between Leonardo and Le Brun on the one hand—both of whom he quoted—and Töpffer on the other. To Leonardo, nature was still the great teacher and rival and the training of memory was just a by-product of his interest in morphology. For Le Brun, art

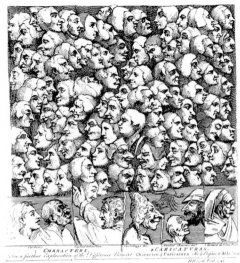

287. HOGARTH: *The Laughing Audience.*
1733. Etching

288. HOGARTH: *Characters and Caricaturas.*
1743. Etching

had become a lofty language from which it was dangerous to depart without loss of caste. Hogarth accepted the idea of art as a language and seized eagerly on the possibilities it offered for the creation of characters with which to people his imaginary stage.

That this was his aim is apparent from such prints as *Characters and Caricaturas* [288], which drives home the difference between a mastery of variety—the know-ledge of character—and the exaggerations of caricature. Later in his life he defined this difference explicitly. Caricature rests on comic comparison. Any scrawl will do if it is found to exhibit a surprising likeness. Hogarth quotes as an example of such a successful caricature the drawing of a singer which consisted of nothing but a stroke and a dot over it. Character, by contrast, rests on knowledge of the human frame and heart. It shows the artist as a creator of convincing types. And here, Hogarth hints, comic art is no less supreme than the much-admired grand manner of Raphael who also did no more—but no less—than create characters.

It would be tempting to trace the development which leads from Hogarth's picture stories to those of Töpffer and from Hogarth's interest in physiognomics to that of his Swiss admirer. The licence given to humorous art, the freedom from restraint, allowed the masters of grotesque satire to experiment with physio-gnomics to a degree quite impossible for the serious artist. This difference becomes clear in and through the story of empirical physiognomics.

The true discoverer of the experimental method in art is Alexander Cozens. We have already encountered his 'new method' of blotting and his configuration of skies that interested Constable. But Cozens published yet another system, and

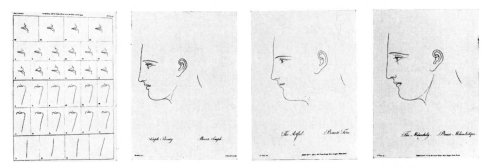

289–292. A. COZENS: *From 'Principles of Beauty Relative to the Human Head'*. 1778

here he anticipated Töpffer—he is thus the joint ancestor of both these discoverers. In an interesting series of prints Cozens presents a standard head of classical beauty and that blankness of expression that often goes with it [289–92]. By systematically varying the proportions, he attempts to investigate the creation of what he calls 'character' through deviations from the canon. His attempt misfired because it was too subtle. It is hard to see much difference between the various types of beauty because he tried to remain within the laws of decorum. But the principle he advocated proved useful in the more robust hands of a humorous artist.

In 1788 Francis Grose, an English antiquarian, published a pamphlet called *Rules for Drawing Caricatures* [293]. It certainly met a demand at the time when the merging of the Hogarthian tradition of comic art with the fashion of portrait caricature led to a popular craze for such drawings among amateurs. Grose combines the diagrams of Le Brun with the variation principle advocated by Cozens. The academic standard face, which corresponds to the canon of Greek art, is experienced as beautiful, he says, precisely because it lacks expression. Try varying the proportions as drastically as you like, and watch what happens. You will soon be equipped with a repertory of funny faces that will be useful in drawing humorous pictures [294].

Historically Grose is the immediate source of Töpffer's theories just as Grose's

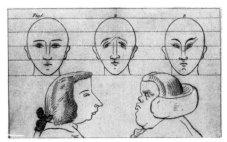
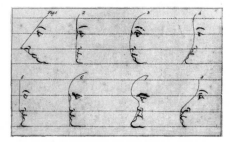

293–294. GROSE: *From 'Rules for Drawing Caricatures'*. 1788

295. ROWLANDSON: *An illustration for
'Dr. Syntax'*. 1810. Pen and water colour

296. DAUMIER: *The Audience Pleased*. 1864.
Lithograph

contemporary, Rowlandson, is the source of Töpffer's types. The comic antics of
Dr. Syntax in search of the Picturesque [295] foreshadow the crazy adventures of
Töpffer's heroes. But artistically the English tradition of humorous art had an
heir much greater than the Swiss inventor of the comic strip. Without Hogarth
and Rowlandson there could have been no Daumier.

Daumier is a master of such stature that he is usually seen in the context of the
French tradition of great art. He can be linked with Delacroix or compared with
Millet. Yet there are perhaps more links between Daumier and the English school
of political pamphleteers than are usually acknowledged. Even so feeble a representative of English political cartooning as H. B. may have contributed something to
the idiom of Daumier's political lithographs [297]. Compare H. B.'s crowds and the
way these physiognomies arise out of careless scribbles, the artist groping his way
through a welter of lines. Rowlandson had done the same thing with much more
gusto. Daumier did it with genius [296]. But the method is the same. It relies not
on pre-existent forms, on the schemata of academic art checked and clarified in
front of the model, but on configurations arising under the artist's hand as if by
accident. Each of these men, like Töpffer's Dr. Festus, is a true creation of the
artist, each owes his life to him alone. Contemporaries tell us that they were struck
by the likeness of the painter Daumier to all his creatures. It is significant that
Leonardo, the inventor of variations of physiognomic themes, was almost obsessed
by the danger of committing this common fault. And need it be an accident that
Rembrandt was constantly returning to his own image as a source of knowledge?
But let Rembrandt remain *hors de concours* in this story of discovery. Daumier,
too, has been praised for his uncannily retentive memory which made him scorn

297. H. B. (J. DOYLE): *Cobbett's Lecture.* 1830

study from the model—but is not his art rather a tribute to his power to project features into the clouds of lines he draws and from which ever new physiognomies emerge as they do from the soft clay under a modelling hand [298]? Daumier started with portrait busts, and something of the modelling habit remained with him in his extraordinary noncommittal drawing technique, the very opposite of

298. DAUMIER: *Two lawyers.* About 1866. Drawing

299. DAUMIER: *Head*. About 1865. Drawing   300. ENSOR: *La Vieille aux masques*. 1889

the schematic forms taught by the Academy. Remembering our formula of schema and correction, we might say that Daumier does not put down on paper more than the merest indications of ambiguous forms, mere clouds of lines in which he will find his schema for modifications. He concentrates on the features which make

301. MUNCH: *The Cry*. 1895. Lithograph

for physiognomic character or gesture or facial expression, but these he brings out with such force that we forget the multiple and ambiguous outlines of the form and invest it with immense vitality [299].

It may seem a little blasphemous to compare this achievement with that of Töpffer, and so far as artistic quality is concerned, I have no such intention. And yet from one point of view such a comparison is illuminating. It helps to define Daumier's historical position. We usually count him a founder-hero of modern art, and we are right in doing so. But his contribution had nothing to do with visual discoveries of the kind Constable made and the impressionists continued.

Daumier made fun of Courbet and despised Monet. To him who never drew from life, the study of "plein-air" effects must have seemed nugatory compared with the study of human reactions. And so it is not surprising that the artists who hailed him as their ancestor were not the impressionists but the expressionists, and in this context, for once, this misleading contrast acquires some meaning. For in and with Daumier the tradition of physiognomic experiment began to be emancipated from that of humour. Very early in his career Baudelaire had noticed that his lawyers, judges, or fauns are far from humorous. They are creations in their own right, often terrifying in their intensity, masks of the human passions which probe deeply into the secret of expression. Without this breaking down of barriers between caricature and great art, a master such as Munch [301] could never have evolved his intensely tragic, distorted physiognomies, nor could the Belgian Ensor [300] in the same period have created his idiom of terrifying masks which so excited the German expressionists.

VI

IT MEANS no disrespect to the achievements of twentieth-century art if we thus link them with the emancipation from the study of nature which was first tried out in the licensed precincts of humour and elucidated in the experiments of Töpffer. Nor need we assume that Töpffer would have been surprised at the course which art was taking. His failing eyesight led him increasingly to meditations on art which were published after his death under the title *Menus propos d'un peintre genevois* and discussed with much respect by Théophile Gautier. Rambling at a leisurely pace through the fields of aesthetics, Töpffer comes to insist increasingly on the conventional character of all artistic signs and concludes that the essence of art is not imitation but expression.

Töpffer's method — to 'doodle and watch what happens'—has indeed become one of the acknowledged means of extending the language of art.

When Picasso says, 'I do not seek, I find', he means, I submit, that he has come to take as a matter of course that creation itself is exploration. He does not plan, he watches the weirdest beings rise under his hands and assume a life of their own. The films which show him at work, and his more playful creations, such as his *papiers déchirés* [302], show that here is a man who has succumbed to the spell of making, un-

302

restrained and unrestrainable by the mere descriptive functions of the image.

It is fitting that a similar claim of discovery through making has been made with

303. JAMES THURBER: '*What have you done with Dr. Millmoss?*' © 1934 *The New Yorker Magazine Inc.*

much charm and humour by one of the most original of contemporary humorists, James Thurber. Thurber describes how some of his most popular drawings arose unplanned. The drawing 'What have you done with Dr. Millmoss?' [303] is a case in point. 'The hippopotamus was drawn to amuse my small daughter,' Thurber says. 'Something about the creature's expression convinced me that he had recently eaten a man. I added the hat and pipe, and Mrs. Millmoss and the caption followed easily enough.'

But what is an accident in art? Are we right when we speak of random movements and random changes only because the artist did not seem aware of his intention beforehand? It is often thought that such an interpretation would contradict the findings of psychoanalysis, which has warned us against attaching too much importance to conscious intention. The forms and expressions found by twentieth-century artists in the course of their experiments with colours and shapes have been popularly accepted as images arising out of the depth of the artist's 'unconscious'. But this is, to my mind, a naïve misunderstanding. What psychoanalysis claims is that our conscious and preconscious mind will always tend to guide and influence the way we react to accidents. The inkblot is a random event; how we react to it is determined by our past. No one could predict where the paper which produced Picasso's ghostly mask would tear—what matters is why he kept it. It must have been almost equally hard to know beforehand how the exact position of the eyebrows would affect the expression of Thurber's hippo— what matters is that he knew how to observe and exploit it. The whole vexing question of what we mean by 'intention' and how far we are ever in control of our movements is in a state of flux. In a way, perhaps, we always control and adjust our movements by observing their effects, similar to those self-regulating mechanisms that engineers call 'feedback'. Skill consists in a most rapid and subtle interaction between impulse and subsequent guidance, but not even the most skilful artist should claim to be able to plan a single stroke with the pen in all its details. What he can do is adjust the subsequent stroke to the effect observed in the previous one—which is, after all, precisely what Thurber has done. In this new process of schema and modification, the artist is one controlling fact, the public another. The artist may fear the accident, the unexpected which seems to endow the created image with a life of its own, or he can welcome it as an ally to expand the range of his language, as Leonardo and Cozens did. The more the public wants to join in this game, the less it will be interested in the artist's intention. Those who attribute to modern art the capacity of trans- cribing the images of our unconscious obviously gravely oversimplify a very complex train of events. We should say rather that it has swept away those restraints and taboos that restricted the artist's choice of means and the freedom of experimentation.

The modern sculptor is free to grope for a global, physiognomic form in shapes which are sisters under their skin to Al Capp's motherly Shmoo. The modern painter may use what he calls 'automatic painting', the creation of Rorschach blots, in order to stimulate the mind—his own and those of others—towards fresh inventions. In this new-found freedom the old divisions created by the social idea of decorum have fallen. We hardly ask ourselves whether to pigeonhole the drawings of William Steig [304] as humour or as serious art. No artist is more characteristic of this

304

ultimate fusion of humorous experiment and artistic search than Paul Klee [305], who described how the artist-creator first builds and shapes the image according to purely formal laws of balance and harmony and then salutes the being that has grown under his hand by giving it a name, sometimes whimsical, sometimes serious, sometimes both.

In turning away from the visible world, art may really have found an uncharted region which waits to be discovered and articulated, as music has discovered and articulated it through the universe of sound. But this inner world, if we may call it so, can no more be transcribed than can the world of sight. To the artist the image in the unconscious is as mythical and useless an idea as was the image on the retina. There is no short cut to articulation. Wherever the artist turns his gaze he can only make and match, and out of a developed language select the nearest equivalence.

305. KLEE: *The Timid Tough.* 1938.
Oil on jute

XI

From Representation to Expression

By their true nature rhythms and tunes are copies of anger and mildness, courage and temperance (with their opposites) and all the other qualities of character. . . . What we perceive by the other senses are not such copies, for instance the things we touch or taste, except for the things we see, because shapes do partake of this character, though only a little. . . .

ARISTOTLE, *Politics*

You need not be in the least afraid of pushing these analogies too far. They cannot be pushed too far; they are so precise and complete, that the farther you pursue them, the clearer the more certain, the more useful you will find them. . . . Affection and discord, fretfulness and quietness, feebleness and firmness, luxury and purity, pride and modesty, and all other such habits, and every conceivable modification and mingling of them, may be illustrated, with mathematical exactness, by conditions of line and colour.

JOHN RUSKIN, *The Elements of Drawing*

I

THE HISTORY of art, as we have interpreted it so far, may be described as the forging of master keys for opening the mysterious locks of our senses to which only nature herself originally held the key. They are complex locks which respond only when various screws are first set in readiness and when a number of bolts are shifted at the same time. Like the burglar who tries to break a safe, the artist has no direct access to the inner mechanism. He can only feel his way with sensitive fingers, probing and adjusting his hook or wire when something gives way. Of course, once the door springs open, once the key is shaped, it is easy to repeat the performance. The next person needs no special insight—no more, that is, than is needed to copy his predecessor's master key.

There are inventions in the history of art that have something of the character of such an open-sesame. Foreshortening may be one of them in the way it produces the impression of depth; others are the tonal system of modelling, highlights for texture, or those clues to expression discovered by humorous art which were the topic of the last chapter. The question is not whether nature 'really looks' like these pictorial devices but whether pictures with such features suggest a reading in terms of natural objects. Admittedly the degree to which they do depends to some extent on what we called 'mental set'. We respond differently when we are 'keyed up' by expectation, by need, and by cultural habituation. All these factors may affect the preliminary setting of the lock but not its opening, which still depends on turning the right key.

The growing awareness that art offers a key to the mind as well as to the outer world has led to a radical change of interest on the part of artists. It is a legitimate shift, I believe, but it would be a pity if these fresh explorations failed to profit from the lessons of tradition. For there is a curious reversal of emphasis in recent critical writings. It has become an accepted fact that naturalism is a form of convention—indeed, this aspect has been somewhat exaggerated. The language of forms and colours, on the other hand, that explores the inner recesses of the mind has come to be looked upon as being right by nature. Our nature.

In conclusion, I should like at least to throw a spotlight on this question. And here as always it seems to me useful to go back to the origins of this type of problem. It was a much-debated question at the time of Plato whether the language of words, the names of things, exists by convention or by nature. Whether there is some real bond between the word 'horse' and a horse, or whether it might also be called by any other name. The question, put in that form, looks to us a little childish. Most of us are convinced that with the exception of such onomatopoeic words as 'moocow,' the names of things are more or less fortuitous labels, noises we have learned to make in order to indicate certain classes of things. It has been traditional in this context to bring out the arbitrary and conventional nature of language by contrasting the accidental name 'horse' or '*cheval*' with the artist's visual image of a horse. This, it was thought, is not conventional but a real likeness, a natural sign, or what is also called an 'icon'.

In Plato's *Cratylus,* which is devoted to this problem, Socrates constantly makes use of this contrast. 'Could a painting, to revert to our previous comparison, be made like any real thing, if there were not pigments out of which the painting is composed, which were by nature like the objects which the painter's art imitates? Is that not impossible?'

'Impossible,' echoes his victim. It is one of the moments in Plato's dialogues when one would like to have been present to thrust the speaker aside. 'O Socrates,' I would have said, 'were you not trained as a sculptor?' 'I was,' he would have admitted. 'And did you find that the stone you used was like the objects you imitated?' 'Not very much, by the dog.' 'Or what about the cups from which you drank at the symposium? Have you not noticed that the old-fashioned ones have black figures on the red burnt clay, while most of your recent pottery uses black for the ground and leaves the natural red of the cup free for the figures? Are objects then both black and red according to the painter's whim? But even if you thought of the coloured paintings by Polygnotus or Zeuxis, we now know, O Socrates, that they could never hope to match their pigments against the reality of a sunlit landscape. Yet sunlit landscapes have been painted, and what you considered impossible has happened.'

In my joy of victory I would not allow the venerable twister to plead that he had never seen sunlit landscapes painted and had never been aware of those perceptual constancies and the miracles of mental set which make the trick possible. I would take him to a nursery and show him children playing with coloured blocks. There would be red, green, and yellow blocks all in a row with one double on top, and the child would push them along shouting 'choo choo'. 'What has this in common with a train?' I would ask triumphantly. 'A what?' he would say. And before I knew where I was he would have his own back. If I told him what trains are, he would believe, or at least pretend to believe, that they move through the country as red, green, and yellow cubes saying 'choo choo'. 'If not,' he would say, 'why do you call this a train? And if it does not say 'choo, choo', what purpose do these strange and senseless syllables serve?'

Perhaps then at last, with both of us a little humbled, we could settle down to the proper argument which is, I believe, that there is more in common between the language of words and visual representation than we are sometimes prone to allow. The train, we would agree, is not a likeness; it is an attempt to arrange the blocks at our disposal in such a way that they can serve as a train on the nursery floor. The child does not say, 'Shall we represent a train in blocks, Daddy?' He says, 'Shall we make a train?' By this he means something like a rudimentary model, a row of units which he can push and which he can people in imagination.

And is it different with the word 'choo choo'? Trains do not make this noise, but within the structure of the child's linguistic medium—which linguists call the phonemes or blocks out of which English is built—the syllable 'choo' matches the noise of a steam engine better than others, and so it has been adopted to represent the thrusts of the piston, a convention, incidentally, which probably continues in countries with electrified railways that never say anything remotely like 'choo'.

In the language of words this type of conventionalized imitation plays a subsidiary part. Yet I believe the student of visual images should consider these so-called onomatopoeic imitations of sound in language for the light they throw on his own problems. Nowhere, I submit, is the link between convention, mental set, and perception more easily analysed than in this restricted field. We have seen that these so-called imitations are not imitations proper but approximations, within the given medium of language, to the sound heard. The sound of the drum, for instance, is imitated as '*rataplan*' in French; English, lacking the nasal phoneme, uses instead the syllables 'rumtitum', which—to me at any rate—is less of an approximation. For that very reason, I believe, we may find it used less than its more successful French equivalent. I would not be surprised if the better match of the French sound results in more projection and illusion—in other words, that more French people hear the drum say '*rataplan*' than English people hear it say 'rumtitum'. To me, at least, the cock says not 'cock-a-doodle-doo' as he calls to the English in the morning, nor '*cocorico*', as he says in French, nor '*kiao kiao*', as in Chinese, but still '*kikeriki*', as he says in German. Or—not to fall into the mistake of Socrates—it is not precisely '*kikeriki*' he says; he still speaks cockish and not Viennese. My percept of the throaty noise of his call is distinctly coloured by habitual interpretation. How much it is coloured would be the problem between nature and convention; to answer that truthfully we would have to be able to compare the sound it really makes with the sound we hear. Put in this way, the difficulty, or perhaps the absurdity, of the problem becomes apparent. There is no reality without interpretation; just as there is no innocent eye, there is no innocent ear.

Take an onomatopoeic word such as 'tick-tock'. Some clocks should really say 'tick-tick', since the units of sound are almost identical, and yet I feel compelled to organize my percepts. But this need to organize and interpret does not mean that we are helplessly caught in our interpretation. We can experiment and through trial and error learn something about such impressions. An alternative interpretation may drive out the accepted one and reveal a glimpse of the reality behind it. Having become critical of my hearing 'tick-tock', I can try to hear something else. I can adopt the tentative hypothesis of making the clock say 'tick-tick-tock', and when I succeed in projecting this alternative, I can conclude that the stimuli I group in these different ways must be neutral. I have made a discovery about reality by trying alternative interpretations. This is what the adventurous artists were doing when, in the face of a tick-tock-believing public, they imposed an alternative reading on reality and thus gradually succeeded in exploring the dazzling ambiguity of vision. In language, of course, the imitation of nature is marginal. What we imitate is one another's speech. But even this process is not without its lessons for the student of mimesis. As readers of this book may have learned to expect, it has proved impossible to analyse speech sound down into its component stimuli however carefully the student of phonetics attends to the noise and disregards the meaning. Those who have tried to produce artificial speech mechanically have made the most astounding observations. When speech is translated into light impulses in special apparatus, it is found that sounds which impress us as identical look very different, while others which we accept as quite different produce identical visible traces. Like the maker of the 'facsimile', the makers of artificial speech found that the context and—in this case—the sequence of sounds affect every element. If we play a recorded speech in reverse we do not hear the same noises simply in a different order; the result is quite unlike human speech. In trying to devise a mimetic machine of speech sounds that would give the illusion of real speech, the engineers had to fall back on the same technique of experimentation which art employed on a secular scale: they devised a 'speech synthesizer' which can translate visible speech into sound, and by this means they are patiently trying

306. VAN GOGH: *Copy after Millet, 'The Cornfield'*. 1890

out the mutual effect of various noises on one another. It is hoped that the speech synthesizer may thus shortly answer the question that the 'innocent ear' could never have solved, the question of what the auditory clues are that make us recognize speech sounds as what we believe we hear.

In learning to speak we follow a path which is also similar to that of art. A few simple schemata are progressively adjusted to match the sound without need for analysis. When confronted with the task of saying 'Lisbeth', a child who had learned to say 'papa' and 'mama' produced the compromise 'Pippa'—a transposition of the sounds he heard into the limited phonemes of his language. What we call a 'foreign accent' is nothing but an extension of this 'Pippa principle'. The foreigner imitates the sounds of the new language as far as the phonemes of his native tongue allow. The motor habits acquired early in life will not only condition his speech but also the way he 'hears' the language. His original schemata have conditioned him to watch out for certain distinctive features while ignoring other variations in sound as irrelevant, and nothing proves harder than articulating the world of sound afresh. Once more the parallel with our findings in this book could hardly be more complete. We have seen the Pippa principle at work in our study of the role of stereotypes in portrayal. An accent, we suspect, has many similarities to those all-pervading qualities we call 'style'.

Few areas in this no man's land between psychology, aesthetics, and linguistics are as unexplored as that of skill, and it is not my intention to open it up here. But

307. MILLET: *The Cornfield.* 1867

I believe the skill of hand in art, like the skill of throat in language, follows the awareness of differences that have to be pointed out to be experienced. Wherever there is a clash of style, where one artist wants to copy the work of a different tradition, the importance of these motor habits becomes apparent.

We have seen, in fact, that the artist who copies will always tend to build up the image from the schemata he has learned to handle. In van Gogh's moving copy of a print after Millet [306], his manner—his motor habits—always breaks through. He repeats Millet's statements [307] in his own accent. It is true that a strong obtrusive accent in its turn can be learned and imitated. Van Gogh's own can be forged with relative ease. But then his swirling lines still belong to the macrostructure of his style. It is in the microstructure of movement and shapes that the connoisseur will find the inimitable personal accent of an artist.

When the Italian physician Morelli first systematically applied such graphological criteria to the study of drawings, his new scientific method aroused great hopes. It consisted precisely of looking at the minute schemata, the habits of the pen in indicating an ear lobe or a fingernail. Why was it that this method produced results only when used by the most gifted of experts and led to absurdities in unskilled hands? Why was it that the true connoisseur, such as Max J. Friedländer, turned away from any pretence at rational analysis and proclaimed that the recognition of personal style was merely a matter of intuition based on experience?

Perhaps the analysis of language perception indicates a direction in which an answer to this puzzle may lie. The personal accent of the artist is not made up of individual tricks of hand which can be isolated and described. It is again a question of relationships, of the interaction of countless personal reactions, a matter of distribution and sequences which we perceive as a whole without being able to name the elements in combination. Friedländer may well have been right in declaring that the trained eye is the most sensitive recording apparatus for such total impressions that defy analysis. By the analogy of the speech synthesizer there would only be one way of probing into the secrets of such total effects: a committee of forgers would have to submit their systematically varied results to a committee of connoisseurs who might then agree on the exact criteria by which they recognize a van Gogh.

II

WITH THE QUESTION of personal style we have reached the frontier of what is usually called 'representation'. For in these ultimate constituents the artist is said to express himself. But is there really such a sharp division between representation and expression? The results of our last chapter have made us doubt it, and a comparison with language will confirm these doubts. For language, like the visual image, functions not only in the service of actual description and subjective emotion, but also in that wide area between these extremes where everyday language conveys both the facts and the emotive tone of an experience.

Indeed, in the *Cratylus*, Socrates toys with the idea that the principle of onomatopoeia, of imitating sounds, might extend beyond the obvious instances I have quoted: that vocal imitation does not stop short where the realm of sound ends but extends beyond into that of sight and movement; that the letter *r* will suggest something flowing or moving, and the letter *i* something sharp or bright. This is dangerous ground, a favourite haunt of cranks and even of madmen, and yet I think it is ground which will have to be traversed. For we all feel that sounds can indeed imitate or match visual impressions—that words like 'flicker', 'blinking', 'scintillating' are at least as good approximations in the language to the visual impression as 'tick-tock' or 'choo choo' were to the auditory ones. What is called 'synesthesia', the splashing over of impressions from one sense modality to another, is a fact to which all languages testify. They work both ways—from sight to sound and from sound to sight. We speak of loud colours or of bright sounds, and everyone knows what we mean. Nor are the ear and the eye the only senses that are thus converging to a common centre. There is touch in such terms as 'velvety voice' and 'a cold light', taste with 'sweet harmonies' of colours or sounds, and so on through countless permutations.

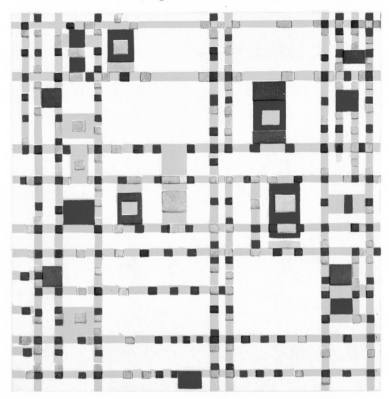

308. MONDRIAN: *Broadway Boogie-Woogie.* 1942/1943

Artists at all times have been interested in these correspondences, which are invoked in a famous poem by Baudelaire, but the Romantics and symbolists were particularly intent on exploring the laws of synesthesia. Rimbaud assigned colours to the five vowels, thus translating auditory impressions into visual ones. Musicians in their turn, were fond of representing the visible world in tones—we need only look down the list of titles Debussy gave to his pieces to see his faith in the efficacy of such evocation: 'Bruyères', 'Clair de Lune', 'Feux d'artifice' all represent or paint visual experiences on the keys of the piano. Some artists indulged in the dream of combining the world of sound and that of sight in higher orders; the fantastic painter Arcimboldo took the lead in the seventeenth century with a colour piano, and the idea persists to Wagner, Scriabin, and Disney's *Fantasia*. Finally painting, in withdrawing from the exploration of pure visibility, took up the challenge and explored the world of sound. Whistler's attempts are still vague and somewhat indefinite, but Kandinsky went further, and in Mondrian's painting labelled *Broadway Boogie-Woogie* [308], we have an example of such a transposition which seems generally accepted and acceptable. I don't know exactly what boogie-woogie is, but Mondrian's painting explains it to me.

309. MONDRIAN: *Painting I.* 1926

And yet can we really compare such renderings of sound patterns in visual terms with the rendering of visual impressions in visual terms? Granted even that most of us experience such synesthetic images with more or less intensity, are they not completely subjective and private, inaccessible and uncommunicable? Can there be real objective discoveries of good and better matches in these elusive spheres as there were in the discovery of visual analogies to visual experience? Can the world of the mind, of the dream, be explored by experiments that result in accepted conventions as was the world of the waking eye? Much of our assessment of twentieth-century art may depend on our answer to this question, for though not all, or even most, of it is concerned with synesthesia proper, all or most of it tries to represent the world of the mind where shapes and colours stand for feelings. I believe the analysis of representation may indeed lead us to understand these attempts better and to assess the chances of any new experiments in that direction.

For this analysis has taught us to remain aware of three factors—the medium, the mental set, and the problem of equivalence. When we talk about art we usually take all these matters for granted—they are the eight-ninths of the iceberg that remain submerged and do not obtrude on our awareness. But many an aesthetician's ship has suffered shipwreck for disregarding them.

To enjoy the Mondrian I need not think of any of these things. But if anyone should ask me seriously if Mondrian had represented a bit of boogie-woogie so accurately that I could now recognize the style if you played it to me, I would have to point to the underwater cliffs—the need, that is, for the context in which the communication takes place. If you made the context sufficiently specific I could. I trust myself to plump for the right piece if one played two contrasting pieces to me—one slow and blue, one fast and noisy. For here the Mondrian would give me a pointer—a pointer for that game which psychologists call 'matching'. Given a simple choice, Mondrian tells me in what class, category, or pigeonhole of music to seek for the equivalent. Without a knowledge of possibilities, this type of representation would work even less than the representation of the visible world that we also found to be dependent on our knowledge of what things might be.

But our analysis is not quite complete yet. For my understanding depends not only on my expectation and experience of possible types of music, but also on my

310. SEVERINI: *Dynamic Hieroglyphic of the Bal Tabarin.* 1912

knowledge of possible types of painting—in other words, on the mental set with which I approach the Mondrian.

In most of us the name of Mondrian conjures up the expectation of severity, of an art of straight lines and a few primary colours in carefully balanced rectangles [309]. Seen against this background, the boogiewoogie picture gives indeed the impression of gay abandon. It is so much less severe than the alternative we have in mind that we have no hesitation in matching it in our mind with this style of popular music. But this impression is in fact grounded on our knowledge of the restricted choice open to the artist within his self-imposed discipline. Let us imagine for a moment that we were told the painting is by Severini [310], who is known for his futuristic paintings that try to capture the rhythm of dance music in works of brilliant chaos. Would we then still feel the Mondrian belongs in the pigeonhole with boogiewoogie, or would we accept a label calling it Bach's *First Brandenburg Concerto*?

I do not think this analysis need speak in any way against the attempt to use forms and colours only as a medium of representing feeling. For if we have learned anything in the course of these chapters it is that a representation is never a replica. The forms of art, ancient and modern, are not duplications of what the artist has in mind any more than they are duplications of what he sees in the outer world. In both cases they are renderings within an acquired medium, a medium grown up through tradition and skill—that of the artist and that of the beholder.

It is my conviction that the problem of synesthetic equivalences will cease to look embarrassingly arbitrary and subjective if here, too, we fix our attention not on likeness of elements but on structural relationships within a scale or matrix. When we say that *u* is dark blue and *i* bright green, we are talking playful nonsense, or serious nonsense if we are in earnest. But when we say that *i* is brighter than *u*, we find a surprising degree of general consent. If we are more careful still and say the step from *u* to *i* is more like an upward step than a downward step, I think the majority will agree, whatever explanations each of us may be inclined to offer. I have chosen this example because I believe that once again the research of linguists offers us the best chance to make this much-discussed problem a little more manageable. It was Professor Roman Jakobson who drew my attention to the fact that synesthesia concerns relationships. I have tried out this suggestion in a party game. It consists of creating the simplest imaginable medium in which relationships can still be expressed, a language of two words only—let us call them 'ping' and 'pong'. If these were all we had and we had to name an elephant and a cat, which would be ping and which pong? I think the answer is clear. Or hot soup and ice-cream. To me, at least, ice-cream is ping and soup pong. Or Rembrandt and Watteau? Surely in that case Rembrandt would be pong and Watteau ping. I do not maintain that it always works, that two blocks are sufficient to categorize all relationships. We find people differing about day and night and male and female, but perhaps these different answers could be reduced to unanimity if the question were differently framed: pretty girls are ping and matrons pong; it may depend on which aspect of womanhood the person has in mind, just as the motherly, enveloping aspect of night is pong, but its sharp, cold, and menacing physiognomy may be ping to some.

In their recent book *The Measurement of Meaning*, Professor Charles E. Osgood and his collaborators have submitted a similar technique to a rigorous statistical analysis. They asked their subjects to place a notion such as 'lady' or 'boulder' along a scale extending between two such contrasting adjectives as 'rough' and 'smooth', 'good' and 'bad', 'active' and 'passive'. Like myself in the game of 'ping' and 'pong', they got a surprising agreement on apparently senseless questions, such as whether a boulder is happy or sad. They conclude that we always place any concept into a structured matrix, what they call the 'semantic space' of which the basic dimensions are 'good and bad', 'active and 'passive', 'strong and weak'. There may be objections to certain of Osgood's methodological assumptions, but I still

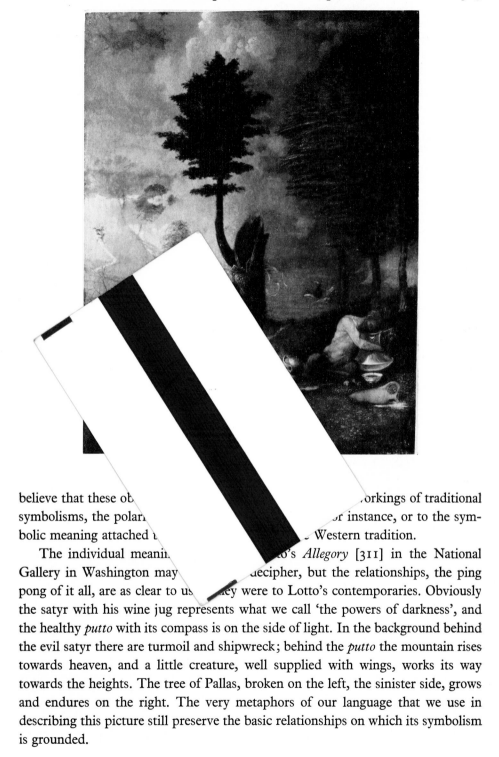

believe that these ob   orkings of traditional
symbolisms, the polar   r instance, or to the symbolic meaning attached   Western tradition.

The individual meani   o's *Allegory* [311] in the National
Gallery in Washington may   decipher, but the relationships, the ping
pong of it all, are as clear to us   ey were to Lotto's contemporaries. Obviously
the satyr with his wine jug represents what we call 'the powers of darkness', and
the healthy *putto* with its compass is on the side of light. In the background behind
the evil satyr there are turmoil and shipwreck; behind the *putto* the mountain rises
towards heaven, and a little creature, well supplied with wings, works its way
towards the heights. The tree of Pallas, broken on the left, the sinister side, grows
and endures on the right. The very metaphors of our language that we use in
describing this picture still preserve the basic relationships on which its symbolism
is grounded.

Lotto's painting proves, if proof be needed, that artists have been aware of the expressive potentialities of shapes and colours long before expressionist theory seized upon that aspect of painting. By the eighteenth century this practical tradition was also a commonplace of the critics. Thus Jonathan Richardson wrote: 'If the subject be grave, melancholy, or terrible, the general tint of the colouring must incline to brown, black, or red, and gloomy; but be gay, and pleasant in subjects of joy, and triumph.' And, 'Generally, if the character of the picture is greatness, terrible, or savage, as battles, robberies, witchcrafts, apparitions, or even the portraits of men of such characters there ought to be employed a rough, bold pencil; and contrarily, if the character is grace, beauty, love, innocence, etc., a softer pencil, and more finishing is proper.'

To some readers these words of an eighteenth-century critic may sound surprisingly modern. They may remind him of similar utterances by Delacroix and van Gogh that led the way to expressionism and Kandinsky's version of abstract art. But I believe this similarity is somewhat deceptive. What Richardson recommends for certain subjects is a deviation from the normal palette and the normal type of brushwork in the direction of darker tones or greater roughness. In giving this advice, he took it for granted that every medium and every convention has its own level of normality that determines the expectations of the connoisseur who would register any subtle emphasis in one direction or another. The identical tone, therefore, that would strike him as expressive of gloom in a water colour might have impressed him as calm and serene in an ink drawing.

It is this awareness of relationships, I feel, that has sometimes been lost in the writings of the expressionists. Anxious as they were to overthrow the hold of conventions, they had to look for absolutes where none can be found. As a consequence, they frequently talked as if a given shape or colour were inherently 'charged' with an expressive meaning that would explode in the mind of the beholder. But artistic communication is quite unlike throwing hand grenades. There must be not only a sender but also a receiver suitably attuned. In our response to expression no less than in our reading of representation, our expectations of possibilities and probabilities must come into play. Given such a keyboard of relationships, a matrix or scale that has intelligible dimensions of 'more' or 'less', there is perhaps no limit to the systems of forms that can be made the instrument of artistic expression in terms of equivalence. The rigid orders of ancient architecture [312] would seem to be a fairly recalcitrant matrix for the expression of psychological and physiognomic categories; still it makes sense when Vitruvius recommends Doric temples for Minerva, Mars, and Hercules, Corinthian ones for Venus, Flora, and Proserpina, while Juno, Diana, and other divinities who stand in between the two extremes are given Ionic temples. Within the medium at the architect's disposal, Doric is clearly more virile than Corinthian. We say that Doric expresses the god's severity; it does, but only because it is on the more severe end of the scale and not because there is necessarily much in common between the god of war and the Doric order. Following a similar trend of thought, Nicolas Poussin compared in a famous letter the expressive qualities of form and colour with the so-called 'modes' of ancient music. The Doric mode is again the severe one and thus suited to stern subjects; the Phrygian mode is passionate and thus comparable to the appropriate treatment of warlike subjects. He compares this change of modes with the methods of poets who attune the sound of the words to the theme of their song. Where Vergil talks of love, his sound is sweet and harmonious; where war is his subject, his verse rushes headlong. The medium is used to express or, as Poussin would have said, 'to paint the passions'. It is not an immediate expression but one

312. VIGNOLA: *The Five Orders of Architecture.* 1562

dependent on conventions. To those of us who do not know the potentialities of Latin verse, the sound of the lines where Vergil speaks of love will not differ much from that where he describes wars; in fact, we might feel inclined to suspect that the critic imagines things. But when we understand that Poussin felt the difference between two Vergilian lines to be analogous to the difference between love and war, we may come nearer to an understanding of what he called the 'depiction of the passions'.

Now here our wanderings have brought us back to the starting-point of this book, the concept of style. It will be remembered from the Introduction that art criticism borrowed this notion from the ancient critics of literature, especially from the teachers of rhetoric. The application of the term to painting and sculpture dates precisely from Poussin's period.

In classical writings on rhetoric we have perhaps the most careful analysis of any expressive medium ever undertaken. Language, to these critics, is an organon, an instrument which offers its master a variety of different scales and 'stops'. Whenever they discuss expression, therefore, they speak of the rich choice of 'expressions'.

This subtle analysis of speech should provide a most valuable supplement and even a corrective to Osgood's investigations. Where he speaks only of concepts,

313. POUSSIN: *The Gathering of the Ashes of Phocion.* 1648

these critics focussed their attention on the influence of words, their sounds and their status in our reactions. Thus Demetrius, in his Greek textbook *On Style* (written, it is believed, in the first century of our era), tells his readers to heed the musical distinction between smooth- and rough-sounding words. When the subject is as rugged and formidable a hero as the Homeric Ajax, the writer will do well to select expressions with harsh and even unpleasant sounds.

But the main distinction which the orator would observe was really a social one, the gamut between noble and lowly. The identical meaning can be expressed in words from different levels along this scale. We can say 'face' or 'countenance', 'girl' or 'maiden'. Cicero, who discusses the fitting choice of language in his dialogues on oratory, elaborates this distinction by establishing three modes of speech, the plain, the medium, and the ornate. 'Boy meets girl' would be humble style; 'youth encounters maiden' is ornate. Then as now, the archaic and obsolete term often sounded more lofty than the word in current usage. This shift in emphasis is known to all students of style: in admiring the force and power of the Authorized Version, we have to remind ourselves that the passage of time has turned the humble speech of the gospels into the lofty style of archaism.

There has always been a temptation in language to treat the social, the historical, and the moral scale as equivalent: to group the ancient with the noble and the restrained, and the modern with the vulgar and the indulgent. Luckily this tendency

314. CLAUDE LORRAIN: *Landscape with Moses and the Burning Bush.* 1664

was sometimes counteracted by those who equated the plain and humble with the good, and the ornate with the stilted, affected, and degenerate.

When Johann Joachim Winckelmann in the eighteenth century first applied the categories of style systematically to the history of art, he projected these shifting categories onto the development of representation. Looking at Greek art through eyes surfeited with Baroque exuberance and rococo frivolity, he exalted it as both simple and noble, the expression of untroubled innocence and moral restraint. The psychological pitfalls of such interpretations need no longer concern us here. We have seen that we cannot judge expression without an awareness of the choice situation, without a knowledge of the organon. I have emphasized in the Introduction how the neglect of skill will deprive the historian of the means to interpret style as expression. Where we have no matrix, no keyboard, we cannot assess the meaning of an individual feature.

The main purpose of the preceding chapters of this book, it will be remembered, was to investigate the limitations in the artist's choice, his need for a vocabulary, and his restricted opportunities for widening the range of representational possibilities. It is the purpose of this present chapter to show why this limitation is not a weakness but rather a source of strength for art. Where everything is possible and nothing unexpected, communication must break down. It is because art operates with a structured style governed by technique and the schemata of tradition that representation could become the instrument not only of information but also of

315. GESSNER: *Woodland scene*. About 1760.   316. WATERLOO: *Woodland scene*.
Etching   About 1650. Etching

expression. Having begun these chapters with Constable's achievement, I should like in conclusion to test these results by returning to his views of art.

III

CONSTABLE is such a crucial witness in our context precisely because of his own ambivalent attitude towards style, the ready-made vocabulary of representation he had inherited. We remember how violently he fought against 'mannerisms', against that obtruding memory of pictures which, he thought, obscured both the artist's and the public's vision of nature. And yet, as Leslie tells us, 'In speaking of a young artist who boasted that he had never studied the works of others, he said "After all, there is such a thing as the art".'

The art, of course, is the language in which the master alone can express his vision. We have seen in previous chapters what this statement means in terms of the history of representation; why it is, in other words, that the art historian is entitled to look for the derivation of any artist's vocabulary in the traditions of the past. It would be the task of a monograph on Constable to refine this research by analysing the elements he took over from the artists he studied and admired. In our present context, however, we are less concerned with these visual derivations than with their meaning in terms of expression, and here the historian will do well to keep to the explicit interpretations he finds in the written sources of the period. In Constable's case they yield a good deal of information.

The subject of Constable's choice, the art of landscape painting, had not begun as a study of natural appearances; it had grown up within such systems of modes or moods as could be reflected in the various genres of poetry, the epic [313] or the idyl [314].

When young Constable opened the book on the art of painting that contained the most detailed account of landscape painting in English, the translation of de Piles, he would read there:

'Among the many different styles of landskip, I shall confine myself to two; the *heroick* and *the pastoral* or *rural*; for all other styles are but mixtures of these. . . . The heroick style . . . is an agreeable illusion, and a sort of inchantment, when handled by a man of fine genius. . . . But if, in the course of this style, the painter has not talent enough to maintain the sublime, he is often in danger of falling into the childish manner.

'The *rural style* is a representation of countries, rather abandoned to the caprice of nature than cultivated: We there see nature simple, without ornament, and without artifice; but with all those graces with which she adorns herself much more, when left to herself than when constrained by art.'

The words here used by de Piles directly echo Cicero's characterization of the 'humble style'. And like the orator, the painter would take it for granted that this style, too, has to be learned.

At the time of Constable's apprenticeship there existed a popular treatise on landscape painting by the Swiss writer and illustrator of idyls Salomon Gessner [315]. To read Gessner's account of his own training is to see the background against which Constable's utterances must be seen, because Gessner still looks at 'The Art' as a system of conventional motifs best picked up from tradition. He tells us, 'Trees were the first things I essayed: and I chose for my model Waterloo [316]. The more I studied this artist the more I found in his landscapes the true character of nature. . . . For rocks I chose the bold masses of Berchem. Lorrain instructed me in the disposition and harmony of foreground and soft fading distance. . . . In returning after these preparations to nature, I found my efforts much less laborious.'

We know that Constable himself explored the same approach to nature. We have seen his copies, and we have his own word for it in that famous letter which records his emancipation.

'For the last two years I have been running after pictures and seeking the truth at second hand . . . I shall return to Bergholt, where I shall endeavour to get a pure and unaffected manner of representing the scenes that may employ me. . . . There is room enough for a natural painture. . . . The great vice of the present day is *bravura*, an attempt to do something beyond the truth. . . .'

There is protest here, and rebellion, but rebellion in terms of existing categories. The 'natural painter' for whom there is room, would cultivate a version of the *style champêtre*. As late as 1824 Constable still wrote to a friend: 'I hold the genuine

pastoral feeling of landscape to be very rare . . . it is by far the most lovely department of painting. . . .'

Now in deciding which mode or style of art he would make his own, Constable
was again following traditional wisdom codified by de Piles: 'It rarely happens',
he would read in de Piles, 'that a painter has a genius extensive enough to embrace
all the parts of painting: there is commonly some one part that pre-engages our
choice, and so fills our mind, that we forget the pains that are due to the other
parts . . . those who practise the pastoral, apply closely to colouring, in order to
represent truth more lively. Both these styles have their sectaries and partisans.
Those who follow the heroick, supply by their imagination, what it wants of truth,
and they look no farther.

'As a counterbalance to heroick landskip, I think it would be proper to put into
the pastoral, besides a great character of truth, some affecting, extraordinary, but
probable effect of nature. . . .'

Now here, it may be, Constable came up against a contradiction in de Piles. We
have seen in a previous chapter that that author advocated different methods of
handling for the two modes: 'As there are styles of thought, so there are also styles
of execution. I have handled the two relating to thought, *to wit* the heroick and
pastoral; and find that there are two also with regard to execution, *to wit* the firm
style, and the polished.'

In de Piles' 'ping pong' the pastoral was the polished. Constable, who followed
the line of truth and natural effects, would reject this categorization. His style of
truth was rough and forceful.

Even this decision, though, would not have surprised any of Constable's contemporaries who had read their classics. The sublimity of truth and of genuine
emotion as distinct from affectation was, after all, the message of one of the most
influential treatises on rhetoric, the one attributed to Longinus.

By this time, I suppose, many a reader may wonder what can possibly be gained
through this intellectual game of pigeon-holing. A good deal, I venture to think.
For the rhetorical tradition may help us to see not only the problem of expression
but even that of self-expression from an unexpected angle. Romanticism has taught
us to talk of art in terms of inspiration and creativity. It was only interested
in what was new and original. The very existence of styles and traditions has
made us doubtful of the value of this approach to the history of art. It is here
that the tradition of rhetoric is such a useful corrective because it supplies a
philosophy of language. In this tradition the hierarchy of modes, the language
of art, exists independent of the individual. It is the young artist who is born
into this system and who has to make his choice. To do so he must study
himself and follow his own bent, and in so far as he succeeds he will also express
his personality.

Now, this view of self-expression as a series of decisions between alternatives certainly over-rationalizes the subtle interactions between an artist and his style. But it has the advantage of presenting precisely that framework of the social situation which Ernst Kris was demanding for a fuller understanding of the psychology of style. In a case such as Constable's it should indeed be possible to reconstruct some of the motivations, social, historical, and psychological, which determined his choice though they did not 'create' his art.

The social factor was strongly felt by Ruskin, who deplored the fact that 'Constable's early education and associations induced a morbid preference of subjects of a low order'. There is no doubt that Constable, the son of a miller, was conscious of his place in the social scale and proud of it. Had not Rembrandt, too, been the son of a miller and become the bogeyman of the over-refined? For him to aspire to the lofty and heroic would seem false and hypocritical. But though Ruskin still thought in terms of strict social hierarchies, times had changed. Perhaps, after all, the future belonged to the lowborn and humble.

We know little of Constable's political sympathies, and it is not these that are here in question. But no one whose youth coincided with the French Revolution could remain unaffected by its challenge to the old hierarchy of values. The 'humble style' had always been associated with truth unadorned. Now this truth had acquired a new pathos. There was too much timidity, too much conformity in the higher ranks of art and society. They had become conservative *from choice*.

There is no more telling document of this attitude against which Constable rebelled than the writings of that lovable and prolific propagandist for picturesque travel, the Reverend William Gilpin. Writing in 1791, Gilpin advised the artist against the search for visual truth:

'The appearance of blue and purple trees, unless in the remote distance, offends, and though the artist may have authority from nature for his practice, yet the spectator, not versed in such effects, may be displeased. Painting, like poetry, is intended to excite pleasure: and though the painter with this view should avoid such images as are trite and vulgar; yet he should seize only those which are easy and intelligible. Neither poetry or painting is a proper vehicle of learning. The painter will do well to avoid every uncommon appearance in nature.'

As the heirs of the Romantic revolution, we find something shocking, almost immoral, in this frank appeal to timid conformity. But the historian does well to remember that his values are not necessarily those of the past. The passage reminds us of the important fact that there must always be two sides to the progress of visual discoveries: the artist who makes them and the public which is ready to share in the game. Perhaps the public will make this effort only in a situation when the idea of innovation, discovery, and progress has acquired some lustre elsewhere. That Constable's was such a period is clear. Did he not himself appeal to the prestige of science to justify his experiments?

Lonely though Constable may have felt when he decided for truth and science against the forces of falsehood and affectation, he was not alone in his decision. We need only open the Prefaces to Wordsworth's poems, the one of 1800 and the other of 1815, to get an inkling of the situation. For Wordsworth, too, was championing the humble mode of speech against the claims of 'poetic diction'; he, too saw the poet 'ready to follow the steps of the Man of Science' in his search for truth, and he, too, demanded, as the first power requisite for the production of poetry, 'the ability to observe with accuracy things as they are in themselves, and with fidelity to describe them'. These are no mere parallels. For it so happens that this last quotation comes from the 1815 edition of Wordsworth's poems, which was dedicated to and illustrated by none other than Sir George Beaumont, Constable's patron and mentor.

Here, in the roughest outlines, is the framework, the situation, which determined the alternatives open to a young artist of Constable's background and generation. But the choice itself could not be fully determined from outside. It was his own, rooted in his past and in his personality. Can the historian pry into these secrets? Constable never fails when we ask him. Indeed, his answer shows so much psychological insight that little need be added to his words in this century of Freud: 'The sound of water escaping from mill-dams, etc., willows, old rotten planks, slimy posts, and brickwork, I love such things. . . . I shall never cease to paint such places . . . painting is with me but another word for feeling, and I associate "my careless boyhood" with all that lies on the banks of the Stour; those scenes made me a painter.'

The observant Leslie tells us even more—a piece of information which needs no further elucidation for those who know how to assess the categories and equivalences of the dreaming mind: in passing some slimy posts near an old mill, Constable said, 'I wish you could cut off and send their tops to me.'

I have invoked Freud. I could also have quoted William James in that wonderful image he used: 'As the bees in swarming cling to one another in layers till the few are reached whose feet grapple the bough from which the swarm depends; so with the objects of our thinking—they hang to each other by associated links, but the *original* source in all of them is the native interest which the earliest one once possessed.'

'The interest suffusing the whole system' of Constable's professional life—for this is the type of interest William James is discussing—rose from this primal and primary interest in the slimy posts of his father's mill. It must have been to the boy Constable a thrilling discovery that there existed a medium in which this original interest could be represented and expanded. Rural scenery in general and

317. CONSTABLE: *Sketch for 'Valley Farm'*. About 1835

watermills [34, 317, 318] in particular had a fixed place in the vocabulary of land-scape art. Let others such as Turner develop the heroic range of the scale; he would press on to make the Dutch rural tradition more and more amenable to the representation of those aspects which make landscape dear to him. We may here gain a glimpse of the deep sources that fed his dissatisfaction with ready-made idyllic schemata, his wish to go beyond them and discover visual truth. Not just any truth. We have learned that all paintings must be interpretations but that not all interpretations are equally valid. The truth Constable was after he has often explained: 'Lights—dews—breezes—blooms and freshness, not one of which has yet been perfected by any painter in the world.' It was for their sake that he looked upon other men's pictures as things to be avoided, for their sake that he looked upon his own as experiments. When old Fuseli made the famous remark that Constable's landscapes made him call for his greatcoat and umbrella, he showed he understood the kind of truth the master was aiming at. Not the dry but the humid, not the linear but the atmospheric, not the lasting but the transient. As Constable himself said in the preface to his published landscapes, to give 'one brief moment caught from fleeting time a lasting and sober existence'. Lasting and sober. We do well to remember these beautiful honest words before we rashly fall in with the view that Constable's finished paintings are less interesting, less artistic than his sketches.

318. CONSTABLE: *Sketch for 'Valley Farm'*. About 1835

The source of this preference is clear. We prefer suggestion to representation, we have adjusted our expectations to enjoy the very act of guessing, of projecting. And we rationalize this preference by fancying that the sketch must be nearer to what the artist saw and to what he felt than the finished work. I do not deny that artists are human and sometimes spoil their works. But I consider it a heresy to think that any painting as such records a sense impression or a feeling. All human communication is through symbols, through the medium of a language, and the more articulate that language the greater the chance for the message to get through. The private meaning of Constable's work is interesting to the psychologist only. Had he been not an artist but a madman incapable of articulate communication, he would have been satisfied with collecting slimy posts. But he was an artist and one born into a situation in which this particular bent could lead to experiment and

319. CONSTABLE: *Valley Farm*. 1835

discovery in the visual arts. One of these discoveries concerned the shift of scale, an adjustment of the palette to greater brightness; another, the dancing highlights that the master's contemporaries, who had not yet learned to see nature in these terms, called 'Constable's snow' [317]. The fact that we know better need not lead us to underrate the achievement which the artist aimed at. 'Sparkle with repose . . . is my struggle just now,' he writes. And of another canvas, 'I have got my picture into a very beautiful state; I have kept my brightness without my spottiness, and I have preserved God Almighty's daylight.' And finally: 'I have been very busy with Mr. Vernon's picture [319]. Oiling out, making out, polishing, scraping, etc. seem to have agreed with it exceedingly. The "sleet" and "snow" have disappeared, leaving in their places silver, ivory, and a little gold.' I know of no more beautiful description of that transfiguration which only art can achieve. Psychoanalysts speak of sublimation here—and indeed the sleet and snow which Constable got out of his unfinished picture must have been nearer the primal satisfaction for the artist to whom painting was but another word for feeling. Constable quoted with approval the definition of one of his friends, calling it useful and comprehensive. 'The whole object and difficulty of the art (indeed of all the fine arts) is to *unite imagination with nature.*'

Constable's *Wivenhoe Park* [5], the painting which has not failed us so far, will help to give a precise and clear-cut meaning to this idea of uniting imagination with nature, the inner with the outer world. Let us see it for a moment in its historical and social context. Wivenhoe Park was a country house owned by General Rebow, who befriended the struggling painter and commissioned the work partly to help him financially, a help which was all the more needed because Constable wanted to marry.

A generation earlier, Gainsborough, whom Constable admired so much, had politely but firmly declined a similar commission to paint the exact view of a country house: 'Mr. Gainsborough presents his humble respects to Lord Hardwicke, and shall always think it an honour to be employ'd in anything for His Lordship. But with regard to *real views* from Nature in this country, he has never seen any place that affords a subject to the poorest imitation of Gaspar or Claude . . . if His Lordship wish to have anything tollerable of the name of Gainsborough, the subject altogether . . . must be of his own Brain.'

We also possess a letter which Constable wrote to his bride while he was working on *Wivenhoe Park:* 'I am going on very well with my pictures. . . . The Park is the most forward. The great difficulty has been to get so much in it as they wanted. On my left is a grotto with some elms, at the head of a piece of water; in the centre is the house over a beautiful wood; and very far to the right is a deer-house, which it was necessary to add; so that my view comprehended too large a space. But today I have got over the difficulty, and begin to like it myself.'

Gainsborough, a man of the eighteenth century, finds the mere imitation of a real view unworthy of the artist who is concerned with the children of his brain, the language of the imagination. Constable is aware of the same difficulty, enhanced by the exacting demand of his literal-minded patron who wanted to have all the notable features of his beautiful estate faithfully recorded on the artist's canvas. The task for him is not an insult but a challenge. Steeped as he is in the love of nature that belongs to the contemporary of Wordsworth, he has forged himself a language that is both truthful and poetic, that makes it possible to fulfil the patron's demand for accuracy and his own urge for poetry.

The purpose of this book was to explain why art has a history, not why its history developed in one direction rather than another. I do not believe that this second question can ever be completely answered. Our evidence for reconstructing the situation in which Constable's *Wivenhoe Park* gained shape is unusually rich, but who would pretend that the few pointers it provides can do more than plot its approximate position on the map of history? And just as the historian can never fully explain the individual work of art with all the decisions involved in making it, so the psychologist can never fully interpret its meaning to the questioning art lover. This admission may come as a surprise to any reader who has felt troubled by so much rationalism in the face of art. Yet it is rational, I think, to maintain that the meaning of human expression will always elude scientific explanation. Have we not seen that our responses in life to the interacting stimuli of light or shape no less than our responses to facial expressions or speech sounds are always immediate, global, unanalysed, and in that sense intuitive? Where we understand we understand directly, as we understand the meaning of a musical phrase or the inflection of a voice. The mystic and irrationalist errs only in thinking that such intuition must always be superior to reason, infallible. There are misunderstandings of expression as there are other false responses. The rational approach can help to eliminate such mistakes by showing what a work of art cannot have meant within the framework of its style and situation. Having thus narrowed down the area of misunderstandings it must retire; for the particular in all its richness is bound to slip through the clumsy net of general concepts which we make by asking our twenty questions. Created as a tool to help us find our way through the world of things, our language is notoriously poor when we try to analyse and categorize the inner world.

In investigating the growth of the language of representation we may have gained some insight into the articulation of other languages of equivalences. Indeed, the true miracle of the language of art is not that it enables the artist to create the illusion of reality. It is that under the hands of a great master the image becomes translucent. In teaching us to see the visible world afresh, he gives us the illusion of looking into the invisible realms of the mind—if only we know, as Philostratus says, how to use our eyes.

Retrospect

SEVERAL FRIENDS who have read the manuscript of this book have urged me to conclude with a recapitulation. They did not want me, however, to start all over again with wire gates and window-panes to prove that the total ambiguity of one-eyed static vision is logically compatible with the claims of geometrical perspective but incompatible with the idea that we 'really' see the world flat or curved. Nor were they anxious for another demonstration of why any representation must of necessity allow of an infinite number of interpretations and why the selection of a reading consistent with our anticipations must always be the beholder's share. These proofs in themselves, after all, have no direct bearing on art, and it was this aspect that the conspectus should bring into focus. Luckily, I found that I had written such a conspectus already—before I ever embarked on this book. I mentioned in the Preface that the plan of this investigation took its origin from certain ideas which I had expressed in *The Story of Art*. They are the passages where I attempted to link the experiments of twentieth-century artists with the problems posed by the triumph of representational skill in the visual discoveries of impressionism. I hope that in reading them in this fresh context the reader may find that what then were rather unsupported assertions can now be read in the light of an explanatory theory:

'But what should a painter experiment with and why can he not be content to sit down before nature and paint it to the best of his abilities? The answer seems to be that art has lost its bearings because artists have discovered that the simple demand that they should "paint what they see" is self-contradictory. This sounds like one of the paradoxes with which modern artists and critics like to tease the long-suffering public; but to those who have followed this book from the beginning it should not be difficult to understand. We remember how the primitive artist used to build up, say, a face out of simple forms rather than copy a real face. . . . We have often looked back to the Egyptians and their method of representing in a picture all they knew rather than all they saw. Greek and Roman art breathed life into these schematic forms; medieval art used them in turn for telling the sacred story, Chinese art for contemplation. Neither was urging the artist to "paint what he saw". This idea dawned only during the age of the Renaissance. At first all seemed to go well. Scientific perspective, "*sfumato*", Venetian colours, movement and expression, were added to the artist's means of representing the world around him; but every generation discovered that there were still unsuspected "pockets of resistance", strongholds of conventions which made artists apply forms they had learned rather than paint what they really saw. The nineteenth-century rebels proposed to make a clean sweep of all these conventions; one after another was tackled, till the Impressionists proclaimed that their methods allowed them to render on the canvas the act of vision with "scientific accuracy".

'The paintings that resulted from this theory were very fascinating works of art, but this should not blind us to the fact that the idea on which they were based was only half true. We have come to realize more and more, since those days, that we can never neatly separate what we see from what we know. A person who was born blind, and who gains eyesight later on, must *learn* to see. With some self-discipline and self-observation we can all find out for ourselves that what we call seeing is invariably coloured and shaped by our knowledge (or belief) of what we see. This becomes clear enough whenever the two are at variance. It happens that we make mistakes in seeing. For example, we sometimes see a small object which is close to our eyes as if it were a big mountain on the horizon, or a fluttering paper as if it were a bird. Once we know we have made a mistake, we can no longer see it as we did before. If we had to paint the objects concerned, we should have to use different shapes and colours to represent them before and after our discovery. In fact, as soon as we start to take a pencil and draw, the whole idea of surrendering passively to what is called our sense impressions becomes really an absurdity. If we look out of the window we can see the view in a thousand different ways. Which of them is our sense impression? But we must choose; we must start somewhere; we must build up some picture of the house across the road and of the trees in front of it. Do what we may, we shall always have to make a beginning with something like "conventional" lines or forms. The "Egyptian" in us can be suppressed, but he can never be quite defeated.'

The main thing I have learned since I wrote these words is that the last sentence is still an understatement. The 'Egyptian' in us ultimately stands for the active mind, for that 'effort after meaning' which cannot be defeated without our world's collapsing into total ambiguity. But it does not quite follow from this that the end result of the artist's representation must be governed by his initial interpretation. The small object close by and the big mountain on the horizon, the fluttering paper and the bird might really be represented through identical shapes on the canvas—though they rarely would be. Strictly speaking, after all, it is because we can make such mistakes and take one thing for another that the eye can be deceived by an illusionist picture. But to see the patch on the close-by canvas as a distant mountain is to transform it in turn according to its meaning. These transformations explain the paradox that the world can never quite look like a picture, but a picture can look like the world. It is not the 'innocent eye', however, that can achieve this match but only the inquiring mind that knows how to probe the ambiguities of vision. I had a hunch when I wrote *The Story of Art* that the explorations by surrealist artists of the ambiguity of shapes, the game of 'rabbit or duck?' would provide the best point of entry into the labyrinth of representation:

'The artist who wants to "represent" a real (or imagined) thing does not start by opening his eyes and looking about him but by taking colours and forms and building up the required image. The reason why we often forget this simple truth is that in most pictures of the past each form and each colour happened to signify only one thing in nature—the brown strokes stood for tree-trunks, the green dots for leaves. Dali's way of letting each form represent several things at the same time may focus our attention on the many possible meanings of each colour and form —much in the way in which a successful pun may make us aware of the function of words and their meaning.'

What I did not know at the time was that the very 'effort after meaning' that enables us to decode those 'cryptograms on the canvas' of which Sir Winston Churchill speaks will tend to hide ambiguity from us as long as possible. This reluctance to recognize ambiguity behind the veil of illusion has also made the path of this investigation a little more arduous for the reader than I would have wished. I must hope all the more that it has helped not only to answer some old questions but also to pose fresh ones.

NOTES

FULL TITLES

OF BOOKS SOMETIMES CITED IN A SHORTENED FORM

ALBERTI, LEONE BATTISTA. *Della Pittura* and *De Statua*, in *Kleinere kunsttheoretische Schriften*. Edited by Hubert Janitschek. (Quellenschriften für Kunstgeschichte, II.) Vienna, 1877.

ALLPORT, F. H. *Theories of Perception and the Concept of Structure*. New York and London, 1955.

ARNHEIM, RUDOLF. *Art and Visual Perception*. Berkeley, Calif., 1954; London, 1956.

BECATTI, GIOVANNI. *Arte e gusto negli scrittori latini*. Florence, 1951.

BORING, EDWIN G. *Sensation and Perception in the History of Experimental Psychology*. New York and London, 1942.

CHERRY, COLIN. *On Human Communication*. Cambridge, Mass., and London, 1957.

D'ALTON, J. F. *Roman Literary Theory and Criticism*. New York and London, 1931.

EVANS, RALPH M. *An Introduction to Color*. New York and London, 1948.

FRIEDLÄNDER, MAX J. *Von Kunst und Kennerschaft*. Oxford and Zurich, 1946. Translated by Tancred Borenius: *On Art and Connoisseurship*. London, 1942, 1943.

GIBSON, JAMES J. *The Perception of the Visual World*. Boston, 1950.

GOMBRICH, E. H. *The Story of Art*. London and New York, 1950.

HAYEK, F. A. *The Sensory Order*. Chicago and London, 1952.

HEBB, DONALD O. *The Organization of Behavior*. New York and London, 1949.

HILDEBRAND, ADOLF VON. *Das Problem der Form in der bildenden Kunst*. Strassburg, 1893. Translated by Max Meyer and Robert Morris Ogden: *The Problem of Form in Painting and Sculpture*. New York, 1907.

IVINS, WILLIAM M., JR. *Prints and Visual Communication*. Cambridge, Mass., and London, 1953.

JUNIUS, FRANCISCUS. *The Painting of the Ancients*. London, 1638.

LEONARDO DA VINCI. *Treatise on Painting*. Edited by A. Philip McMahon. Princeton, 1956.

LESLIE, C. R. *Memoirs of the Life of John Constable* (1st edn., 1843). Edited by Jonathan Mayne. London, 1951.

MALRAUX, ANDRÉ. *La Psychologie d'art*. Vols. I, II: Geneva, 1947–48; Vol. III: Paris, 1950. Translated by Stuart Gilbert: *The Psychology of Art*. 3 vols. New York (Bollingen Series XXIV) and London, 1949–51. Revised as: *Les Voix du silence*. Paris, 1951. Translated by Stuart Gilbert: *The Voices of Silence*. New York, 1953; London, 1954.

METZGER, WOLFGANG. *Gesetze des Sehens*. 2nd edn., Frankfurt am Main, 1953.

OSGOOD, CHARLES E. *Method and Theory in Experimental Psychology*. New York, 1953.

POPPER, KARL R. *The Open Society and Its Enemies*. London, 1945; Princeton, 1950.

REWALD, JOHN. *The History of Impressionism*. New York, 1946.

RUSKIN, JOHN. *Modern Painters* (London, 1843) and *The Elements of Drawing* (London, 1857). Both included in: *The Works of John Ruskin*. Edited by E. T. Cook and Alexander Wedderburn. 39 vols. London and New York, 1903–1912.

SAKANISHI, SHIO. *The Spirit of the Brush*. (The Wisdom of the East Series.) London, 1939.

SCHÄFER, HEINRICH. *Von ägyptischer Kunst*. 3rd edn., Leipzig, 1930.

SZE, MAI-MAI. *The Tao of Painting: A Study of the Ritual Disposition of Chinese Painting, with a translation of the Chieh Tzŭ Yüan Hua Chuan (Mustard Seed Garden Manual of Painting), 1679–1701*. 2 vols. New York (Bollingen Series XLIX) and London, 1956.

VASARI, GIORGIO. *Le Vite de' più eccellenti pittori, scultori ed architettori* (1st edn., 1550). Edited by Gaetano Milanesi. Florence, 1878–85.

VERNON, M. D. *A Further Study of Visual Perception*. Cambridge, 1952.

WEIZSÄCKER, VIKTOR VON. *Der Gestaltkreis: Theorie der Einheit von Wahrnehmen und Bewegen*. 4th edn., Stuttgart, 1950.

WÖLFFLIN, HEINRICH. *Die klassische Kunst*. Munich, 1899. Translated by Peter and Linda Murray: *Classic Art*. London, 1952.

WÖLFFLIN, H. *Kunstgeschichtliche Grundbegriffe*. Munich, 1915. Translated by M. D. Hottinger: *Principles of Art History*. New York, and London, 1932.

WOODWORTH, R. S., and HAROLD SCHLOSBERG. *Experimental Psychology*. New York, 1954; London, 1955.

WRESZINSKI, WALTER. *Atlas zur altägyptischen Kulturgeschichte*. Leipzig, 1923.

ZANGWILL, O. L. *An Introduction to Modern Psychology*. London, 1950.

NOTES

For the full titles of books sometimes cited in abbreviated form,
see page 334.
LCL = Loeb Classical Library.

INTRODUCTION

p.3 MOTTO: 'Da das Kunstschaffen, was es sonst immer sei, jedenfalls ein seelisch-geistiger Vorgang ist, muss die Wissenschaft von der Kunst Psychologie sein. Sie mag auch etwas anderes sein, Psychologie ist sie unter allen Umständen.' Friedländer, *Von Kunst und Kennerschaft* (Oxford and Zurich, 1946), p.128. (Cf. tr. Tancred Borenius: *On Art and Connoisseurship*, London, 1942, 1943, p.145. The translation in the text is mine.)

p.4 HEINRICH WÖLFFLIN, *Kunstgeschichtliche Grundbegriffe* (Munich, 1915), tr. M. D. Hottinger: *Principles of Art History* (New York and London, 1932), foreword to the 7th German edn.

AESTHETICS AGAINST ILLUSION: See my predecessors in the Mellon Lectures, especially Etienne Gilson, *Painting and Reality* (New York [Bollingen Series XXXV:4] and London, 1957), Ch. VIII.

RABBIT OR DUCK? Ludwig Wittgenstein, *Philosophical Investigations*, tr. G. E. M. Anscombe (Oxford, 1953), p.194 (II.11).

p.5 THE MIRROR IMAGE: There is a simple diagram in the *Encyclopaedia Britannica*, 14th edn. (1929), XV, 590; and an illustration of the size illusion in G. A. Storey, *The Theory and Practice of Perspective* (Oxford, 1910), p. 262.

KENNETH CLARK, 'Six Great Pictures, 3: "Las Meninas" by Velázquez', London *Sunday Times*, June 2, 1957, p.9.

p.6 THEORIES OF NONFIGURATIVE ART: See my article 'The Tyranny of Abstract Art', *Atlantic Monthly*, April 1958. The title was the editor's; my own title was 'The Vogue of Abstract Art'.

p.7 PLATO, *Sophist* 266C, tr. H. N. Fowler (LCL, 1921), pp.450–51.

ICONOLOGY: Erwin Panofsky, *Studies in Iconology* (New York, 1939).

THE VISIBLE AND INVISIBLE WORLD: The allusion is to Rembrandt's pupil Samuel van Hoogstraeten, who gave his book *Inleyding tot de Hooge Schoole der Schilderkonst* (Rotterdam, 1678) the subtitle *De zichtbare Werelt* (The Visible World). According to Houbraken he planned a sequel, *De onzichtbaere Werelt* (The Invisible World), that would have dealt with religious and secular imagery.

BOOKS BY ARTISTS AND ART TEACHERS: Frédéric Schmid, *The Practice of Painting* (London, 1948), on eighteenth-century works. Further bibliography in my Ch. V.

p.8 STILUS: 'Artifex stilus', Cicero, *Brutus* 96. More references in Charlton T. Lewis and Charles Short, *A Latin Dictionary* (Oxford, 1879).

RHETORIC AND CRITICISM: J. F. D'Alton, *Roman Literary Theory and Criticism* (New York and London, 1931), with rich bibliography.

CATEGORIES OF EXPRESSION: Key passages are Cicero, *Orator 20* and *De oratore* III, 199. For further references see D'Alton, *Roman Literary Theory*, Ch. II, and the lucid survey by W. Rhys Roberts in his introduction to Demetrius, *On Style* (LCL, 1953).

METAPHORS: Larue van Hook, *Metaphorical Terminology of Greek Rhetoric and Literary Criticism* (Chicago, 1905). Many Latin examples in Giovanni Becatti, *Arte e gusto negli scrittori latini* (Florence, 1951), with rich bibliography.

APPLICATION TO THE VISUAL ARTS: Some historical references in Heinz Weniger, *Die drei*

Stilcharaktere der Antike in ihrer geistesge-schichtlichen Bedeutung (Göttinger Studien zur Pädagogik, 19; Langensalza, 1932), and in Werner Hofmann, '"Manier" und "Stil" in der Kunst des 20. Jahrhunderts', *Studium Generale* (1955).

QUINTILIAN, *Institutio oratoria* XII, 10, 1–10. For bibliography see Becatti, *Arte e gusto*.

ASIANISM: See D'Alton, *Roman Literary Theory*, Ch. IV. The key passage is in the preface to Dionysius Halicarnassus, *Ancient Orators* (Ad Ammaeum), tr. in J. D. Denniston, *Greek Literary Criticism* (London, 1928), pp. 150–53.

SENECA, *Ad Lucilium, Epistolae morales*, CXIV, tr. Richard M. Gummere (LCL, 1925), III, 300 ff.

p.9 TACITUS: 'Vidit namque . . . cum condicione temporum et diversitate aurium formam quoque ac speciem orationis esse mutandum.' *Dialogus de oratoribus* 19.

CICERO, *Academica* II, 20 and 86.

MIMESIS: H. Koller, *Die Mimesis in der Antike* (Dissertationes Bernenses, Ser. I, fasc. 5; Berne, 1934).

PLINY: *The Elder Pliny's Chapters on the History of Art*, tr. K. Jex-Blake, ed. E. Seller (London, 1896); a more recent annotated edition with Italian tr., ed. Silvio Ferri (Rome, 1946). For Pliny's sources see also Carl Robert, *Archäologische Märchen* (Berlin, 1886), Ch. II: 'Die Kunsturteile des Plinius', and, most recently, Becatti, *Arte e gusto*.

VASARI: Julius von Schlosser, *La Letteratura artistica*, tr. Filippo Rossi (Florence, 1956), with rich bibliography brought up to date by Otto Kurz. For background see also my paper 'The Renaissance Concept of Artistic Progress and Its Consequences', *Actes du XVIIme Congrès International d'histoire de l'art, Amsterdam, 23–31 Juillet 1952* (The Hague, 1955).

GIORGIO VASARI, *Le Vite de' più eccellenti pittori, scultori ed architettori*, ed. Gaetano Milanesi (Florence, 1878–85), I, 453.

p.10 VASARI ON GADDI: *Vite*, I, 585.

VASARI ON MASACCIO: *Vite*, II, 288.

JONATHAN RICHARDSON, *The Theory of Painting* (London, 1715), here quoted from *The Works of Jonathan Richardson* (London, 1792), pp. 61–62.

BARRY: *The Works of James Barry* (London, 1809), I, 521.

p.12 CONSTABLE'S LECTURE AT HAMPSTEAD, 1836, in C. R. Leslie, *Memoirs of the Life of John Constable*, ed. Jonathan Mayne (London, 1951), p.327.

JOHN RUSKIN, *Modern Painters* (London, 1843), Vol. I, Part II, Sec. I, Ch. II; *The Works of John Ruskin*, ed. E. T. Cooke and Alexander Wedderburn (London and New York, 1903–12), III, 140.

PLINY, *Natural History*, XI, 146, tr. H. Rackham (LCL, 1938), III, 523. I am indebted to Professor Harry Bober for this reference.

HISTORY OF EARLY OPTICS: A useful conspectus in Gezenius ten Doesschate, *De Derde Commentaar van Lorenzo Ghiberti in Verband met de Middeleeuwsche Optiek* (diss. Utrecht, 1940).

PTOLEMY: *L'Optique de Claude Ptolémée*, ed. Albert Lejeune (Louvain, 1956).

p.13 ALHAZEN: Hans Bauer, 'Die Psychologie Alhazens auf Grund von Alhazens Optik', *Beiträge zur Geschichte des Mittelalters*, X, 5 (Münster in Westphalen, 1911). The only edition of Alhazen is still in the garbled Latin translation included in A. F. Risnerus, *Opticae thesaurus* (Basel, 1572). The passage quoted is based on Alhazen, II, 17.

PERCEPTUAL THEORY FROM LOCKE TO HELMHOLTZ: Edwin G. Boring, *Sensation and Perception in the History of Experimental Psychology* (New York and London, 1942), especially Ch. III.

KONRAD FIEDLER, 'Moderner Naturalismus und künstlerische Wahrheit', in *Schriften über Kunst* (Leipzig, 1896), p.177.

ADOLF VON HILDEBRAND, *Das Problem der Form in der bildenden Kunst* (Strassburg, 1893), p.14. (Cf. tr. Max Meyer and Robert Morris Ogden: *The Problem of Form in Painting and Sculpture* [New York, 1907], p.31.) The influence of Fiedler and Hildebrand is discussed in Lionello Venturi, *History of Art Criticism* (New York, 1936).

p.14 THE RISE OF ART HISTORY: See my chapter on 'Kunstwissenschaft', in *Das Atlantisbuch der Kunst*, ed. Martin Hürlimann (Zurich, 1952), pp.653–64, with further bibliography.

BERNARD BERENSON, *The Florentine Painters of the Renaissance* (New York and London, 1896), pp.4 ff.

HEINRICH WÖLFFLIN, *Die klassische Kunst* (Munich, 1899), tr. Peter and Linda Murray: *Classic Art* (London, 1952).

WÖLFFLIN, *Kunstgeschichtliche Grundbegriffe.*

ALOIS RIEGL, *Stilfragen* (Berlin, 1893).

p.15 FRANZ WICKHOFF AND WILHELM RITTER VON HARTEL, *Die Wiener Genesis* (Vienna, 1895), tr. Mrs. S. Arthur Strong: *Roman Art* (New York and London, 1900).

RIEGL ON HILDEBRAND: 'Naturwerk und Kunstwerk', in *Gesammelte Aufsätze* (Augsburg and Vienna, 1929), pp.65–70.

ALOIS RIEGL, *Die spätrömische Kunstindustrie nach den Funden in Österreich-Ungarn* (Vienna, 1901; 2nd edn., Vienna, 1927). The Italian tr. by B. Forlati Tamaro and M. T. Ronga Leoni, *Industria artistica tardoromana* (Florence, 1953), has a detailed introduction by Sergio Bettini, with bibliography.

p.16 RIEGL ON STYLE: *Kunstindustrie*, 2nd edn., p.394. For a discussion of Riegl's psychological ideas on tactile perception see G. Révész, *Die Formenwelt des Tastsinnes* (The Hague, 1938), II, 74 ff., and Viktor Lowenfeld, *The Nature of Creative Activity* (London, 1939).

MEYER SCHAPIRO, 'Style', in *Anthropology Today*, ed. A. L. Kroeber (Chicago, 1953), p.302. See also my inaugural lecture at University College: *Art and Scholarship* (London, 1957), reprinted in *College Art Journal*, XVII (1958).

THE LIFE CYCLE OF THE ARTS: Vasari, *Vite*, I, 243.

EXPRESSION OF THE AGE: Georg Wilhelm Friedrich Hegel, *Vorlesungen über die Philosophie der Geschichte*, ed. F. Brunstäd (Leipzig, 1907), pp.94, 107 of the Intro.; tr. J. Sibree: *The Philosophy of History* (New York, 1944), pp. 53, 63–64.

CARL GUSTAV CARUS, *Neun Briefe über die Landschaftsmalerei* (1815–1834) (Leipzig, 1835), 5th letter, p.81.

DANGER OF MYTHOLOGICAL EXPLANATIONS: See my lecture *Art and Scholarship*, cited above.

p.17 HANS SEDLMAYR, 'Die Quintessenz der Lehren Riegls', in Alois Riegl, *Gesammelte Aufsätze* (cited for p.15), pp. xxxi ff.

KARL R. POPPER, *The Poverty of Historicism* (Boston and London, 1957), p.149.

FACILE EXPLANATIONS: For more specific criticisms of these tendencies see my papers on Giulio Romano, *Jahrbuch der kunsthistorischen Sammlungen in Wien*, n.s., VIII (1935), especially p.140, and my discussion with E. von Garger, 'Wertprobleme und mittelalterliche Kunst', *Kritische Berichte*, VI, parts 3–4 (1937); more recently in my review of Arnold Hauser's *The Social History of Art*, in *Art Bulletin* (March 1953), p.82, and my Ernest

Jones Lecture on 'Psycho-Analysis and the History of Art', *International Journal of Psycho-Analysis*, XXXV, part IV (1954), now reprinted in Benjamin Nelson, ed., *Freud and the Twentieth Century* (New York, 1957 [Meridian paperback], and London, 1958). For similar criticisms in related fields see Edward Sapir, *Culture, Language and Personality*, ed. G. Mandelbaum (Berkeley and Los Angeles, 1957), p.177; Ernst Robert Curtius, *European Literature and the Latin Middle Ages*, tr. Willard R. Trask (New York [Bollingen Series XXXVI] and London, 1953), p.15; and René Wellek and Austin Warren, *Theory of Literature* (New York, 1956), especially Chs. XI and XIV.

p.18 BIOLOGICAL UNITY OF MANKIND: For a discussion of this problem from the point of view of psychoanalysis, see H. Hartmann, Ernst Kris, and R. M. Loewenstein, 'Some Psychoanalytic Comments on "Culture and Personality",' in *Psychoanalysis and Culture*, ed. George B. Wilbur and Werner Muensterberger (New York, 1951). For the anthropologist's approach, see Franz Boas, *Primitive Art* (New York, 1955), where all explanations of primitive cultures in terms of 'primitive mentality' are forcefully dismissed in the preface.

EMANUEL LOEWY, *Die Naturwiedergabe in der älteren griechischen Kunst* (Rome, 1900), tr. John Fothergill: *The Rendering of Nature in Early Greek Art* (London, 1907). For a recent appreciation of Loewy's theories, see Schapiro in *Anthropology Today* (as cited for p.16), p. 301.

p.19 MEMORY IMAGES: For the elusiveness of this concept, see R. S. Woodworth and Harold Schlosberg, *Experimental Psychology* (New York, 1954; London, 1955), pp.720 and 816.

JULIUS VON SCHLOSSER, 'Zur Kenntnis der künstlerischen Überlieferung im späten Mittelalter', *Jahrbuch der kunsthistorischen Sammlungen in Wien*, XXIII (1903), 279, and his book, *Die Kunst des Mittelalters*, ed. A. E. Brinckmann (Berlin, 1923). For a recent appreciation, see O. Kurz, 'Julius von Schlosser: Personalità—Metodo—Lavoro', *Critica d'arte* XI/XII (1955), 402–19.

ABY WARBURG, 'Dürer und die italienische Antike' (1905), *Gesammelte Schriften*, ed. Gertrud Bing (Leipzig and Berlin, 1932), II, 445–49; for other examples of his use of the term, see under *Antike: Wirkungen* and

Pathosstil in the index of that edn. For a recent appreciation, see Fritz Saxl, 'Three Florentines', in *Lectures* (London, 1957), I, 331–44.

p.20 INVESTIGATION OF CONTINUITIES: In addition to the writings of Warburg's immediate followers, especially Fritz Saxl and Erwin Panofsky, and to many papers printed in the *Journal of the Warburg and Courtauld Institutes*, see Henri van de Waal, *Drie Eeuwen vaderlandsche Geschieduitbeelding, 1500–1800, Een iconologische Studie* (The Hague, 1952). ANDRÉ MALRAUX, *La Psychologie d'art* (Vols. I, II: Geneva, 1947–48; Vol. III: Paris, 1950), tr. Stuart Gilbert: *The Psychology of Art* (3 vols., New York [Bollingen Series XXIV] and London, 1949–51). Revised as *Les Voix du silence* (Paris, 1951), tr. Stuart Gilbert: *The Voices of Silence* (New York), 1953; London 1954). See my review, 'André Malraux and the Crisis of Expressionism', *The Burlington Magazine* (December 1954). CURTIUS, *European Literature*, as cited above for p.17. QUINTILIAN: 'Tradi enim omnia, quae ars efficit, non possunt. Nam quis pictor omnia, quae in rerum natura sunt, adumbrare didicit? Sed percepta semel imitandi ratione adsimulabit quidquid acceperit. Quis non faber vasculum aliquod, quale nunquam viderat, fecit?' *Instituto oratoria* VII, x, 9. See Becatti, *Arte e gusto*, p.180.

p.21 FAMILY OF FORMS: William Morris in his lecture *The Lesser Arts* (1877) answers Quintilian across the centuries: 'I do not think it is too much to say that no man, however original he may be, can sit down today and draw the ornament of a cloth, or the form of an ordinary vessel . . . that will be other than a development or a degradation of forms used hundreds of years ago.' William Morris, *On Art and Socialism*, ed. Holbrook Jackson (London 1957), p.20. JAMES J. GIBSON, *The Perception of the Visual World* (Boston, 1950), p.129. DONALD O. HEBB, *The Organization of Behavior* (New York and London, 1949), p.44. RALPH M. EVANS, *Introduction to Color* (New York and London, 1948), p.181.

p.22 WOLFGANG KÖHLER, *Dynamics in Psychology* (New York, 1940; London, 1942), pp.89 and 87 in the later edition.

RUDOLF ARNHEIM, *Art and Visual Perception* (Berkeley, Calif., 1954; London, 1956). CUBISM: Arnheim, p.93. WILLIAM M. IVINS, JR., *Prints and Visual Communication* (Cambridge, Mass., and London 1953). ANTON EHRENZWEIG, *The Psycho-analysis of Artistic Vision and Hearing* (London, 1953).

p.23 K. R. POPPER, *The Open Society and Its Enemies* (Princeton, 1950; 3rd edn., London, 1957), II, 213 ff. in the later edition; see also his chapter, 'The Philosophy of Science: A Personal Report', in *British Philosophy in the Mid-Century*, ed. Cecil A. Mace (London 1957), pp.155–94. GIBSON, *Perception of the Visual World*, p.222. L. VON BERTALANFFY, 'Theoretical Models in Biology and Psychology', in *Theoretical Models and Personality Theory*, ed. David Krech and George S. Klein (Durham, N. C., 1952), p.28. PIAGET: E.g., Jean Piaget, *The Child's Construction of Reality*, tr. Margaret Cook (London, 1955), especially pp.350 ff. FREUD AND HIS DISCIPLES: E.g., H. Hartmann and Ernst Kris, 'The Genetic Approach in Psychoanalysis', *The Psychoanalytic Study of the Child* (New York), I (1945), 11–30; H. Hartmann, Ernst Kris, and R. M. Loewenstein, 'Comments on the Formation of Psychic Structure', ibid., II (1946), 11–38. MACHINES THAT LEARN: W. Sluckin, *Minds and Machines* (Harmondsworth [Penguin], 1954), pp. 32 ff. CATEGORIZING: For a recent lucid statement, see Jerome S. Bruner, 'On Perceptual Readiness', *Psychological Review*, LXIV, no. 2 (1957), 64; reprinted in David C. Beardslee and Michael Wertheimer, eds., *Readings in Perception* (New York and London, 1958) with further bibliography.

p.24 FRIEDRICH AUGUST VON HAYEK, *The Sensory Order* (Chicago and London, 1952). BRUNER AND POSTMAN: As summarized in Floyd H. Allport, *Theories of Perception and the Concept of Structure* (New York and London, 1955), p.376, with further bibliography. The pioneers of this approach were Edward C. Tolman and Egon Brunswik, to whose joint paper, 'The Organism and the Causal Texture of Environment', *Psychological Review*, XLII (1935), I have referred in the Preface. POPPER, *The Logic of Scientific Discovery* (London and New York, 1959).

p.25 ERNST KRIS, *Psychoanalytic Explorations in Art* (New York and London, 1952), p.21.

FASHIONS AND TASTE: See my papers: 'Visual Metaphors of Value in Art', in *Symbols and Values: An Initial Study*, Thirteenth Symposium of the Conference on Science, Philosophy, and Religion, ed. Lyman Bryson and others (New York, 1954); 'Psycho-Analysis and the History of Art', cited above for p.17; and 'The Tyranny of Abstract Art', cited for p.6.

CHAPTER ONE

p.29 MOTTO: 'La peinture est la plus étonnante magicienne; elle sait persuader, par les plus évidentes faussetés, qu'elle est la vérité pure.' Liotard, *Traité . . . de la peinture*, first pub. at Geneva, 1781 (modern edn., 1945), Ch. I.

CONSTABLE IN 1816: Michael Kitson, 'John Constable, 1810–1816: A Chronological Study', *Journal of the Warburg and Courtauld Institutes*, XX (July–December 1957).

PAINTING A SCIENCE: Constable's fourth lecture at the Royal Institution (1836), in Leslie, *Memoirs*, p.323.

p.30 PIGMENT MATCHING LIGHT: The most recent discussion is in Evans, *An Introduction to Color*, pp. 92–93 and 309–310 (with bibliography). The history of the problem has still to be written. Wolfgang Schöne, *Über das Licht in der Malerei* (Berlin, 1954), concentrates on the luminosity of colours and mostly bypasses the issue of representation. Some historical notes are to be found in Wilhelm Seibt, *Helldunkel* (Frankfurt am Main, 1885). Key passages are Leone Battista Alberti, *Della Pittura*, ed. H. Janitschek, pp. 77 and 136–37; Vasari, *Vite*, ed. Milanesi, VII, 657; Ruskin, *Modern Painters*, Vol. I, part 1, sec. 2, Ch. I: 'Of Truth of Tone'; Vol. IV, part 1, sec. 1, Ch. III: 'Of Turnerian Light'; Hippolyte Taine, *Philosophie de l'art* (Paris, 1865), I, iv; Hermann van Helmholtz, 'Optisches über Malerei', in *Vorträge und Reden II* (Braunschweig, 1884); Georg Hirth, *Aufgaben der Kunstphysiologie* (Munich and Leipzig, 1891), pp. 171–84; M. Luckiesh, *Light and Shade and Their Applications* (New York, 1916), Ch. X; Arthur Pope, *The Language of Drawing and Painting* (Cambridge, Mass., 1949), and remarks by Matisse quoted in Alfred H. Barr, Jr., *Matisse* (New York, 1951), p.552.

p.34 DIORAMA: Leslie, *Memoirs*, p.106.

WINSTON S. CHURCHILL, *Painting as a Pastime* (London, 1948; New York, 1950), pp. 28–29.

THE POST OFFICE ASPECT: For general background in information theory, see Colin Cherry, *On Human Communication* (Cambridge, Mass., 1957); for psychological aspects see Fred Atteneave and Malcolm D. Arnoult, 'The Quantitative Study of Shape and Pattern Perception', *The Psychological Bulletin*, LIII:6 (1956) (with bibliography on earlier papers); see also Osgood, *Method and Theory*, pp. 229 and 237, for the neurological aspect. An example of engineering wizardry with gradations: K. Bischoff and O. Schott, 'Eine neue Kontrastverstärkungseinrichtung für Röntgenaufnahmen', *Fortschritte auf dem Gebiete der Röntgenstrahlen*, LXXXVII/2 (1957).

p.35 DISCOVERY OF LIGHT AND SHADE: Ernst Pfuhl, *Malerei und Zeichnung der Griechen* (Munich, 1923), Index 7, *Licht und Schatten*, p.948.

p.38 GRAPHIC NOTATIONS: Masterly discussions in Erwin Panofsky, *Albrecht Dürer* (Princeton, 1943), pp. 47–48, 63–68, 133–35; and Ivins, *Prints and Visual Communication*, p.66.

p.40 CREMONA FIDDLE: See my *Story of Art* (London and New York, 1950), pp.374–75, after Leslie, *Memoirs*, p.114.

THE FARINGTON DIARY (May 8, 1799), quoted from *Great Paintings from the National Gallery of Art*, ed. Huntington Cairns and John Walker (Washington, 1952), p.114.

THE CLAUDE GLASS: Christopher Hussey, *The Picturesque* (London and New York, 1927), p.107.

p.41 EVANESCENCE: E.g., Leslie, *Memoirs*, p.100.

'NASTY GREEN THING': Sidney J. Key, *John Constable* (London, 1948), p.88.

ERNST WILHELM VON BRÜCKE, *Bruchstücke aus der Theorie der bildenden Künste* (Leipzig, 1877), p.157.

THE DAZZLE: Wilhelm Ostwald, *Malerbriefe* (Leipzig, 1904), p.151; tr. H. W. Morse: *Letters to a Painter* (New York. 1907) pp. 147–51.

p.45 RELATIONSHIPS: For the history of this discovery see Boring, *Sensation and Perception*, especially p.255.
WOLFGANG KÖHLER, *Gestalt Psychology* (New York, 1929), pp. 167–68; for related experiments, see Osgood, *Method and Theory*, p. 279; for a critical view, see D. W. Hamlyn, *The Psychology of Perception* (London, 1957), p.61.
WHAT WE GET ON THE RETINA: See Osgood, p. 197.

p.46 THE STABLE WORLD: Gibson, *Perception of the Visual World*, especially Ch. III.
THE CONSTANCIES: Osgood, pp. 271 ff.; M. D. Vernon, *A Further Study of Visual Perception*, Ch. VI; Gibson, Ch. IX; Woodworth and Schlosberg, Ch. XV; Metzger, *Gesetze des Sehens*, Ch. IX; all with bibliographies.
PICTURES SEEN FROM THE SIDE: D. Katz, 'Zwei Beiträge zur Theorie der Wahrnehmung', *Theoria* (Gothenburg, 1951), pp. 89–102.

p.47 GRIME IT DOWN: Leslie, *Memoirs*, p.96.
RUBBED OUT: Ibid., p.218.

p.48 THE END OF ART: Ibid., p.97.
PICTURE CLEANING: For the chemical aspect, see Gilson, *Painting and Reality* (as cited for p.4, above), Ch. III, Part 3 (with bibliography).

See also: National Gallery (London), *An Exhibition of Cleaned Pictures* (1947).

p.51 CICERO, *De oratore* III, 98.
APELLES' DARK VARNISH: 'Unum imitari nemo potuit, quod absoluta opera atramento inlinebat . . . ne claritas colorum aciem offenderet veluti per lapidem specularem intuentibus et e longinquo eadem res nimis floridis coloribus austeritatem occulte daret.' Pliny, *Historia naturalis* XXXV, 97. I have previously drawn attention to this passage in a letter to the *Burlington Magazine*, XCII (1950).

p.53 THE WAX IMAGE: Julius von Schlosser, 'Porträtbildnerei in Wachs', *Jahrbuch der kunsthistorischen Sammlungen in Wien*, XXXI, (1911).
MENTAL SET: For recent discussions and bibliography, see Woodworth and Schlosberg, *Experimental Psychology*, esp. pp.830 ff.; Allport, *Theories of Perception and the Concept of Structure*, pp.208 ff.; and J. S. Bruner, 'On Perceptual Readiness', cited for p.23 above. The German tradition of 'Einstellung' is summarized in Hubert Rohracher, *Einführung in die Psychologie* (Vienna, 1946), p.336.
HORIZON OF EXPECTATIONS: I owe this phrase to K. R. Popper.
BOCCACCIO, *Decamerone*, Giornata VI, Novella 5.

p.54 MALRAUX, *The Voices of Silence*, and my review, 'André Malraux and the Crisis of Expressionism', in the *Burlington Magazine*, as cited for p.20, above.

CHAPTER TWO

p.55 MOTTO: 'Dieser Schematismus unseres Verstandes, in Ansehung der Erscheinungen . . . ist eine verborgene Kunst in den Tiefen der menschlichen Seele, deren wahre Handgriffe wir der Natur schwerlich jemals abraten . . . werden.' Kant, *Kritik der reinen Vernunft* (Riga, 1787), pp.180–81. The passage is also referred to in the beginning of Heinrich Wölfflin's *Principles of Art History*.
LUDWIG RICHTER (Adrian Ludwig), *Lebenserinnerungen eines deutschen Malers*, ed. Heinrich Richter, introd. Ferdinand Avenarius (Leipzig, 1909), pp.176–77. The passage is also referred to in the beginning of Heinrich Wölfflin's *Principles of Art History*.

EMILE ZOLA, *Mes Haines* (Paris, 1866); see *Collection des Œuvres complètes Emile Zola* (Paris, n.d.), XXIII, 176.

p.56 PHOTOGRAPHS OF PAINTER'S MOTIFS: See John Rewald's comparisons of Cézanne's paintings, with photographs of his subjects, in *Art News*, XLIII (1944), Nos. 1, 11, 12, and a similar treatment of van Gogh's motifs in the *Art News Annual*, 19 (1949). Also Erle Loran, *Cézanne's Compositions* (2nd edn., Berkeley, 1946) and Josiah de Gruyter, *Vincent van Gogh* (The Hague, 1953). For a deliberate challenge to the camera, see Pietro Annigoni and Alex Sterling, *Spanish Sketch-book* (London, 1957).

p.57 THE IMAGE ON THE RETINA: See above, notes for p.45. One of the first to protest against the naïve assumption that the mind looks at this image was Thomas Reid, *An Inquiry into the Human Mind, on the Principles of Common Sense* (Edinburgh, 1764).

p.58 GEORGE INNESS, JR., *Life, Art and Letters of George Inness* (New York, 1917), as quoted in *Great Paintings from the National Gallery of Art*, ed. Huntington Cairns and John Walker (New York, 1952), p.174.

p.59 LOGICIANS: A strict definition of a statement and, therefore, of truth is only possible in what is called a 'formalized' language, as has been first shown in a famous paper by Alfred Tarski, 'The Concept of Truth in Formalized Languages', now available tr. by J. H. Woodger in A. Tarski, *Logic, Semantics, Meta-Mathematics* (Oxford, 1956).
FALSE CAPTIONS: Arthur Ponsonby, *Falsehood in War-time* (New York and London, 1928), pp.135–39.
PIG EMBRYO: The reference is to Ernst Haeckel; see Richard B. Goldschmidt, *Portraits from Memory* (Seattle, 1956), p.36.
TRUTH IN CAPTIONS: See my review of Charles W. Morris, *Signs, Language and Behavior* (New York, 1946), in *The Art Bulletin*, XXI:1 (1949).
ALTERED PORTRAITS: George S. Layard, *Catalogue Raisonné of Engraved British Portraits from Altered Plates* (London, 1927).

p.60 SCHEDEL'S 'NUREMBERG CHRONICLE': V. von Loga, 'Die Städteansichten in Hartman Schedel's Weltchronik', *Jahrbuch der preussischen Kunstsammlungen*, IX (1888). This was one of the favourite examples of Julius von Schlosser; see his 'Portraiture', *Mitteilungen des österreichischen Instituts für Geschichtsforschung*, Ergänzungsband XI (Festschrift zu Ehren Oswald Redlichs; 1929), 882–94.

p.63 SIMILE: See the works of Julius von Schlosser discussed in the notes for pp.19 and 60.

p.64 SCHEMA AND CORRECTION: Woodworth and Schlosberg, *Experimental Psychology*, p.715. A somewhat fuller account is contained in the earlier edition of Woodworth, *Experimental Psychology* (New York, 1938; London, 1939), pp.73 ff., based on an article by F. Kuhlmann, *Psychological Review*, XIII (1906), 316–48. The importance of this formula was stressed by D. O. Hebb, *The Organization of Behavior*, pp.46 and 111.
O. L. ZANGWILL, 'An Investigation of the Relationship between the Processes of Reproducing and Recognizing Simple Figures, with Special Reference to Koffka's Trace Theory', *British Journal of Psychology*, XXVII (1937), 250–75.
LABEL INFLUENCING DRAWING: L. C. Carmichael, H. P. Hogan, and A. A. Walter, 'An Experimental Study of the Effect of Language on Visually Perceived Form', *Journal of Experimental Psychology*, XV (1932), 73–86. For a critical discussion of their findings, see W. C. H. Prentice, 'Visual Recognition of Verbally Labelled Figures', *The American Journal of Psychology*, LXVII (June 1954), 315–20.
F. C. BARTLETT, *Remembering: A Study in Experimental and Social Psychology* (Cambridge, 1932), p.180; see also Gibson, *The Perception of the Visual World*, pp.209–10.
CONSEQUENCES: Bartlett, p.19.
CELTIC COPIES OF CLASSICAL COINS: Julius von Schlosser, 'Zur Genesis der mittelalterlichen Kunstanschauung' (1901), in *Präludien* (Berlin, 1927), p.198; Malraux, *The Voices of Silence*, pp.132–44; see also R. Bianchi Bandinelli, *Organicità e astrazione* (Milan, 1956), pp.17–40, the source of our illustration.

p.67 THUTMOSE: Walter Wreszinski, *Atlas zur altägyptischen Kulturgeschichte* (Leipzig, 1923), II, 226, with a translation of the inscription.

p.68 VILLARD'S LION: Hans R. Hahnloser, *Villard de Honnecourt* (Vienna, 1935); see also Schlosser, in *Präludien*, p.199, and his *Die Kunst des Mittelalters*, p.83.

p.69 STRANDED WHALES: A. B. van Deinse, 'Over de potvissen in Nederland gestrand tussen de jaren 1531–1788', *Zoologische Mededeelingen . . . s'Rijks Museum van Natuurlijke Historie te Leiden*, IV (1918). The drawing for our print by Goltzius, now in the Teylers Stichting, Haarlem, is listed in the catalogue of the exhibition 'H. Goltzius als Tekenar', Museum Boymans Rotterdam (May/July 1958), as No. 90 (with full bibliography).

p.70 RHINOCEROS: F. J. Cole, 'The History of Albrecht Dürer's Rhinoceros in Zoological Literature', *Science, Medicine, and History* (Essays Written in Honour of Charles Singer), ed. E. Ashworth Underwood (New York and London, 1953), I, 337–56.

p.71 JAMES BRUCE, *Travels to Discover the Sources of the Nile in the Years 1768, 1769, 1770, 1771, 1772 and 1773* (Edinburgh, 1790), V, 86–87.

p.72 ELEPHANTS: A. E. Popham, 'Elephantographia', *Life and Letters*, V (1930), and in *The Listener* (April 24, 1947).
NICON'S HORSE: Franciscus Junius, *The Painting of the Ancients* (London, 1638), p.234.
EYES: W. Reitsch, 'Das Dürer-Auge', *Marburger Jahrbuch für Kunstwissenschaft*, IV (1928), 165–200.
LEONARDO: K. D. Keele, *Leonardo da Vinci on the Movement of the Heart and Blood* (London, 1952).
SCIENTIFIC ILLUSTRATIONS: Ivins, *Prints and Visual Communication*; Claus Nissen, *Die naturwissenschaftliche Illustration* (Bad Münster am Stein, 1950), with rich bibliography.

p.73 CHINESE EYES: The allusion is to Chiang Yee's beautiful book *The Chinese Eye* (London, 1935).

p.75 F. W. NIETZSCHE, *Scherz, List und Rache,* no. 55, in *Die fröhliche Wissenschaft, Nietzsche's Werke*, V (Leipzig, 1895), 28. The German reads:
'Treu die Natur und ganz !'—Wie fängt er's an:
Wann wäre je Natur im Bilde abgethan ?
Unendlich ist das kleinste Stück der Welt !—
Er malt zuletzt davon, was ihm gefällt.
Und was gefällt ihm ? Was er malen kann !
DUTCH TYPES: See the beautiful chapter on 'Individualität und Typus' in Max J. Friedländer, *Von Kunst und Kennerschaft*, pp.74–76 (tr. Tancred Borenius, pp.85–86).
NO NEUTRAL NATURALISM: Malraux, *The Voices of Silence*, pp.315 ff.

p.76 CONVENTIONAL AND NATURAL SIGNS: For some remarks on the history of this distinction, see my lecture on 'Lessing' in the Series on Master Minds, in *Proceedings of the British Academy*, XLIII (1957), 139.

CHILDREN'S DRAWINGS: Gustaf Britsch, *Theorie der bildenden Kunst*, ed. Egon Kornmann (Munich, 1926, 1930); Arnheim, *Art and Visual Perception*, esp. pp.128–30. See also Helga Eng, *The Psychology of Children's Drawings* (London, 1937), with rich bibliography.
FLEXIBLE SCHEMA: Popper, 'The Philosophy of Science' (as cited for p.23 above), esp. pp.171–75.
TWENTY QUESTIONS: Cherry, *On Human Communication*, p.85.

p.77 MACHINE LEARNING: See W. Sluckin, as cited above for p.23; Donald M. McKay, 'Towards an Information-Flow Model of Human Behaviour'. *British Journal of Psychology*, XLVII:1 (1956), 30–43. Recent applications of related ideas to the theory of perception are surveyed in D. T. Campbell, 'Perception as Substitute Trial and Error', *Psychological Review*, LXIII (September 1956), 330–42, and J. S. Bruner, 'On Perceptual Readiness', as cited above for p.23; to expression, in René A. Spitz, *No and Yes* (New York, 1957), pp.15 ff.
ARBORIFORM STRATIFICATION: O. G. Selfridge, 'Pattern Recognition and Learning', *Information Theory* (Papers read at a symposium on information theory held at the Royal Institution, London, September 12–16, 1955), ed. Colin Cherry (New York and London, 1956), p.349.
POLICE DRAFTSMEN: *The Sunday Pictorial* (London), May 14, 1950, p.9; the name of the artist referred to is Al Valanis. A more recent instance was reported and illustrated in *The New York Times*, August 5, 1958, p.28.
LANGUAGE: Stephen Ullmann, *The Principles of Semantics* (Glasgow, 1951), with rich bibliography. See now also C. Rabin, 'The Linguistics of Translation', in *Aspects of Translation*, Studies in Communication 2 (The Communication Research Centre, University College, London, 1958).

p.78 B. L. WHORF, *Language, Thought and Reality*, ed. John B. Carroll (Cambridge, Mass., 1956). For a critical discussion of Whorf's views, see C. Levi-Strauss, R. Jakobson, C. F. Voegelin, and T. A. Seboek, 'Results of the Conference of Anthropologists and Linguists' (in Bloomington, Indiana), *International Journal of American Linguistics*, XIX (April 1953).

CHAPTER THREE

p.80 MOTTO: Ernst Vatter, *Die religiöse Plastik der Naturvölker* (Frankfurt am Main, 1926), after Walter E. Roth, 'An Inquiry into the Animism and Folklore of the Guiana Indians', *Thirtieth Annual Report of the Bureau of American Ethnology, 1908–1909* (Washington, 1915), p.130.
LUCIEN FREUD, 'Thoughts on Painting', *Encounter*, 10 (1954).

p.81 DONATELLO'S CURSE: Vasari, *Vite*, II, 404.
THE PAINTER LORD OF ALL THINGS: Leonardo da Vinci, *Treatise on Painting*, ed. A. Philip McMahon (Princeton, 1956), No. 35 (or J. P. Richter, ed., *The Literary Works of Leonardo da Vinci* [Oxford, 1939], No. 19).

p.82 ART ROUSING PASSIONS: Leonardo, *Treatise*, ed. McMahon, No. 33 (or Richter, *Literary Works*, No. 28).

p.83 PAINTERS IN DESPAIR: Leonardo, *Treatise*, ed. McMahon, No. 220.
LEONARDO THE MAKER: See my article, 'Leonardo's Grotesque Heads', in *Leonardo, Saggi e ricerche*, ed. Achille Marazza (Rome, 1954), esp. p.216. and 'Conseils de Léonard sur les esquisses de tableaux', *Etudes d'art*, 8–10 (Paris-Alger, 1954).
PLATO, *Republic* X, 596–98, tr. Paul Shorey (LCL, 1930, 1935), II, 420–35.

p.84 ICONIC SIGNS: For this term (coined by C. S. Peirce), see Charles Morris, *Signs, Language and Behavior*, and my review cited above for p.59.
REINS AND BIT: Plato, *Republic* X, 601C; Shorey, II, 442–43.
THE WORLD OF THE CHILD: See my paper, 'Meditations on a Hobby Horse', in *Aspects of Form*, ed. L. L. Whyte (New York and London, 1951), which partly supplements this chapter.

p.85 ARTIFICIAL SINGING BIRDS: For the early history and popularity of such automata, see Paul Jacobsthal, *Ornamente griechischer Vasen* (Berlin, 1927), pp.102–109. See also A. Chapuis and E. Droz, *Les Automates; Figures artificielles d'hommes et d'animaux* (Paris, 1949), and J.

Huizinga, *The Waning of the Middle Ages* (Harmondsworth [Penguin], 1955; also in an Anchor paperback, New York, 1957), Ch. XIX.
THE SNOWMAN IN OUR HEAD: See my criticism of Loewy above, p.19.
DEFINITIONS LAID DOWN IN HEAVEN: The philosophical consequences of Plato's and Aristotle's theories of universals are discussed by K. R. Popper, *The Open Society*, especially in Ch. XI. See also F. A. Hayek, *The Sensory Order*, pp.48–49.

p.86 COPY THE IDEA OF A MOUNTAIN: Erwin Panofsky, '*Idea*', *Ein Beitrag zur Begriffsgeschichte der älteren Kunsttheorie* (Studien der Bibliothek Warburg 5, ed. Fritz Saxl; Leipzig and Berlin, 1924).
WE LEARN TO PARTICULARIZE: See above, Introduction, p.23, and Ch. II, p.77.
THE CHICKEN: See above, Ch. I, p.45.
THE EGG: O. L. Zangwill, *An Introduction to Modern Psychology* (London, 1950), p.126, after K. S. Lashley's findings published in *Psychological Review*, XLV (1938).
ANIMAL BEHAVIOUR: Nikolas Tinbergen, *The Study of Instinct* (Oxford, 1951). For a popular presentation, see Konrad Lorenz, *King Solomon's Ring: New Light on Animal Ways*, tr. M. K. Wilson (New York and London, 1952). For the theoretical foundations (even more interesting but also more vulnerable from the point of view of ethics and methodology), see Konrad Lorenz, 'Die angeborenen Formen möglicher Erfahrung', *Zeitschrift für Tierpsychologie*, V (1943). A note on the early history of these ideas by J. B. S. Haldane is in the *British Journal of Animal Behaviour*, IV (October 1956). For tentative applications of these findings to the problems of primitive art, see my paper on the 'Hobby Horse' (cited above for p.84) and Katesa Schlosser, *Der Signalismus in der Kunst der Naturvölker: biologischpsychologische Gesetzlichkeiten in den Abweichungen von der Norm des Vorbildes* (Arbeiten aus dem Museum für Völkerkunde der Universität Kiel I; Kiel, 1952).

p.87 RESPONSE TO FACES: A brief summary of Lorenz's views (with illustrations) in Tinbergen, *The Study of Instinct*, p.209. A paper by

R. A. Spitz and K. M. Wolfe on first reactions to faces is discussed by Gibson, *The Perception of the Visual World*, p.207.

p.89 RORSCHACH TEST: A full bibliography in Bruno Klopfer and others, *Developments in the Rorschach Technique* (2 vols., Yonkers, 1954–1956).
RORSCHACH ON PERCEPTION: H. Rorschach, *Psychodiagnostik* (Berne and Leipzig, 1921), p.18. (Cf. tr. Paul Lemkan and Bernard Kronenberg, New York, 1942.)

p.90 LEONE BATTISTA ALBERTI, *De Statua*, in *Kleinere kunsttheoretische Schriften*, ed. Janitschek, p.173.
THE SPELL OF THE STARS: Georg Thiele, *Antike Himmelsbilder* (Berlin, 1898), and Aby Warburg, *Gesammelte Schriften*, ed. Gertrud Bing (Leipzig and Berlin, 1932), II, especially 464 ff. and 491.
THEODOR KOCH-GRÜNBERG, *Anfänge der Kunst im Urwald* (Berlin, 1905).

p.91 DISCOVERED SHAPES AS STARTING POINT: Kurt Heinrich Busse, 'Die Ausstellung zur vergleichenden Entwicklungspsychologie der primitiven Kunst bei den Naturvölkern, den Kindern und in der Urzeit,' *Kongress für Aesthetik und allgemeine Kunstwissenschaft* (Berlin, 1913). For the use of accidental shapes in cave art, see G. H. Luquet, *The Art and Religion of Fossil Man*, tr. J. Townsend Russell (New Haven, 1930), p.119, and K. Schlosser, *Der Signalismus* (cited above for p.86), p.12 (with further bibliography).
CAVE ART A CULMINATION: Gene Weltfish, *The Origins of Art* (Indianapolis, 1953), pp. 229–32.

p.92 THE UNSPOILT HUNTERS: A recent exposition of this traditional view, with bibliography, is A. R. Willcox, *Rock Paintings of the Drakensberg* (London, 1956), Ch. XII.
EVOLUTIONISM: See above, Introduction, p.18.

p.93 ASSUMPTIONS ABOUT NEOLITHIC ART: Arnold Hauser, *The Social History of Art* (New York and London, 1951), p.34.
THE JERICHO SKULLS: K. M. Kenyon, *Digging Up Jericho* (London, 1957; New York, 1958).

p.94 THE KAYAK SPELL: Hans Himmelheber, *Eskimokünstler* (Eisenach, 1953) pp.43 and 62.

The author does not illustrate this type of decoration, and inquiries at the Smithsonian Institution in Washington failed to produce an example. A letter to the author elicited no reply, but at least I have no reason to doubt the existence of the legend.
ERNST KRIS AND OTTO KURZ, *Die Legende vom Künstler* (Vienna, 1934).

p.95 SACRED WORDS: Ludwig Traube, *Nomina Sacra, Versuch einer Geschichte der christlichen Kürzung* (Quellen und Untersuchungen zur lateinischen Philologie des Mittelalters, II; Munich, 1907).
INCOMPLETE HIEROGLYPHS: Pierre Lacau, 'Suppressions et modifications de signes dans les textes funéraires', *Zeitschrift für Aegyptische Sprache und Altertumskunde*, LI (1914), 1–64.
FRONTAL FIGURES IN EGYPT: Wreszinski, *Atlas zur altägyptischen Kulturgeschichte*, pl. 91(with commentary).
THE IMAGE IN JUDAISM: For a full discussion of various interpretations, see Karl Heinz Bernhardt, *Gott und Bild* (Berlin, 1956).

p.96 THE IMAGE IN EASTERN CHRISTIANITY: Edwyn R. Bevan, *Holy Images* (London, 1940).
THE EVIL EYE: W. Staude, 'Die Profilregel in der christlichen Malerei Aethiopiens und die Furcht vor dem bösen Blick', *Archiv für Völkerkunde*, IX (1954), 287; Otto Demus, *Byzantine Mosaic Decoration* (London, 1948; Boston, 1951), p.8.
PICTURES THAT FOLLOW WITH THEIR EYES: Classical instances mentioned by Pliny, *Historia naturalis* XXXV, 10 (37) (a Minerva by the painter Famulus or Amulius) and by Lucian, *De Syria Dea*, quoted in Franciscus Junius, *The Painting of the Ancients*, p.233. A fifteenth-century example connected with Rogier van der Weyden is discussed with other texts in Kurt Rathe, *Die Ausdrucksfunktion extrem verkürzter Figuren* (Studies of the Warburg Institute, 8; London, 1938), pp. 48–50. For ancient and modern explanations of the illusion, see below, Ch. VIII, note for p.234.
THE MIND ON VARIOUS LEVELS: Bevan, *Holy Images* (as cited above), p.31.

p.97 MALRAUX, 'The Imaginary Museum', in *The Voices of Silence*, Part I.

p.98 PALISSY: Ernst Kris, 'Der Stil Rustique', *Jahrbuch der kunsthistorischen Sammlungen in Wien*, n.s., I (1926).

MATISSE: For the master's own version of the anecdote, see his 'Notes d'un peintre sur son dessin', *Le Point* IV, XXI (1939), 14. 'J'ai répondu à quelqu'un qui disait que je ne voyais pas les femmes comme je les représentais: Si j'en rencontrais de pareilles dans la rue, je me sauverais epouvanté. Avant tout, je ne crée pas une femme, *je fais un tableau.*'

CHAPTER FOUR

p.99 MOTTO: Plato, *Greater Hippias* 282A.

PLATO AGAINST MIMESIS: Alexander W. Byvanck, *De beeldende Kunst in der Tijd van Plato* (Mededelingen der Koninklijke Nederlandse Akademie van Wetenschappen, Afd. Letterkunde, n.s., part 18, 16; 1955), pp.429–75.

AWAKENING OF GREEK ART: The best introduction from the point of view of this chapter is John Davidson Beazley and Bernard Ashmole, *Greek Sculpture and Painting to the End of the Hellenistic Period* (Cambridge, 1932).

p.100 EVIDENCE FOR DATING GREEK SCULPTURE: Gisela M. A. Richter, *The Sculpture and Sculptors of the Greeks* (rev. edn., New Haven, 1950).

E. LOEWY, see Introduction, p.18.

p.101 UNIQUENESS OF GREEK ART: For the most detailed and searching discussion, fundamental to this chapter, see Waldemar Deonna, *Du Miracle grec au miracle chrétien* (3 vols., Basel, 1945–48).

HEINRICH SCHÄFER, *Von ägyptischer Kunst* (3rd edn., Leipzig, 1930).

p.102 MOSAIC TEST: Margaret Lowenfeld, *The Lowenfeld Mosaic Test* (London, 1954), p.52.

p.103 THE SPHINX: I. E. S. Edwards, *The Pyramids of Egypt* (Harmondsworth [Penguin], 1947), p.107.

THE PLANTS BROUGHT BY THUTMOSE: See above, Ch. II, p.67.

AMARNA AND THE GREEK MIRACLE: Deonna (as cited for p.100), pp.337 ff.

p.104 H. A. GROENEWEGEN-FRANKFORT, *Arrest and Movement* (London, 1951).

p.105 MERERU-KA: My interpretation is based on William S. Smith, *A History of Egyptian Sculpture and Painting in the Old Kingdom* (London, 1946), p.355, who refers to the opinions of Schäfer and Sethe. See also Wreszinski, *Atlas zur altägyptischen Kulturgeschichte*, III, Pl. 1 and text. Prentice Duell, *The Mastaba of Mereruka* (Publications of the Oriental Institute, University of Chicago, XXXI, XXXIX; Chicago, 1938), gives a somewhat different interpretation of the painting scene as an invocation to the seasonal gods to protect the crops. The same author, however, also regards the totality of the scenes depicted in the tomb as 'both retrospective and prospective', which tallies well with my interpretation.

p.106 THEY SHOULD BE READ: Groenewegen-Frankfort, *Arrest and Movement* (as cited for p.104), pp.33, 34.

p.107 ONE WHO KEEPS ALIVE: Heinrich Schäfer and Walter Andrae, *Die Kunst des alten Orients* (Propyläen-Kunstgeschichte, 2; Berlin, 1925), p.33.

CYCLIC IDEA OF TIME: Mircea Eliade, *The Myth of the Eternal Return*, tr. Willard R. Trask (New York [Bollingen Series XLVI] and London, 1954). For the serpent biting its own tail, see Ficino after Iamblichus as discussed in my article 'Icones Symbolicae, The Visual Image in Neo-Platonic Thought', *Journal of the Warburg and Courtauld Institutes*, XI (1948), and George Boas, tr., *The Hieroglyphics of Horapollo* (New York [Bollingen Series XXIII], 1950). Some material on seasons, eternity, and funerary art in late antiquity in G. M. A. Hanfmann, *The Season Sarcophagus in Dumbarton Oaks* (Dumbarton Oaks Studies, 2; Cambridge, Mass., 1951 [i.e., 1952]), especially p.234.

EURIPIDES, *Alcestis*, 348–54. (I am indebted for the translation to Richard Gombrich.)

PLATO, *Laws* II, 656D, tr. R. G. Bury (LCL, 1926), I, 101–3.

p.108 THE COUCH: Plato, *Republic* X, 598, tr. Paul Shorey (LCL, 1930–1935), II, 430–31.
OPTICAL ILLUSIONS: *Republic* X, 602C–D, tr. Shorey, II, 448–49.
PLATO AGAINST MODERN ART: See above, note for p.99.

p.109 FICTION IN GREEK THOUGHT: Edgar John Forsdyke, *Greece before Homer* (London, 1955), Ch. VIII.
CHICAGO SYMPOSIUM: Helene J. Kantor, George Hanfmann, and others, 'Narration in Ancient Art: A Symposium', *American Journal of Archaeology*, LXI (January 1957).

p.110 HANFMANN, *Greek Narration*, p.74.
JUDGMENT OF PARIS: Christoph Clairmont, *Das Parisurteil in der antiken Kunst* (Zurich, 1951), with bibliography.

p.112 SCENIC ART AND ILLUSION: Ernst Pfuhl, *Malerei und Zeichnung der Griechen* (Munich, 1923), Index 10, under *Bühnenmalerei*.

p.113 HOMER, *Odyssey* XIX, 227–31, tr. E. V. Rieu (Harmondsworth [Penguin], 1945), p. 303. See H. L. Lorimer, *Homer and the Monuments* (London, 1950).

p.114 PLATO ON EGYPTIAN ART: See above, p. 107.
HELIODORUS: *Aethiopica* III, 13. The passage is discussed and elaborated in the appendix to Lessing's *Laokoon*: see *Gotthold Ephraim Lessings sämtliche Schriften*, ed. Karl Lachmann and Franz Muncker (Leipzig, 1898), XIV, 420.
PHILOSTRATUS, *The Life of Apollonius of Tyana*, Bk. IV, Ch. XXVIII, tr. F. C. Conybeare (LCL, 1912), I, 413 (paraphrased).

p.118 PLATO'S COUCH: See above, p.108.

p.119 PLINY ON PARRHASIOS: 'Parrhasius . . . in liniis extremis palmam adeptus. Haec est picturae summa subtilitas . . . Ambire enim se ipsa debet extremitas et sic desinere, ut promittat alia post se ostendatque etiam quae occultat.' (*Hist. nat.* XXXV, 67, 68.) For comment, see B. Bandinelli, 'Parrasio', *Critica d'arte* (1938),

p.5; Karl Borinski, *Die Antike in Poetik und Kunsttheorie* (Leipzig, 1914–24), II, 50–54.
AUSTRALIAN ABORIGINES: M. A. McElroy, 'Aesthetic Ranking Tests with Arnhem Land Aborigines', *Bulletin of the British Psychological Society*, No. 26 (1955), p.44.
EGYPTIAN HIEROGLYPHS: See the article by P. Lacau cited above for p.95.

p.120 TIMANTHES: Pliny, *Hist. nat.* XXXV, 73. The description occurs also in Cicero, *Orator* 74, and in Quintilian, *Inst. oratoria* II, XIII, 12. It became the stock example of postmedieval writers on expression in painting.
QUINTILIAN: '. . . distortum et elaboratum in qua vel praecipue laudabilis est ipse illa novitas ac difficultas.' *Inst. or.* II, XIII, 10.
ANECDOTES: See Ernst Kris and Otto Kurz, *Die Legende vom Künstler* (Vienna, 1934).

p.122 FORMULAS IN GREEK ART: E. Loewy, 'Typenwanderung', *Archaeologische Jahreshefte*, XII (1909), 243; XIV (1911), 1.
FORESHORTENING IN MEXICAN ART: An impressive example is the newly discovered wall painting of Bonampak: Augustín Villagra Caleti, *Bonampak, la ciudad de los muros pintados* (Supplement to *Anales del Instituto Nacional de Antropología e Historia*, III; Mexico City, 1949), to which Mr. P. Dark kindly drew my attention.

p.123 PLINY ON LYSIPPUS: *Hist. nat.* XXXIV, 65.

p.124 QUINTILIAN ON CONNOISSEURS: 'Polygnotus atque Aglaophon, quorum simplex color tam sui studiosos adhuc habet, ut illa, prope rudia ac velut futurae mox artis primordia maximis, qui post eos exstiterunt, auctoribus praeferant, proprio quodam intelligendi, ut mea opinio est, ambitu.' *Inst. or.* XII, x, 3.
BREAKDOWN OF CLASSICAL STANDARDS: For a fresh assessment of late antique currents, D. Levi, 'L'arte Romana: Schizzo della sua evoluzione e sua posizione nella storia dell'arte antica', *Annuario della Scuola Archeologica Italiana di Atene*, XXIV–XXVI, n.s. VIII–X, 1946–48 (Rome, 1950), pp.229–304.

p.125 THE ICON: See E. Bevan, *Holy Images* (London, 1940), p.145.
BYZANTINE CYCLES: Otto Demus, *Byzantine Mosaic Decoration* (London, 1948; Boston, 1951), p.145.

CHAPTER FIVE

p.126 MOTTO: W. H. Auden, in *The Collected Poetry* (New York, 1945), p.267. This quotation came to my attention through the kindness of Dr. Giorgio Tonelli.

THE PERFECT CANON: Erwin Panofsky, 'The History of the Theory of Human Proportions as a Reflection of the History of Styles', in *Meaning in the Visual Arts* (New York [Anchor], 1955), pp.55–107, with bibliography supplemented on p.vi.

FRED C. AYER, *The Psychology of Drawing, with Special Reference to Laboratory Teaching* (Baltimore, 1916).

p.128 CHINESE TEXTBOOK: Mai-mai Sze, *The Tao of Painting: A Study of the Ritual Disposition of Chinese Painting, with a translation of the Chieh Tzŭ Yüan Hua Chuan (Mustard Seed Garden Manual of Painting) 1679–1701* (2 vols., New York [Bollingen Series XLIX], 1956). See also Henry P. Bowie, *On the Laws of Japanese Painting* (San Francisco, 1911).

LEARNING TO WRITE: *The Mustard Seed Garden Manual of Painting*, in *The Tao of Painting*, II, 323–24.

p.129 DRAW FOUR LEAVES: Ibid., II, 328.

MOOD FOR INSPIRATION: Ibid., II, 327.

CHINESE CRITICAL TERMS: An interesting discussion in William Reynolds Beal Acker, *Some T'ang and Pre-T'ang Texts on Chinese Painting* (Leiden, 1954), introduction.

MEDIEVAL TRADITIONALISM: Adolph Goldschmidt, 'Das Nachleben der antiken Formen im Mittelalter', *Vorträge der Bibliothek Warburg*, I (1921–1922) (Berlin, 1923), 40–50. See also the writings of Julius von Schlosser referred to in the notes for pp.19 and 60. For the bibliography of medieval patternbooks see Hans Huth, *Künstler und Werkstatt der Spätgotik* (Augsburg, 1923), notes 56, 57, 63.

p.130 VILLARD FOR AMATEURS: I owe this suggestion to Professor Harry Bober.

p.131 THE WINDOW: Leone Battista Alberti, *Della Pittura*, ed. Janitschek, p.79.

p.132 LEONARDO'S LAW OF GROWTH: J. P. Richter, *The Literary Works of Leonardo da Vinci* (2nd edn., London and New York, 1939), I, 126 (Nos. 394, 395); I have paraphrased and condensed Leonardo's notes.

LEONARDO THE MAKER: See above, p.83.

p.133 INFLUENCE OF PLATONISM: Erwin Panofsky, '*Idea*', as cited for p.86. The fundamental text of this doctrine, Giovanni Pietro Bellori's lecture of 1664 on 'Idea', is now easily accessible in Elizabeth G. Holt, *A Documentary History of Art*, II (New York [Anchor], 1958).

p.134 TEACHING METHODS: The best account is in Joseph Meder, *Die Handzeichnung; ihre Technik und Entwicklung* (Vienna, 1919); see also Nikolaus Pevsner, *Academies of Art* (Cambridge and New York, 1940).

MICHELANGELO, ON A DRAWING IN THE BRITISH MUSEUM: Johannes Wilde, *Italian Drawings in the British Museum; Michelangelo and His Studio* (London, 1953), no. 31ʳ.

JOACHIM VON SANDRART, *L'Academia tedesca della architectura, scultura & pittura: oder, Teutsche academie der edlen bau- bild- und mahlerey-künste* (Nürnberg, 1675), Book I, Part 3. The passage derives from the chapter on *disegno* in Vasari, *Vite*, intro., xv. For similar formulations see also Panofsky, *Albrecht Dürer* (Princeton, 1943), p.273.

DRAW 'A MAN': Max Liebermann's teacher Steffeck used to say, 'What you can't paint out of your head you can't paint at all'. Max Liebermann, *Gesammelte Schriften* (Berlin, 1922), p.42.

p.135 DRAWING BOOKS: Some more are listed in H. L. Boersma *Kunstindustrieele Literatur* (The Hague, 1888) and in the catalogues of the great art libraries, notably those of Conte Cicognara (Pisa, 1821), Nos. 288–369; of the Österreichische Museum für Kunst und Industrie (Vienna, 1883), Section D and of the Amsterdam Rijksmuseum (Amsterdam 1934), I, 221–28.

VOGTHERR: See the List of Illustrations for the titles of the drawing books discussed in this chapter. The bibliography of Vogtherr's book is worth mentioning because it testifies to the enormous demand: after its appearance in

1538, the book was reprinted in 1539 and in 1540, twice in German, twice in Latin. There is also a pirated Antwerp edition with French and Spanish letterpress and new editions in 1545, 1559, and 1572. A facsimile was published in the Zwickauer Facsimiledrucke, 19 (1913).

p.136 DÜRER'S QUEST: Erwin Panofsky's article on proportion and also his *Albrecht Dürer*, cited for pp.126 and 134, above.
CAREL VAN MANDER, *Den Grondt der Edel vry Schilder-Const*, ed. Rudolf Hoecker, in *Quellenstudien zur holländischen Kunstgeschichte*, VIII (The Hague, 1916), 56 (II, 6–7).

p.138 AGOSTINO CARRACCI: Rudolf Wittkower, *The Drawings of the Carracci in the Collection of Her Majesty the Queen at Windsor Castle* (The Italian Drawings at Windsor Castle; London, 1952), p.13.

p.140 EUCLIDIAN BIRDS: 'Havendosi per long' esperientia di studio osservato d'entr' a' segreto della natura, che ciascuna cosa da Dio creata ha simpatia alle figure d'Euclide, si come imparai per esperientia dall'osservazione ch'io feci all hora, ch'andavo alle scuole, mentre un mio compagno, naturalmente, et senz' alcuno studio disegnava uccelli sopra la carta. Non sarà dunque fuor del nostro principio . . . il seguir la naturalezza di detto mio compagno, la quale sarà vera mascina, et vero modo per disegnar qualsisia uccello con ogni giusta proportione.' Crispyn van de Passe, *La Luce del dipingere* (Amsterdam, 1643), Part V, p.1.
BIRDS AND EGGS: Sze, *The Tao of Painting*, II, 535.

p.141 JAPANESE TRICK DRAWINGS: The bird from the egg: Henry P. Bowie, *On the Laws of Japanese Painting* (San Francisco, 1911), Pl. XXII; Hokusai's schemata: Jack R. Hillier, *Hokusai* (London, 1955).
RUBENS: See Julius von Schlosser, *La Letteratura artistica* (Florence, 1956), p.644. Mr. Michael Jaffé is preparing a critical edition of the book.

p.144 VAN MANDER, *Schilder-Const* (cited above for p.136), p.56 (II, 5).

p.147 PETRUS CAMPER, *The Connexion between the Science of Anatomy and the Arts of Drawing, Painting, Statuary, etc.* (London, 1794), p.94.

p.148 MODIFICATION OF ANTICIPATION: J. R. Beloff, 'Perception and Extrapolation', *Bulletin of the British Psychological Society*, No. 32 (May 1957), p.44.
LEONARDO'S SKETCHING METHODS: See my article in *Etudes d'art*, cited above for p.83.

p.149 DEGAS: John Rewald, *The History of Impressionism* (New York, 1946), p.156.
MEDER: *Die Handzeichnung* (as cited above for p.134), pp.258–59.
LYSIPPUS AND CARAVAGGIO: Roger Hinks, *Michelangelo Merigi da Caravaggio* (London, 1953), p.32.
THE MODERN DILEMMA: A searching discussion in Joyce Cary, *Art and Reality* (New York and Cambridge, 1958), sections 7–10.
CONSTABLE: Leslie, *Memoirs*, p.279.

p.150 CHARDIN: Charles Nicolas Cochin, 'Essai sur la vie de Chardin', in *Documents sur la vie et l'œuvre de Chardin*, ed. A. Pascal and R. Gaucheron (Paris, 1931), p.5. The essay was not published in Constable's lifetime but the parallel with his wording is striking: 'Voilà, se disait-il à lui même, un objet qu'il est question de rendre. Pour n'être occupé que de le rendre vrai, il faut que j'oublie tout ce que j'ai vu, et même jusqu'à la manière dont ces objets ont été traités par d'autres.'
POUSSIN: André Félibien, *Entretiens sur les vies et sur les ouvrages des plus excellens peintres anciens et modernes* (Trevoux, 1725), IV, 81 (Entretien VIII, on Poussin): 'Il veut que lorsqu'il vient à mettre la main à l'oeuvre, il le fasse d'une manière qui n'ayt point encore executée par un autre, afin que son ouvrage paroisse comme une chose unique et nouvelle.'
JOHN CONSTABLE, *Various Subjects of Landscape* (London, 1832).
PAINTING A SCIENCE: Leslie, *Memoirs*, p.323.
COZENS AND CONSTABLE: Paul Oppé, *Alexander and John Robert Cozens* (London, 1952), p.70. One of a set of fifteen other copies by Constable after Cozens was included in the *Exhibition of Works from the Paul Oppé Collection* at the Royal Academy of Arts (London, 1958); as no.44 in the catalogue.

p.151 CLOUDS: Kurt Badt, *John Constable's Clouds*, tr. S. Godman (London, 1950).
GOETHE ON HOWARD:
Was sich nicht halten, nicht erreichen lässt,
Er fasst es an, er hält zuerst es fest;

Bestimmt das Unbestimmte, schränkt es ein,
Benennt es treffend !—Sei die Ehre dein !
The cycle 'Howards Ehrengedächtnis' is in the section of Goethe's collected poems called 'Gott und Welt'.

CHAPTER SIX

p.154 MOTTO: Shakespeare, *Antony and Cleopatra*, IV, xii, 2–7.
PHILOSTRATUS, *Life of Apollonius of Tyana*, Bk. II, Ch. 22. My version is based on the tr. by F. C. Conybeare (LCL, 1912), I, 175–79.

p.155 PROJECTION: See above, Ch. III, esp. note for p.89.

p.156 PAUL OPPÉ, *Alexander and John Robert Cozens* (London, 1952), p.167. The book contains a reprint of Alexander Cozens' *A New Method of Assisting the Invention in Drawing Original Compositions of Landscape*, 1st edn., 1785.

p.157 JUSTINUS KERNER, *Kleksographien* (Stuttgart, 1853).
INKBLOT READING: O. L. Zangwill, 'A Study of the Significance of Attitude in Recognition', *British Journal of Psychology*, XXVIII (1937), 12–17.
PICTURESQUE MOTIFS: Christopher Hussey, *The Picturesque* (London and New York, 1927). See also my article 'Renaissance Artistic Theory and the Development of Landscape Painting', *Gazette des beaux-arts*, XLI (May 1953); reprinted in *Essays in Honor of Hans Tietze* (Paris and New York, 1958).

p.158 SAMUEL VAN HOOGSTRAETEN, *Inleyding tot de Hooge Schoole der Schilderkonst* (Rotterdam, 1678), p.237.
CHINESE BLOTTING: Ch'ên Yung-chih, quoted from H. A. Giles, *An Introduction to the History of Chinese Pictorial Art* (Shanghai and Leiden, 1905), p.100.

p.159 LEONARDO DA VINCI, *Treatise on Painting*, ed. McMahon, No. 76.
LEONARDO'S METHOD: See my article 'Conseils de Léonard', cited above for p.83.
AYER, *Psychology of Drawing*, as cited above for p.126.

p.160 LEONARDO ON BOTTICELLI: *Treatise on Painting*, ed. McMahon, No. 93.
THE SPONGE: Pliny, *Hist. nat.* XXXV, 103.
ALBERTI ON ORIGINS: See his *De Statua*, as cited above for p.90.
LUSUS NATURAE: Jurgis Baltrušaitis, *Aberrations* (Paris, 1957), Ch. II. Many examples in Michael Bernhard Valentini, *Museum museorum*, II (Frankfurt am Main, 1714), Ch. VII.
PEARLS: Peter Stone, 'Baroque Pearls', *Apollo* (December 1958).

p.161 PLATO: See above, Chs. III and IV.
DISTORTED PROPORTION: Plato, *Sophist* 23, 236.
TZETZES, Chiliad xl, hist. 381, and viii, 193; quoted from Franciscus Junius, *The Painting of the Ancients*, p.232; see also Jurgis Baltrusaitis, *Anamorphoses; ou perspectives curieuses* (Paris, 1955), p.12.

p.162 HORACE, *Ad Pisones* (*Ars poetica*) 361–62.
THE ROMANCE OF THE ROSE, lines 19383–93; tr. Frederick S. Ellis (Temple Classics; London, 1903), III, 131–32.
DONATELLO: Vasari, *Vite*, ed. Milanesi, II, 170–71.

p.163 BALDASSARE CASTIGLIONE, *Il Libro del Cortegiano* (1st edn., 1527), ed. Vittorio Cian (4th edn., rev., Florence, 1947), p.69 (Bk. I, Ch. 28).

p.165 TITIAN: Vasari, *Vite*, ed. Milanesi, VII, 452. Vasari's allusion to careless imitators is probably aimed at Tintoretto, whose technique is later defended on similar lines in Carlo Ridolfi, *Meraviglie d'arte* (Venice, 1648). For the technical aspects, see Vojtěch Volavka, *Painting and the Painter's Brushwork* (Prague, 1954).
GIOVANNI PAOLO LOMAZZO, *Trattato dell'arte della pittura, scultura ed architettura*, Bk. VI, Ch. LXII (1st edn., 1584) Rome, 1844, II, 446.
CAREL VAN MANDER, *Schilder-Const*, XII, 26 (p.274 of the edn. cited for p.136).

REMBRANDT: Arnold Houbraken, *De Groote Schouburgh der nederlantsche Konstschilders en Schilderessen* (1st edn., 1718; The Hague, 1753), I, 269.

VELÁZQUEZ: Antonio Palomino de Castro y Velasco, *El Museo pictorico, y escala optica*, Bk. III, Ch. III (1st edn., 1714; Madrid, 1947), p.905. I am indebted for this reference to Mrs. Enriqueta Frankfort.

p.166   TWO MANNERS:

> *Vedo un impasto, un sprezzo de penelo,*
> *Un certo che inefabile, e amirando,*
> *Che soto l'ochio me và a bulegando*
> *Si che scovegno dir: questo è'l più belo.*
> *In fin quelo xè un sforzo, un voler far*
> *Con tempo, con paciencia, e con amor:*
> *E forsi anche a quel segno ogni Pitor,*
> *Che habia bon'ochio ghe puol arivar.*
> *Ma l'ariva a la maniera, al trato*
> *(Verbi gratia) del Paulo, del Bassan,*
> *Del vechio, Tentoreto, e de Tician,*
> *Per Dio, l'è cosa da deventar mato.*

Marco Boschini, *La Carta del navegar pitoresco* (Venice, 1660), pp.296–97.

MARCO BOSCHINI, *Descrizione del tutte le pubbliche pitture della Città di Venezia*, ed. A. M. Zanetti (Venice, 1733). p.11.

p.167   ROGER DE PILES, *The Principles of Painting*, tr. by a painter from *Cours de peinture par principes avec un balance des peintres* (1st edn., 1709; London, 1743), p.156.

CAYLUS: 'La vérité de cette opération de l'esprit est fondée sur la nature. En agissant ainsi, il flatte l'amour-propre de celui qu'il veut persuader. Loin de le dégouter ou de le révolter par une répétition détaillée, il le traite en homme éclairé qui croit sentir et imaginer par lui-même ce qu'on vient de lui suggérer.' Anne Claude Phillippe, Comte de Caylus, *Discours sur la peinture et la sculpture*, ed. A. Fontaine (Paris, 1910), p.153. I am indebted for this reference to Mr. H. Lester Cooke. Similar reflections with regard to writing occur in Demetrius, *On Style* 222.

JOSHUA REYNOLDS, *Discourses* (1769–90; New York and London, 1928), pp.239–41 (Discourse XIV).

p.168   J. E. LIOTARD, *Traité des principes et des règles de la peinture* (Geneva, 1945), p.97.

p.169   THE LOADED BRUSH: Maurice Grosser, *The Painter's Eye* (New York, 1955), pp.66 ff.

NEW FUNCTION OF ART: See my lecture on 'Psycho-Analysis and the History of Art', cited above for p.17.

CONUNDRUMS OF MODERN ART: According to Jean Limbourg, in his introduction to the *Catalogue of Works by Jean Dubuffet* (exhibited at Arthur Tooth & Sons Ltd., London, April–May 1958), the 'first principle' of that artist's method is to appeal to the imagination of the spectator, 'who will give to each painting the meaning he wants . . . that is why lazy minds are not attracted by Dubuffet's painting; it leaves them to do half the work'.

CHAPTER SEVEN

p.170   MOTTO: Maximus Tyrius, *Philosophumena*, ed. H. Hobein (Leipzig, 1910), pp.123, 124; in Franciscus Junius, *The Painting of the Ancients*, p.344.

PHILOSTRATUS: See above, p.154.

PICTURE READING: Some bibliography in M. D. Vernon, *A Further Study of Visual Perception*, pp.28–40 and 262.

WILLIAM JAMES, *Talks to Teachers on Psychology and to Students on Some of Life's Ideals* (New York and London, 1899), p.159.

p.171   INFORMATION THEORY: Colin Cherry, *On Human Communication*.

SELECTIVE FUNCTION: D. M. McKay, 'The Place of Meaning in the Theory of Information', in *Information Theory, a Symposium*, ed. Colin Cherry (New York and London, 1956), p.219.

p.172   EXPERIMENTS IN SUGGESTION: Vernon, *A Further Study of Visual Perception*, p.241; C. E. Osgood, *Method and Theory*, p.640. A parallel experiment on the perception of heat is described by G. W. Williams, 'Suggestibility in the Normal and Hypnotic States', *Archives of Psychology* (1930).

CULT IMAGES: Bevan, *Holy Images* (as cited for p.96).

p.173   ZEUXIS AND PARRHASIOS: Pliny, *Hist. nat.* XXXV, 36.

p.174   THEON'S SOUND FILM: Claudius Aelianus,

Var. hist. II, 44. Delacroix commented on this story in his *Journal*, May 16, 1857.
CHINESE THEORY: Sze, *The Tao of Painting*, II, 250–51.

p.175 BRUSH SPARED PERFORMANCE: *The Tao of Painting*, I, 104.
THE PAGODA: Treatise attributed to Wang Wei in Shio Sakanishi, *The Spirit of the Brush* (The Wisdom of the East Series; London, 1939), p.71.
SHADOW ANTIQUA: Raymond Cohn and Michael Estrin, *101 Ornamental Alphabets* (New York, 1956), p.83.
SUBJECTIVE CONTOUR: Osgood, *Method and Theory*, p.232.

p.176 X RAYS: G. Spiegler, *Physikalische Grundlagen der Röntgendiagnostik* (Stuttgart, 1957), Ch. 7, with bibliography.
'BELIEVING IS SEEING': I take this excellent formulation from M. L. Johnson, 'Seeing's Believing', in *New Biology*, XV (October, 1953), 60–80.
LINE OF PARRHASIOS: See above, p.119.
PHILOSTRATUS: ἀναλογία ταῦτα, ὦ παῖ· δεῖ γὰρ κλέπτεσθαι τοὺς ὀφθαλμοὺς τοῖς ἐπιτηδείοις κύκλοις συναπιόντας. *Imagines* I, 4.
WILLIAM SHAKESPEARE, *The Rape of Lucrece*, stanza 204, lines 1422–28. The similarity does not appear to have been noticed; the name of Philostratus does not occur in the rich bibliography to T. W. Baldwin, *On the Literary Genetics of Shakspere's Poems and Sonnets* (Urbana, 1950). I hope to return to this problem elsewhere.

p.177 THE CARRACCI: R. Wittkower in *Studies in Communication* by A. J. Ayer and others; intro. by B. Ifor Evans, Studies in Communication (The Communication Research Centre, University College, London, 1955).

p.179 DROODLES: Roger Price, *Droodles* (New York, 1953); see also Osgood, *Method and Theory*, p.214, and Arnheim, *Art and Visual Perception*, p.33.
HILDEBRAND: *Das Problem der Form in der bildenden Kunst*, p.5.

p.181 WHISTLER ON FRITH, after William Gaunt, *The Aesthetic Adventure* (Harmondsworth [Penguin], 1957), p.115.

p.182 NIETZSCHE: See Ch. II, p.75.

p.185 THE FRASER SPIRAL: Metzger, *Gesetze des Sehens* (2nd edn., Frankfurt am Main, 1953),

p.18. I do not wish to imply that my remarks dispose of the mystery of this and similar illusions.
GIBSON, *The Perception of the Visual World*, p.65.
ROY CAMPBELL, *Broken Record* (London, 1934), p.27.
VASARI, *Vite*, ed. Milanesi, IV, 9 (Preface to Part III).
BARBARO: 'È la perfettione dell' arte, fare i contorni di modo dolci, et sfumati, che ancho s'intenda, quel che non si vede, anzi che l'occhio pensi di vedere, quello ch'egli vede, che e un fuggir dolcissimo una tenerezza nell orizonte della vista nostra, che e, et non e, et che solo si fa con infinita pratica, et che diletta à chi non sa più oltra, et fa stupire, chi bene l'intende.' Daniele Barbaro, in Vitruvius Pollio, *I dieci libri dell' architettura* (Venice, 1556), Bk. VIII, Ch. V, p.188.

p.186 CHINESE TREATISE: Attributed to Wang Wei, in Sakanishi, *The Spirit of the Brush*, p.71.
HENRY PEACHAM, *The Compleat Gentleman . . . To which is added The Gentleman's Exercise* (London, 1634), p.39. I have adopted the easier spelling of the London 1661 edition, p.339.

p.187 THE CONSTANT PRINCE, I, i, in *The Dramas of Calderón*, tr. Denis Florence McCarthy (London, 1853), I, 12–13.

p.189 VERNON, *Visual Perception*, p.130, after G. K. Adams in *American Journal of Psychology*, XXXIV (1923), 359.
LEAF OR DONKEY?: Vernon, *Visual Perception*, pp.130–31. For a detailed discussion of similar experiments in the light of perceptual theory, see Jerome S. Bruner, Leo Postman, and John Rodrigues, 'Expectation and the Perception of Color', *American Journal of Psychology* (Austin, Tex.), LXIV (1951), 216–27, reprinted in David C. Beardslee and Michael Wertheimer, *Readings in Perception* (New York and London, 1958).

p.191 READING AN IMAGE: A good introspective analysis in Jean-Paul Sartre, *The Psychology of Imagination* (London and New York, 1950), p.43. See also Karl Hofer, *Über das Gesetzliche in der bildenden Kunst* (Berlin, 1956), pp.49–51, and G. T. Buswell, *How People Look at Pictures* (Chicago, 1935), on eye movements.

ACTIVATION OF PHANTOMS: Vernon, *Visual Perception*, Appendix B.

RECENT EXPERIMENT ON PERSISTENCE: C. Fisher, 'Dreams and Perception, the Role of Preconscious and Primary Modes of Perception in Dream Formation', *Journal of the American Psychoanalytic Association*, II (1954), 389–445. DISCARDED MISREADINGS: Gudmund Smith, 'Visual Perception, an Event over Time', *Psychological Review*, LXIV (September 1957), with bibliography. The two papers here quoted confirm the interesting introspective accounts of Anton Ehrenzweig, *The Psycho-analysis of Artistic Vision and Hearing* (London, 1953), without necessarily supporting his interpretation.

PUZZLE PICTURES: R. S. Woodworth and Harold Schlosberg, *Experimental Psychology*, p.716, with bibliography.

IMAGE OF POINTING HAND: E. E. Jones and J. S. Bruner, 'Expectancy in Apparent Visual Movement', *British Journal of Psychology*, XLV (1954), 157–65. S. E. Kaden, S. Wapner, and H. Werner, 'Studies in Physiognomic Perception II: Effects of Directional Dynamics of Pictures, Objects and of Words on the Position of the Apparent Horizon', *The Journal of Psychology*, XXXIX (January 1955), 61–70.

PHILIP ANGEL, *Lof der Schilder-Konst* (Leiden, 1642), p.41. There is a discussion of this effect in Ptolemy's *Optics*, p.55 of the edn. cited for p.12.

p.192 MOBILITY AND SPACE: Hans Wallach, D. N. O'Connell, and Ulric Neisser, 'The Memory Effect of Visual Perception of Three-dimensional Form'. *Journal of Experimental Psychology*, XLV (May 1953), 360–68; and the interesting discussion in Metzger, *Gesetze des Sehens*, pp.448–55.

p.193 POTENTIAL LIVING SPACE: For some historical consequences, see above, pp.118–120 and 131, and my review of J. Bodonyi, 'Entstehung und Bedeutung des Goldgrundes in der spätantiken Bildkomposition', in *Kritische Berichte zur kunstgeschichtlichen Literatur*, V (1932-33), esp. p.74.

p.194 REMBRANDT: Johann Plesch, *Rembrandts within Rembrandts*, tr. Edward Fitzgerald (New York, 1953).

p.200 THE AMBIGUOUS HAND: See M. L. Johnson in *New Biology*, cited above for p.176.

p.201 METALANGUAGE: See A. Tarski, as cited above for p.59.

CHAPTER EIGHT

p.204 MOTTO: 'Naturalis quidem compositio visus res est mirabilis in casu suo qui ordinate fit cum extensione sua, et sensibilitate quam exhibet videndi et discernendi diversitates subjectarum figurarum, quomodocumque posite fuerint. Facit autem hoc velociter, sine tarditate aut intermissione, et utitur diligenti ratiocinacione cum mirabili virtute fere incredibili, et agit hec insensibiliter propter celeritatem suam. . . . Sensus ergo, cum non poterit videre subiectam rem eo modo qui ei convenit, cognoscit eam per manifestationem ceterarum diversitatum. Et sic quandoque apparet ei res vere, et quandoque ymaginatio falsa. . . .' Ptolemy, *Optics*, Bk. II, 74 and 136, quoted after Albert Lejeune, ed., *L'Optique de Claude Ptolémée* (Louvain, 1956), pp.50 and 81. PHILOSTRATUS: See above, p.154.

p.205 RECENT WRITINGS ON PERSPECTIVE: The criticism of traditional perspective owes most of its impetus to the writings of G. Hauck, *Die*

subjektive Perspektive und die horizontalen Curvaturen des dorischen Styls (Stuttgart, 1879), and *Die malerische Perspektive* (Berlin, 1882). Its philosophical consolidation is due to Erwin Panofsky, 'Die Perspektive als symbolische Form', *Vorträge der Bibliothek Warburg* (1924-1925). Panofsky's interpretation was developed and applied in John White, *The Birth and Rebirth of Pictorial Space* (London, 1957). The conclusions of these and other critics of projective perspective were challenged by M. H. Pirenne, 'The Scientific Basis of Leonardo da Vinci's Theory of Perspective', *British Journal for the Philosophy of Science*, III:10 (1952), and by Decio Gioseffi, *Perspective artificialis* (Istituto di Storia dell'arte antica e moderna, No. 7; Trieste, 1957), whose historical and logical arguments cannot easily be bypassed.

p.206 M. C. ESCHER: See the *Catalogue of the Stedelijk Museum Amsterdam*, No. 118

(Autumn 1954), and L. S. Penrose and R. Penrose, 'Impossible Objects: A Special Type of Visual Illusion', *British Journal of Psychology*, XLIX (1958).

p.209 HERBERT READ, *The Art of Sculpture* (New York [Bollingen Series XXXV:3], and London, 1956), pp.66 f.
LABORATORY TROMPE L'ŒIL: William H. Ittelson, *The Ames Demonstrations in Perception* (Princeton, 1952), with further bibliography.

p.210 PERCEPTIONS, NOT DISCLOSURES: A. Ames, Jr., 'The Rotating Trapezoid', in F. P. Kilpatrick, *Human Behavior from the Transactional Point of View* (Hanover, N. H., 1952), p.65. See also William H. Ittelson, and Franklin P. Kilpatrick, 'Experiments in Perception', *Scientific American* (New York), 185 (1952), reprinted in David C. Beardslee and Michael Wertheimer, *Readings in Perception* (New York and London, 1958), especially the concluding paragraphs.

p.211 'WE CANNOT SEE ROUND CORNERS': I owe this formulation to Mr. M. H. Pirenne, whose article is cited above for p.205.

p.213 ANAMORPHOSIS: See Jurgis Baltrušaitis, *Anamorphoses; ou perspectives curieuses* (Paris, 1955).

p.214 PLATO'S PROTEST: In the *Sophist*, as cited above for p.161.
THE VAULTED SKY: Hermann von Helmholtz, *Handbuch der physiologischen Optik* (Hamburg and Leipzig, 1896), III, No. 28, p.673; No. 30, p.775.

p.215 PARADOXICAL RESULTS: See White, *Pictorial Space* (as cited for p.205), Ch. XIV, esp. pp.209–10 and notes.

p.217 THE MELODY OF PERCEPTION: James J. Gibson, 'Visually Controlled Locomotion and Visual Orientation in Animals', *British Journal of Psychology*, XLIX (1958). A brief, well-illustrated discussion of the practical aspect is Roger Hinks, 'Peepshow and Roving Eye', *Architectural Review* (London), CXVIII (September, 1955), 161–64.

p.218 THE CURVED STRING: Helmholtz, *Handbuch* (cited for p.214), III, No. 28, p.686.

ARGUMENT FROM ARCHITECTURE: See Hauck, *Subjektive Perspektive*, cited above for p.205.
LEONARDO ON THE MIRROR: *Treatise on Painting*, ed. McMahon, No. 432.
'OBSERVING DIFFERENCES': Norman L. Munn, *Psychology: The Fundamentals of Human Adjustment* (Boston, 1946), p.331. See also above, Ch. V, p.148.

p.219 SIZE-DISTANCE: A Babylonian example, Etana's flight to heaven, in Schäfer, *Von ägyptischer Kunst*, p.84 and appendix, pp.348–49; see also White, *Pictorial Space* (as cited for p.205), pp.127–28 and introduction.
BATHYSCAPHE: In a newspaper report on the British Association meeting in Dublin in the autumn of 1957.
'THERENESS-THATNESS': Ittelson, *The Ames Demonstrations* (as cited for p.209), pp.21 ff.
SUBJECT-PREDICATE CHARACTER: A., Prinz Auersperg, after Viktor von Weizsäcker, *Der Gestaltkreis: Theorie der Einheit von Wahrnehmen und Bewegen* (4th edn., Stuttgart, 1950), p.87.

p.220 AFTERIMAGES IN SPACE: See the discussion of Emmert's Law in Woodworth and Schlosberg, *Experimental Psychology*, pp.487–88.

p.221 THE GESTALT SCHOOL: Arnheim, *Art and Visual Perception*, esp. pp.205–6, and Wolfgang Metzger. See also, however, the article by E. C. Tolman and E. Brunswik cited for p.24.

p.225 WILLIAM HOGARTH, *The Analysis of Beauty* (1st edn., 1753), ed. Joseph Burke (Oxford, 1955), pp.110–11.
CONVEX AND CONCAVE: Hogarth, ibid., p.117.
PLATO, *Republic* X, 602D, tr. Paul Shorey (LCL, 1930–1935), II, 449.

p.226 AMBIGUOUS STAIRS: A visual commentary is M. C. Escher's lithograph *Relativity*, illustrated in the catalogue of the artist's work (cited above for p.206), No. 29.

p.227 YOSHIO MARKINO, *When I Was a Child* (Boston, New York, and London, 1912), pp. 272–74.

p.228 JOHN RUSKIN, *Modern Painters*, Vol. I, Part II, Sec. I, Ch. II.

CATLIN'S ACCOUNT: George Catlin, *Letters and Notes on the Manners, Customs and Conditions of the North American Indians* (London, 1841; New York, 1842–1844), II, 190–94 in the British edition.

THE SHADOWED FACE: For similar stories of misinterpretation, see Lucien Arréat, *Psychologie du Peintre* (Paris, 1892), p.80; Julius von Schlosser, *Präludien* (Berlin, 1927), p.211; Schäfer, *Von ägyptischer Kunst*, p.92; and Joyce Cary, *Art and Reality* (New York and Cambridge, 1957), p.67.

CHINESE TREATISE: Attributed to Han Fei, d. 233 B.C., in Shio Sakanishi, *The Spirit of the Brush*, p.19.

p.229   LIGHT FROM THE LEFT: Metzger, *Gesetze des Sehens*, pp.377 ff.; J. J. Gibson, *The Perception of the Visual World*, p.99.

p.231   EINSTEIN AND THE AMOEBA: K. R. Popper, 'The Philosophy of Science', in *British Philosophy in the Mid-Century* (as cited for p.23), p.179. For further bibliography, see my Introduction, pp.23 f.

STRATEGY: The term is used in the theory of games and applied to psychology in J. S. Bruner, J. J. Goodnow, and G. A. Austin, *A Study of Thinking* (New York and London, 1956).

VALUE OF SIMPLICITY: K. R. Popper, *The Logic of Scientific Discovery* (New York and London, 1959), especially Ch. VII and Appendix VIII. My suggestion to interpret the findings of the Gestalt school in this light converges with the conclusions of Julian E. Hochberg, 'Effects of the Gestalt Revolution: The Cornell Symposium on Perception', *Psychological Review*, LXIV (1957), reprinted in D. C. Beardslee and Michael Wertheimer, *Readings in Perception* (New York and London, 1958), especially n.4 referring to Kohler's experiments with inverted vision.

p.232   VAUGHAN CORNISH, *Scenery and the Sense of Sight* (Cambridge, 1935), p.61. See also the passage in Helmholtz cited above for p.214.

TEXTURE: Gibson, *Perception of the Visual World*, especially Chs. V and VI.

SERIAL ORDERS: Gibson, *Perception of the Visual World*, especially Ch. VII; Hans Wallach and D. N. O'Connell, 'Kinetic Depth Effect', *Journal of Experimental Psychology*, XLV (1953), 205–17; and the article by Gibson cited above for p.217.

UNITY OF PERCEPTION AND MOVEMENT: Viktor von Weizsäcker, *Der Gestaltkreis*, as cited above for p.219.

p.233   REDUNDANCIES: Cherry, *On Human Communication*, Ch. V, section 4.

TROMPE L'ŒIL MUST BE FLAT: J. E. Liotard, *Traité des principes et des règles de la peinture* (Geneva, 1781; mod. edn., 1945), Ch. I.

p.234   PICTURES THAT FOLLOW WITH THEIR EYES: For early instances see above, p.96. The correct explanation of the illusion is already given by Ptolemy in his *Optics*, Bk. II, 133 (p.7 of the edition cited for p.204): 'Putatur etiam quod ymago faciei depicte in tabulis respiciat parum in aspicientes illam sine motu ipsius ymaginis, quoniam vera respectio non dinoscitur nisi per stabilitatem forme eiusdem visibilis radii qui cadit super depictam faciem. Visibilis ergo sensus non novit hoc, sed respectio fit ad locum radii qui est propinquus axi tantum, quoniam ipse partes faciei aspiciuntur per radios visus qui sunt ordine consimiles. Cum ergo aspiciens elongabitur, putat quod ymago respiciat cum eo respiciente.' For recent discussions of the illusion, see W. H. Wollaston, 'The Apparent Direction of Eyes in Painting', *Philosophical Transactions of the Royal Society* (London, 1924), and A. Neumeyer, 'Die aus dem Bilde blickende Figur', *Kunstchronik*, VII (1954), 287.

p.235   BERNARD BERENSON: See my Introduction, p.14.

p.236   DANTE, *Purgatorio*, X, 58–63.

A. C. QUATREMÈRE DE QUINCY, *Essai sur la nature, le but et les moyens de l'imitation dans les beaux arts* (Paris, 1823), p.128; tr. J. C. Kent: *An Essay on the Nature, the End, and the Means of Imitation in the Fine Arts* (London, 1837), p.147. The translation in the text is mine.

MAURICE DENIS, *Théories* (Paris, 1913).

p.237   BLACK MAN: Metzger, *Gesetze des Sehens*, p.313; a similar design is discussed in Gibson, *Perception of the Visual World*, pp.181 ff.

CHILDREN LESS PRONE TO THIS ILLUSION: A. R. E. Chapanis, W. R. Garner, C. T. Morgan, *Applied Experimental Psychology* (New York and London, 1949), p.113.

p.238 KONRAD VON LANGE: *Das Wesen der Kunst* (2nd edn., Berlin, 1907), pp.383, 385.

p.239 CUBISM AND SPACE: For quotations and criticisms of some early formulations, see Christopher Gray, *Cubist Aesthetic Theories* (Baltimore, 1953). The most consistent interpretation of cubism in these terms is Daniel Henry Kahnweiler, *The Rise of Cubism* (New York, 1949). For a recent formulation of the cubist aim 'to discover a means of representing space and volume without recourse to illusionism', see the introduction by Douglas Cooper to the catalogue of the Georges Braque exhibition at the Tate Gallery, London, 1956, p.10.

CUBISM AND HILDEBRAND: Mr. Kahnweiler kindly told me in a letter, however, that he did not know Hildebrand's book till later. He doubts if it was known to any of the early protagonists of cubism.

CONTRADICTORY CLUES: A description of some of these effects, which he terms 'iridescence', is given by Winthrop Judkins, 'Towards a Reinterpretation of Cubism', *The Art Bulletin*, XXX (1948).

p.240 SPATIAL INCONSISTENCY: The modern specialist in this game is M. C. Escher. See illus. 210, and note for p.206.

p.244 ACTION PAINTER: For an early interpretation see Harold Rosenberg, 'The American Action Painters', *Art News*, December, 1952.

CHAPTER NINE

p.246 MOTTO: 'Je näher die Hieroglyphe—und alle bildende Kunst ist Hieroglyphe—dem sinnlichen Eindruck der Natur kommt, desto grössere Phantasietätigkeit war erforderlich, sie zu erfinden.' Max Liebermann, 'Die Phantasie in der Malerei', *Gesammelte Schriften* (Berlin, 1922), p.41.

ROGER FRY, *Reflections on British Painting* (London, 1934), pp.134-35.

p.247 FROM THE SCHEMATIC TO THE IMPRESSIONIST: See my book *The Story of Art* and the literature cited for pp.76 and 99. For the bibliography of impressionism, see the standard work by John Rewald, *The History of Impressionism*.

p.250 JOHN RUSKIN, *The Elements of Drawing*, note to par. 5.

p.251 BERKELEY: Boring, *Sensation and Perception*, pp.5 ff., and above, Introduction, p.13.

CÉZANNE ON MONET: Ambroise Vollard, *Paul Cézanne* (Paris, 1914), p.88.

BLIND GAINING SIGHT: The sources are collected in Marius von Senden, *Raum und Gestaltauffassung bei operierten Blindgeborenen* (Leipzig, 1932). For differing interpretations of this material, see Hebb, *The Organization of Behavior*, and Gibson, *The Perception of the Visual World*.

p.252 SENSATION AND PERCEPTION: Boring, *Sensation and Perception*, pp.12 ff.

p.253 ALBERTI: See above, citation for p.131.

LEONARDO: Richter, *The Literary Works of Leonardo da Vinci*, No. 83.

THE MIRROR: See my Introduction, p.5.

p.254 ALL THINKING IS SORTING: See Introduction, especially notes for pp.23, 24.

'PHENOMENAL SIZE IS RELATIVE': E. G. Boring, 'The Gibsonian Visual Field', *Psychological Review*, LIX (1952), 246.

p.255 HERBERT READ, *Art Now* (rev. edn., New York and London, 1948), Ch. IV.

H. THOULESS, 'Phenomenal Regression to the Real Object', *British Journal of Psychology*, XXI (1931), 339-59; XXII, 1-30.

CONSTANCY AND MEDIEVAL OPTICS: See Hans Bauer, 'Die Psychologie Alhazens', p.60, after *Alhazen*, II, 36, and Gezenius ten Doesschate, *De Derde Commentaar van Lorenzo Ghiberti*, p.77; cited for pp.12 and 13.

p.256 OSGOOD, *Method and Theory*, p.284.

TRANSFER EXPERIMENT: See Evans, *An Introduction to Color*, p.149.

p.258 SEEING THE WORLD AS A PICTURE: A famous description of this experience is in Goethe's *Dichtung und Wahrheit*, II, Book 8;

earlier examples in my article on 'The Development of Landscape Painting' cited above for p.157.

CÉZANNE'S ADVICE: *Cézanne's Letters*, ed. John Rewald (London, 1941), p.234. For the methods of art teaching in France, see Horace Lecoq de Boisbaudran, *Lettres à un jeune Professeur* (Paris and Abbeville, 1874); tr. L. D. Luard, *The Training of the Memory in Art and the Education of the Artist* (London, 1911).

p.260 ILLUSIONS THE RULE: Metzger, *Gesetze des Sehens*, Ch. VII.
'ILLUSION NO PLACE IN PSYCHOLOGY': Boring, *Sensation and Perception*, p.238.
THE SPREADING EFFECT: Evans, *Introduction to Color*, p.181.
RUSKIN, *Elements of Drawing*, par. 152.

p.262 EIDETIC FACULTY: For bibliography, see Woodworth and Schlosberg, *Experimental Psychology*, p.722; applications to art history in G. A. S. Snijder, *Kretische Kunst, Versuch einer Deutung* (Berlin, 1936); a more sceptical evaluation in H. Schäfer, *Von ägyptischer Kunst*, p.99.
KEEPING MANY RELATIONSHIPS IN MIND: L. S. Hearnshaw, 'Temporal Integration and Behaviour', *Bulletin of the British Psychological Society*, September 1956 (with bibliography). Winston Churchill, *Painting as a Pastime* (London, 1948; New York, 1950), p.23, and Alfred H. Barr, *Matisse* (New York, 1951), p.122.

p.263 MOUNTAIN RANGES: Metzger, *Gesetze des Sehens*, p.153.
CÉZANNE AND THE PHOTOGRAPH: See above, note for p.56.
CÉZANNE: Meyer Schapiro, *Paul Cézanne* (New York and London, 1952).

p.264 ROLAND FRÉART DE CHAMBRAY, *Idée de la perfection de la peinture* (Mans, 1662), p.20.
STIMULUS CONCENTRATION: Vernon, *Visual Perception*, p.145.

p.265 BRAQUE ON AMBIGUITY: In statements made to John Richardson, *The Observer*, December 1, 1957.
KONRAD FIEDLER: See above, note for p.13.
MOBILIZING MEMORIES OF PICTURES: A good description in Konrad von Lange, *Das Wesen der Kunst* (2nd edn., Berlin, 1907), pp.456–57.

SIR WINSTON CHURCHILL: See above, note for p.34.

p.266 ROGER DE PILES, 'Dialogue sur le Coloris' (1673), in *Conversations sur la Connoissance de la Peinture* (1677), p.61. I am indebted for this reference to Miss Jennifer Montagu.
THE PICTURESQUE: Christopher Hussey, *The Picturesque* (London and New York, 1927), and N. Pevsner, 'Richard Payne Knight', *The Art Bulletin*, 1949.

p.267 CONSTABLE: Lecture in Leslie, *Memoirs*, p.323.
BEAUMONT: See above, note for p.40.
GAINSBOROUGH IN EVERY HEDGE: Constable in Leslie, *Memoirs*, p.9.

p.268 GAINSBOROUGH'S COPIES: Mary Woodall, *Gainsborough's Landscape Drawings* (London, 1939).
HEINRICH WÖLFFLIN, *Kunstgeschichtliche Grundbegriffe*, p.249.
LESLIE ON CONSTABLE: C. R. Leslie, *A Handbook for Young Painters* (London, 1855), p.274.

p.271 AN ASH: Leslie, *Memoirs*, p.239.
CONSTABLE ON CUYP: Ibid, pp.234–35.
CONSTABLE ON LANDSCAPE PAINTING: See above, p.27.
POPPER: See above, notes for pp.23f.

p.272 HENRY RICHTER, *Daylight, a Recent Discovery in the Art of Painting, with Hints on the Philosophy of the Fine Arts and on that of the Human Mind as first dissected by Emmanuel Kant* (London, 1817), pp.2–3. For bibliography, see W. Schöne, *Über das Licht in der Malerei*, as cited above for p.30.

p.273 LECOQ DE BOISBAUDRAN, tr. Luard: *The Training of the Memory in Art* (as cited above for p.258), p.301.
MANET AND RAPHAEL: Ernest Chesneau, *L'Art et les artistes modernes* (Paris, 1864), p.190; Rewald, *The History of Impressionism*, p.151. The fame of the print is attested by Fréart de Chambray, who uses it to demonstrate the perfect composition. (See above, note for p.264.)

p.274 MANET'S TRIAL AND ERROR: There is a beautiful page on this aspect in Joyce Cary, *Art and Reality* (New York and Cambridge,

1958), p.86, that I would have quoted if I had known of it at the time of writing.

ONE THING AT A TIME: See my lecture *Raphael's Madonna della Sedia* (Oxford, 1956), pp.22–23.

p.275 CICERO: See above, citation for p.9. Constable chose the passage as a motto for his *Various Subjects of Landscape* (London, 1832).

p.276 ANDRÉ MALRAUX, *The Voices of Silence*, p.279.

ORIGINAL SIN IN THE WAY OF TRUTH: I owe this interpretation to K. R. Popper.

GIBSON, *The Perception of the Visual World*, Ch. 11.

THE JUMPING SQUIRREL: N. Pastore, 'An Examination of the Theory That Perceiving

Is Learned', *Psychological Review*, LXIII (September 1956), 309.

NATIVISM VERSUS EMPIRICISM: According to O. L. Zangwill, 'Psychology', in *The New Outline of Modern Knowledge*, ed. Alan Pryce-Jones (New York and London, 1956), p.173, it looks as if the nativists had scored an important success with Sperry's experiments on animals. See also Eckhard H. Hess, 'Space Perception in the Chick', *Scientific American* (New York), 195 (1956), reprinted in David C. Beardslee and Michael Wertheimer, *Readings in Perception* (New York and London, 1958).

p.277 BERNARD BERENSON, *Seeing and Knowing* (London, 1953).

J. J. GIBSON, 'The Visual Field and the Visual World', *Psychological Review*, LIX (1952), 148–51.

CHAPTER TEN

p.279 MOTTO: Lewis Carroll, *Alice in Wonderland*, Ch. VI.

PLINY AND VASARI: See above, Introduction, pp.9–10.

p.280 VASARI ON TITIAN: See above, note for p.165.

REMBRANDT'S TECHNIQUE: A. P. Laurie, *The Brushwork of Rembrandt and His School* (London, 1932), and Vojtěch Volavka, *Painting and the Painter's Brushwork* (Prague, 1954).

CHINESE FORMULA: See above, p.175.

p.281 VAN EYCK'S TEXTURES: See above, note for p.185.

LOMAZZO, tr. Richard Haydock, *A Tracte Containing the Arts of Curious Paintings, Carvings and Building* (Oxford, 1958), p.136.

p.282 ALBERTI, *Della Pittura*, ed. Janitschek (Bk. II), p.121.

MAX J. FRIEDLÄNDER, *Von Kunst und Kennerschaft*, p.217. (Cf. tr., p.238.)

READING FACES: A famous experiment with schematic faces discussed and interpreted in Egon Brunswik, *Perception and the Representative Design of Psychological Experiments* (2nd edn., Berkeley, 1956), pp.100 ff.

MONA LISA'S SMILE: See George Boas, 'The Mona Lisa in the History of Taste', in *Wingless Pegasus* (Baltimore, 1950); for other

examples (and some bibliography), see my article, 'Botticelli's Mythologies', in the *Journal of the Warburg and Courtauld Institutes*, VIII (1945), 11–12.

p.284 R. TÖPFFER: A vigorous interest in Töpffer and Töpfferiana survives in Geneva, where Editions des Centenaire Albert Skira publish the *Petite Collection Rodolphe Töpffer*, ed. Pierre Cailler and Henri Darel, with works by and on the artist.

RODOLPHE TÖPFFER, *Essai de physiognomie* (Geneva, 1845); *Œuvres complètes de R. Töpffer*, ed. Pierre Cailler and H. Giller, XI (Geneva, 1945), 14.

p.286 TÖPFFER'S IMITATORS: The first of these was Cham (Amédée de Noé), for whose contracts with Töpffer see F. Ribeyre, *Cham, sa vie et son œuvre* (Paris, 1884) and L'Abbé Relave, *La Vie et les Œuvres de Töpffer* (Paris, 1886), esp. p.194. I am indebted for these references, new to this edition, to Mr. David M. Kunzle.

p.288 INBORN RESPONSES: See above, notes for pp.86f.

p.289 CARICATURE: E. H. Gombrich and Ernst Kris, *Caricature* (Harmondsworth [Penguin],

1940), and 'The Principles of Caricature' (first published 1938) in Ernst Kris, *Psychoanalytic Explorations in Art* (New York, 1952), with bibliography.

p.290 FILIPPO BALDINUCCI, 'Caricare', in *Vocabulario Toscano dell'arte del disegno* (Florence, 1681).

p.292 ARNOLD HOUBRAKEN, *De Groote Schouburgh der Nederlantsche Konstschilders en Schilderessen* (1st edn., 1718; The Hague, 1753), I, 263–67. Houbraken derived his argument on expression from Giovanni Pietro Bellori, 'Idea' (1664), in *Le Vite de'pittori, scultori ed architetti moderni* (Rome, 1672), p.9; for translation, see above, note for p.133.

p.293 OTTO BENESCH, *Rembrandt Drawings: A Critical and Chronological Catalogue* (London, 1954), II, 113 (Cat. C5).

p.294 LEONARDO DA VINCI, *Treatise on Painting*, ed. McMahon, II, No. 415.
LEONARDO'S DOODLES: See my article on his grotesque heads, cited above for p.83.

p.295 LE BRUN: A Ph.D. dissertation on Le Brun's theory and practice by Jennifer Montagu, London, is deposited in the Library of London University.
HOGARTH: Draft for *The Analysis of Beauty*, ed. J. Burke (Oxford, 1955), p.185.
HOGARTH ON CARICATURE: In the inscription on the print *The Bench*.

p.296 COZENS' SYSTEMS: See Paul Oppé, *Alexander and John Robert Cozens* (London, 1952).

p.297 FRANCIS GROSE, *Rules for Drawing Caricatures* (London, 1788).

p.298 DAUMIER'S LIKENESS: 'Il se représentait continuellement lui-même, sans doute à son insu. C'était toujours son nez!—et quel nez en virgule! et ses petits yeux pénétrants et luisants comme les diamants.' Jean Gigous, *Causeries sur les artistes de mon temps* (Paris, 1885), p.55.
LEONARDO'S OBSESSION: See my article on Leonardo's grotesque heads, cited above for p.83.

p.301 BAUDELAIRE ON DAUMIER: 'On the Essence of Laughter' (1855), in *The Mirror of Art: Critical Studies by Charles Baudelaire*, tr. and ed. Jonathan Mayne (New York and London, 1955), pp.159 ff.
RODOLPHE TÖPFFER, *Reflexions et Menus propos d'un peintre genevois* (Geneva, 1846–47), Book V, Ch. XXXV. Gautier's review (*Revue des deux mondes*, 1847) was republished in Geneva, 1943.
PICASSO: 'Pablo Picasso: An Interview' (1923), in Robert Goldwater and Marco Treves, *Artists on Art from the XIV to the XX Century* (New York, 1945), pp.416–17.

p.302 JAMES THURBER, *The Beast in Me and Other Animals* (New York, 1948), p.73.

p.303 PSYCHOANALYSIS: For a concise summary of the Freudian view, see Edward Glover, *Freud or Jung?* (London and New York, 1950), p.13.
MOVEMENT AND INTENTION: Viktor von Weizsäcker, *Der Gestaltkreis*, Ch. I; Colin Cherry, *On Human Communication*, p.300.
PAUL KLEE, *On Modern Art* (*Über die moderne Kunst*), tr. Paul Findlay (London, 1948).

CHAPTER ELEVEN

p.304 MOTTOES: Aristotle, *Politics* VIII, 1340A. John Ruskin, *The Elements of Drawing and Perspective*, par. 135.

p.305 NATURAL AND CONVENTIONAL SIGNS: See above, note for p.76.
PLATO: *Cratylus* 434, tr. H. N. Fowler (LCL, 1939), p.169.
SUNLIT LANDSCAPES: See above, notes for pp. 30 and 272.

p.306 PHONEMES AND ONOMATOPOEIA: Cherry, *On Human Communication*, especially Ch. III.

p.307 SPEECH SOUND AND SPEECH SYNTHESIZERS: Cherry, *On Human Communication*, Ch. IV (with bibliography), and D. B. Fry, 'The Experimental Study of Speech', in *Studies in Communication*, by A. J. Ayer et al. (as cited above for p.177), pp.147–67.

p.309 COPYING: See above, Ch. II, pp.65–66, and Ivins, *Prints and Visual Communication*, p.61.

MORELLI'S METHOD: Ivan Lermolieff, pseud. (Giovanni Morelli), *Italian Painters; Critical Studies of Their Works*, tr. C. J. Ffoulkes, introd. A. H. Layard (London, 1892–93).

p.310 VAN GOGH'S CRITERIA: M. M. van Dantzig, *Vincent ?* (Amsterdam, 1953).

SYNESTHESIA: For early studies see E. G. Boring, *Sensation and Perception in the History of Experimental Psychology*, p.49; for later studies, Charles E. Osgood, *Method and Theory in Experimental Psychology*, pp.642–46; F. A. von Hayek, *The Sensory Order*, pp.19–24. For synesthetic metaphors, see also Stephen Ullmann, *The Principles of Semantics* (Glasgow, 1951), pp.266–89, and the same author's *Style in the French Novel* (Cambridge, 1957), Ch. V (both with rich bibliography). An historical study is Erika von Erhardt-Siebold, 'Harmony of the Senses in English, German and French Romanticism', *Publications of the Modern Language Association of America*, XLVII (1932).

p.311 ARCIMBOLDO: F. C. Legrand and Felix Sluys, *Arcimboldo et les arcimboldesques* (Aalter, Belgium, 1955).

WASSILY KANDINSKY, *Über das Geistige in der Malerei* (Munich, 1912); tr.: *Concerning the Spiritual in Art* (New York, 1947).

p.314 MATCHING: Reinhard Krauss, 'Über den graphischen Ausdruck', *Beihefte zur Zeitschrift für angewandte Psychologie*, 48 (Leipzig, 1930), where the possibility of matching abstract design against concepts and moods is demonstrated in a restricted-choice situation. This precaution is neglected in the discussions on 'The Representative and Expressive Effects of Music', in Leland W. Crafts and others, *Recent Experiments in Psychology* (New York and London, 1938), Ch. VIII. Results are accordingly negative.

SYNESTHESIA AND RELATIONSHIPS: Gladys A. Reichard, R. Jakobson, E. Weiss, 'Language and Synaesthesia', *Word*, II (1949).

'PING-PONG': Peter H. McKellar, *Imagination and Thinking* (New York and London, 1957), pp.65–66, reports on experiments he made according to my suggestions. For a comparable procedure, see Osgood, *Method and Theory*, pp.712–14.

CATEGORIES OF ARTISTS: For similar contrasts, see Max J. Friedländer, *Von Kunst und Kennerschaft*, p.44 (cf. tr., p.50), where painters are paired as 'warm' and 'cool'.

CHARLES E. OSGOOD, George J. Suci, Percy H. Tannenbaum, *The Measurement of Meaning* (Urbana, 1957).

p.315 METAPHORS: See my paper 'Visual Metaphors of Value in Art', cited above for p.25.

p.316 JONATHAN RICHARDSON, *The Theory of Painting*, in *The Works of Jonathan Richardson* (London, 1792), p.65 (colouring), p.70 (handling).

EXPRESSIONISTS: See Bernard S. Myers, *Expressionism* (London, 1957), esp. Ch. 4.

VITRUVIUS, *De architectura*, Bk. I, Ch. II.

p.317 POUSSIN'S LETTER of Nov. 24, 1647, is translated and annotated in Elizabeth G. Holt, *A Documentary History of Art*, II (New York [Anchor], 1958), pp.154–56. See also P. Alfassa, 'L'Origine de la lettre de Poussin sur les modes d'après un travail récent', *Bulletin de la Société de l'histoire de l'art français*, 1933, pp.125–43.

p.318 DEMETRIUS, *On Style* 105 and 176. The theory is expounded and applied in Pope's *Essay on Criticism:* 'The sound must seem an echo to the sense.'

CICERO'S CATEGORIES: See Introduction, p.8.

p.319 WINCKELMANN's link with the tradition of rhetoric: Heinz Weniger, *Die drei Stilcharaktere*, as cited for p.8.

p.320 'THE ART': Leslie, *Memoirs*, p.279.

p.321 LANDSCAPE MODES: See my article on 'The Development of Landscape Painting', cited for p.157.

DE PILES, *Principles of Painting* (as cited for p.167), p.124.

CICERO, *Orator* XXIII, 78. The same treatise, X, 36, also contains a comparison of the contrasting manners of oratory with tastes in painting.

SALOMON GESSNER, 'A Letter on Landscape Painting' (1st English edn., 1770). I quote from the edition of the *Works I* (Liverpool, 1802), pp.180–89.

ROOM FOR NATURAL PAINTURE: Leslie, *Memoirs*, p.15.

p.322 PASTORAL FEELING: Ibid., p.132.

DE PILES, *Principles of Painting* (as cited for p.167), p.125.
STYLES OF EXECUTION: Ibid., p.156.
GIFTS AND STYLE: Cicero, *De oratore* III, IX, 35.

p.323 E. KRIS: See above, Introduction, p.25.
RUSKIN, *Modern Painters*, Part II, Sec. I, Ch. 7.
W. GILPIN, *Forest Scenery*, quoted after C. Hussey, *The Picturesque* (London and New York, 1927), p.124.

p.324 WORDSWORTH, *Poems* (London, 1815). The first quotation comes from the Preface to 'Lyrical Ballads', Vol. II, p.381, of the edition cited; the second from Vol. I, p.viii.
SOUND OF WATER: Leslie, *Memoirs*, pp.85–86.
SLIMY POSTS: Ibid., p.237.
WILLIAM JAMES, *Talks to Teachers on Psychology and to Students on Some of Life's Ideals* (New York and London, 1899), p.99.

p.325 DUTCH RURAL TRADITION: Fisher on 'Dutch Forest School', Leslie, *Memoirs*, p.37.
'LIGHTS—DEWS': Ibid., p.218.
PICTURES TO BE AVOIDED: Ibid., p.218.
FUSELI'S UMBRELLA: Ibid., p.100.

ONE BRIEF MOMENT: John Constable, *Various Subjects of Landscape* (London, 1832), introd.

p.327 SPARKLE WITH REPOSE: Leslie, p.123.
BRIGHTNESS WITHOUT SPOTTINESS: Ibid., p.240.
A LITTLE GOLD: Ibid., p.247.

p.328 UNITE IMAGINATION WITH NATURE: Ibid., p.179.
GAINSBOROUGH'S LETTER: William T. Whitley, *Thomas Gainsborough* (London, 1915), p. 358–59.
WIVENHOE PARK: Leslie, p.68.

p.329 INTUITION AND REASON: For a rational comparison between the achievements of global perception and analytical thought, see Egon Brunswik, *Wahrnehmung und Gegenstandswelt* (Leipzig and Vienna, 1934), pp.127 and 224 ff.
ELIMINATING FALSE RESPONSES: A similar function is assigned to scholarship by T. S. Eliot in 'The Frontiers of Criticism' (1956), in *On Poetry and Poets* (London, 1957), p.114. I need hardly emphasize once more that this interpretation tallies with the general methodology of this book derived from K. R. Popper, *The Logic of Scientific Discovery* (New York and London, 1959).

RETROSPECT

p.330 STORY OF ART: pp.421–22.

p.331 SURREALISTS: Ibid., p.443.

p.332 RELUCTANCE TO RECOGNIZE AMBIGUITY: An attempt to evaluate the degree of this reluctance as a test for rigidity is Else Frenkel-Brunswik, 'Intolerance of Ambiguity as an

Emotional and Perceptual Personality Variable', in Howard Brand, *The Study of Personality* (New York and London, 1954). For the philosophical aspects, see K. R. Popper, 'Philosophy of Science' (as cited above for p.23), esp. pp.175–76. The applications to image reading were first brought to my attention by Dr. Gottfried Spiegler.

LIST OF ILLUSTRATIONS

Unless otherwise indicated, the photographs have in general
been furnished by the respective institution
or collection.

IV. Reflections on the Greek Revolution

V. Formula and Experience

VI. The Image in the Clouds

IX. The Analysis of Vision in Art

X. The Experiment of Caricature

XI. From Representation to Expression

INDEX

INDEX

abbreviation, 94, 95 & *n*, 145; *see also* simplification

abstract art, *see* nonfigurative art

'abstraction', 23, 87, 140–41; *see also* 'generalisation'

academy figure, 141

accent, 308, 309–10

accidental forms, 154–161, 176, 194, 251, 302–3; in projective tests, 191–92

Acker, W.R.B., 129*n*

'action painting', 243–44

Adams, G.K., 189*n*; quoted, 189

advertising, *see* posters

Aelianus, Claudius, 174*n*

after-images, 192, 219, 220*n*

Alain, (Daniel): cartoon, 3, 4, 8, 20, 21, 24, 25, 258, fig. 1

Alberti, Leone Battista, 30*n*, 90 & *n*, 91, 131 & *n*, 160 & *n*, 253 & *n*, 282 & *n*; quoted, 90

Alcamenes, 162

Alcestis, 107

Alexander's victory over Darius, mosaic 115, Fig. 96–97

Alfassa, P., 317*n*

Alhazen, 13*n*; quoted, 13

Allen, Arthur B., from *Graphic Art in Easy Stages*, 127, fig. 104

Allport, Floyd H., 24*n*, 53*n*

Altdorfer, Albrecht: *The Virgin amidst Angels*, 181–82, figs. 181 & 182

ambiguity: deliberate, 4–5, 181, 222, 225–26, 240–43, 331–32, fig. 220; hidden, 24, 198–200, 210–13, 215, 216, 219–44, 264–65, 278, 331–32 & *n*; *see also* projection

Ames, Adelbert, Jr.: chair demonstrations, 209–11 & *n*, 213–14, 217, 218–19, 227, 232, 233, 278, fig. 213; size-distance demonstrations 219 & *n*, 230–31

'anamorphosis', 213 & *n*–14

'anchorage', 169, 191, 192

Andokides amphora, figs. 12, 13

Andrae, Walter, 107*n*

Angel, Philip, 191*n*; quoted, 191

angle of vision, 45, 46, 131, 217, 234, 248, 249–50, 250–51

animals: behaviour, 45, 48, 86 & *n*–87 & *n*, 276 & *n*, 288; representations of, 68–72, 139–41

animation, 283

Annigoni, Pietro, 56*n*

Anscombe, G.E.M., 4*n*

anticipation: colour, 189–92; and illusion, 50, 53–54, 170–74, 184–85, 191–93, 197, 220–22, 233–34, 235, 237–38, 256–57, 278, 304, 316, 326; in perception, 23, 77, 148, 157, 170–71, 187, 188–90, 211, 232, 251, 254–55; in science, 271–72

Antioch: mosaic from, 37, 240 ,241, figs. 16, 225

Apelles, 51 & *n*, 120

Apollo of Piombino, 99, fig. 86

Apollo of Tenea 99, fig. 85

'appearances': 'discovery of', 246–78, 279; Platonic, 84–85, 99, 108–9; in stimulus psychology, 219, 221

archaic art, *see* pre-Greek Art; primitive art

architecture: classic orders, 316–17, fig. 312; curvatures, 218

Arcimboldo, 311 & *n*

Aristotle, 85*n*, 186, 304; Politics quoted, 304

Arnheim, Rudolf, 22 & *n*, 76 & *n*, 179*n*, 221*n*

Arnoult, Malcolm D., 34*n*

Arréat, Lucien, 228*n*

art: emancipation of, 98, 108, 120, 161, 172, 176, 195, 236–38, 278, 289, 303; history of, 3–4, 9–12, 14–20, 24, 54, 66–67, 75, 99–101, 123–25, 127–28, 129–30, 208–9, 227, 246–47, 265–71, 278, 279, 304, 320, 328–29, 330–31; language of, 7–8, 20, 76, 78, 114, 122, 157, 175, 200–1, 294, 295, 296, 301, 303, 305, 319, 320, 328, 329; *see also* Byzantine art; cave art; child art; Chinese art; classical art; Cretan art; cubism; Dutch painting; Egyptian art; German art; Greek art; Italian art; Japanese art; medieval art; Mesopotamian art; Mexican art; narrative art; neolithic art; nonfigurative art; pre-Greek art; primitive art; Renaissance art; Roman art; twentieth-century art; Victorian art

art criticism: academic, 4; Chinese, 129 & *n;* classical theories of, 8–10, 120–21, 316–17

art nouveau, 18

art teaching, 10–12, 126–28, 134–44, 149, 258–59

Ashmole, Bernard, 99*n*

associations, 24

assumptions, *see* hypothesis

Assur-bani-pal; lioness from palace of, 122, fig. 101

Atteneave, Fred, 34*n*